INSCRUTABLE BELONGINGS

ASIAN AMERICA

A series edited by Gordon H. Chang

The increasing size and diversity of the Asian American population, its growing significance in American society and culture, and the expanded appreciation, both popular and scholarly, of the importance of Asian Americans in the country's present and past—all these developments have converged to stimulate wide interest in scholarly work on topics related to the Asian American experience. The general recognition of the pivotal role that race and ethnicity have played in American life, and in relations between the United States and other countries, has also fostered the heightened attention.

Although Asian Americans were a subject of serious inquiry in the late nineteenth and early twentieth centuries, they were subsequently ignored by the mainstream scholarly community for several decades. In recent years, however, this neglect has ended, with an increasing number of writers examining a good many aspects of Asian American life and culture. Moreover, many students of American society are recognizing that the study of issues related to Asian America speak to, and may be essential for, many current discussions on the part of the informed public and various scholarly communities.

The Stanford series on Asian America seeks to address these interests. The series will include works from the humanities and social sciences, including history, anthropology, political science, American studies, law, literary criticism, sociology, and interdisciplinary and policy studies.

A full list of titles in the Asian America series can be found online at www.sup.org/asianamerica

INSCRUTABLE BELONGINGS

QUEER ASIAN NORTH AMERICAN FICTION

STEPHEN HONG SOHN

STANFORD UNIVERSITY PRESS • STANFORD, CALIFORNIA

Stanford University Press
Stanford, California

©2018 by the Board of Trustees of the Leland Stanford Junior University. All rights reserved.

No part of this book may be reproduced or transmitted in any form or by any means, electronic or mechanical, including photocopying and recording, or in any information storage or retrieval system without the prior written permission of Stanford University Press.

Printed in the United States of America on acid-free, archival-quality paper

Library of Congress Cataloging-in-Publication Data

Names: Sohn, Stephen Hong, author.
Title: Inscrutable belongings : queer Asian North American fiction / Stephen Hong Sohn.
Other titles: Asian America.
Description: Stanford, California : Stanford University Press, 2018.
Series: Asian America | Includes bibliographical references and index.
Identifiers: LCCN 2017046518 | ISBN 9781503604018 (cloth : alk. paper) | ISBN 9781503605923 (pbk.) | ISBN 9781503605930 (epub)
Subjects: LCSH: Gays' writings, American—History and criticism. | Gays' writings, Canadian—History and criticism. | American fiction—Asian American authors—History and criticism. | Canadian fiction—Asian authors—History and criticism. | American fiction—21st century—History and criticism. | Canadian fiction—21st century—History and criticism. | Asian Americans in literature. | Families in literature. | Gays in literature.
Classification: LCC PS153.G38 S64 2018 | DDC 813/.5409895—dc23
LC record available at https://lccn.loc.gov/2017046518

Typeset by Bruce Lundquist in 10/14 Minion Pro

CONTENTS

Acknowledgments	ix
A Note on Usage	xv
Introduction: Imagining Queer Asian North American Lives	1
1 Tactical Diversions: Toward Queer Asian North American Formalisms	27
2 Narrative Endurance: Queer Asian North American Storytellers, Survival Plots, and Inscrutable Belongings	59
3 Inscrutable Belongings in Pathology: Infectious Genealogies in Alexander Chee's *Edinburgh*	87
4 Inscrutable Belongings in Cinema: Filmic Lineages in Noël Alumit's *Letters to Montgomery Clift*	123
5 Inscrutable Belongings in Hunting: Interracial Surrogacies in Nina Revoyr's *Wingshooters*	159
6 Inscrutable Belongings in Bondage: Degenerate Descendants in Lydia Kwa's *Pulse*	197
Coda	235
Notes	241
References	267
Index	307

ACKNOWLEDGMENTS

I always begin any acknowledgments with an apology. A book is so big that I can't even recall how many people have read portions or drafts along the way (which in part explains the length of this section), so I apologize if I have forgotten anyone who had a hand in seeing this thing through to the end. I have tried to be diligent about giving credit where it is due, but I know I have probably failed in one massive way or another.

First, let me proceed with official permissions necessary to complete this book. The third chapter in *Inscrutable Belongings* was previously published in a shorter and earlier form:

> Sohn, Stephen Hong. "'Burning Hides What It Burns': Retrospective Narration and the Protoqueer Asian American Child in Alexander Chee's *Edinburgh*." *Journal of Asian American Studies* 17:3 (2014), 243–271. © 2014 Johns Hopkins University Press. Reprinted with permission of Johns Hopkins University Press.

I also acknowledge Groundwood Books for providing me permission to reprint an image that originally appeared in Mariko and Jillian Tamaki's *Skim*:

> Text copyright © 2008 by Mariko Tamaki
> Illustration copyright © 2008 by Jillian Tamaki
> First paperback edition published in Canada and in the USA in 2010 by Groundwood Books. Third paperback printing 2015.

With official business and apologies out of the way . . . the very nascent beginnings of this book really originated as a proposal draft for the UC President's Postdoctoral Fellowship sometime in 2004. This draft was aggressively edited with the help of Julie Carlson at UC Santa Barbara, and I'm not sure I ever got the chance to thank her. While on that fellowship, I worked closely with Glen C. Mimura, who was absolutely instrumental in giving this book the time to evolve and to percolate.

Once I got to Stanford, I didn't work on this project as much, but toward the last couple of years I had to get myself in high gear and was able to get the majority of it drafted. First off, I was part of a lovely reading and writing group that I wish I could have stayed in forever, which involved dinners and conversations with Yvonne Yarbro-Bejarano. Also, I have to mention the absolutely heroic support of Andrea Lunsford, who read very early and very rough drafts of this manuscript. There are not enough things I can say to express my infinite gratitude for all that she has done and continues to do for me. I wish I could bottle up that energy and good spirit and sell it. It was also during this period that I established a number of key friendships that were instrumental in the eventual publication of this book. I'm deeply indebted to Alyce Boster, Nicole Yun Bridges, Judy Candell, Katie Dooling, Dagmar Logie, Ivan Lupic, Stephen Orgel, Nelia Peralta, Elizabeth Tallent, Sau-ling C. Wong, Karen Tei Yamashita, and others in this regard. Alyce, I have to say that I so much appreciate that one conversation we had when you said something to this effect: "Please don't make this book too depressing." I hope I have captured the sense of possibility that is still apparent when one endures. While finishing up my time at Stanford, I was lucky enough to work with a number of wonderful (and now former) students, many of whom no doubt influenced my line of thinking for this book. I wanted to name some of them here (with the caveat that there are many others that could be added to this list): Sarah Chang, Trac Dang, Mark Flores, Sunli Kim, Iris Law, Tenyia Lee, Annabeth Leow, Henry Leung, Cynthia Liao, Jennifer H. Liu, Thanh Nguyen, Debra Pacio, Annie Phan, Henry Tsai, Sammie Wills, and Victoria Yee.

Min Hyoung Song deserves a line of credit for this book all on his own. Min: thank you so much for taking a chance on what would become a chapter of this book and providing critical support in a very difficult professional time.

I finished the earliest full draft of the book while at UCR amongst a whole new set of energizing colleagues. The transition to the new job was made possible by the indefatigable efforts and teamwork of Gavin Jones and Deborah Willis (and others involved in that search). My scholarly life has been scaffolded by superbly social department members, who remind me of balance and that there is life beyond editing, research, and teaching. Thanks especially to Traise Yamamoto, Sherryl Vint (wow, you are a saint for that super late-stage read on the Introduction, and I bow down to you), and Robb Hernández in this regard. Traise and Sherryl: those trips to Los Angeles were always the lifeboats in a too-busy academic year. Osito: sparkle, spirits, and spandex forever. I am incredibly blessed that you are always there to remind me about what it means to live, especially on Halloween.

I have had a chance to work in more focused contexts with a number of inspiring faculty and staff at UCR, including the English Department more broadly, and more specifically, Jennifer Doyle, Perla Fabelo, Tina Feldmann, Leann "Lightning" Gilmer, Christy Gray, Weihsin Gui, George Haggerty, Regina "Gina" Hazlinger, Jennifer Morgan, Linda Nellany, and Lauren Savord. Also, it was a wonderful pleasure to work with the graduates (including but not limited to José Alfaro, Kai Hang Cheang, Xiomara Forbez, Brian Stephens, MT Vallarta) and undergraduates at UCR.

The Center for Ideas and Society has been especially supportive of this particular book through the HIP interdisciplinary grant and its Senior Fellows Award. I especially need to recognize Georgia Warnke and Katharine Henshaw for their support. I also received critical grant monies for this book through UC Riverside's Academic Senate.

I need to name the many individuals who provided critical feedback (and research support) for me along this long, windy path. I am in serious debt to them because they continually read and re-read portions of my book, researched and created important annotated bibliographies, and pushed me to make my arguments better, so often under the duress of short deadlines: Yanoula Athanassakis, Crystal Mun-hye Baik, Karli Cerankowski, Stewart Chang, Johaina Crisostomo, James Matthew Estrella, Christopher Fan, Tara Fickle (sorry you had to read the whole thing), Allen Frost, Donatella Galella, Donald C. Goellnicht, Nadeen Kharputly, Sue J. Kim, Paul Lai, Raechel Lee, Long Le-Khac, Liz Przybylski, Vanessa Seals, and Haerin Shin. A billion zillion trillion infinity thank-yous to everyone!!

I was given the excellent opportunity to present portions of this book at an early stage to a working group up at UC Berkeley at the invitation of Johaina Crisostomo and Daniel Vallela.

Early on, I was lucky enough to meet a person who made me understand the need for endurance, so I express my deep gratitude toward Shawn Lynn

Keller. Wherever you are now, I hope your life is filled with light and love, and many dogs.

Lisa Wehrle, OWFOE: your talents are unreal. Thank you for being there for the entire book-writing process and for taking the time to get to know me beyond the page. You have been a beacon of positive energy always and have continually led me away from the dark editorial cornfields.

The four anonymous readers who provided critical and extensive comments on the draft of this book are to be celebrated for their truly impressive efforts. Many editors along the way have been instrumental in the development of this book, and I thank the feedback of the ever-responsive Sara Jo Cohen and Cathy Schlund-Vials in this regard. A huge thanks goes to the folks at Stanford University Press, including but not limited to Nora Spiegel and Margo Irvin. And Margo: wow, I so much appreciate the overall and line-item feedback you provided at a very late stage. You've been amazing, and I hope I get the chance to work with you many times over. Gordon Chang: yet again, you have shown me the importance of mentorship and support at the most crucial of times. The production team over at Stanford University Press helped usher this book toward its final, pristine phase; these wonderful people include (but are not limited to) Stephanie Adams, marketing manager; David Horne, copyeditor; Jessica Ling, production editor; Bruce Lundquist, compositor, and Kate Templar, sales and exhibits manager.

I wanted to also thank the *Spa Night* movie team for their permission to use an image from their brilliant, provocative, and groundbreaking movie: Andrew Ahn, David Ariniello, Giulia Caruso, Ki Jin Kim, Joe Seo, and Kelly Thomas. Though I do not engage in a lengthy analysis of the film in this particular book, the arresting image that graces this study's cover is appropriate given the themes and issues raised in the film.

I have to mention what I could call the many manifestations of my own inscrutable belongings: the many teachers, scholars, and mentors who have influenced me and given so much of their time to me, the many generations of students whom I have had the honor to instruct. I need to give a special shout-out to Shirley Geok-lin Lim, who has always been an extended family member to me and who has always set the highest bar for mentorship and generosity in academia, while also understanding that I am more than just my scholarly parts. Along those lines, I have benefited so much from the continuing friendship and siblinghood I share with Celine Parreñas Shimizu. A host of others have been formative for this book: many thanks to Aimee Bahng,

Juliana Chang, Tina Chen, Kandice Chuh, Nguyen Tan Hoang (thanks for that article!), Joseph Jonghyun Jeon, James Kyung-jin Lee, Rachel C. Lee, Arnold Pan, and the many others both inside and out of the field.

I have gotten so much outside of classroom and the home, and I begrudgingly admit my tendency to devote my time to athletic ventures: the BayLands Frontrunners and the Rainbow Recreation volleyball players. Albert Cheng, Roger Drummond, Stephen "Bunsen" Keteltas, Peter Kuykendall, Bill Lewis, Curt McDowell, Oliver "Ollie" Northrup, Bill Steiglemann, the tennis "boys," and the yogis over at Yoga Belly and Yoga is Youthfulness: thanks so much for your friendship and camaraderie always; the Bay Area is always hard to visit knowing that I can only spend so much time there catching up with you all. The folks in Riverside, who play tennis, also have been instrumental in my happiness beyond the book: big kudos to the Hampton Indoor Tennis Center (sadly closed since 2015), and the Andulka Tennis Center folks, coaches, staff, and recreational players for keeping me sane on and off the court.

Certainly I would like to acknowledge the ever-growing Sohn clan in its many branches and iterations. In particular, I must always mention my parents, Soon Ho Sohn and Yunpyo Hong Sohn, who have given so much in the process of raising me and my three siblings (Richard, Julianne, and John) and who have set the highest standard possible for what it means to create a family (and variations thereof). Mom, Dad: you are both truly the ultimate survivors and incredibly tough cookies.

A special shout-out to my destination birthday sisters: Jules, Krystal Young, and Gina Valentino; may there be many more travel-based celebrations in the future. You three have seen me through thick and through thin, and there's nothing I can say that can properly address how much you have done for and mean to me. I only wish I had more time for our (mis)adventures together. As was noted on that beach in Waikiki during Virgo-pocalypse, we are S.A.P.

A NOTE ON USAGE

Throughout this manuscript, I have generally chosen to standardize the use of the term *Asian North American* when referring to scholarly studies originally written or conducted within a specific national context. As I mention in my introduction, the tenor and the ethos of this book, given its larger argument, is to promote the overlaps in Asian American Studies and Asian Canadian Studies, even while I do acknowledge the distinct need to separate these fields in certain contexts and under particular analytical conditions. As a gesture to those scholars seeking more specificity, I've noted some key pages and citations involving Asian North American Studies from a United States context: 5 (Du, Ton, and Kramer; M. Ng), 18 (Aguilar-San Juan; Hom), 19 (Takagi; Kumashiro), 72 (N. Shah), 80 (C. Shimizu), 92 (Chuh), 152 (Feng), and 163 (JeeYeun Lee).

INSCRUTABLE BELONGINGS

INTRODUCTION

IMAGINING QUEER ASIAN NORTH AMERICAN LIVES

"**IT GETS BETTER**," a project founded in 2010 by Dan Savage and Terry Miller, promotes what cultural critics and theorists might call queer optimism. Addressing a rash of gay teen suicides that rocked the nation, outspoken activists released public service announcements and video messages in which they reassured younger gays and lesbians that their lives as sexual minorities would improve over time. The rhetoric underlying the "It Gets Better" campaign is one of *survivorship*: the suffering queer subject must live for the chance to experience a better future. And yet, the short messages—often no more than a minute or two—do not always detail how and why things actually do "get better." This campaign's progressive message, one that proclaims an eventually happy life, offers some concrete evidence of the sea change that has occurred within the past decade, particularly in attitudes concerning same-sex marriage and other issues, in which queers—and queer cultures—are increasingly tolerated by the mainstream public in North America. With the repeal of "Don't Ask, Don't Tell" in 2011 (the law banning openly queer service members from participating in the U.S. armed services) and the 2016 Federal Drug Administration decision to reconsider banning blood donations by queer individuals, the move toward equality seems to continue unabated.[1] Most notably, same-sex marriages were federally recognized by Canada and the United States in 2005 and 2015, respectively. The future for queer people looks, for perhaps the first time, promising.

The advent of legislative equality is no doubt fortuitous, but the "It Gets Better" campaign can function with a reductive ethos that homogenizes the LGBTQI community, especially from a frame that overshadows and even undercuts the persistence of social inequalities. As David L. Eng reminds us in *The Feeling of Kinship*, this story of queer activism is wrapped up in many other narratives, especially those coterminous with the unfinished project of the civil rights movement. Eng highlights the danger of regarding the injustices embedded in race relations as something from a bygone era in order to promote a different, apparently more pressing cause such as queer equality (4).[2] Instead, race and queerness are indelibly and historically linked, as a host of scholars have shown, including Ian Barnard, Siobhan Somerville, Nancy Ordover, and Margot Canaday. The continuing struggles of both racial and sexual minorities emerge in forms that exist beyond the bounds of legislation and judicial precedents.[3] Here cultural productions provide necessary correctives because they destabilize the fantasy of queer progress in a postracial milieu.[4] Such narratives draw attention to the more private spheres of romantic entanglements and family rupture while gesturing to the ways that elements of everyday life have an impact on how we understand the dynamics of power and oppression as they unfold at local, urban, regional, national, and transnational scales, and at momentous historical intervals.

The interventions that fictional narratives can make to discourses of progress and futurity have become conspicuously evident to me, particularly as I have developed new course preparations concerning narrative and narrative theory. One common text I include in these courses is Jane Austen's *Northanger Abbey*. In one instance, I recall lecturing on courtship and marriage plots, discussing why exactly Henry Tilney is the appropriate choice for the heroine, Catherine Morland. Henry's witty, he's handsome, he's virtuous, and, perhaps most important, he comes from the appropriate class background. Although Catherine is a woman with limited means, she manages to snag her wealthy romantic foil and, of course, lives happily ever after with him. A lecture on a novel such as *Northanger Abbey* reminds me how much I enjoy the matrimonial dilemma at the center of courtship and marriage plots. But not one of the books I have been reading most fervently for my research—fiction penned by queer writers of Asian North American backgrounds—possesses even remotely similar plots. In fact, courtship and something like marriage seem secondary given that these books offer few, if any, appropriate and safe venues in which to express queer desire. Certainly I am aware that the contexts for a contemporary queer Asian North American fiction cannot be equated with nineteenth-century British cultures, but the comparison germinates political questions about the issue of courtship and marriage, and their relationship to larger national concerns about social recognition and familial constructs. Austen's heroines could no doubt be seen as marginalized subjects, seeking forms of security through heterosexual marriage. An allied problem arises with the arrival of the queer Asian North American protagonist in fiction because he or she also strives to achieve some measure of social integration. Though scholars show that the institutions of the monogamous, heterosexual marriage and the nuclear family are far less relevant (and prevalent) in this contemporary period than during earlier epochs (including most famously the 1950s),[5] *the fantasy* and *idealizations* of these normative social constructs on both sides of the U.S.-Canadian border remain firmly embedded in their respective national cultures.[6]

Given these paradigms, my concerns have evolved: If courtship and marriage plots are not readily available or perhaps not always preferred by characters, then what narrative sequences are most prominent in queer Asian North American literatures? The answer to this question is the catalyzing point for this book, as I critically consider the correspondence between queer Asian North American protagonists in fictional works and the plots that emerge from these narratives. Two patterns become most evident: queer Asian North American protagonists are lucky simply to survive, and their survival depends on a community of other characters (including nonliving entities) who do not come from the protagonists' biological families. Reading these stories against the "It Gets Better" campaign produces a jarring dissonance: things may improve, but the path to that point is littered with incredible trials, physical harm, and antagonistic forces. In some cases, things arguably do not improve at all. In other words, it can and often does get worse.

Inspired by the endurance of these characters and the dynamic social formations that they construct, *Inscrutable Belongings* is an extended study of queer Asian North American fictions that have emerged alongside the rise of activism concerning LGBTQI equality, postracial thought, and the evolving discourses undergirding normative family values and kinships.[7] Reading queer Asian North American fictions demonstrates that optimism must be guarded: these stories relay the ongoing dangers of racial and sexual minority existences. Russell Leong's "Camouflage," for instance, a short story I will return to in Chapter 2 for a lengthier critical engagement, establishes a far more ambivalent depiction of a queer Asian North American's life. For the Filipino American protagonist-storyteller, Bernard Amador Angelo Tan, queer desire is set within the frame of physical brutality and the possibility of death. Bernard performs as a Japanese exotic dancer at the titular bathhouse, where he may be contributing, however indirectly, to higher HIV infection rates; he volunteers at a local AIDS clinic; and he cruises for sex at Griffith Park. He struggles with many issues: the aftereffects of childhood molestation by his uncle, his failure to become a filmmaker, and his response to the recent murder of a gay man whom he knew. Romance seems hardly an option, as Bernard battles drug dependency and job insecurity. Further, Bernard retains no sustained connection to biological family members. In Leong's depiction, the future is always in question. Though Bernard survives to tell his tale, the story's last scene is of Bernard having sex with a patient at the AIDS clinic whom he knows is HIV positive. "My thirst," explains Bernard, "drives me to do crazy things" (100). Even the short story's title performs a metaphorical layering by asking us to think about visibility and how camouflage defends against capture, consumption, and ultimately death.[8]

Social Death, Material Violence, and the Queer Asian North American

"Camouflage" illuminates the central question of my book: How is the queer Asian North American protagonist's livelihood depicted in a fictional world filled with the menace of corporeal violence and antagonistic social forces? The cultural productions I analyze in detail—Leong's "Camouflage," Nina Revoyr's *Wingshooters*, Noël Alumit's *Letters to Montgomery Clift*, Alexander Chee's *Edinburgh*, and Lydia Kwa's *Pulse*—all deal explicitly with queer Asian North American figures who manage to survive to their narrative conclusions. These texts outline the desperate need for expansive social recognitions for their vulnerable protagonists, so that something like the affective fulfillment—that is, happiness, assumed longevity, security, and a sense of home—so integral to the Austenian romance might one day supplement such existing survival plots. I focus on fictions published around 2000 and beyond because they complicate and critique the contemporary discourses of postracial thought and queer optimism that overstate narratives of progress concerning equality. Even when one's humanity is codified through law, other barriers persist that undermine the queer Asian North American's sense of inclusion. If death and injury in both literal and metaphorical forms stalk the everyday lives of racialized queer subjects and the many people they associate with, then the price of desiring another of the same sex is already too high. On this level, we can understand the desperate acts initiated by queer Asian North American characters as they navigate a perilous world in which desire and sexual intimacy are deemed pathologically deviant. Rather than revel in pessimism, these fictions chronicle the precarious balancing act negotiated by the queer Asian North American who seeks to find a larger community to claim as a kind of family but who contends with the heavy burden of existing as a figure beset by multiple threats.

To begin with, the queer Asian North American faces *material violence* in myriad forms, such as school bullying, physical assaults, hazing, and associated hate crimes (Nadal 223). The body's endangerment is exacerbated by oppressive forces—often cultural, structural, and legislative in scope—that render this individual as a subject mired in *social death*. I redeploy this phrase with respect to queer Asian North American contexts, taking inspiration from historian Orlando Patterson, who defines social death in relation to the slave: "Alienated from all 'rights' or claims of birth, [the slave] ceased to belong in his own right to any legitimate social order" (5).[9] As Patterson notes, the slave faces "natal alienation," which manifests as "the slave's forced alienation, the loss of ties of birth in both ascending and descending generations" (7). Patterson's conception has been reimagined and more broadly applied by other scholars, notably in relation to cultural annihilation (Card 63; Spivey and Robinson 69) and the ongoing clashes over civil rights (Cacho).[10] For queer Asian North Americans, social death occurs on a variety of fronts. For example, queer Asian North Americans' romances and sexual relationships have only recently achieved recognition in the realm of state-sponsored forms of legislation.[11] While these changes portend the possibility of new forms of kinship and family, the legal realm can offer only so much support for the maintenance and construction of novel social formations.[12]

In addition, queer Asian North Americans exploring their identities as racial and sexual minorities cannot necessarily expect support from their biological families. As Nang Du, Hendry Ton, and Elizabeth J. Kramer convey, the possibilities of reformulating Asian North American heteronuclear family structures to adapt to any forms of same-sex relationships are highly limited (338).[13] A number of scholars and cultural critics further denote that queer Asian North Americans who come out of the closet can face familial disownment, expulsion from the home, physical harm, and psychological distress (Aguilar-San Juan 38; Chung and Szymanski 88; Fung 238). The influence of Asian culture on the maintenance of traditional heterosexual and intergenerational social roles is compounded by North American investments in normative family and kinship formations. Mark Tristan Ng explains that the challenge of dealing with racial and sexual differences leads queer Asian North Americans to live "double lives—the racial versus the sexual. Many live in silence and secrecy, and often find themselves in situations where they are forced to compromise the multiplicity of their identities" (270).[14] The most salient issue here is the problem of community formations for the queer Asian North American who must balance the weight of both biological family expectations and sociocultural pressures against individual desires and romantic relationships.[15] Mainstream film and television often function as dubious places for the representational inclusion of the queer Asian North American, as he or she most often surfaces in comic or sidekick roles that reinscribe his or her eccentricity.[16]

The queer Asian North American is a figure in danger of being written out of traditional kinship systems, which are encompassed by two core elements: (1) biological relations to entities such as parents and siblings and (2) an appropriate, often assumed-to-be heterosexual, monogamous marriage partner.[17] This treacherous position is amplified by the queer Asian North American's simultaneously constructed sexual and racial formations. The queer Asian North American man, for instance, is often considered as the submissive, obedient partner, mainly matched in an interracial relationship with a Caucasian man (K. Chan 179).[18] His relative status as the "bottom" is linked to the longer racialization of Asian North American men as effeminate, sexually deviant, and undesirable.[19] Chong-suk Han argues, "Not only are gay Asian men marginalized, they are made invisible by a new process of racial formation—stressing Asian American 'family' values and perpetuating the model minority image for Asian Americans—that simply denies the existence of gay Asian Americans" (13). In a similar fashion, the queer Asian North American woman is most often read as invisible or as impossible, precisely because her relationship to another of the same sex is misinterpreted as sisterhood or platonic friendship.[20] Given the hypersexual stereotype that filters through popular culture concerning the Asian North American woman (C. P. Shimizu, *Hypersexuality*), her queerness is potentially overwritten by an assumed heterosexuality (JeeYeun Lee). This hypersexuality functions contradictorily in the sense that she must act submissively with respect to her male partner, even as she is assumed to be sexually insatiable. In either case, queer Asian North American men and women both suffer from a distorted form of social recognition, most often predicated by a figurative ghostliness.

The collective positioning of queer Asian North Americans of either gender as spectral nonentities reinforces the importance of reading these fictions as a collective grouping, one that can address the multipronged nature of racial, sexual, cultural, and associated marginalizations. Indeed, if there is a kind of ghostliness attached to queer Asian North Americans, then I follow Avery Gordon's point that this spectrality maintains a resistive force, a "seething presence" (8) that materializes in literary depictions.

Inscrutable Belongings examines how formal and contextual modes of critique intertwine and how these fictions prescribe the need to imagine alternative social formations. At the same time, this book tasks American studies with the continuing project of interdisciplinary engagement, involving the "strange affinities" (Hong and Ferguson 18) that bind cultural critique with disciplines such as narratology, sociology (via family studies), anthropology (via kinship studies), history, race and ethnic studies, and gender and sexuality studies. By uniting these areas, we can target the increasingly intricate ways in which exploitation and subjugation are represented within cultural productions. The fictions I analyze are not merely symptomatic in their portrayal of the ambivalence accorded to the survival of the queer Asian North American protagonist. They also foreground the need to articulate how fictional worlds can deploy both the promise and the peril that dynamic, localized community formations offer for the collective recognition of those who have been bound painfully together by the omnipresence of physical brutality and social death.

The writers I study choose a narrative form that enables them to revisit and supplement the literary construct of the first-person storyteller, who in this case is a queer Asian North American. The choice to imagine such a life and voice in the narrative space offers these writers a chance to recenter a figure radically unrepresented in fictional worlds. Given the specific formal and contextual issues that arise in fictional depictions of queer Asian North Americans, this project takes into account narratological innovations, dynamic communal formations, and multiple registers of social difference to establish the revolutionary nature of these cultural productions. As Judith Butler notes in *Undoing Gender*,

> The struggle to survive is not really separable from the cultural life of fantasy, and the foreclosure of fantasy—through censorship, degradation, or other means—is one strategy for providing for the social death of persons. Fantasy is not the opposite of reality; it is what reality forecloses, and, as a result, it defines the limits of reality, constituting it as its constitutive outside. The critical promise of fantasy, when and where it exists, is to challenge the contingent limits of what will and will not be called reality. Fantasy is what allows us to imagine ourselves

and others otherwise; it establishes the possible in excess of the real; it points elsewhere, and when it is embodied, it brings the elsewhere home. (28–29)

I take the time to quote this passage because it models why fictions are the subject of this study: they create the fantasies of what should be "possible." Queer Asian North American writers invent storytellers who are aspirational in some sense: to invigorate narrative trajectories in order to expand which lives should exist, which tales can be told from so rarely heard voices, which homes and communities can be nurtured. In this process, multiple resurrections take place: (1) the ghostly queer Asian North American finds some measure of vibrancy through a survival plot and through a retrospectively positioned, first-person narrative discourse, and (2) his or her recounting illuminates a larger assemblage—that is, an *inscrutable belonging*—that demands recognition as a "constitutive outside" to traditional constructs such as the nuclear family and the heterosexual, monogamous marriage. Chapter 2 explains this term in more detail, but I invoke it here to introduce its central feature, as a collective that exists beside traditional North American family systems composed of a father, a mother, and their biologically conceived offspring.

The inscrutable belonging possesses multiple scales of social intervention. On the local level, the queer Asian North American storyteller finds an actual community that can sustain him or her, however temporarily, as a refuge from the forces of social death and threat of material violence. But this inscrutable belonging further emphasizes the ways in which the queer Asian North American storyteller demands larger acknowledgments and concessions for these dynamic, imperiled fellowships. In other words, whether the novels are set in the United States, Canada, or Asia, they all reveal queer Asian North American protagonists who are not necessarily seen as ideal citizen-subjects; they are metaphorical national children who require recognition beyond that offered by a figurative state-father, who does not deem their romances and their alternative kinships worth legitimizing either through law or through cultural norms.

These fictions and their considerations of such novel social formations generate creative interventions into the larger discourse surrounding queer equality movements. A number of scholars (such as Russell K. Robinson and Suzanne Lenon) working on both sides of the U.S.-Canada border have noted that same-sex marriage equality advocates employ an implicitly postracial paradigm to justify their demands for policy changes.[21] Racial injustice becomes a relic of the past, but same-sex marriage equality advocates simultaneously create a homogenous view of the queer community with one common goal: the desire to be wedded in legally codified matrimonial bliss. The underlying framework is that the queer only wants to be like any other "normal" North American, just with the right to marry someone of the same sex. But this homonormative perspective also functions in insidious ways.[22] In the context of U.S. transnational dynamics, Jasbir K. Puar notes, "US patriotism momentarily sanctions some homosexualities, often through gendered, racial, and class sanitizing" ("Homonormativities" 71) with the intent of denigrating individuals such as terrorists, who are deemed (at least situationally) to be the most antithetical to the nation-state. The queer can achieve a tentative form of social inclusion in part by advocating for a lifestyle modeled on normative heterosexual dynamics (such as the monogamous marriage), but this recognition is instrumentalized as a way by which other communities and groups are then savagely compared. The coalitional ruptures generated by homonormativity are instructive for my argument because they reveal that only certain forms of queerness are rendered legible, while both queer *and* racial difference continue to exist as coupled identity markers targeted by the nation-state and other institutional entities for violent regulation.

In relation to these fictions, the queer and racial intersectionalities that define the lives of the protagonists and their survival plots also influence the development of their social formations. Indeed, the radical articulations of family and kinship offered by these narratives require widespread recognition both within and beyond queer and racialized communities. In some sense, then, these fictions charge us with the need to move beyond marriage equality as a means by which queers of any color can achieve forms of justice and inclusion. In this way, the marriage plot (with its potentially homonormative investments) should be only one of many available narrative sequences for the queer Asian North American protagonist, as more writers imagine diverse life trajectories for their characters. To be sure, though many of the cultural productions I analyze are set before the federal recognition of same-sex marriage in the United States and in Canada, I do not believe that future queer Asian North American fictions will be centered on the marriage plot. Instead, I expect that narratives concerning alternative families and kinships; nontraditional relationships, courtships, and romances; and idiosyncratic communities, genealogies, and lineages will only continue to proliferate, always pushing us to imagine more ways to endure and to belong.

Configuring the Queer Asian North American

I have already noted that this project is configured around queer Asian North American storytellers, their tales of survival, and their associated inscrutable belongings. Now I will explain the essential reason I bring together queer Asian Canadian and queer Asian American fictions.

To be sure, I am well aware of some key differences between queer Asian Canadian and queer Asian American populations, especially with respect to the distinct dimensions of racial formation. In the United States, Asian American populations have typically been understood through a panethnic model that links migrants hailing from countries roughly from Afghanistan to Japan. Asian American racial formation theory largely coheres around the ways in which certain ethnic groups were determined to be unassimilable through a series of anti-immigration laws and legislative acts first passed in the late nineteenth century, which extended well into the twentieth (Lowe). Panethnicity further enabled the possibility of race-based community organizing that emerged in light of civil rights movements in the 1960s, which has correspondingly led to the widespread institutionalization of Asian American studies as part of college and university curricula.

In contrast, a panethnic model has not been a driving factor for framing Asian Canadian populations, due to differing social tensions and historical events that hindered race-based classification systems and community activism (Goellnicht, "A Long Labour"). Iyko Day further notes the centrality of comparative racial formation and census designations to the inception of Canadian identity categories.[23] As Day asserts, the presence of Aboriginal peoples and associated organizing around Indigenous issues has exerted a significant impact on the emergence of a "roots"-based identity paradigm that privileges multiethnic backgrounds over monoracial designations (63–64).[24] These various issues help explain the tenuous institutionalization and evolution of Asian Canadian studies as a distinct field.[25] More recently, minority groups in Canada have achieved significant forms of recognition, at least through legislative paradigms that offered a political stance on diversity (through the Canadian Multiculturalism Act of 1988) and that, in 2005, sanctioned same-sex marriage.[26] The United States, in contrast, has never officially endorsed a legislative policy concerning diversity and only recently (2015) fully recognized same-sex marriage on the federal level.[27]

Despite obvious dissimilarities in these national paradigms, my larger concern remains the interlocking ways in which individuals marked with multiple forms of social difference become rendered as Other and are often treated as such through forms of exclusion that move beyond the bounds of law. And although both countries have shown a progressive shift in their policies toward minorities—specifically those of Asian descent and identifying as queer—we must nevertheless understand these nations as being constituted by longer histories of incredible violence directed toward these populations, primarily in the context of transnational racialized labor economies, on the one hand, and medical mistreatment, on the other. In relation to the former issue, one does not need to look beyond the multitude of anti-immigration laws that were passed on more localized (state and provincial) and federal levels on both sides of the U.S.-Canadian border.[28] On the latter issue, the treatment by both the United States and Canada of queer individuals is stained by traumatic medicalization. In a study involving gay men in both countries, Roy Cain notes that "[t]he dominant clinical position on homosexuality during the 1950s and 1960s held that it was a psychopathological condition" (26).[29]

Such homophobic perspectives obviously presented a great challenge for the nascent gay and lesbian liberation movements developing in both countries in that same time period.[30] Furthermore, the AIDS crisis of the 1980s generated another systematic wave of anti-queer sentiment and medical misconduct on both sides of the border, often necessitating binational activism. Such coalitional efforts were apparent in the organizing initiated by ACT UP (AIDS Coalition to Unleash Power, founded in New York) and AAN! (AIDS ACTION NOW!, founded in Toronto) at the June 1989 international AIDS conference held in New York.[31]

These mutually constitutive histories and conditions inspire and influence the fictions of queer Asian Canadian and queer Asian American writers, as the ensuing chapters will show in great detail. *Inscrutable Belongings* follows the lead of other cultural critics, including Eleanor Ty, Donald C. Goellnicht, Rocío Davis, and Monica Chiu, who have convincingly argued for the need to consider Asian American and Asian Canadian writings as a textual collective given the "general similarities in historical treatment, experiences, cultural categorization, and social perception of subjects we call Asian Americans and Asian Canadians" (Ty, *Unfastened* xix).[32] At the same time, I move beyond these studies to argue that queer identities can be explored alongside racial differences to engage more fully the archive that is at the center of this book. Indeed, the larger corpus of queer Asian Canadian and queer Asian American narratives reveals protagonists whose racial and sexual backgrounds bring their mortalities into sharper relief.

In this sense, these cultural productions, though distinguishable via national taxonomies, communicate very similar concerns about the challenges related to the survival of social relationships that exist beside the bounds of the North American heteronuclear family.

A comparison between SKY Lee's *Disappearing Moon Cafe* and Lysley Tenorio's "Save the I-Hotel" (from the short story collection *Monstress*) illuminates the important connections between Asian American and Asian Canadian frames of reference, as they appear in fictional worlds. Both texts show how Asian North American bodies historically have been framed as queer vis-à-vis legislative policies and cultural norms that defined racialized sexualities as aberrant. Both also feature prominent characters who come to their respective North American countries in search of better economic opportunities, but who find harsh working conditions and racist environments that stymie trajectories of upward mobility. Finally, each fictional work involves major characters who can be identified as queer due to same-sex orientations and relationships.

Disappearing Moon Cafe is an intergenerational family saga anchored primarily by a first-person storyteller, Kae Ying Woo. Interspersed throughout the novel are third-person perspectives often following previous generations of the Woo family.[33] The novel's early sections detail how Gwei Chang, the family patriarch, attempts to make a living in Canada as a newly arrived migrant. As Donald C. Goellnicht notes, "The Canadian Dream—literally the railway that opened up the western part of the country for others of European origin to claim as their own—turns nightmare for these Chinese laborers" because of deplorable working conditions and unethical wage practices ("Of Bones and Suicide" 310). Even as Gwei Chang manages to gain a level of economic stability once he becomes proprietor of the titular Disappearing Moon Cafe, he must contend with newly implemented Canadian legislative policies adopted in 1923 that restrict Chinese immigration and accordingly hamper the institution of heteronuclear family structures. As the third-person narrator explains about the possible incest that occurs between two of her family members in a previous generation, "There was such a meagre number of young people—no new immigrant blood. What few there were, were native-born. Since 1923 the Chinese Exclusion Act had taken its heavy toll. The rapidly diminishing chinese-canadian community had withdrawn into itself, ripe for incest" (198, lowercase in original). In this sense, Lee's novel gestures to the ways in which one family's genealogical quandaries exist in concert with legislative forces that wreak havoc on social formations, relationships, and romances. As Chinese Canadian communities attempt to retain a measure of ethnic cohesion amid restrictive immigration laws, the limited romantic options for individuals of marriageable age are evident as incestuous relationships emerge. To be sure, Lee's novel is not suggesting that incest is unavoidable in these circumstances, but that endogamy is exacerbated by legislative conditions.

While Asian Canadian heterosexual romances are regulated and rendered as queer social formations, the novel productively enables the possibility of other orientations to emerge. As I see it, Kae Ying narrates her family's queer racialized history in order to trace out the potentiality of her own same-sex romance. Though the novel never clearly delineates Kae Ying's connection to her former classmate, Hermia Chow, something more than a platonic friendship transpires, especially when Kae Ying gives up a lucrative career to meet Hermia in Hong Kong with the intent of pursuing a new career as a writer. In one of the novel's most explicit homoerotic moments, Kae Ying reveals her intimacy with Hermia, as she "leaned forward and pressed a long kiss against the thin nape of [Hermia's] neck" (282). Lee's novel codes queerness in such understated instances, an appropriate style given a family background shrouded in so much instability. Arnold E. Davidson argues that the novel "contains a lesbian coming-out account within a five-generation family saga" (32), but there is never any definitive labeling of the relationship between Kae Ying and Hermia. This subtle erasure is important given the many ways in which Chinese Canadians have put up with ostracism, sexual regulation, and outright racism. For Kae Ying and Hermia's relationship to have a chance, one might argue, they cannot be too forthright with their same-sex relationship. Through an intergenerational family saga, the novel makes apparent how racial difference, queerness, and sexual relationships must be understood as relational constructs.

In a similar manner, though set in different historical and national domains, Lysley Tenorio's "Save the I-Hotel" imagines the critical intertwinement of race and queerness through a constellation of star-crossed romances. In this case, the story is focalized primarily from the third-person perspective of a Filipino migrant, Fortunado, who migrates to the United States just prior to 1934.[34] After working for a time in the fields of Stockton, he travels to San Francisco and strikes up a friendship with a fellow Filipino migrant named Vicente. Their fellowship is cemented by their collective status as racial Others, who work long hours with inadequate pay. Vicente eventually encourages Fortunado to quit his job and become a bellhop for the Parkdale Hotel, where Vicente is already employed.

During this period, Vicente engages in a romantic liaison with a white woman named Althea from Wisconsin. Althea works as a maid at the same hotel; she and Vicente often take advantage of her possession of spare room keys, which allows the couple access to restricted areas. Given the many anti-miscegenation laws instituted in California by 1931, Fortunado is concerned about their being caught together, asking Vicente, "What do you think they'll do to you if they find you with a white girl? This is your life, Vicente" (184). Such laws eventually take their toll on Filipino men during this period: the combination of restrictive immigration policies and anti-miscegenation statutes makes it virtually impossible to marry and to create traditional family structures: "Neither [Fortunado nor Vicente] married. No one in the I-Hotel ever did, and when they wanted to, the law forbade them. No Filipino could bring a wife or fiancée to the States back then, and there were no Filipinas here. Marrying white women, even dating them, was illegal, and always dangerous. The same week he arrived in California, a Filipino field worker was beaten to death for swimming in a lake with his white girlfriend" (168). Much like in *Disappearing Moon Cafe*, even heterosexual romances are considered unacceptable, as they are obstructed by legislative policies and racist paradigms. And as this passage so baldly notes, pursuing interracial liaisons of any kind can result in death.

Notably, the protagonists of both fictional works can be identified as queer, even as their sexual acts remain coded. In the short story's case, Fortunado develops strong feelings for Vicente, especially after they share a kiss one night, an act that is never repeated. While Vicente steers his sexual energies toward Althea, Fortunado seeks respite from his loneliness through transitory sexual encounters with other men. Vicente's relationship with Althea is eventually discovered, which leads to their job dismissals and ostensibly ends their romance. During this tumultuous period, Fortunado struggles with his feelings for Vicente: "Hours later, alone on the third-floor fire escape of the I-Hotel, Fortunado drank through a bottle of Du Kang, remembering the kiss he shared with Vicente, how it happened in darkness, in silence. And he thought of Vicente and Althea's kiss on the sidewalk, so reckless and unhidden, which perhaps was the point: Fortunado understood how difficult love could be, how its possibility hinged on a delicate balance between complete anonymity and the undeniable need to be known" (187). In this sense, the heterosexual, interracial romance between Vicente and Althea is resolutely linked to Fortunado's same-sex desires for Vicente. The short story enables us to understand how transnational laborers are frustrated by the conditions that deny their romances, both heterosexual and queer, any chance to blossom.

As both Tenorio's "Save the I-Hotel" and Lee's *Disappearing Moon Cafe* convey, even heterosexual relationships among Asian North Americans are regulated, as migrant populations become marked as deviant and polluted. In addition, similar to *Disappearing Moon Cafe*'s portrayal of Kae Ying's fledgling attachment to Hermia, the short story only vaguely sketches out the challenges that could arise for someone like Fortunado, if he were to seek to replicate in his own same-sex romance the "reckless and unbidden" displays of affection occurring between Vicente and Althea. Fortunado's queer desire is effectively closeted, and he never initiates a sustained same-sex relationship over the course of the short story's plot. Both Fortunado and Vicente ultimately remain bachelors, and the tenuousness of their lives is made clear through their evictions from the I-Hotel and the building's eventual demolishment. These historical conditions and social tensions, in both Canada and the United States, offer a racially informed sexual genealogy that showcases the rich tapestries of these fictional worlds. Migrants, queers, racial Others, and other such figures overlap due to their collective status as bodies and lives that are unfairly targeted by destructive social forces, which in turn imperil viable communal, romantic, and interpersonal attachments. This study of queer Asian North American fictions will operate with these various affinities in mind.[35]

Queer Asian North American Fictions

I now turn to a review of queer Asian North American cultural productions as a unique and multinational literary tradition.[36] My bibliographic research shows that queer Asian North Americans have produced well over one hundred different creative texts in all genres—ranging from novels, short story collections, memoirs, poetry, plays, and anthologies—over a period of about half a century, beginning most distinctly in the 1970s.[37]

With respect to single-authored fictions, a modest output of creative work cropped up in the 1980s, most prominently Willyce Kim's novels *Dancer Dawkins and the California Kid* and *Dead Heat*. It was in the 1990s that queer Asian North American fictions gained more visibility. Some notable works to surface include Shyam Selvadurai's *Funny Boy*, Wayson Choy's *The Jade Peony*, Hiromi Goto's *Chorus of Mushrooms*, SKY Lee's *Disappearing Moon Cafe*,

Shani Mootoo's *Cereus Blooms at Night*, R. Zamora Linmark's *Rolling the R's*, Lawrence Chua's *Gold by the Inch*, Nina Revoyr's *The Necessary Hunger*, and Bino Realuyo's *The Umbrella Country*. Strikingly, a number of these earlier works were produced outside of mainstream publishing houses. Such independent, smaller presses (such as Alyson Books and Kaya in the United States, and NeWest Press and Douglas & McIntyre in Canada) often offered these queer Asian North American writers the first opportunities to showcase their talents to a wider readership. The need for such presses was (and continues to be) paramount given their abilities to support publications that might be seen as too experimental or specialized for general audiences.

The years since the new millennium have seen a steady rise of publications by LGBTQI-identified Asian North American fiction writers, including Larissa Lai's *Salt Fish Girl*, Ghalib Shiraz Dhalla's *Ode to Lata*, Han Ong's *Fixer Chao*, Brian Leung's *World Famous Love Acts*, Kazim Ali's *Quinn's Passage*, Abha Dawesar's *Babyji*, Shani Mootoo's *Out on Main Street: & Other Stories*, Hiromi Goto's *The Kappa Child*, Noël Alumit's *Talking to the Moon*, Nina Revoyr's *Southland*, Rahul Mehta's *Quarantine*, and Rakesh Satyal's *Blue Boy*. Since 2011, publications have continued apace, with notable works including Justin Chin's *98 Wounds*, Philip Huang's *A Pornography of Grief*, Malinda Lo's *Huntress*, Shani Mootoo's *Moving Forward Sideways Like a Crab*, Tamai Kobayashi's *Prairie Ostrich*, Shyam Selvadurai's *The Hungry Ghosts*, Manil Suri's *The City of Devi*, James Sie's *Still Life Las Vegas*, Mariko Tamaki's *Saving Montgomery Sole*, Rahul Mehta's *No Other World*, Kazim Ali's *The Secret Room*, and Viet Dinh's *After Disasters*. This impressive list is by no means exhaustive,[38] and queer Asian American cultural productions are increasingly being published by commercial presses, including McClelland & Stewart, Doubleday Canada, W. W. Norton, St. Martin's Press, Picador, and Little, Brown.

The historical emergence of these queer Asian North American cultural productions as a collective grouping can clearly be traced to the period following the civil rights movement and the development of a new political consciousness that occurred throughout the 1980s as a direct result of the AIDS epidemic. The opening of immigration in 1965 in the United States and in 1967 in Canada has allowed a robust generation of writers to come of age. Finally, many of these writers undoubtedly have benefited from the widespread institutionalization of ethnic studies courses as well as the expansion of creative writing programs in colleges and universities.[39] But, most crucially, many of the aforementioned writers have established networks among their authorial and editorial peers, a fact that becomes evident in the acknowledgments pages of these books and in the routes that manuscripts take to eventual publication.[40]

Queer Critical Genealogies

Central to my arguments are various strains of queer critical practices and scholarship, and I accordingly move to a fuller investigation of these genealogies. The term *queer* initially appeared as an epithet leveraged against the deviancy of homosexuals and other such sexually non-normative peoples. The term was reclaimed and transformed by those it targeted, while being employed by academics to enable new ways of reading cultural productions, historical moments, and social movements and communities. Feminist studies scholar Suzanna Danuta Walters attributes queer theory's germination to a particular materialist and political context derived out of "the AIDS crisis, the rise of postmodern/poststructural theory, the politics of academia, the sex debates, and recent critiques of feminism" ("From Here" 837). Because the term *queer* is so fluid, queer theoretical work and analysis have been fraught with debates about how it should be deployed. *Queer* finds itself shouldering the weighty burden of having to represent multiple sexual categories, acts, practices, individuals, groups, and communities. As an umbrella term, *queerness* further struggles to encapsulate non-heteronormative sexualities, including homosexuality and bisexuality, as well as those individuals identifying as lesbian, gay, transgender, and intersex. In a semiautobiographical essay, Didi Khayatt writes, "The category 'queer' did not work for other people because it seemed to flatten the very diversity it purposed to acknowledge. 'Queer' embraced differences while not quite coming to terms with issues of power that are intrinsic to each sexual category included under the rubric 'queer' as it intersects with race, gender, class, disability, and so on" (497). Khayatt's statement denotes the importance of power and intersectionality in deploying queerness as an analytic. My study takes into account the fluidity of the term *queer* and places it in conversation with other registers of social difference, such as race, ethnicity, class, and nationality.[41]

As part of the overwhelming proliferation of scholarly studies concerning sexuality, queer Asian North American cultural studies in the 1990s offered a number of key contributions. For instance, groundbreaking scholarship in this area could be found in anthologies and essay collections, most prominently

Russell Leong's *Asian American Sexualities* in 1995 and David L. Eng and Alice Y. Hom's *Q&A* in 1998. These two works mapped out central concerns for queer Asian North Americans, ranging from the dangers of coming out to the challenges of developing a sense of community.

In the years following the new millennium, David L. Eng's *Racial Castration* (2001) and *The Feeling of Kinship* (2010), Martin Manalansan's *Global Divas* (2003), Gayatri Gopinath's *Impossible Desires* (2005), Jasbir Puar's *Terrorist Assemblages* (2007), Martin Joseph Ponce's *Beyond the Nation* (2012), Amy Sueyoshi's *Queer Compulsions* (2012), Eng-Beng Lim's *Brown Boys and Rice Queens* (2013), Nguyen Tan Hoang's *A View from the Bottom* (2014), and C. Winter Han's *Geisha of a Different Kind* (2015) have addressed critical issues related to the queer Asian North American experience in a variety of cultural, ethnic, and generic arenas. These studies provide obvious precursors to *Inscrutable Belongings* and influence my arguments in their varied articulations of sexuality as it becomes enmeshed with Asian and Asian North American racialization.

Not surprisingly, a common theme among these studies is the queer Asian North American's search for and desire to find a home, however that place might be defined. For instance, *Asian American Sexualities* and *Q&A* contain early chapters investigating the precariousness of family and kinship. In a study published in the former, Alice Y. Hom immediately diagnoses the fragile place of the queer Asian North American in the domestic space. Though Hom finds the possibility of familial reparation even amid the disclosure of sexuality, the piece begins from the standpoint that the home is made unstable for the queer Asian North American who dares to come out of the closet ("Stories").[42] From the latter anthology, Karin Aguilar-San Juan ominously explains, "Like many others who refuse the privileges associated with heterosexuality, queer Asian Americans come out and go home only at the risk of great loss, sometimes terror, even death. Gestures toward home and family seem both necessary and impossible: necessary for a sense of completion, impossible because family requires heteronormativity" ("Going Home" 38).[43] For Aguilar-San Juan, the queer Asian North American must "push toward the other side" (38) in order to create a haven that can exist external to the traditional home. Richard Fung notes in addition, "As is the case for many other people of color and especially immigrants, our families and our ethnic communities are a rare source of affirmation in a racist society. In coming out, we risk (or feel that we risk) losing this support, though the ever-growing organizations of lesbian and gay Asians have worked against this process of cultural exile" (238). For Fung, because the biological family cannot always function to provide the "affirmation" the queer Asian North American needs, alternative communities must be formed, but this process is riddled with complications. Indeed, these modes of organizing are not always available for queer Asian North Americans, often because such individuals may not reside in large urban centers where such coordination can germinate.[44]

The strain of solidifying a sense of home is so severe for many queer Asian North Americans that one of the most robust areas of emerging research relates to psychological distress and counseling.[45] The problems arising for queer Asian North Americans are made clear by Dana Takagi: "In other words, many of us experience the worlds of Asian America and gay America as separate places—emotionally, physically, intellectually" (25). And in one case study involving young queer Asian North Americans, Kevin Kumashiro notes that for his participants, queerness often gets marked as white, while one's ethnoracial background signifies as heterosexual (502). Both Takagi and Kumashiro make evident the ways in which the bifurcation between sexuality and racial identity leaves the queer Asian North American in a state of incoherence.

The search for inclusivity is all the more disquieting because of the limited ways in which we have come to define what constitutes a viable and welcoming collective, and a place one might consider another home. Of these myopic ways of thinking, David L. Eng explains that "a retheorization of family and kinship relations after poststructuralism" is "still largely absent in current debates in queer theory and anthropological accounts of kinship" (*Feeling* 16). Eng's overarching thesis finds traces of poststructural kinships in social formations such as transnational adoptee families. He makes a compelling case for the lack of psychosocial support that would enable a Korean adoptee to possess, for instance, a biological and an adoptive mother at the same time (164–165). Reading such dual maternity as a queer diasporic construct, Eng leaves us with the sense that we require but are not prepared to institute sustained alterations in the heteronuclear family structure.[46] While taking into account these queer Asian North American cultural studies, it is equally important to analyze dynamic assemblages as they emerge in queer Asian North American fictions.[47] Eng's study offers much to intervene in discourses of kinships through readings of texts such as legal policies and documentary films. But it leaves out the archive at this study's center: queer Asian North American fictions that vigorously retheorize heteronuclear family formations and that dramatize the first-person storyteller's survival plot. And while some of the aforementioned scholars devote sections of their books to the analysis of queer Asian North American novels, none fully engage this literary body as a distinct grouping that requires both contextual and formal attention.

Given the centrality of material histories, cultures, and contexts embedded in these fictional representations, my overarching critical methodology is influenced by what Roderick Ferguson calls a "queer of color critique," which investigates "how intersecting racial, gender, and sexual practices antagonize and/or conspire with the normative investments of nation-states and capital" (4). In *Aberrations in Black*, Ferguson analyzes a broad selection of cultural productions that unveils the limits of canonical American sociological studies.[48] Ferguson's intervention helps situate the pioneering work first completed by feminist lesbian writers and scholars in the 1970s and 1980s, forming a queer of color genealogy that links these earlier publications with the ongoing critical explorations of both race and sexuality.[49] Though Ferguson's study concentrates primarily on queer African American cultures and how they must be read to supplement existing accounts of pervasive social ills, a queer of color critique can also be applied to Asian North American fictions. In this case, a queer of color critique showcases the continuing subjugation of queer Asian North American characters as nonentities who struggle for multiple forms of recognition and to create communities of refuge.

At the same time, given the highly transnational nature of many fictions at this study's center, I employ another methodological branch of cultural analysis known as queer diasporic critique. Existing scholarship (penned by the aforementioned Eng, Gopinath, and Manalansan) focuses primarily on transnational and global paradigms for analyzing queer Asian North American cultures and cultural productions. These studies explore Asian North American masculinity and associated textual representations (Eng, *Racial Castration*), the everyday lives of queer Filipino American men residing in New York City (Manalansan), the im/possibility of same-sex female desire as depicted in South Asian Anglophone literature and film (Gopinath), and the tenuous emergence of poststructural kinships (Eng, *Feeling*). A queer diasporic critique offers an additional tool to examine the highly mobile lives of Asian North American characters depicted in fictional worlds and how their travels, often across national boundaries, inform their developing sexual subjectivities and their quests to find communities who accept them.

Ferguson, Eng, Manalansan, and Gopinath model how race, ethnicity, class, culture, and sexuality (and other associated identity markers) can be studied in tandem. Queer of color and queer diasporic critiques help contour traditionally heteronormative disciplines such as American studies while augmenting queer theory through an emphasis on ethnoracial discourses. These lines of thinking offer a way to examine the queer Asian North American's search for home, however that place and community might be defined, and to make sense of his or her ongoing displacement and alienation.

While my work takes much inspiration from queer Asian North American cultural studies, and queer of color and queer diasporic critiques, it also draws on one major debate that has arisen in queer theory between Lee Edelman and José Esteban Muñoz. Edelman's *No Future* promotes the discourse of queer pessimism, specifically through psychoanalytic methodologies and a form of active refusal. Edelman bristles at the centrality of the figural Child, a being that is coded into the social fabric as the Thing that we must protect at all costs because this youthful entity is innocent and pure. The queer is alternatively positioned as a form of excess that society repeatedly (and unsuccessfully) attempts to expunge; the queer exists as the diametric opposite to this Child. For Edelman, the urgency of a queer political project (in all of its manifestations) appears in embracing the negativity related to this social death. Responding in part to Edelman's thesis, Muñoz's *Cruising Utopia* contests the antirelational foundations of queer pessimism. Muñoz notes, "Queerness is the thing that lets us feel that this world is not enough, that indeed something is missing. Often we can glimpse the worlds proposed and promised by queerness in the realm of the aesthetic" (1). For Muñoz, then, the function of cultural productions is the potential to create "concrete utopias" (3), moving beyond the constraints of the material world, which is already mired in so many queer negations.

Inscrutable Belongings takes into account both Edelman's and Muñoz's perspectives, attempting to carve out a middle way. The disclamation of the Child, as encouraged by Edelman, is powerful, especially for queers and others who are marginalized. But my project confronts a different depiction of the child, one found in queer Asian North American fictional narratives. This child complicates existing discourses related to infants, youths, and family values through elaborating on the prospects of protoqueerness. By *protoqueer*, I define a term that speaks to the child who will later grow up and pursue same-sex yearnings. These fictions offer us this child figure and remind us of the possibility that sexual identifications cannot be assumed. At the same time, these narratives grant us a rare opportunity to analyze the nature of the protoqueer Asian North American child's survival, how he or she manages to mature, despite facing so many forms of antagonism and physical violence. In this sense, these fictions ask us to reconsider the figure of the child, this protoqueerness, and the eventual negotiation of a tenuous path to adulthood.

My study draws from Muñoz's conception of "concrete utopias" (3) precisely because they can be related "to historically situated struggles, a collectivity that is actualized or potential" (3). The inscrutable belongings at the center of these readings exist as a corollary to these "concrete utopias" because they form "the hopes of a collective, an emergent group" (3), which in this case are found in the fictional worlds imagined by queer Asian North American writers. At the same time, so many of the dynamic social formations that enable the protagonists to survive are fragile, often transitory, and sometimes destructively terminated. These fictions remind us that the queer Asian North American storyteller's endurance is conditional, never finally assured. Though the storyteller lives to tell his or her tale, the future remains ambivalently unscripted, plagued by material violence and social death on the one hand, and buoyed by utopic potential on the other.

Reading Retrospectively: Survival Plots, Inscrutable Belongings, and Queer Asian North American Fictions

As our queer Asian North American storyteller narrates retrospectively, we understand that he or she has negotiated a survival plot. But we can make comprehensive sense of what this sequencing means only after the tale is finally told: this recounted life is continually jeopardized. As I have introduced only my central interventions, methodologies, and key terms, I use the first two chapters of this book to establish more expansively the contextual, historical, critical, and theoretical grounds upon which my overall argument rests. In Chapter 1, I articulate the emergence of three formal and thematic patterns that I call *tactical diversions*. I choose this name because these patterns move away from the author's autobiographically imbued fictional double—a queer Asian North American—to incorporate other discursive viewpoints, characters, and social issues.

These tactical diversions sometimes overlap with the extended analytical focus of this study, which repeatedly emphasizes two key elements: *survival plots* that significantly involve queer Asian North American characters as storytellers and an associated community of individuals (and associated entities), what I earlier termed as *inscrutable belongings*. In contrast to the narrative patterns and motifs explored in Chapter 1, survival plots exhibit a distinctive element in their focus on an embattled narrator who shows a progressive arc typified by a movement from youth to adulthood. But because of the ways in which this speaker is regarded as both physically and socially deviant, he or she is always in danger of being written out of the story. In this way, the first-person narrator maintains a crucial insurgency by refusing to be moved into the margins, upholding the "I" that is under threat of dematerialization. At the same time, I am centrally invested in how this storyteller's fortitude is connected to a set of individuals (and entities) who are not necessarily biologically related to him or her and who together constitute an *inscrutable belonging*. This community provides the storyteller with a dynamic collective that exists as a potential tool that can be wielded to withstand the violent forces, both physical and structural, that embattle him or her.

Thus, in the second chapter, I elaborate on the queer Asian North American storyteller as a radical character type, one who journeys through a survival plot, on the one hand, and constructs inscrutable belongings, on the other. First, I outline exactly why this speaking entity and associated narrative sequencing are such visionary constructs in light of existing advances in cultural studies and formalist criticism. Second, I flesh out my conception of inscrutable belongings, which is indebted to the scholarship of sociologists, historians, and anthropologists who investigate forms of alternative kinships and family structures. Third, I use the chapter to complete a lengthier reading of Leong's aforementioned short story "Camouflage," which dramatizes the storyteller's ambivalent but pressing need to generate multiple nourishing fellowships among his queer brethren.

The remaining chapters all take on readings of novels that bring to mind foundational struggles for queer Asian North Americans (and other marginalized groups) and confront a broad range of issues, including interracial desire, the AIDS/HIV epidemic, and transnational mobility. Chapters 3 to 6 follow one major ordering conceit: I first analyze the novel that presents the storyteller with the shortest life span as it unfolds within the fictional world and end with the one that presents the storyteller with the longest. While these fictional characters' life spans lengthen, their narrative trajectories become increasingly fraught. This trend suggests that the most intricate survival plots are simply more difficult to imagine, as the narrator is in jeopardy for a more extended period. In this way, the later novels in this study more directly question the viability of same-sex romance over the long term and arguably are imbued with a deeper ambivalence. All four fictions further find an ordering conceit related to a serious trauma occurring in what I call a "protoqueer" period, a time in which the narrator has not yet explicitly delved into his or her queer sexuality. In this sense, my analyses are influenced by discourses and philosophical approaches to the child, as advanced by Lee Edelman and others. Finally, this chapter order enables my argument to unfold with the actual publication chronology of these fictions in mind.

The third chapter, "Inscrutable Belongings in Pathology: Infectious Genealogies in Alexander Chee's *Edinburgh*," involves a storyteller named Fee who becomes the research assistant to a historian. During this period, he finds strength in letters that were penned by a bubonic plague victim who had been entombed alive. The importance of this finding is not fully made clear until after Fee is an adult and reflects back on his childhood and teen years. He accordingly recounts a harrowing tale in which he—along with numerous other young boys—is molested by a choir director. While many of his fellow choirboys commit suicide, the narrator manages to reach adulthood. However, existing under the weight of these traumas, Fee finds himself struggling to work through his troubled past. I argue that the novel demonstrates how the Black Plague survivor transforms into Fee's metaphorical progenitor, allowing him to reframe the sexual abuse he endured as a preteen and to reconstitute notions of family and kinship through the logic of a community of individuals who have braved a calamitous outbreak. I also investigate the ways in which the novel critically links earlier pandemics to the AIDS/HIV crises in the 1980s. Acknowledging these infectious genealogies enables Fee to disengage from his own participation in abusive intergenerational relationships.

Chapter 4, "Inscrutable Belongings in Cinema: Filmic Lineages in Noël Alumit's *Letters to Montgomery Clift*," considers the metaphorical ancestries and alternative social formations developed by a storyteller named Bong. He spends much of his time mooning over Hollywood movie stars, especially Montgomery Clift. In this sense, this chapter explores the novel's source of spectral haunting by moving forcefully into the Golden Age of Hollywood cinema.[50] Here I am interested in how the protoqueer Asian North American boy employs his imagination to deal with childhood traumas. The narrator recounts the centrality of Clift as part of an inscrutable belonging that helps restore order in a chaotic and dangerous period in which he is abused by a family member and left abandoned. Eventually he is adopted, allowing him a chance to foster lasting attachments, but these changes also come with others: Bong's relationship to Clift alters, and the nature of such social affinities must evolve for him to emerge as the survival plot's heroic center.

The specters of the bubonic plague victim and Montgomery Clift remain palpable as I move to Chapter 5, "Inscrutable Belongings in Hunting: Interracial Surrogacies in Nina Revoyr's *Wingshooters*," in which the narrator, Michelle, obsessively reflects on one period of her youth. During that time, an African American couple named Garrett move to Michelle's hometown, which is a bucolic but segregated midwestern location during the 1970s. A period of heightened racial tensions ensues during which Mrs. Garrett is targeted and then murdered by a townsperson. This moment is traumatic because the storyteller, casting back to this time, had imagined the possibility of an inscrutable belonging based on the bonds she had forged with Mr. and Mrs. Garrett. The novel reveals Michelle's need to reconceptualize her life through what I call "interracial surrogacies," a phrase that calls attention to the desire for this protagonist to construct a makeshift family, however ephemeral and unlikely, in a racially homogenous agrarian setting.

And the final chapter, "Inscrutable Belongings in Bondage: Degenerate Descendants in Lydia Kwa's *Pulse*," takes us to Singapore, where the storyteller, Natalie, grapples with the suicide of a close friend's son. Whereas earlier chapters focus on marginalized subjects who act as metaphorical progenitors, Chapter 6 shows how Natalie reconfigures her relationships through healing and alternative therapies. These therapeutic approaches are necessary to deal with her past traumas, which come to light after she acknowledges the unexpected parallel she shares with the suicide victim. In this case, the ghost that haunts this chapter belongs not to someone who died long ago but to a figure who was born a generation after her. The storyteller comes to embrace this phantom through their collective status as "degenerate descendants" of the postcolonial nation. The novel's Singaporean setting elucidates the transnational stakes in my critique, as these two characters function to undercut national ideologies that promote technological progress and ethnoracial factionalism.

Each fictional work centrally involves a dead subject from the past—in "Camouflage," a queer man who succumbs to the AIDS virus; in *Edinburgh*, a Black Plague survivor from the 1300s; in *Letters*, Montgomery Clift, who dies in 1966; in *Wingshooters*, an African American woman murdered in the seventies; in *Pulse*, a young man who commits suicide in Singapore a scant handful of years into the new millennium. Indeed, these texts conjure specters from the past as a way for the queer Asian North American storyteller to reconstitute ghosts as metaphorical ancestors, symbolic family members, and/or figurative descendants, as what we might call an intertextual set of *inscrutable belongings*. Such social formations operate as a key asset that enables the storyteller to endure and to survive. As *Inscrutable Belongings* moves forward with its emphasis on such dead subjects, the overlaps among all of the inscrutable belongings become ever more apparent. The diseased and the monstrous, the apparitional and the haunted, the racially impure, and the alternative healers all find a measure of transitory recognition in their respective fictional worlds. And in the process, these novels diagnose the need for unconventional assemblages that enfold the queer Asian North American beside and beyond the bounds of the heteronuclear family.

A short coda sums up the book's major insights and mulls over the continued importance of analyzing these pioneering cultural productions. If from such varied fictional worlds we can extrapolate any kind of future, however ambivalently portrayed, it emanates from the communicative act of storytelling between the narrator and his or her implied audience, one that extends to readers who can begin to imagine the multiplicity of lives that demand our attention. Thus the novels encourage us to confront the social death of queer Asian North American protagonists in light of other expendable "eccentrics" and to link them relationally as part of inscrutable belongings. As the storytellers shift to the narrative center, they remind us that marginality can still emerge in other dangerous forms and that our critical lenses must always be attuned to power and oppression as they manifest so catastrophically in cultural productions.

CHAPTER 1

TACTICAL DIVERSIONS

TOWARD QUEER ASIAN NORTH AMERICAN FORMALISMS

IN THE INTRODUCTION I briefly mentioned that the deviance associated with queer Asian North American storytellers pervades the fictional world through their fragility in the *survival plot*. The ever-present danger for narrative figures of such social eccentricity is that they will be terminated from the story. Nevertheless, the concept of *inscrutable belongings* provides these narrators a tool and a community, however transitory and ambivalent in its formation, that allow them to last to the final page.

This chapter establishes the survival plot's significance and its complementary assemblage of eccentric entities by charting the larger archive of queer Asian North American fictions. I remain attentive to how a wide set of cultural productions fashions the expansive diversity of queer Asian North American fictions, while concomitantly revealing why tales of endurance and inscrutable belongings remain so elusive to depict. Though these cultural productions do not necessarily offer sustained depictions of queer Asian North American characters, they do constitute a significant textual grouping in their exploration of pressing social issues such as interracial romance, childhood guardianship, and familial dynamics.

I begin this chapter's analysis by considering how queer Asian North American formalisms have evolved in general. To this end, I survey what I term *tactical diversions*: three formal and thematic patterns—*narrative elliptics, protoqueer narratives*, and *ensemble narratives*—found in queer Asian North American fictional works. These fictions spotlight characters who must be *tactical* in the ways that they negotiate power relations arising in specific spaces (de Certeau 37). Indeed, the many characters who appear in these fictions often are subjected to violent forms of domination produced out of socially constituted locations such as the court, the educational facility, and the home. In this sense, their movements through the plot cannot always be planned and must show adaptability in the face of obstacles. In many cases, these hindrances are too significant, and the characters cannot withstand such destructive forces despite their calculated choices. Notably, these fictions do not involve a queer Asian North American storyteller as the primary narrating entity. I assess this choice of aesthetic discourse as a mode of *diversion*, not only in the sense of a moving away from queer Asian North American themes, but also in the productive way that this shift allows for a purposeful reorientation of the fictional world. Diversions enhance the complexity of how we understand these fictions as an archive depicting various social problems, threatened communities, and imagined lives. At the same time, these diversions signal the challenge of centering the queer Asian North American character, who bears so much social eccentricity that his or her place within the fictional world is constantly in question.

Toward a Queer Racial Formalism

A queer racial formalism considers the impact social difference has on the structure of fictional worlds. One question immediately arises: What kinds of narratives involve the sexual and racial differences of Asian North Americans? To answer this question, readers can look to model minority stereotypes through an emphasis on their construction. In such a stereotype, the Asian North American exists as an imaginary figure imbued with signifying properties that inform unidirectional sequencing.

The post-1965 model minority narrative on first glance seems to present the Asian North American in a positive light: he or she is not so malevolent. From birth forward, this child receives the proper, strict parenting that enables him or her to achieve. In this plotting, the model minority must show inexorable progression in his or her studies, eventually reaching adulthood as an unqualified success. As part of the rising action, this figure scores exceptionally on standardized exams and later receives admittance into a prestigious college or university. His or her work ethic and diligence are evidenced by the attainment of a white-collar job position in a respectable field such as medicine, law, or engineering. Despite ceaseless toil, the model minority somehow has time to procreate with a heterosexual partner, giving birth to a child that of course will go on to become a model minority as well.

Though many scholars make persuasive cases dismissing the model minority paradigm as a false construct (for example, Chou and Feagin; Yook; Ty, *Asianfail*) or contextualizing this stereotype through historical developments (Wu; Hsu), this reductive mode by which Asian North Americans are rendered continues to persist. Some writers, in fact, uphold the model minority stereotype, advising readers on how they can raise equally high-achieving children. One infamous example is Amy Chua's *Battle Hymn of the Tiger Mother*; other prominent examples include Soo Kim Abboud and Jane Kim's *Top of the Class: How Asian Parents Raise High Achievers—and How You Can Too* and Quanyu Huang's *The Hybrid Tiger: Secrets of the Extraordinary Success of Asian-American Kids*. All three publications portray reproduction as perfunctory rather than passionate or romantic. Sex is simply a mechanism for parents to replicate the model minority child in their own heteronuclear families. These how-to guides apparently envision a mode of figurative parthenogenesis, as any parents apparently can "raise high achievers," so long as they follow the methodical continuity essential in the procurement of model minority accomplishments. Deviations to the "plot" are not allowed; absolute obedience to diligence and improvement are expected. At the same time, the heterosexuality of the Asian or Asian North American parent exists only as a function of raising the model minority child from birth to overachieving adulthood. In this sense, the model minority plot implicitly precludes the possibility of the queer subject, while promoting the centrality of the monogamous, heterosexual marriage and nuclear family formation.

Not surprisingly, model minority progeny must adhere to a rather strict regime when it comes to sexuality. In *The Hybrid Tiger* Huang describes his own entry into the world of romance and marriage, which exists in contrast to his lesser-achieving friends: "My friends at the factories also married and had children, which meant that they'd stay factory workers forever. I was the only one who went to college. Of course, after I graduated from college, it was finally my turn: I found love and established a happy family" (217). Huang clarifies that the model minority can succeed only with the appropriate ordering, in which heterosexual desires are acted upon only after the achieving of at least a college degree. To provide an example of an undesirable trajectory, Abboud and Kim discuss a woman named Susan, who "attended college and began dating an older artist halfway through her sophomore year. Months later, Susan announced that she had taken up painting and that her boyfriend had convinced her that she was good enough to make a living off her new vocation. Since Susan had never picked up a paintbrush or shown any interest in the arts before, her parents were understandably worried" (20). Susan's downfall becomes complete when "she dropped out of college and married the artist. As it turned out, her parents' fears were confirmed: her career as an artist floundered. Susan is now divorced and trying to get a degree in communications at a small community college" (20). Abboud and Kim are quick to point out that they "are not saying that people with a love and talent for art should not pursue their dreams" (21), but instead use Susan's parents as an example of a couple who did not instill in their child that "education and learning provided (at least some) happiness, pride, and security" (21). In these how-to guides, Asian North American heterosexuality revolves around model minority dynamics. In both Huang's and Abboud and Kim's examples, heterosexuality must be restricted in favor of a proper veneration of educational achievement first. If heterosexual desires become rampant at too early a stage, success will be endangered. Though heterosexual desires must at first be curtailed, these stories also convey the necessity of reproduction to the model minority child who will eventually grow up and establish his or her own "happy family." The expectation, then, is that the cycle of model minority reproduction can be reborn *ad infinitum*.

Even as Asian North Americans move out of the monstrosity and perverted sexuality embedded in racist designations such as the yellow peril, forms of racial and sexual circumscription come attached to their new visibility as the model minority. In this new plot, the path is unyieldingly unidirectional and suggests that racialized heterosexuality is contained within a controlled, nonthreatening paradigm. Asian North Americans apparently will have sex, but only insofar as they attempt to produce the model minority child, who can then be the template for other parents to produce their own high-achieving offspring.[1]

Tactical Diversions

The model minority plot informs and overshadows the entire corpus of queer Asian North American cultural productions. Because the model minority plot involves a strict regulation, but necessary extension, of sexuality, the queer Asian North American cannot participate in this sequencing. His or her queerness endangers the next generation of model minorities. Not only does biological reproduction become questioned, but his or her sexuality, too, bears negative signifying power, polluting the narrative of progress. Not surprisingly, *Battle Hymn of the Tiger Mother*, *Top of the Class*, and *The Hybrid Tiger* all implicitly employ heteronormative dynamics and traditional social structures to scaffold the model minority plot. And despite the fact that these how-to guides employ a decidedly queer dimension by promoting metaphorical parthenogenesis as a mode by which any parent can replicate the overachieving child, such non-normative, non-intergenerational reproductions are categorically disavowed in order to shore up the spectacle of the pristinely exceptional, ever-advancing Asian North American family.

In this way, an Asian North American exits this narrative ordering as soon as his or her queer orientation manifests, but what new representational path then follows this expulsion? Queer Asian North American writers—most of whom have published their work in the period in which this stereotype has predominated—must generate fictional narratives that are tasked with the responsibility of bringing other potential plots into being. What other stories can be told? What other fictional trajectories can be created? These questions are difficult to answer only insofar as such narratives offer no single unifying theme, content, or formal approach.

Nevertheless, as I have found while researching this literary corpus, certain patterns materialize. The patterns that concern me here are what I earlier termed tactical diversions. These cultural productions offer fictional worlds informed by, but not directly or explicitly engaging, a queer Asian North American figure who is the center of the narrative discourse. The first type, narrative elliptics, involves plots in which no major character can be identified as both queer *and* Asian North American. At the same time, the cultural productions that invoke narrative elliptics still explore the complications of social difference, as they influence characters' lives in deleterious ways. In this sense, these narratives foreground some of the issues that will entangle the queer Asian North American storyteller as a figure stymied by material violence and social death. The second type, protoqueer narratives, comprises stories in which the main Asian North American character might be assumed to exhibit non-normative sexual tendencies, but because of his or her age, usually in the preadolescent or early teenage years, nothing explicitly indicates that the character categorically identifies or could be labeled as queer. There is no extended plot that sees this youthful character mature into his or her adult years. The final form, ensemble narratives, involves a queer Asian North American who is one part of a larger character-system. His or her developmental trajectory must be balanced alongside the fates of other characters. In this set of fictions, narrative perspectives are consistently fractured among multiple viewpoints through the use of shifting focalization.[2] Characters who exhibit same-sex desires in these ensemble narratives may face catastrophic consequences from the pursuit of their queer liaisons. There exists the possibility of death or expulsion from the family.

Tactical diversions, along with the survival plots I will analyze in other chapters, counter conceptions of linear narrative progression as it relates to Asian American families. These cultural productions invoke the relationality between forms of queerness and racial difference, undermining the presumed heterosexuality of model minority constructs. At the same time, they often depict romances that are not foregone conclusions and resist the reproductive futurism inherent to the model minority sequencing. Whereas model minority plots are invested in a presumptive tomorrow filled with overachieving children, these fictions are far more attentive to a larger historical tapestry in which the past comes to inform how queer sexuality and racial difference are intimately connected. Though these cultural productions provide an important representational alternative to the model minority, they also diagnose the fragility of those deemed to be outcasts and signal the challenge of centering the queer Asian North American character in narrative discourse. In the next three sections, I undertake short readings of numerous fictions; my point in drawing out these concatenated analyses is twofold. I first show the aesthetic depth, thematic range, and contextual heterogeneity of work being produced by queer Asian North American writers as a larger grouping. Second, my analyses clarify the exceptional nature of the queer Asian North American protagonist who not only commands the plot as the retrospective storytelling foundation but also matures from child to adult within the space of that same narrative.

Narrative Elliptics: Into the Queer/Racial Past

The first form of tactical diversion unites themes of racial and sexual difference in the fictional world, falling in line with scholars who have sought to redefine Asian North American studies through intersectional methodologies. For instance, Eng's conclusion to *Racial Castration* provocatively reorients the field through queer diasporic discourses. Migrant Asian bodies and sexualities have long been targeted by legislation that forbade, for instance, interracial marriage. Constructed by law as a non-normative sexual being, the Asian becomes queer. Eng's points are germane to this first form of tactical diversion in which there is no figure within the fictional world who might be seen as the queer Asian North American author's autobiographical shadow. Even as the queer racialized protagonist is absent, these narratives humanize characters who also encounter ostracism and prejudice. In this first form, the primary romance plots do not endure because they continually signify as non-normative in some way. I commence pithy readings of Brian Leung's *Take Me Home*, Nina Revoyr's *The Age of Dreaming*, and Malinda Lo's *Huntress* to investigate some choice examples.

Brian Leung's *Take Me Home* leads readers into the late nineteenth century in a historical fiction set in the Wyoming Territory. Addie, one of the protagonists, is an anomaly because she is one of the few women willing to brave the unyielding environment of the frontier, a landscape so harsh that her brother, Tommy, at first hesitates to invite her despite his own need for help. Addie eventually moves to Wyoming, leaving behind an alcoholic father in Kentucky. This radical shift to such an austere place forces her to develop an independent identity, one that is clearly feminist in its construct. Addie eventually marries a miner of Finnish background, Muuk. Her marriage is never consummated. Instead, Addie's most significant romantic liaison and sexual partner is a Chinese cook named Wing Lee. Given the era in which the novel is set, an interracial romance between a white woman and a Chinese man emerges as its own form of deviant sexuality. The third-person narrator spotlights the murky nature of Addie and Wing's sexual relationship: "What were they doing? They understood it simultaneously. They were friends who talked and gutted game, closer than this other thing that brought them both a sense of freedom but seemed less. It wasn't love between Addie and Wing, could not be in any case, but it was something akin and just as important" (262). Here their attraction to each other cannot be understood as "love," precisely because such feelings would be outlawed. Nevertheless, their link to each other is "just as important" as "love," something "akin" and something a little bit queer in its construct.

The novel's conclusion sees an elderly Addie revisiting Wyoming (after having settled in California) to confront Muuk about a terrible period of racially motivated rioting and unrest that had occurred many decades prior. Muuk may have shot Addie during one of these riots, and because of her gunshot wounds she lost an unborn child. Also, it was during this period of unrest that Wing was burned alive and many other Chinese butchered.[3] Addie suspects that Muuk took revenge for her affair with a Chinese man and for carrying a mixed-race child that Muuk could not then claim as his own. As Addie discovers on her return, Muuk's mental capacities have deteriorated due to senile dementia, but he still bears a strong memory of a man named Panu Lankinen. This moment allows Addie to recontextualize her own experiences with Muuk: "On their wedding night he'd been on top of her and said, 'I cannot,' but today, beneath the murkiness of his bathwater, she saw that he could, even years after everything else about who he was had melted away. He did it while thinking about someone named Panu Lankinen" (284). Though Leung's work never directly labels Muuk a queer character, Addie concludes that Muuk's primary sexual drives were same-sex-oriented. This information casts their marriage in a new light: Muuk was using Addie as evidence of his heterosexuality, and he had wanted the baby Addie lost in order to prove his socially sanctioned paternity to others in the community. Despite what Addie discovers, the novel provides a pessimistic rendering of both queer and interracial romances. Indeed, neither Addie nor Muuk sustain their connections to the people who most matter to them in their youth, and the mixed-race child becomes a casualty of social strife.

As with Leung's novel, Revoyr's *The Age of Dreaming* is roughly based on real-world referents embedded in a fictional world in which queer sexuality and racial difference are coded through the experiences of multiple characters. The protagonist and first-person storyteller is Jun Nakayama, a Japanese American actor who gains acclaim during America's silent film period. In this case, the fictional Jun serves as a hazy refraction of Sessue Hayakawa, one of the most popular silent-era movie stars.[4] The novel's main temporality is 1964, the period in which it opens. At this point, Jun is an elderly man. But occasionally the novel moves back into the past, delving into Jun's recollections of his time as a movie star. The novel begins with a request by Nick Bellinger, an advisor to the opening of a retro-themed theater, to interview Jun about his work in silent cinema productions (14). Although reluctant at first, Jun eventually agrees to meet Nick. As Jun comes to discover, Nick boasts numerous networking contacts with other industry professionals, and he encourages Jun to audition for a minor but crucial role in an upcoming film. Though Jun has been retired for some time, he thinks about the opportunity as a way to rekindle his career. Jun's storytelling fills in the details concerning his rise and eventual fall from the Hollywood film industry. His abrupt retirement from silent cinema occurs in the wake of an unsolved murder, which functions as a central mystery.

In the latter half of the novel, we learn for the first time about this homicide. Harriet Cole, the enraged mother of a young ingénue named Nora Minton Niles, murders a talented actor-director, Ashley Bennett Tyler. Nora has become pregnant, and her status as an unwed mother will likely destroy her career. Harriet assumes that Ashley is the father because he has spent so much time mentoring and working with Nora. However, it is Jun who, in a brief fit of passion, has impregnated Nora (and, in fact, as Jun comes to later discover in 1964, Ashley was actually a closeted, queer man). When Harriet learns that Jun, not Ashley, is responsible for impregnating her daughter, she threatens to ruin Jun's career by revealing what he has done. Given the anti-miscegenation laws and rising sentiment against Asians at the time, Jun rationalizes that his best choice is to make a hasty retreat from films. As Jun finds out at the novel's conclusion, his mixed-race son is alive, having been institutionalized in a facility for the mentally challenged.

As does Leung's *Take Me Home*, Revoyr's novel strikes a rather bleak picture for those who engage in interracial or queer relationships. In this case, the negative connotations of queer sexuality correspond, however indirectly, to interracial desire, especially as Ashley is mistakenly targeted and murdered because Jun had impregnated Nora. Like Addie and Wing's star-crossed relationship, Jun's interracial romance with Nora is thwarted. Jun's other primary possible romance is with a fellow movie star, a white actress named Elizabeth Banks. Though they exhibit great chemistry together, Jun notes that their relationship needed to be cloistered from public view: "We never went out in public together—we couldn't have, of course—and when I drove to her house, I took care to park my new Pierce Arrow in the back garage where nobody could see it. In truth, I did not mind these inconveniences. If we were alone, away from our fans, then I had her completely to myself" (187). The fact that they "couldn't have" gone out in public together is attributable again to the negative publicity their interracial romance would have generated. In both *Take Me Home* and *The Age of Dreaming*, then, queer and interracial couplings are marked as nonnormative sexualities that must be regulated and terminated. In each novel, too, being murdered is the possible price for pursuing such desires.

In contrast to *Take Me Home* and *The Age of Dreaming*, *Huntress* seems completely divorced from actual historical events or figures. The plot centers on a group of humans who travel to a distant land populated by various fairy races to address a regional climate crisis that threatens the livelihood of all kingdoms.[5] The narrative perspective centers on two young teenage sages, Taisin and Kaede, who are gifted with magical powers and who help lead their fellow humans into the fairy kingdom. Importantly, Taisin and Kaede exhibit sexual feelings for each other, though they never go further than sharing a kiss. The novel's central antagonist is a mixed-race, fairy-human hybrid woman named Elowen. She attempts to create a superior race by experimenting on other living beings. In the process, she catastrophically alters the weather patterns. The fairy-human hybrid's desire to modify other creatures genetically in order to make them more like her evokes the questions of belonging that have long been an issue for individuals who can claim multiple ancestries, and it further calls attention to ethics issues related to eugenics. Her motivation to engender these apparently more enlightened, more powerful beings stems from the rejection she experiences when her full-blooded fairy mother reveals that Elowen cannot ever claim a place in the royal kingdom because of her hybridity. From Elowen's perspective, subjecting other fairies to experiments and drastically affecting the climate in that process is a small price to pay to make a place for those with fairy-human ancestries. Elowen is intent on populating an army that can subdue both fairy and human kingdoms, so she will be the undisputed ruler of all living beings. Though Elowen's patently evil and self-indulgent quest is derailed when she is killed, her characterization seems to paint a portrait that makes mixed-race beings out to be psychologically unhinged. But the novel also portrays a very chastened fairy queen, one who realizes her approach toward her daughter was certainly flawed. Kaede "saw [the fairy queen] for who she truly was, and she wept to see the Queen's love for her dead daughter [Elowen], and what difference there was between fay and human was erased, for both understood the sorrow of loss" (362).

The narrative does not end up superficially celebrating a hybrid culture, nor does it assume that miscegenation is an evil that cannot occur. Although "difference" is momentarily "erased," this bridge emerges only in the aftermath of Elowen's death and the almost total destruction of the fairy kingdom. The novel shows that for an inter-being coalition to be preserved, such a radical change requires a more judicious approach to fairy and human relations. Indeed, by that point, readers understand that the divisions between fairy and human kingdoms have stood for so long that the queen's mixed-ancestry daughter stands as an exceptional and isolated example of a cross-being offspring. The queen's willful rejection of Elowen's place as heir to the fairy kingdom further speaks to a larger divide at work: there is no structure, culture, or society in place to allow Elowen to develop a more nuanced understanding of her mixed ancestry. She is presented as impure and bears this background as a racialized trauma that unfolds in her desire to claim superiority over both humans and fairies. It is not an accident that fairies and humans must work together to destroy Elowen and restore order to both kingdoms; this coalition portends the possibility of a society in which fairies and humans maintain active and generative contact with each other. The promise of this future is one that could account for mixed-race populations and enable a multifaceted reconsideration of fairy-human ancestries. Of course, given that the rupture between humans and fairies remains even more apparent in Lo's *Ash*, a novel that is set in the same world but centuries later, the potential for uniting humans and fairies seems unattainable.

Though *Huntress* provides a more positive account of same-sex relationships in the strong bond between Taisin and Kaede, *it* never explores this romance with the kind of depth it devotes to the central plot concerning climate change and the divide between fairies and humans. The novel's conclusion acknowledges the importance of overcoming the long-standing schism between mystical and mortal beings, but it also sees the definitive termination of Taisin and Kaede's relationship. Indeed, for Taisin to succeed fully in her trained discipline as a mystic, she must forgo any sexual liaisons. In this sense, the promise of queer futurity is foreclosed, a theme that the novel shares with *Take Me Home* and *The Age of Dreaming*. Further still, in all three novels, interracial—or inter-being in the case of *Huntress*—romance is provisional and unsettled by reproductive failure or complications. Rather than cast queerness or interracial desire as inherently perverted, the novels help to diagnose social conditions, both fictional and actual, that produce a milieu in which non-normative sexual relationships of all types cannot blossom. None of the three novels includes a character who is defined as both queer and Asian North American. Nevertheless, each novel continually links queer and racialized forms of sexuality, revealing how social differences must be considered through intersectional analytical perspectives. Hence, this first form of tactical diversion, narrative elliptics, involves a larger, heterogeneous continuum of individuals who have suffered from radical social oppressions at different historical points and under unique sets of circumstances. These novels remind us of the multitude of ways in which marginalization takes shape: an individual can be defined by others as a sexual deviant, a racial outcast, or even an otherworldly, subhuman creature.[6]

Protoqueer Narratives: Budding Desire and the Asian North American Minor

The second form of tactical diversion involves narratives in which queerness is mapped only as a kind of possibility because their Asian North American protagonists are under the age of eighteen and generally considered to be legal minors. Given the controversies and issues surrounding child and adolescent sexuality, I am careful to label such figures as protoqueer, as a nod to the ways in which youths may have not come to any sort of definitive understanding of their own sexualities even as they may engage in acts that suggest same-sex erotic attractions.[7] This tactical diversion never grants a lengthy trajectory for its protoqueer Asian North American characters. For this reason, we cannot be sure that they will ever come to identify as queer, nor can we be entirely sure that they will survive to adulthood, given the traumas and modes of abuse they must confront. *Huntress* provides a bridge into thinking about these issues. Even though none of its characters are explicitly identified as Asian North American, the novel does include a fledgling same-sex romance that cannot be nurtured. The eventual foreclosure of a fully figured queer future suggests the challenge of creating a fictional world conducive to and constitutive of non-normative sexualities. Other fictions such as R. Zamora Linmark's *Rolling the R's*, Rakesh Satyal's *Blue Boy*, Mariko and Jillian Tamaki's *Skim*, and Hiromi Goto's *Half World* all gesture to the perils and the productive possibilities of protoqueer yearnings.

In the corpus of the aforementioned fictions, *Rolling the R's* is probably the most well known, with a number of critical articles devoted to its meticulous depictions of a 1970s-era Hawaiian community.[8] The mixed-genre novel defies simple categorization. The narrative perspective is fractured among a number of characters, the primary of which are protoqueer children around ten years of age, who must navigate a childhood filled with inattentive teachers and parents. The friendship between Edgar Ramirez and Vicente de los Reyes anchors the novel. Without much oversight, Edgar, Vicente, and their peers must wrestle with their sexual and racial identities on their own. In the very first chapter, narrated by Edgar, readers are confronted with the heteronormative and gender-normative standards set forth by Edgar's parents and the school system. In one tirade, Edgar's father yells at him for his interest in Scott Baio and Baio's role in *Happy Days*: "And from now on, I don't want to hear anymore Scott Baio or Chachi from your filthy mouth. Do you want your classmates to start calling you a fag? A mahu?" (4). This invective absolutely embodies the constricting milieu in which Edgar struggles to explore his burgeoning erotic attachments and typifies the hostile parenting that at-risk children might receive when exhibiting protoqueer orientations. In the educational system tasked with the instruction of these children, the teachers employ suspect evaluation standards that do little to address the various difficulties these students face.

For instance, in a progress report concerning Vicente—who goes by the nickname Vince—Ms. Takara and Mrs. Takemoto grade his performance primarily on the basis of his penmanship, while they push Vince's parents to discourage him from reading teen idol magazines such as *Tiger Beat* and from hanging out with Edgar and another student named Katrina (51). Other adults associated with the school, such as the janitor, are discovered to be having pederastic relationships with the children.

Given these contexts, the children often turn to each other to formulate their own sense of community. The limitations of this youth-based fellowship are made apparent in a harrowing chapter titled "Mama's Boy" in which Vince recounts a sexual trauma. Vince accompanies Edgar on an excursion that involves prostitution (138–139). Vince is an unwilling participant, and he places much of the blame for this experience on Edgar. The adult man in the encounter certainly should be understood as the outright villain (and criminal), but the first-person narration casts Edgar as a betrayer, one who welcomes the salacious advances of this anonymous man and then later abandons Vince to the man's pederastic sexual appetite. But the question of abandonment crops up at numerous other points throughout the novel, as parents fail to supervise their children and as teachers employ rather ineffectual forms of pedagogy. In other words, Vince's plaintive cry for support from his friend largely speaks to the rather fragile connections between the youths and their adult counterparts, who presumably are charged with overseeing them. In this miseducation of protoqueer Asian North Americans, these children must school one another in the rules of sex and sexuality, and they occasionally fail.

If any promise exists for the protoqueer child in *Rolling the R's*, then it appears in the ambivalent guise of pop culture. For Edgar and Vince (and many of the other protoqueer Asian North American characters), well-known cultural productions of the day such as *Happy Days* and *Tiger Beat* offer the opportunity to role-play and provide an outlet that moves them beyond the limitations inherent in their communities. Disco music is another rallying point, as they express their zeal for Donna Summer and Studio 54.[9] Certainly the 1970s is understood as the height of an era in which popular culture helped to promote the so-called sexual revolution. But their interest in such iconic television shows, thumping club tracks, and magazines is questionable insofar as it can only partially refract their developing erotic attachments. Indeed, Linmark's novel reveals a pop cultural landscape infused by white, cisgender figures and communities. The cover of the novel, which shows an Asian face superimposed on the body of a figure meant to invoke Farrah Fawcett, conveys the desperate need for the youths to find models that more directly reflect their own protoqueer, genderqueer, and racialized social positions.

The sense of isolation that pervades *Rolling the R's* is put on a more extreme display in Satyal's debut novel, *Blue Boy*. Kiran Sharma, the first-person narrator, is twelve years old, is Indian American, and has a predilection for gender-bending habits, reminding us of Edgar Ramirez from *Rolling the R's*. He likes to wear makeup, takes ballet classes, is a gifted artist, and looks forward to performing in the school talent show. Perhaps the most dynamic element that Satyal explores in relation to Kiran's character trajectory is the linking of religious figures with non-normative sexual desires. In this case, Kiran is inspired by Krishna, a Hindu deity. For Kiran, this deity, despite being strange for his blue skin, still possesses uncommon power and agency. Given the constant harassment that Kiran experiences from other Indian American youths and from fellow schoolchildren, the realm of the divine provides him with constitutive terrains from which to build a positive, life-affirming protoqueer, ethnoracial identity.

His mother strongly supports most of Kiran's interests and hobbies. But when it is publicly acknowledged that Kiran is experimenting with women's makeup and his family is subsequently shamed in front of their local Indian American community, Kiran's pastimes become circumscribed, especially by his father. He reprimands Kiran for his identification with feminine culture, pushes him to act more like a man, and finally punishes him by decreeing that he cannot be in the school talent show. Nevertheless, Kiran stages a form of rebellion and surreptitiously decides to participate anyway. The novel's conclusion sees Kiran pass out right after his performance, a result of a slight overdose from a medication that he had been taking. As his doctor explains, silver medications accumulate in the body over time and result in poisoning; the physical manifestation of this overdosing is a slight blue gray tinge seen on the epidermis. Kiran at first notices this change, but attributes it to Krishna's blessing. The final pages see Kiran and his family achieving a rapprochement.

Though the final pages resound optimistically, the novel gestures to the hazards faced by the protoqueer Asian North American child. His ethnic community, family, and school friends and acquaintances rarely provide him with the support he needs. At one point, echoing the model minority rhetoric that enforces a strict regime on the life of the child, Kiran's father reminds him about all the sacrifices their family has made so that Kiran could have an easier road to success, and they disavow Kiran's propensity for genderqueerness by stating that he is not a girl (223). Kiran divulges after this moment, "I have never felt so ineffective as a boy. My crying proves right everything my father is accusing me of" (224). Here Kiran internalizes the shame he brings on the family for not taking on a proper masculine role. At school, Kiran finds some support from Mrs. Buchanan, a teacher whose kindness offers him brief solace in an antagonistic school atmosphere. Mrs. Buchanan helps him understand his status as an ethnic minority, but as Kiran notes later, "Being a minority implies being part of a group. But to what group do I belong? Yes, I am Indian, but my recent experiences have only reiterated that I am not really part of that group. There are so many unique qualities about me that I can't be put into one category" (211). Indeed, Kiran's protoqueer sexuality, his gender-bending predilections, his youthful age, and his ethnic background make him out to be someone so "unique" that he feels an acute sense of dejection after this conversation with Mrs. Buchanan (212). Without a parental or educational entity to guide him through the intersections of these social differences, Kiran must navigate his identity-based predicaments on his own.

The novel provides one subtle indication that Kiran eventually comes to terms with his queer identity in a moment that suggests that the narration is retrospective. After one particular manifestation of his same-sex desires, Kiran admits, "Only now am I able to fully understand what being called gay means" (203). However, we are not provided a sense of how he comes to "understand" his status as a "gay" individual, nor do we get any indication of the ways his family, so heteronormatively depicted in the novel, might have reacted to his queerness. Further, the "now" of the narrative perspective is never defined, so we do not know how old Kiran is when he comes to this realization. The one concrete way that the novel spotlights Kiran's attempt to contextualize his protoqueer sexuality occurs in relation to spirituality and fantasy. In this case, Kiran primarily looks to his religious beliefs to forge a protoqueer identity.[10] As Kiran believes, "Every time I see a picture of Krishna, I cannot help but see myself. I cannot help but recognize something glowing—hurt, but glowing—in His beautiful, made-up eyes and in His brilliant skin. The way my body burns with longing can only be the work of some Greater Force—a divine force" (205). Kiran employs Krishna as a spiritual template upon which to model his protoqueer sexuality, especially as this deity sports a physicality that marks him as strikingly different, yet still impressive in construct. Kiran's metaphorical burning is later mapped onto his growing awareness of his same-sex orientations: "For the first time in my life, I wonder if there might be people just like me in my school, other 'flamers' who have the same sexual desires I do, just not overtly. I am the figurehead of a secret, sacred brotherhood of blue flame souls—the first blue boy" (244). Again, Kiran carries over the spiritual significance of blue skin from Krishna to make sense of his sexual desires and the possibility that there may be others like him. Thus the novel has much in common with *Rolling the R's*, as Kiran must look beyond his immediate family and the educational institution to make his protoqueer life more bearable.

Mariko and Jillian Tamaki's graphic novel *Skim* portrays the angst-filled teen life of its heroine, Kimberly Keiko Cameron, otherwise known by her titular nickname. Skim is a tenth-grade student at a Toronto high school. The novel's plot is set in motion once Skim hears the news that her classmate John Reddear has killed himself. The reverberations of his suicide are felt throughout the high school, as students respond by creating clubs focusing on the celebration of life. Guidance counselors are put on alert for students exhibiting signs of depression. John's ex-girlfriend, Katie Matthews, is the subject of much scrutiny, especially when she arrives at school one day with two casts on her arms. There is some gossip surrounding her injuries, that she may have attempted suicide herself. At the same time, rumors abound that John might have been queer. As Skim notes, "he was MAYBE a star volleyball player and depressed person who was also in love with a boy who was on the St. Michael's second string volleyball team" (94). This moment is critical because it establishes a cultural milieu in which Skim's high school may not have embraced those exploring queer attachments.

Skim, who identifies as part of the goth subculture, finds most of her peers to be somewhat off-putting and intentionally embraces her status as an outsider. While Skim deals with the changes in high school, she also navigates the perilous waters of protoqueer desires. She develops a significant crush on her English teacher, Ms. Archer, feelings that are somewhat reciprocated, at least insofar as we perceive them through Skim's perspective.

In a two-page panel from the book (Figure 1), Skim and Ms. Archer kiss, but because this panel transpires in non sequitur form—that is, the panels that occur before and after this section do not prepare the reader for this event—this act may be read as Skim's adolescent fantasy. As Skim's feelings for Ms. Archer grow, Ms. Archer becomes far more ambivalent about any contact between them. Ms. Archer eventually quits her high school job, as she receives an art fellowship in New Mexico, thereby effectively ending any possibility of a romance with Skim. During this period, Skim grows distant from her best friend, Lisa Soor, but a chance encounter with Katie Matthews provides her a new and deeper platonic connection. The graphic novel ends with the implication that Skim and Katie have become much closer.

Though set in Canada, this cultural production contains many similarities to both *Rolling the R's* and *Blue Boy*, especially in relation to the lack of parental guidance. Skim's mother and father are separated, and they seldom appear within the graphic narrative. Her mother comes off as a cold and unemotional parent, who is very focused on her career. Her father seems loving, but not attentive to his daughter's teenage exploits. In one scene, Skim is having a meal with her father and the woman he is dating. Their conversation is minimal, but at one point, he does ask Skim whether she has a boyfriend (67). The question reflects a presumption that Skim would be exploring heterosexual feelings and serves to, however unintentionally, disregard the possibility of queer attachments (such as her exploits with Ms. Archer). Not surprisingly, Skim's body language communicates her sense of discomfort: her eyes are downcast

Figure 1. Illustration from *Skim* by Mariko Tamaki and Jillian Tamaki used with permission from Groundwood Books, Toronto. Illustration copyright © 2008 by Jillian Tamaki.

and her shoulders are slumped. Her response to her father's question is an obvious no.

Her relationship to Ms. Archer is far from set in stone. Though Ms. Archer does present a strong role model for Skim at first, the teacher's involvement with Skim borders on the unprofessional and suggests possible misconduct. Skim's infatuation with Ms. Archer derives not only from a sense of sexual attraction but also from her perception of a possible unspoken intimacy. Intriguingly, Skim's same-sex orientations are never explicitly divulged; instead, readers are continually encouraged to read between the lines. This elliptical representation of protoqueer desires is intentional: Skim struggles to name the nature of her attachments to Ms. Archer precisely because they could be labeled as deviant, a fact made apparent in the salacious rumors that abound in the wake of John's suicide.

Similarly to the youths depicted in *Rolling the R's* and *Blue Boy*, Skim looks to fantastical and mystical realms to gain a sense of her own alternative identity. Not only does she identify with the counterculture goth crowd, but she also practices Wicca, a pagan religion. Certainly contemporary pagan and goth subcultures are known for their more liberal ideals toward sexuality and social deviance.[11] In this way, Skim finds an outlet to explore her protoqueer attachment to Ms. Archer; she cultivates this erotic dynamic through the use of altars, spells, and tarot cards. At one point, Skim employs her tarot card deck to read her own fortune and discovers that the Lovers card repeatedly turns up. As Skim explains, the Lovers card denotes "love and relationships, new beginnings, and new connections, but when it appears in reverse, it denotes a bad decision, an untrustworthy person, a state of imbalance." Skim's analysis is that she may have "an untrustworthy person in her life" who may be Lisa or that she has done her "fortune too many times" (59). She does not consider the circumstance that Ms. Archer, a teacher who might be romantically involved with a student, could be this problematic person. In this sense, Skim selectively employs the cards to make meaning out of her life. Notably in the panel in which she shares her tarot-based interpretations, she is lying in bed reading *Romeo and Juliet*, implying that her relationship with Ms. Archer may be star-crossed.

The conclusion of the graphic novel appropriately sees Skim seemingly putting her interest in witchcraft on the backburner, especially given the fact that her relationship with Ms. Archer never develops into anything weighty. But the last image provided for the reader is an origami fortuneteller, suggesting that the occult will remain in Skim's life in one way or another.

One unique entry in this narrative grouping is Hiromi Goto's *Half World*, which involves a young teenage protagonist named Melanie Tamaki. But Melanie's relationship to protoqueerness unfurls through her affiliation with other characters and to reproductive dynamics rather than through any same-sex yearnings or tendencies she personally exhibits. This young adult novel is not unlike *Huntress* in that it contains paranormal elements. The story is focalized from the third-person perspective. The novel opens with Melanie being pursued by teenage bullies. As with the protoqueer Asian North American characters in the previous three novels, Melanie is a social outcast. Fortunately, she finds refuge in the local market owned by the older but kind Ms. Wei, a migrant who hails from a long line of scholars. The plot thickens when Melanie discovers her mother is missing and that a mysterious man named Mr. Glueskin may have kidnapped her. It is through Ms. Wei's knowledge of the occult and the supernatural that Melanie comprehends that she must travel to another world in order to save her mother. And once she finds the entry point, located inside the Cassiar Tunnel in Toronto, Melanie realizes that she's stepped over into the titular Half World, a location between life and the afterlife in which souls exist in a state of limbo. The novel's prologue reveals that Half World is undergoing disintegration because its souls have become trapped, forced to live and relive the moment of their mortal deaths without being able to cross over into the Realm of Spirit, which is the afterlife.

Melanie's quest to retrieve her mother is also wrapped up in a strange prophecy suggesting that she may be the key to ending the cycle of torment in which Half World entities are mired. What she eventually discovers is that her birth is considered to be miraculous because her parents are both Half World entities, beings who should not be capable of producing life within that purgatory-type realm. Indeed, her mother, Fumiko, takes Melanie away from Half World precisely for this reason, but her excessive years away from Half World mark Fumiko as a fugitive (and a target for Mr. Glueskin's ire). Further still, Fumiko, because of her status as a non-living entity, cannot sustain her energy in the human world and must eventually return to Half World. The novel's resolution involves Melanie's battle with Mr. Glueskin, whom she eventually defeats. In that process, Mr. Glueskin transforms into a baby, revealing another miraculous conception of a human subject in Half World. By the rules of the realm, Melanie and Mr. Glueskin, who then is rechristened as Baby G, must leave for the human world. Being only a teenager and now having to care for an infant, Melanie's transition to the human world is no doubt daunting, but Goto leaves her in the capable hands of Ms. Wei.

Following the patterns of other protoqueer narratives, this novel intertwines multiple rubrics of social difference alongside the portentous journey faced by a young protagonist. In this case, race and ethnicity function more elliptically. Because Melanie's parents hail from Half World, it is difficult to demarcate definitively their ethnic or racial identities, yet the novel repeatedly hints at a specific background. For instance, Melanie's last name, Tamaki, and her parents' first names (Shinobu and Fumiko) suggest a Japanese ancestry. In addition, toward the novel's conclusion, the Japanese word *hinotama* is used as a description for the soul of Melanie's mother (194). Finally, the illustrator of this work (whose sketches appear occasionally throughout) chooses to render Melanie in a way that further points to an East Asian ancestry. I bear out these observations precisely because Melanie is implied to be Japanese Canadian. Melanie's status as a racial Other provides one possible motive behind the bullying she experiences. Indeed, the early sections of the novel see her being tormented by teenagers who call her a "fat crow" (11) while pelting her with tomatoes.

Given Melanie's status as teenage pariah and racial minority, Ms. Wei conveys her support at just the right moments. For her part, Ms. Wei is explicitly described as queer: she admits to Melanie that she once was in a same-sex relationship with a woman named Nora Stein, who has since passed on. Ms. Wei's ethnic background, much like Melanie's, is only suggested. In this case, numerous references to Chinese and Asian cultures accompany her introduction to the plotting. Through Melanie's perspective, we see that Ms. Wei's bookshelves are "completely lined with books, the titles on the spines written in Chinese, French, German and English" (34) and that she herself commands knowledge of Japanese and Chinese languages (43). Yet these scholarly tomes also hold an extra level of significance because they emphasize that Ms. Wei possesses knowledge of the supernatural. Ms. Wei's ethnic, queer, and occultist backgrounds are important because they enable her to mentor Melanie as she comes to terms with her unique, otherworldly heritage.

As in other protoqueer narratives, the protagonist cannot always rely on the adults around her for persistent support. Indeed, though Ms. Wei ends up being a trusted maternal figure, Melanie must leave the living world—and Ms. Wei—in order to find a way to survive. While Half World is certainly a dangerous location, ruled by a being intent on killing Melanie, it is also a place that provides her with a more expansive genealogy. Her birth as the first living entity in Half World spotlights her mother's reproductive power as anomalous. Melanie herself is imbued by this exceptional state of conception, as she is a being unlike her own mother, so much so that they cannot inhabit the same realm. Reproductive queerness occurs in another instance once Melanie defeats Mr. Glueskin and he transforms into an infant filled with vital non–Half World–based energies. As in Melanie's case, the forces contained in supernatural beings are repatterned to create life. Thus Mr. Glueskin, as Baby G, becomes a kind of figurative kin to Melanie, as they both derive out of miraculous, seemingly impossible birthing events. The novel defines protoqueerness through non-normative reproductive cycles, as Melanie and Baby G are living entities despite having originated in a spiritual limbo.

Readers also discover that Mr. Glueskin's attempt to master Half World is due to his own cycle of torment. One of the grotesque beings from this realm notes that in Mr. Glueskin's "cycle, he was killed by his father while his mother was trying to birth him. That's the cycle that formed him. That's the cycle that he stretched. He was the first who understood that we could change, stretch, reshape our Half Lives" (172). In this case, the origin point for Mr. Glueskin's monstrosity is actually a death that occurs as a by-product of traditional heterosexual reproduction gone awry. For Mr. Glueskin, being trapped in this cycle is brutal because the time between his life and death is apparently so short that he is constantly in agony. Only through his ability to "stretch" does Mr. Glueskin allow himself longer periods of painlessness. But the novel's largest conflict resolves when Melanie terminates Mr. Glueskin's traumatic repetitions. As Melanie restructures his cycle into one of a protoqueer rebirth, she simultaneously legitimates her own magical conception. For Melanie and even Baby G, then, Half World is a space of fantastic possibility rather than of familial destruction.

Goto's novel is not content to leave these sorts of non-normative reproductions within the realm of the supernatural. Indeed, Ms. Wei anchors the text's final pages by offering Melanie and Baby G a home. This novel perhaps offers the most progressive vision of the protoqueer narratives considered in this study because it generates a social formation closest to the inscrutable belongings that will be analyzed at length in upcoming chapters. Though the mystical realms of Half World seem to be long gone, Melanie retains a magical pendant in which survives a fraction of her mother's spirit essence. In this sense, the supernatural links that Melanie once possessed remain central to her narrative resolution. At the same time, some of the magical spirit-animals that still populate the text are skeptical. The epilogue reveals one such creature, a white cat, that states, "So the girl saves the Realms, loses her parents, and ends up living with an old woman while they raise a baby," and adds, "Human lives are so pitifully pedestrian. You have to admit it. There is nothing spectacular about them. How awful it is to be human" (225). Here the white cat's viewpoint casts a critical gaze upon this alternative kinship, one that can be rationalized given the many ways in which these characters will face further social ostracism and prejudice due to their new standing as a makeshift family of misfits and oddballs.

All four novels I have discussed represent only a sliver of the characters' developmental arcs, leaving the question of how these protoqueer Asian North American youths will come to identify as adults in terms of their sexualities, genders, racial backgrounds, and other such categories of social difference. Further, given the traumas that so many of these characters face—bullying, molestation, sexual assault, and parental neglect, among others—there is no guarantee that all such characters will even survive into adulthood. John Reddear's ultimate fate, one that might have been connected to queer yearnings, situates the perilous trajectory that may follow these characters as they grow up. This form of tactical diversion reveals the fragility of the protoqueer Asian North American's youth, one that is often devoid of proper guardianship, especially from adults who hail from the characters' educational institutions and from their nuclear families. To find coping mechanisms, these youths look beyond their immediate communities—sometimes even escape to other realms, as in the case of Goto's *Half World*—to constitute their emerging erotic attachments and to begin to construct fellowships beyond the traditional home space. These novels forcefully spotlight the need for young characters to make their desires manifest through the elastic boundaries of the popular imaginary, the spiritual, and the occult. Without the constraints and logics of the so-called real world, protoqueer desires and social dynamics can blossom in these more fanciful realms.

Ensemble Narratives: The Queer Asian North American Versus the Not-So-Heterosexual Family

The final form of tactical diversion involves cultural productions that explicitly contain queer Asian North American characters, but only as part of a number of interdependent plots. The reader's narrative attention is divided among multiple storytelling perspectives and an expansive character-system. Because of the decreased space given to any one character, his or her position in the fictional world is inevitably compared to other characters and their associated plots. Not surprisingly, the queer Asian North American's trajectory in these novels is often cut short, as such characters do not necessarily live to the concluding pages. And when they do act upon their sexual desires, they often do so at great cost. These novels, which include SKY Lee's *Disappearing Moon Cafe*, Ghalib Shiraz Dhalla's *The Two Krishnas*, Sandip Roy's *Don't Let Him Know*, and Mala Kumar's *The Paths of Marriage*, are incisive in their critique of the heteronormative and homophobic foundations of the family. Indeed, the queer Asian North American character's biological relations often produce the most violent forms of brutality, trauma, and silencing. The importance of distributed narrative perspectives is further made apparent because the use of various focalizers reveals how the so-called traditional family is far less heteronuclear than it at first appears. In this sense, these novels show how the seemingly straight characters who compose the family still can be resituated with respect to queer sexualities and themes.

Recall that I provided a short analysis of SKY Lee's *Disappearing Moon Cafe* in the Introduction. My purpose there was to frame queer Asian Canadian and queer Asian American literatures as part of a larger coalitional archive, but I briefly return to that novel now in order to show how it perfectly models the ensemble narrative. As I noted earlier, the novel involves a number of different perspectives, following various Woo family members. One of the main viewpoints is given to Kae Ying Woo, who immediately invites the reader to ponder the problem of the queer Asian North American in a larger family and genealogical structure. As she reveals, "I'm so very disappointed. I've been brought up to believe in kinship, or those with whom we share. I thought by applying attention to all the important events such as the births and the deaths, the intricate complexities of a family with chinese roots could be massaged into a suant, digestible unit. Like a herbal pill—I thought I could swallow it and my mind would become enlightened" (25, lowercase in original). Kae Ying's frustration stems from the multiple ways in which her ancestors and relatives involve themselves in extramarital affairs or romances, while others engage in incest, albeit unknowingly. The family tree is at best only partial. Consequently, reader attention is distributed across multiple generations of the Woo family, as this expansiveness helps clarify how genealogy extends beyond marriage ties, legitimate children, social norms, and culturally sanctioned relationships.

As I also established in the Introduction, the social deviancy mapped onto Chinese Canadian families in earlier historical periods provides a valuable precursor to Kae Ying, a queer Asian North American, whose life story eventually unfolds in this ensemble narrative. Her budding romance with Hermia Chow then seems not so strange in light of her ancestors, many of whom settled into surreptitious relationships as a result of sociocultural pressures exerted both within the Chinese Canadian migrant community and by racist legislative acts. At the same time, the novel's rather bleak depiction of the Woo family's attempt to sustain itself across multiple generations suggests that Kae Ying's connection to Hermia may itself be embattled. Perhaps this foreshadowed instability is made apparent in the ways that queer desire cannot be expressed openly. Indeed, Kae Ying and Hermia's relationship remains so coded that cultural critics describe it in conflicting terms. Leslie Bow calls Hermia only a "potential lover" (101), while Caroline Chung Simpson altogether dismisses any homoerotic dynamics, asserting that the novel "d[oes] not include any lesbian characters or themes" (72). But these inconsistencies are more largely telling of the inscrutability of queer desire within this novel, which remains vulnerable precisely because of the logic that defines any Asian North American sexuality as potentially aberrant and fit to be regulated. As Kae Ying exists as one figure in an ensemble narrative, the tenuousness of her relationship mirrors the larger instability of the Woo family across many generations.

While I have focused on a Chinese Canadian family in my brief discussion of *Disappearing Moon Cafe*, the next three examples of ensemble narratives depict South Asian and South Asian American social formations. Though these novels are not the only ones that create ensembles in which the queer Asian North American participates,[12] they do gesture to the importance of ethnic contexts that inform the construction of transnational lineages. Specifically, in South Asian Indian culture, as noted by Rakesh K. Chadda and Koushik Sinha Deb, the traditional family structure involves multiple generations, often including aunts, uncles, and cousins, all potentially living under the same roof.[13] Even following migrations, Asian families continue to show a strong disposition toward a more elaborate intergenerational formation involving "grandparents, parents, children, and sometimes even unmarried aunts or uncles" (Xia, Do, and Xie 706). Of course, the transnational development of South Asian families is further influenced by longer historical and cultural conditions, such as a patrilineal inheritance system, the prevalence of castes (in the case of Hindus), and the centrality of filial piety. These cultural frames of reference are essential in order to engage how these novels broker narrative perspective across a larger character-system comprising multiple individuals in a South Asian American household.

Ghalib Shiraz Dhalla's *The Two Krishnas* is a depressing but admirably depicted social realist work set in a transnational Indian community. The trajectory of the main characters in Dhalla's novel underscores how the fragility of survival predominates as a theme in so many publications penned by queer Asian North Americans. The omniscient narrator for the most part follows three principal characters: Rahul Kapoor; Rahul's wife, Pooja; and Rahul's lover, Atif. Rahul and Pooja also have one son named Ajay. Pooja has a couple of acquaintances, including a neighbor named Sonali and a man named Charlie who runs a local yoga center. Much of the novel's first half establishes the conflicts that arise from a romantic triangle that leaves all three primary characters feeling bereft. Pooja wonders what she can do to make herself more attractive to her husband and to make her family life more fulfilling; the home space essentially becomes oppressive, a constant reminder that her life in the United States has not been all that she imagined it would be. Rahul attempts to navigate a double life as the married man who wants to stay in the closet and retain his family, while keeping his young, same-sex lover satisfied. Atif, having fallen madly in love with Rahul, yearns to spend more time with him. Son Ajay, though given much less narrative space, exemplifies a teenager struggling to find his place in the household as the child of Indians who immigrated to the United States via Kenya. Late in the novel, Dhalla adds an integral flashback portion that focuses on Pooja and Rahul's life in Kenya in the early 1980s, a time of incredible political unrest in which violence was directed at those deemed to wield the most power.[14] This significant temporal and geographical shift, one that at first seems disarticulated from the main narrative, gestures to the ways in which secrets in all forms will come to surface. In this case, traumatic ethnic pasts and queer sexuality both emerge as closets that cannot remain shut.

In the final arc, Pooja discovers Rahul's affair with Atif. Given Pooja's own past, in which much of her family was killed during ethnic violence and unrest in Kenya, knowledge of her husband's indiscretion strikes as another obvious way in which her American life has been calamitous. One of Pooja's initial responses to learning of her husband's trysts with another man is to fantasize about Atif dropping out of the picture: "Something horrible could happen to him. Maybe the boy would die tomorrow. While crossing the teeming boulevard, he could be struck by a speeding car, tossed up in the air like a rag doll, his body mangled up, bloody like her heart" (219). Atif's imagined death would then preserve the heterosexual bounds of the family: "Neither by word nor by deed would she make a reference to his tendency and the shame it had brought on them, and in time they would continue the ritual of aging together, that ritual which is the rightful dividend of every marriage" (219). Though Pooja eventually realizes that Rahul is leaving her, the projection of Atif's death ominously foreshadows the place of queerness in relation to a normatively conceived family. It must be stamped out and killed, a pollutive force bringing shame.

Ajay also realizes that his father is having an affair, but it is not until he and a thuggish friend trespass into Atif's home that Ajay comprehends that his father's extramarital liaisons are with a man. Atif's response to Ajay's newfound understanding is "to comfort the person who had not just resembled, but came from the man he loved. [Atif] wished that rather than defending himself, he could have allayed his assailant's pain. But something, a long-suppressed suspicion of how his luck would eventually run out, his own distrust of life or just the pure, unalloyed hate in Ajay's face told him that things would not work out well" (323). Atif's impulse reveals his attempt to broach the confines of the heteronormative Asian North American family, an affective response that Ajay violently deconstructs by killing Atif with a candle-holder. The word *unalloyed* is quite apt to describe the family's inability to transform into a hybrid construct that is able to accommodate both heterosexual desires and queer romances. In the wake of Atif's death, Ajay and his accomplice endeavor to evade police officers. The chase results in Ajay being shot and killed. Pooja's response to having lost her son is to cast Rahul out of her life for good. The last pages show her swallowing a bottle of pills, but the novel ends before readers discover whether her suicide attempt succeeds.

The fact that Rahul's biological son is the one to terminate his father's queer love affair figuratively charges the family with an inflexible heterosexuality that is catastrophically destructive. Certainly my reading is not meant to absolve Rahul of his responsibilities. At the same time, the novel gestures to the insurmountable challenge of integrating queer sexuality within or beside the Asian North American home. Queerness is apparently such a toxic force that homicide must be employed to regulate it, even at great cost to the family unit. My reading is not to suggest that Pooja should have been open to a polyamorous marriage, but rather that the novel presents no possible way for the family to move forward—perhaps find a new structure amid a divorce—once queerness is introduced in any iteration.

Billed as a novel in stories, *Don't Let Him Know* begins with a chapter involving a South Asian mother named Romola, as she discovers that her adult son Amit has come upon a letter purportedly written by a former male lover of Romola's named Sumit. Romola immediately blanches at the letter, thus evidencing a guilt-ridden face that Amit assumes is proof that she once had been in love with someone other than his father, Avinash. By this point, Avinash has died, and Romola moves in with Amit, making the difficult choice to relocate from India to San Francisco. If it seems as though Romola's response suggests she once had a relationship with this man before she married Avinash, the second chapter reveals another secret entirely. The letter was actually penned by a former male lover of Avinash; Romola had found the letter by accident, but never confronted her husband about its contents or returned it to him. This chapter also clarifies that Romola covers up her husband's same-sex romance by misleading her son into believing she was the one to have an affair with Sumit.

The second chapter shifts backward in time to a moment when Romola and Avinash are living in India, the married couple having moved back there after Avinash finished his schooling in Carbondale, Illinois. Narrative perspective centers on Sumit, the figure named in the letter from the previous chapter. After being settled in San Francisco for many years, Sumit travels back to India and drops in to see Avinash. We discover critical information about these two characters from their youth. For instance, as children, Sumit and Avinash were a part of a tight-knit group of boys who vowed that they would never get married (49). This group also included an individual named Abhijit, who Sumit, later as an adult, will discover has killed himself. The motive is unclear, but the novel suggests that Abhijit was queer, perhaps his death a result of an unrequited same-sex love affair. As part of this fondly recalled boys' group, Sumit and Avinash often met in a "storage room on the roof" of Avinash's home. In the story's present, Sumit requests to see that space again and reminisces about the past, "where as young boys they'd once had secret clubs" and where "they would reach for each other, the darkness guiding their hands. Later that night as he rode his bicycle home through the shadowy sleeping streets, he'd lift his hand to his face and smell Avinash still clinging to him, his fingers, his lips, his neck, and he would start to sing as well" (57). The pivotal importance of this scene appears in the fact that their queer desire blooms in the space of the home. Indeed, the novel gestures to the ways in which queerness is central to the familial experience, though secrecy and darkness are required to maintain its potentialities. Given Avinash's new life as a married man and father to a young child, it is not surprising that the chapter ends without any romantic reconciliation between these characters.

The closeted queer romance that is revealed early on reflects many other concealed sexual experiences that surface repeatedly in other instances: an interracial coupling between Amit and an African American woman; the budding love affair between Romola and a man who would later become a Bollywood star; Avinash's childhood crush on his barber; and his later experience during which he is sexually assaulted by a man he meets at a function designed to bring together queer South Asians who first connected over the Internet. The novel outlines the asymmetrical but interlinked ways that characters harbor clandestine desires that can be labeled as deviant or unacceptable, especially by family members. In one of the chapters in which Amit acts as the primary focalizer, he shocks his mother by saying that he might date someone who is African American (137). Her response indicates her wish for Amit to marry someone of Indian descent. The novel never clarifies whether Amit goes on to tell anyone in his family of his later sexual encounter with an African American woman, but it is evident that his mother would not approve. With respect to Romola's teen romance with an aspiring movie star, it is her mother who pushes her to end the relationship (157), as her mother assumes that such a man would be involved in "dirtiness" (157). The novel depicts the direct descent of maternal control and expectation over the child's developing heterosexuality from the way Romola's mother treats her flirtation with an actor to the way that Romola herself treats her son's possible interracial dating life.

Unlike Atif from *The Two Krishnas*, Avinash does not suffer from a violent death, though his assault reveals the dangers inherent in acting on queer desires within the space of the proverbial closet. Beyond the gaze of the public and his family, Avinash's yearnings repeatedly lead him to seek out anonymous sexual encounters to satisfy certain needs. The novel further implies that a queer relationship cannot be sustained in the face of familial power dynamics. Sumit's ability to engage his queerness in San Francisco perhaps signals that Avinash might have found more acceptance had he remained in the United States after the completion of his degree, but a novel like *The Two Krishnas* reminds us that exploring queer sexuality even in the United States is perilous. Both novels end with queer Asian or Asian North American characters dead in some form or another and with the key same-sex romance plot terminated.

In contrast to *The Two Krishnas* and *Don't Let Him Know*, Mala Kumar's *The Paths of Marriage* depicts a queer Asian North American character whose same-sex romance survives to the story's end. Kumar's debut novel involves four different narrators. Three occur in the first person and track the intergenerational lives of South Asian and South Asian American women. Lakshmi grows up poor, part of the Shudra caste of the Hindu faith. Though she pursues her educational options, members of higher castes and classes seek to limit her academic achievements. Lakshmi sees an arranged marriage as perhaps the only viable option to escape an impoverished life, especially once her educational opportunities come to an end. She therefore marries an Indian man of a higher caste who moves her to the United States, and she bears two daughters.

The older daughter is named Pooja, who gets a turn as our storyteller in the second part of the novel. Growing up in West Virginia, Pooja confronts racial prejudice in her community and finds the expectations of her parents to be oppressive. Her parents, for instance, push her into an arranged marriage. Pooja at first attempts to rebel, but eventually she assents to be wed to an ambitious man named Anand. Anand and Pooja eventually settle in Florida. During her early years of married life, Pooja is determined to get an education, but this drive creates tension with Anand, who is pursuing a career of his own. Eventually their marriage crumbles under these divergent trajectories, but just before they are divorced, Pooja realizes that she is pregnant with a daughter, whom she will come to name Deepa.

The third section begins to shift the stakes, as Deepa takes her turn as our storyteller. Deepa identifies as a lesbian, and when she begins a long-term relationship with a French national named Audrey, who is pursuing a professional degree in the United States, she promises her lover that she will tell her mother about their relationship. Deepa eventually does come out to her mother, but only long after she tells Audrey she will. In the ensuing period, Pooja breaks ties with Deepa, while Audrey feels betrayed by Deepa's delay in telling her mother. Deepa ends up being estranged from both her mother and Audrey.

Once Deepa is given her opportunity to narrate, this novel can be categorized within the third form of tactical diversion. As a queer Asian North American character, she must share the storytelling space. This fracturing of narrative attention is increased one step further, as the final section of the novel shifts to a third-person perspective. This choice by Kumar perhaps is meant to provide the distance the characters need to emotionally recover, as they reconcile certain expectations they have had about their closest loved ones. This section and the ensuing epilogue arguably set the novel apart from any other fiction in that its same-sex romance plot comes to a firm resolution. Indeed, Pooja's mother, Lakshmi, encourages her daughter to take a path to motherhood that she herself could not. That is, she tells Pooja to allow her daughter to marry the partner of her choice. Lakshmi's ability to accept Deepa's queer sexuality before Pooja does is an important one, as she tells Deepa, "many people in India said I did not deserve an education. Many people said educating a girl was unnatural. Just because there were many people does not mean they were right. I will not be a part of the many against you" (322). Lakshmi links her experience of social marginality rooted in the caste system to Deepa's queerness. The crux of Lakshmi's perspective is that the definition of the natural must be widened, a viewpoint that she extends to Deepa's sexuality. This striking moment reminds us of our first tactical diversion in which interracial romance and queerness are depicted as non-normative. In this case, Kumar's *Paths of Marriage* moves one step further in its inclusion of a character who comes to benefit from a figurative inheritance, one based on her grandmother's ability to connect the caste system to queer sexuality.

At the same time, Audrey comes to understand that she pushed Deepa too quickly and too hard with respect to the process of coming out. The last pages see Deepa and Audrey married, with Pooja supportive of their union. As Deepa tells it, "The announcement of federally recognized same-sex marriage was made sixty-five days ago. I proposed to Audrey sixty-four days ago. She said yes before I finished my sentence" (331–332). Kumar makes an interesting choice in her 2014 novel by placing the story in a slightly alternative temporality, one that foreshadows the June 26, 2015, Supreme Court decision to legalize gay marriage in all states. Yet the fictive and future-oriented temporality that Kumar generates for her characters also suggests that queers—and, in this case, a queer Asian North American—can only successfully enter a courtship plot that can come to a form of narrative closure once gay marriage is federally recognized. In this sense, the novel provides a stark and optimistic contrast to *The Two Krishnas* and *Don't Let Him Know*.

It remains to be seen whether *The Paths to Marriage* marks a significant turning point for queer Asian North American fictional productions and associated plots, but I identify many parallels to *The Two Krishnas* and *Don't Let Him Know*. Inasmuch as the novel resolves the queer romance conundrum through a federally sanctioned marriage, the significant barriers that emerge to stymie that developmental narrative trajectory are important to acknowledge. Deepa's primary antagonist to her same-sex relationship is her mother, Pooja. In the pivotal coming out scene, Deepa narrates, "I begged her to see me, her child, her Deepa. But centuries of discrimination backed her reasons. She could not handle an uprooting of her expectations" (283). This scene is punctuated by her physical removal from the home: "I had no chance at negotiating a peaceful recess. As she pushed me out the front door back into the pouring rain, she cupped both of her hands over her mouth at the sight of our broken family. The sobs rushed out as though she were mourning the death of her child" (283). The diction Deepa provides here is critical to establish the rupture that occurs in the process of uncloseting queer sexuality within the framework of the Asian North American family. Her status as child is foreclosed, and Deepa undergoes a figurative death, at least with respect to her place and her status as a biological descendant. While the novel's ending suggests that the queer Asian North American eventually can be welcomed into the familial fold, the vast majority of cultural productions I have already analyzed in this chapter do not offer such an optimistic inclusion.

If the Asian North American family cannot be reformulated or transformed to accommodate the possibility of the queer descendant, then where can this outcast find a new home, another community, and a sense of refuge? The majority of works that hallmark tactical diversions cannot fully answer this question. Queer racialized figures may not be directly depicted in the fictional world, or they do not mature into independent adults, or they are part of a larger character-system in which the twinned forces of social death and material violence prematurely terminate their romances or fleeting sexual liaisons.

Beyond Tactical Diversions

The cultural productions that have helped me lay out these three tactical diversions offer much to contextualize the archive that is at this book's focus. Narrative elliptics clarify the ever-important historical inheritances for queer Asian North Americans, who are critically affiliated with pasts littered with interracial violence and sexual brutalities. Protoqueer narratives remind us that vulnerable protoqueer Asian North American youths must find ways to grapple with their racial and sexual differences among families and communities that offer them little support. Without models to follow, these characters must move beyond their immediate realities to find ways to negotiate their multifaceted identities. Ensemble narratives institute queer Asian North American characters who are not always the primary protagonists or characters in their novels, but whose narrative arcs still reveal how their sexual desires are made tenuous in light of the traditional family's heteronormativity.

These tactical diversions help map out key themes and narrative patterns in the larger corpus of queer Asian North American fictions. Indeed, these three modes of queer racial formalisms predominate in extant publications. At the same time, this preponderance of depictions that give queer Asian North American characters only short trajectories gestures to both the challenge and the need to center this figure in the fictional world. Thus the remainder of this study focuses on the queer Asian North American storyteller and an associated narrative trajectory I call the *survival plot*, which couples the narrator to the alternative social formations I have coined *inscrutable belongings*.

CHAPTER 2

NARRATIVE ENDURANCE

QUEER ASIAN NORTH AMERICAN STORYTELLERS,

SURVIVAL PLOTS, AND INSCRUTABLE BELONGINGS

WHAT NARRATIVE FORM might best address how it is that the queer Asian North American character manages to last to the final page? The narrative types considered in the preceding chapter do not fully answer this question, and thus I move to a distinctive fictional structure involving the queer Asian North American character as a primary storyteller, who recounts experiences in a retrospective fashion. Unlike the tactical diversions spotlighted in Chapter 1, this narrative form allows the protoqueer protagonist a longer arc in which there is an explicit indication that the child has grown up to become an adult and has faced significant struggles along the way. He or she has survived, but at great cost.

The fictions I investigate in this book—Russell Leong's short story "Camouflage," Nina Revoyr's *Wingshooters*, Noël Alumit's *Letters to Montgomery Clift*, Alexander Chee's *Edinburgh*, and Lydia Kwa's *Pulse*—are all penned by North American writers of Asian descent who, at some point, have been vocal about their queer status. This open identification is important precisely because these writers establish a political connection to their fictional works, especially as they create characters who hail from racial and sexual backgrounds similar to their own. The overlap between authorial background and first-person narrator of course is crucial; we can see the potential autobiographical influence on these writers' fictional worlds. These writers, I argue, accept the burden of representation that falls on those daring to create characters who are rarely given centrality in fictional worlds. To imagine the narratorial "I" is to bring into cultural and social visibility a queer Asian North American character-storyteller who, though entirely fictive, boasts an incredible fortitude despite the menacing presence of social death and the possibility of physical harm.[1]

The revolutionary nature of these fictions cannot be understated, especially because of what they offer to diverse readerships. I briefly turn to Claudia Tate's exploration of late-nineteenth-century African American romance novels and their relationship to the newly emergent black middle class, which enables us to understand what is at stake when authors' backgrounds have an impact on the meaning and the larger social value of their publications. Tate notes, "The popularity . . . of black women's post-Reconstruction novels, as evidenced by their preponderance during the decade of the 1890s, suggests that their first readers found in them personal and social meaning with which they had decided affinity" (6). Tate points out that despite the "formulaic domestic plots," these narratives were momentous for their ability to provide middle class black readers "pleasurable self-affirmation that reflected their racial and gender aspirations to live in a world where such stories were possible" (6). Tate focuses on the rise of middle class black readership in the post-bellum period and the need for such an audience to find reflections of themselves both in writers' racial ancestries and in their associated cultural productions. Tate's contentions influence my analyses, as I investigate plots of survival that imagine and validate complex life trajectories for queer Asian North Americans. Such cultural productions would be valuable not only for queer Asian North American readers, but also for a wide array of audiences who must be introduced to a world in which "such stories" are possible, shown that "such stories" can model how actual lives can and should be lived, and encouraged to believe that "such stories" might even evolve to offer more expansive possible outcomes and futures.

Queer Racial Formalisms

Queer Asian North American fictions are intriguing for their retrospective nature and their anachronic discursive progressions. These texts feature a nonlinear narrative form that contrasts with other, more common constructs, such as the traditional courtship and marriage plots.[2] A nonlinear narrative is certainly not unique to queer Asian North American fictions, but I argue that this mode of storytelling unfolds in concert with the sociohistorical circumstances that exert pressure on the ways that certain tales are most effectively told. I draw here on the work of Patricia P. Chu, who tackles how the bildungsroman is revised in Asian American cultural productions. Chu, "viewing the Anglo-American bildungsroman as a genre that depicts and privileges certain subjects as exemplary of the nation," argues that "Asian Americans rewrite the genre [of the bildungsroman] to register their vexed and unstable positions in America" (6).[3] Chu's thesis advances the incompatibility between the narrative of progress hallmarked by the traditional bildungsroman and the coming of age of the Asian American protagonist who encounters barriers often intimately arising from his or her racial background. As Chu's many analyses show, narrative form must itself be altered to invite the tentative inclusion of the Asian American.[4]

From another standpoint, queer formalists and feminist narratologists have deliberated on the ways in which sexuality and identity exert pressures on narrative structures.[5] According to Marilyn Farwell, the representation of the "lesbian subject" forces a disruption of some common discursive practices (61–62). More generative still is Farwell's exploration of "different power relations" (62), especially as they are apparent when a queer character takes on a more central position within the plot that in turn catalyzes changes in the narrative: "Multiple plots or voices heighten our awareness of the arbitrariness of the traditional plot by either imitating it, or parodying it, or referring obliquely to it, or recalling it through images. It is as if the story is instead a series of stories, telling and retelling itself. These counterplots often occur in the multiple voices of the narrators who direct the story's internal strategy" (62). Judith Roof similarly argues that narrative implicitly functions under the structure of marriage and heterosexuality, which results in "stories where homosexualities can only occupy certain positions or play certain roles metonymically linked to negative values within a reproductive aegis" (*Come As You Are* xvii). To combat the heteroideology of narrative, Roof suggests engaging fictional worlds by attending to nonprogressive narrative structures: "In concrete terms this means emphasizing, privileging, locating the repetitions that constitute the terminally unfinished presence of existence, putting repetition, alternation, and accrual in place of progress and closure" (182–183). For Roof, reading narrative for an element such as "repetition" or "accrual" is a political act that helps constitute queer aesthetic practices.

Despite the differences in identity categories used and the nuances in their arguments, Chu, Farwell, and Roof are united in asserting the incommensurability of a traditional, linear plot with the minority subject, whether Asian

North American or queer. They all look to revision and, in the case of queer narrative, repetition and recounting of the past to disrupt the move toward closure and resolution. To conceive of a *queer racial formalism* is to think of the ways that social forces push writers to reconfigure elements such as narrative structures and the characters who travel through fictional worlds. While influenced by Chu's work and other formalists such as Elda Tsou, Christopher Lee, and Amy C. Tang, I already made evident in the Introduction the acute need to cohere Asian Canadian and Asian American literatures.[6] In addition, the pioneering work of contextual narratologists such as Marilyn Farwell and Judith Roof can be enriched through a consideration of race and how it, too, can have an impact on the sexual and gender dynamics of narrative construction.

I use the phrase *reproductive past* to connote how a queer Asian North American storyteller recalls traumatic experiences and memories through retrospective narration. This discourse enables a critical intervention: the narrator's survival depends on his or her ability to concatenate personal experiences to a larger field of social relations existing within an expansive historical continuum. This process is inherently a mode of relationality, one that de-emphasizes forms of traumatic exceptionalism and foregrounds a communal spirit strengthened by the acknowledgment of collective structural losses.[7] The importance of such comparisons appears not in the ability to equate one loss with another, one form of social marginality to another, but in the ability to initiate spectral solidarities, to remind us that a multitude of threatened and expired lives demand representational resurrections.[8] These cultural productions attend to the politics and aesthetics of survivorship for queer Asian North Americans, but also extend how one character's survival is intertwined with the systemic fragility of so many other lives and communities.[9]

The queer Asian North American narrator's attempt to survive confronts a number of historical circumstances and structural inequalities, expressly related to racial oppression and queer struggles. Looking back to the previous chapter, we recall that the first form of tactical diversion often appears in novels depicting a past that links themes of racial oppression to queer sexuality, though not necessarily through the experiences of a single character. The fictions at this study's center take into account multiple inheritances, but here they critically influence and direct the life of a single protagonist. This protagonist faces a panoply of historically positioned hauntings: for instance, the queers who succumbed to AIDS in the late 1970s and early 1980s, or Asian migrants subjected to racist policies as they attempted to make new homes in North

America. The question of the fictional present is one mediated by how these traumatic pasts, imbued with phantoms that seem to follow at every turn, can be made usable—tools, if you will—to negotiate the possibility of new social formations. The queer Asian North American's place in this intricate historical tapestry provides metaphorical ancestries and progenitors; these are lineages that move beyond the biological realm and enfold those who have struggled and perhaps died due to their connection with identity categories deemed racially and sexually perverse.

Inscrutable Belongings is indebted to the fruitful interdisciplinary engagements concerning social difference, time, and history. A host of books have explored, for instance, queer temporality, including but not limited to Elizabeth Freeman's *Time Binds*, Judith Halberstam's *In a Queer Time and Place*, Heather Love's *Feeling Backward*, and Nishant Shahani's *Queer Retrosexualities*. What these books share is an investment in the queer subject who interrupts the inexorable linearity that defines our modernized existence, a time signature that Freeman calls "chrononormativity" (3). Yet the intersectionalities emphasized by this book and that are embodied by the queer Asian North American storyteller require us to account for the impact of multiple social differences, processes, and forces on the disruption of chrononormativity. That is, as much as the narrator's sexuality comes to influence how stories can be told retrospectively, so too do racial status and the quest to find a refuge beyond the heteronuclear home bear weight upon the discursive features of the fictional narrative. To read these works for their reproductive pasts is to institute a temporally sensitive analytical practice that takes into account the storyteller's multifaceted identity and positionalities.

Survival Plots

Fictions concerning fortitude amid arduous circumstances present us with queer Asian North American storytellers who physically endure while simultaneously illuminating the role of *social death* in obscuring any final narrative resolution. As mentioned in the Introduction, I diverge from Orlando Patterson's original formulation of this term and apply it to contemporary forms of "natal alienation" (7) in which the socially marginalized subject is held in a tenuous position with respect to his or her heteronuclear family, as it is defined by and codified by biology, law, and cultural norms. Even if queer racialized characters find a measure of inclusion on a personal level, systemic inequalities remain omnipresent. The cultural productions at the center of *Inscrutable Belongings* take into account the social death of the queer Asian North American, who is marked by figurative invisibility, disappearance, ghostliness, and historical connections to broader racial and sexual oppressions. Though the queer Asian North American character appears as a pivotal figure in the fictional world, his or her place is never assured, which is the basis of the *survival plot*. He or she must contend with tangible forces, such as an abusive family member, while also navigating a larger social realm that designates racial and queer livelihoods as aberrant and fit for termination.

Affirming a literary genealogy broadly aligning queer Asian North American narratives to British novels, my study draws from the argument of Alex Woloch's *The One vs. the Many*, which grapples with the relationship between the protagonist and the multitude of characters who surface in nineteenth-century fictions. In the battle for attention and the protagonist's quest toward a particular resolution—in Jane Austen's novels, for instance—minor characters may exist as either supportive or antagonistic forces. Woloch argues that the rise of the industrial revolution and the shifting nature of class relations in the nineteenth century necessitated a fictional form that would reflect these social dynamics. The realist novel, with its emphasis on a diversity of characters who struggle for attention and a central protagonist who must somehow maintain her elevated position within the narrative, offers itself as a suitable form to depict (1) the rapidly changing nature of industrializing England and (2) the dilemma to improve one's social status through marriage, for example, amid a population explosion, rising urban centralization, and concomitant resource scarcity. Antagonistic minor characters are defined as eccentrics, because they get in the way of the protagonist's quest and thus must be written out of the plot. For instance, characters seen as libertines or rakes (such as Mr. Wickham from *Pride and Prejudice*) imperil the successful resolutions of courtship and marriage plots through their threatening sexualities and cannot remain in the narrative.

Woloch's argument is germane for the fictions in this study precisely because a figure who might be labeled as an antagonistic force now moves to the narrative center. Of course, we cannot apply Woloch's framework too liberally. In the contemporary narrative, a threatening sexuality extends beyond the heterosexual-based seduction stratagems of an untoward gentleman that might be found in the nineteenth-century novel. Lesbian desire, for example, becomes coded alongside the homicidal impulse of female characters, as noted by both Lynda Hart and Sherrie Inness, and these same-sex-oriented characters are not surprisingly given catastrophic narrative trajectories, often ending in gruesome, elaborate death sequences. In an allied manner, the queer Asian North American, tainted by social deviancy, sexual perversity, and racial difference, exemplifies a highly eccentric character, one uncommonly granted narrative centrality and persistently a target for violence and brutality. If given any representational space at all, he or she might have existed in other fictional worlds as a minor character who retains only a limited impact on the plot. But my larger point is that, once this figure is positioned as the protagonist, this storyteller's survival is revolutionary because he or she must take possession of so much narrative space that the creative writer must map out a life path that has heretofore rarely existed in fictional worlds. The seemingly simple task, then, of charting this extended journey is made increasingly fraught because of the storyteller's connection to real-life referents that make this narrative path riddled with danger. The structure of the *survival plot* is founded on the critical intertwinement of possible physical death and the omnipresence of social death. Jeopardy persists in these fictional worlds in myriad constructs. One character might attempt to abuse the queer Asian North American protagonist, or the protagonist may face discriminatory social policies. The very motivation behind a hate crime directed at a queer Asian North American appears rooted in the desire to make corporeal the fact of his or her social death: this figure should be stamped out, made unrecognizable and therefore unworthy not only of life but also of being mourned.

The survival plot is not necessarily unique to queer Asian North American fictions, so I take time to parse out why this progression is crucial to understanding this set of texts. The most traditional definitions of plot involve two components: the author's deliberate ordering of events in a narrative and the reader's ability to make sense of this sequence (Fludernik 5). A plot, which necessarily involves a causally conceptualized sequence of events, typically is distinguished from story, which does not account for a specific order.[10] There are various narratological studies concerning plot,[11] but the progression of queer Asian North American fictions necessitates another understanding of narrative temporality. Survival plots, in particular, require the endurance of the storyteller until the last page. In the texts that are here given extended analytical deliberation, all survival plots roughly function with a similar narrative sequencing. The fiction begins with the queer Asian North American storyteller as an adult. Each fiction then involves some mode of retrospective storytelling or extended analepses (flashbacks). That is, the adult narrator recounts events in the past—typically ones that occur in childhood—in which his or her life was placed in mortal danger. Each fiction details how the storyteller goes on to mature despite these difficult circumstances and provides a trajectory that moves the reader into the diegetic present and toward the temporal point which first began the narrative. That is, we see that the protagonist is able to negotiate his or her way to adulthood, despite this dangerous period in his or her youth. Though the storyteller endures, this survival is questionable as he or she remains bound by social death: large-scale and systemic social oppressions remain, even if the protagonist charts his or her individual way through a fictional world corroded by antagonistic forces. Notably, the actual age of a queer Asian North American storyteller at the conclusion never exceeds the fifth decade, implying that there is a longer plot still waiting to be told.

Retrospection provides the discursive mode by which the storyteller and reader reconstruct the survival plot and make meaning out of it in new ways. This approach enables readers to reconsider a narrative in light of the storyteller's racialized queerness only expressed belatedly or explicitly in adulthood. Consequently, reader engagement also involves revisiting childhood sequences with the understanding that this youthful figure will one day mature into a figure who will confront his or her queerness and racial background. As the queer Asian North American takes center stage in this tenuous survival plot, he or she assumes a position in the narrative space that allows his or her life to unfold through the act of first-person storytelling. While this figure ascends to the narratively inscribed position of power, other characters accordingly seem more marginal and eccentric, and they take on roles that move them into trajectories that may lead to their exit from the plot. But they also attain significance beyond their status as narratively expendable figures and are not what Woloch would label as antagonistic. The recursive nature of these fictions reveals a narrator-protagonist driven to look back, which also affects his or her relationship to this group of minor characters who may also face subjugation, disempowerment, death, or termination from the plot. Here the past becomes even more reproductive. The recounting offered by the queer Asian North American character makes the fictional world more expansive and enables my analytical intervention to be made: this protagonist becomes part of a larger fellowship, brought together with narratively and socially threatened figures as part of inscrutable belongings.

Inscrutable Belongings

An inscrutable belonging is the aggregation of a group of individuals (and related entities) in the fictional world who are directly connected to the queer Asian North American protagonist's movement through the survival plot. They—in one way or another—enable the queer Asian North American to make it to the very end, so that he or she may come to tell the story in the first place. An inscrutable belonging deviates from the more traditional forms of human relationships and communities studied by anthropologists, sociologists, and legal scholars. As anthropologist David Schneider notes, North American kinship is defined through genealogy (such as parents and their biological offspring) and legally binding relationships (most commonly through marriage): "In sum, the cultural universe of relatives in American kinship is constructed of elements from two major cultural orders, the *order of nature* and the *order of law*. Relatives in *nature* share heredity. Relatives *in law* are bound by custom, by the code of conduct, by the pattern for behavior. They are relatives by virtue of their *relationship*, not their biogenetic attributes" (*American Kinship* 27, emphasis original).[12] The North American family system is a unit of kinship, which is based on the nuclear model. As Sarkisian and Gerstel note, "The family is the basic unit of American society. Family values are at the core of American culture. Or so many social commentators have said for at least a century. However, the family that they argue is the basic unit of American society is not just any family. It is the *nuclear family*, consisting of a mother, a father, and their young children still living at home" (1, emphasis original). The primacy of the nuclear family in the Canadian context is also made evident in the legal scholarship of Dawn Bourque, Fiona Kelly, and Harder and Thomarat.[13] Though the practical variations on the North American family and kinships are obviously numerous and remarked upon by a number of scholars, my larger concern is how the traditional heteronuclear model becomes a social norm and idealized fantasy to which other communities and group formations are (often violently) compared.

The storytellers in this study complicate traditional kinship and family models not only because of their racial and sexual differences, but also because of cultural traditions carried over from lands of ancestral origin, which may offer social structures distinct from the North American heteronuclear model.[14] Informed by many local, national, and transnational paradigms, these narrators must create inscrutable belongings, which are communities most often comprising individuals who are not biologically affiliated (through traditional reproductive modes) or legally bound (such as through marriage). These alternative social formations are "inscrutable" in so far as they are unrecognized by larger cultural and legislative entities and are imbued by a racialized queer genealogy of oppression attached to Asian North Americans (R. Chang 954). From this historical standpoint, inscrutability reminds us of the ways that Asians are physically rendered as unreadable, while their psyches are understood to be traitorous. Underlying this racist formulation is a sexual deviancy: if Asians cannot be trusted, their bodies and desires must be regulated. Thus inscrutability bears an implicit queer component: this Asian not only looks treasonous,[15] not only thinks in duplicitous ways, but also desires that which is salacious.

While inscrutability is not so explicitly tied to Asian North Americans today, queer identifying or otherwise, my point in employing this term is to modify how we understand the dynamic social formations that correspond with survival plots. Because inscrutable belongings defy traditional conceptions of family and kinship, they also cannot easily be harnessed under regimes of normalization and occasionally are able to flourish beyond the reach of official power structures and regulatory apparatuses. Hence, inscrutability as it is attached to modes of communion and fellowship also operates as a mode of resistance. But the idiosyncratic nature of inscrutable belongings also necessitates a critical practice that will actively look for them. In this sense, my own place as cultural critic is to root out unexpected affinities and collectives, as the queer Asian North American storyteller may not always be directly conscious of the ways in which he or she attempts to create such communities of refuge.

In the case of Asian North Americans who identify as queer, the opportunity to long for something like a romance and to find "belongings" is essential given the many ways they exist as marginalized subjects. The gerund form of "belonging" is especially pressing because it connotes that the desire to find a community of refuge is a process, one that simultaneously conveys a developmental narrative and a precariousness that comes with daring to try to sustain an assemblage of outcasts and outlaws. For queer Asian North Americans and these dynamic social formations, to generate such inscrutable belongings is to demand the right to live—and even to find some sense of larger fulfillment—despite possible material violence and ongoing systemic oppressions. Although making idiosyncratic communal constructs transparent would seem to make belongings *not* inscrutable but instead something recognizable, I retain the term precisely because such belongings are often so ephemerally depicted. My readings convey the challenge in nurturing these aggregations, given the still-embattled existences facing the characters and the lack of institutionalized power structures that would enhance the longevity of these organizations.

My conception of inscrutable belongings is beholden to a number of scholars who have explored alternative social formations that deviate from white North American heteronuclear models.[16] Consequently, I highlight how alternative kinship and family studies enable a critical engagement of these cultural productions. At the same time, such studies, variously focusing on queer parenting, transracial adoptees, and innovative reproductive technologies, do not address the sociohistorical and cultural forces that are most evident in queer Asian North American fictions.[17] My critical interventions emphasize the need to extend these arguments and methodologies further by theorizing alternative social formations through humanistic critical analyses.

Christopher Peterson and Elizabeth Freeman ("Queer Belongings") survey the potentials and the limits of integrating alternative kinship theory with queer studies. As both point out in separate studies, kinship at its core may be a fundamental mode of relationality that operates by defining the self with or against others: you are either like me (as kin and family) or not like me (as stranger, foe, or outlander). Any alternative kinship could be said to operate in part by exclusion and becomes a social formation that is constituted through violence and power. The problem with this shortsighted theoretical formulation of kinship is the way that it universalizes all such aggregations as social formations that necessitate the same kinds of exclusions. Kinships—as we must pluralize them—are not all created equal, and the specific connotation that I see as most relevant here is that the term conjures up the notion that there is a possibility for a sense of belonging, especially for those deemed to be outcasts.

Fortunately, both Peterson and Freeman still find productive possibilities in alternative kinship structures, expressly as they arise in queer cultures. Peterson, for example, reminds queer theorists and scholars that any kinship created by those defining themselves as sexually non-normative cannot only be future-oriented. Such a kinship must also make strong claims to the past, by expanding the network of ancestors to those who are affiliated to the queer community despite no necessary blood or legal relationship. For Peterson, the danger of a queer community moving toward homonormativity (for example, through same-sex marriage rights) is that it disavows or covers over a queer past constituted by death and loss, especially with respect to the HIV/AIDS epidemic (140–151). Freeman sees alternative kinship as offering a new vocabulary for queer studies, one that focuses on the habits and practices of social groupings based simultaneously on renewal and historicism. She critically reformulates the foundation of normative kinships and families, which are both future-oriented with respect to reproduction and past-oriented with respect to idiosyncratic lineages and ancestries. In these dynamic social formations, renewal functions as a metaphorically generative process, which might occur through the community-building inherent in artistic creations or performances (such as the production of a drag show).[18] Freeman's considerations of such assemblages inspire my argument, as she details the more figurative modes by which non-normative social collectives are constructed and maintained. At the same time, following the viewpoint of Peterson, I am cognizant that any conception of such social formations must be tempered with an attentive eye to the queer's place within the larger historical spectrum, one informed by inescapable material and structural losses.

As with queer studies, Asian North American studies have also been influenced by understandings of alternative kinships and families. The early history of Asian migrants routinely involved familial rupture, as young men immigrated to work on a plantation, as farm hands or in some other service capacity, potentially leaving behind parents who might still be dependent upon them for income and financial support. As Imogene L. Lim notes, "During this first notable wave of Asian immigration, mainly Chinese, Gum Saan (Gold Mountain) was the destination—not a specific place called Canada or the United States" (15). The movement of whole families to North America (portions of the continent were called "Gold Mountain" by Chinese migrants because of the location's implied wealth of resources) was rare during the late nineteenth- and early twentieth-century periods, so much so that Chinatown bachelor communities emerged, as did other social formations that were predominantly male and labor-oriented.[19] Because later migration patterns in the United States included other ethnic groups such as South Asians, Filipinos, and Japanese, Nayan Shah argues that "together transient migrants forged relations of 'stranger intimacy' that shaped more than random and quixotic rapport. Certainly migratory work and transportation crossroads produced environments of compulsory sociality, but it was the appetite for passionate engagement, the determination to smash alienation, and the desire for visceral solidarity that created both fleeing and enduring relationships" (55). As Shah details, beyond work and toil, Asian North Americans who sought economic opportunities also found other ways to interact in "visceral solidarity" (55). The cultural critic Christopher Lee also details the importance of the transnational flows that often bound Asian immigrants together: "The first group of Chinese immigrants to Canada arrived from San Francisco in 1858 and members of the Washington State–based Asiatic Exclusion League were instrumental in instigating the 1907 anti-Asian riots in Vancouver" ("Lateness" 4). As anti-Asian sentiment increased in both the United States and Canada, the ushering in of widespread legislative restrictions on immigration (on state, provincial, and/ or national levels) resulted in the use of false documentation to create paper families.[20] Here kinship and family formations themselves became fictions to subvert legal boundaries. Other official policies and hostile cultures often prevented Asian North American men from interracial marriage, limiting the romantic choices available in already gender-unbalanced communities.

Even as Asian North Americans have gained more rights, to the point at which they can claim full-fledged citizenship and even construct heteronuclear families,[21] issues related to alternative kinship continue to surface. One of the fields in contemporary Asian North American studies that has scrutinized the issue of alternative kinships and families has been orphan and adoptee studies.[22] SooJin Pate, for instance, makes clear how transnational Korean adoption creates a dilemma at the heart of American normative kinship systems. Part of the process by which the adoptee becomes pacified as an American citizen is through her reconstruction as an individual who is strongly encouraged to relinquish all ties to a birth family. This forced amnesia upholds the primacy of white normative forms of American kinship while disavowing the potential for an adoptee to have multiple families and multiple ancestries.[23] Engaging analyses of adoptee narratives (138–151), Pate shows how adoptees can resist the restructuring of kinship into a white heteronormative form through feats of the imagination undertaken in memoirs and creative works. My study follows the scholarly work of Shah, Pate, and others, who show us that immigrant and Asian North American families hardly take shape in one standard way.[24]

Queer Asian North Americans must be understood beyond a biologically circumscribed notion of family and kinship, so as to extend and reformulate the nature of lineages and genealogies; in other words, to recognize their inscrutable belongings. Rather than being permanent refuges from harm and violence, inscrutable belongings are delicate in their designs. Their fragility reminds us that such community configurations are often seen as subversive and tend to disintegrate under the forces associated with material violence and social death. These cultural productions are ultimately fictions of suspension, a liminal position indicative of the queer Asian North American's place and time with respect to inscrutable belongings. Not surprisingly, the storyteller is connected to motifs of the undead and the afterlife because he or she is subjected to violence in so many forms. While the storyteller does not evacuate the space of negativity so central to Edelman's thesis in *No Future*, he or she also does not succumb to a kind of *ressentiment* leading to apathetic inaction or unending melancholy, even in this state of living death and living among the dead.[25] Storytellers must withstand such circumstances to chronicle their journeys, while remaining cognizant of the many others' lives that inform and enable them to remain steadfast.

Revisiting Russell Leong's "Camouflage"

Inscrutable Belongings critically links Asian North American studies with queer studies and theory through the ways in which fiction imagines the possibilities for non-normative social collectives. Having drawn out the core argument, critical genealogies, methodologies, and key terms for this book, I return to Russell Leong's short story "Camouflage." Though I have summarized the major thematic concerns of this story in the Introduction, I now spend a lengthier time parsing out how the narrative intricately maps the storyteller's survival plot and his associated inscrutable belongings. I must also briefly note that Leong's story comes from a larger collection, *Phoenix Eyes & Other Stories*, reminding us that this work exhibits a form of tactical diversion, as many of the other stories elucidate plots that do not explicitly feature queer Asian North American characters or contexts. Story collections by queer Asian North American writers often can be categorized as ensemble narratives given the fact that each individual story's character-system accrues greater meaning once they are compared against each other. The story "Daughters," for example, focuses on the life of a sex worker named Haishan, who hails from an impoverished background in China but eventually finds a measure of stability in Los Angeles. "Daughters" features a key parallel to "Camouflage," as both stories concern the plight of transnational sex workers who struggle to make a living, despite the fact that the former predominantly involves heterosexual Asian North American women and the latter is based on queer Asian North American men.

At the same time, "Camouflage" stands out in this collection because it condenses an extended period of the storyteller's life into a tight narrative arc. The short story makes effective use of analepses, or flashbacks, to draw out a capacious trajectory for its narrator, Bernard, who provides vital information about his sexual development as a child and his later life as an adult. And, most important, the story cements the vital necessity of inscrutable belongings for the narrator's existence, his ability to create a sense of inclusion, however flawed or ephemeral, beside the bounds of the heteronuclear family.

One of the central conflicts in "Camouflage" involves queer sex acts. At the AIDS clinic where Bernard volunteers, he bumps into Chino, a Japanese American HIV-positive man who has seen Bernard performing at the Camouflage bathhouse while using the stage name of Sakoi. Bernard is momentarily perturbed by Chino's knowledge because it means that many of the clinic patients probably know about his bathhouse exploits. Given Bernard's willingness to work at the bathhouse, Chino perceives that Bernard possesses liberal attitudes toward sex, figuring that his own HIV status will not be a barrier for a potential relationship between them. However, Bernard rebuffs Chino's advances, leading to a brief moment of discord. As Bernard recovers from this encounter, he narrates, "My stomach is churning. My breakfast spills out of my mouth and splatters everywhere. Chino has a point. Technically, I don't have sex with any of the customers. No penetration. But I bring customers into the spa where they have sex with each other. So, what's the difference? Maybe I'm adding to the caseload of men who become infected in these places" (97). This scene illuminates the thorny issue of survival, as it relates to the livelihood of bathhouse patrons, who may be more willing to initiate unsafe sex practices during Bernard's performance.

Bernard's musings bring up a moral code of sexual conduct that he may be violating. He volunteers his time at an AIDS clinic, demonstrating a committed awareness of key health challenges affecting the queer Asian North American community. Here he works to lessen the emotional burden and isolation that accompany chronic and life-threatening illnesses. Yet at the same time, he engages in bathhouse sex work that could be increasing HIV transmission rates. Therefore, Bernard's involvement with the AIDS clinic comes off as potentially hypocritical and hollow. If Bernard really cares about stopping the spread of AIDS, why does he work in a bathhouse? The contradiction reflects more broadly the bipolar reactions occurring in queer theoretical and political circles toward gay sexual conduct in an age of rising conservatism, homonormative discourses, and a renewed focus on the nuclear family.[26] The story gives readers the sense that Bernard, as a politically invested queer Asian North American man, does the right thing by volunteering his time for others in his community who are struggling and may even be dying. But deciphering his sexual choices becomes more difficult once made public; his cruising practices and choice of bathhouse work reveal an individual seemingly not invested in HIV prevention and awareness. His carelessness is made more fraught because this historical period—the early 1990s—is a time in which retroviral therapies are not yet widely available, and HIV infection still can lead to eventual death.

Given the complicated nature of his encounter with Chino, it is not surprising that Bernard's body undergoes a sort of revolt right after, as his breakfast "spills out of [his] mouth and splatters everywhere." On one level, we understand this corporeal reaction as a result of his poor eating habits and consistent drug use. But on another, this physical expulsion operates metaphorically as a war being waged inside his body, at the location where his queer desires emanate. This scene perversely rewrites and revises the early sexual climax he experiences at the end of his bathhouse performances. Instead of being produced by sexual satisfaction, this unwelcome bodily "ejaculation" erupts due to the responsibility that comes with thinking about how his sex work might be having a negative impact on others. At this point, a key question springs forth: even if Bernard navigates the plot to the end, what is the price of survival if he is contributing to the caseload of infections that might shorten the lives of other queer men?

The short story's ending unsettles this question even further: Bernard cruises for sex at Griffith Park, his actions generating more concerns. Bernard narrates, "Leaves and branches camouflage our faces, bodies, and identities. He inches forward, around to the throbbing below my belly. I glance down. A dark-haired head bobs up and down. It's Chino. So my cover's blown. I take a capsule from my pocket and finger his lips until I can slip it down his throat. My thirst drives me to do crazy things" (100). The narrative returns to the motif of camouflage, moving it from the bathhouse where patrons are hidden behind the club's doors to the outside, where cruising men are concealed by trees and shrouded in shadows. I want to pause for a moment to think about what Bernard means when he states, "leaves and branches camouflage our faces, bodies, and identities." It makes sense on the literal level that the leaves and branches can camouflage the faces and bodies of those participating in these discreet sexual encounters, but what exactly does he mean that "identities" are camouflaged? In the darkness, where the differences between him and the next person become moot, the histories and trajectories of those individuals also seem similarly opaque, unable to be read. The encounter, infused so much with the desire for sexual release, also brings with it an anonymity that Bernard finds liberating. Here the terrain of moral sexual conduct might also be escaped until he realizes that the man giving him a blowjob is Chino, the same man who had given him a hard time for not going on a date with him. Only after his "cover's blown" does Bernard make the statement that "my thirst drives me to do crazy things." This admission places questionable value once again on his cruising escapades: he is doing something "crazy" by participating in sexual acts with an HIV-positive man in a semi-public space. His actions might be read as evidence that he has overwritten his earlier code to avoid dating patients at the AIDS clinic because of a "conflict of interest." This moment, moreover, compromises the survival plot. Bernard has made it to the ending of the short story, but only insofar as we know he is engaging in sex acts with an HIV-positive man at a time in which retroviral therapies are not widely available. Thus multiple survivals seem to be endangered: the lives of bathhouse patrons, on the one hand, and Bernard's own, on the other. And of course, given Chino's seropositivity, we know that the status of his health may change should his infection progress.

To tangle with the intricacies of the survival plot—even in the context of queer moralism—I suggest that Leong's story asks for a much more nuanced reading of this last sexual act, one that requires us to think about why Bernard is attracted to these "crazy" actions, ones that seem to undermine his activist-oriented agenda as an AIDS clinic volunteer. The story actually asks us to do the opposite of what the character is doing in his "camouflage." My analyses employ a queer of color and queer diasporic critique in order to confront how Bernard brings with him traumas sustained from his upbringing in the Philippines and later discovers a new set of obstacles in his acculturation to the United States. I further show how his present-tense narration must be placed into conversation with tactical uses of analepsis, shifts backward in time that highlight Bernard's postcolonial and transnational migration history. These anachronic movements establish how Bernard's sex acts are an attempt to reconfigure an earlier period in which he was sexually assaulted. In addition, they clarify how the survival plot has more contours and extends beyond the ethical issues around HIV transmission rates in relation to his bathhouse occupation. Consequently, I turn to extended analyses of Bernard's flashbacks, which focus on his childhood and teenage years, and place these occurrences in critical conversation with his adult actions and choices in order to establish the multifaceted nature of his survival plot.

As I discussed at a prior point in this chapter, a plot is distinct from a story precisely because of causal links in the sequencing of events. For "Camouflage," this definition seems straightforward because the story proceeds chronologically for the most part: (1) Bernard performs at the bathhouse, (2) volunteers at the AIDS clinic, (3) is confronted by Chino, and (4) ends with cruising at Griffith Park, where he bumps into Chino again. But interspersed throughout this narrative progression are short flashbacks, which interrupt a unified timeline. They function to establish why the story is a plot precisely because these moments account for Bernard's actions as an adult and how they may actually derive from a traumatic past. In this sense, Bernard's endurance is understood to be not only a story but also a narrative that generates meaning from its ordering. And I accordingly tackle three key scenes from Bernard's childhood, a period of time during which he resides in the Philippines, that demonstrate exactly what is at stake for him as he manages to make it to adulthood.

In one harrowing recollection, Bernard reveals his molestation as a young child by his Uncle Apostol. He recalls, "We'd bathe together. He'd ask me to soap up his scrotum and between his thighs. A few years later, he would push his penis into my mouth. The first time I bit on it. He knocked me against the green tiled wall, blasting cold water on me until I shivered and cried for him to stop. Smiling, he just tightened his grip around my throat and said that my father would kill me if I spoke one word" (91). What first stands out in this excerpt is the wealth of contradictions. The passage begins with the simple phrase "we'd bathe together" as if to suggest the quiet intimacies between family members, but soon this description gives way to a sexualized and violent account, as the young boy Bernard gets introduced to his uncle's genitals, one part at a time, from the touch of his hand to the engagement of oral sex. There is a sort of reeducation going on, as bathing becomes eroticized and serves as a pretext for sex acts. Bernard's resistance to this change is made most clear when instead of performing oral sex on his uncle, he bites his uncle's penis. He is punished for his inability to act in the required way, "knocked . . . against the green tiled wall," a memory so acute that he recalls the chilling bodily sensations during that time. Most insidiously, queer sexuality is introduced in the context of guardianship. An adult man who is entrusted to bathe with him is the very same man who molests him; resistance comes with the threat of violence and death. This moment must be read from the vantage point of power and subjection to highlight Bernard's sexual formation. As Judith Butler reminds us, "the desire to survive, 'to be,' is a pervasively exploitable desire. The one who holds out the promise of continued existence plays to the desire to survive" (*The Psychic Life of Power* 7). In Bernard's sexual molestation, his "existence" is not only exploited but predicated on the development of a queer sexual knowledge, one that is produced through both physical and promised future violence and possible death (if the abuse is disclosed). But, of course, we might also play into a Freudian reading of his action to bite his uncle's phallus, one that suggests an unconscious desire to rob his uncle of the ability to penetrate and continue with these incestuous acts.

The negotiation of Bernard's childhood survival plot first begins with a tactical choice: he must remain silent so that no one discovers what is going on between him and his uncle. At the same time, once Bernard is able to move away from his uncle, how does he deal with the aftermath of what has occurred? To answer this question, I shift briefly to an analysis made by queer theorist Ann Cvetkovich in her investigation of trauma, abuse, and incest in Dorothy Allison's novel *Bastard Out of Carolina*. Cvetkovich concentrates on reading the protagonist, ominously named Bone, as an individual who is able to put her trauma to a productive use by reorganizing its psychically damaging features. She contends, "Out of the pain and shame of being beaten, Bone is able to salvage the pride of pleasure in her fantasies and orgasms. To call these fantasies masochistic in a simply derogatory sense, or to consider them the 'perverse' product of sexual violence, is to underestimate their capacity to provide not only pleasure but power.... Bone is able to seek and find solace in the masturbatory repetition of the violence she has experienced ... she acquires power by putting her body in motion" (103). Cvetkovich's argument reveals how, in the psychic ruins of sexual abuse, Bone finds a way to direct her own imagination so that she can find gratification. Cvetkovich works to suspend judgment in this act, by refusing to call it the "perverse product of sexual violence" and thereby granting Bone a more complex agency. I employ Cvetkovich's reading as a model for thinking about how Bernard is able to reconfigure an earlier sexual trauma. Bernard's sexual acts might be seen at the contradictory intersections of shame, pain, pleasure, and pride, and beyond this viewpoint, they are what Cvetkovich calls the power of "putting" the "body in motion."

Sexual pleasure is certainly absent in Bernard's initial molestation given the violent nature of this encounter. But Bernard later divulges that after he had finally left home for boarding school at the age of twelve, and after enduring years of sexual abuse, he fantasizes about certain aspects of this moment. As he recalls, "There, I had my first wet dream. I dreamt that a man with dark arms walked out of a glistening wet wall and pressed me against his chest until I grew aroused, then suffocated . . . the other boys sensed I was different. They could smell me out, I think, the layers of lye, sperm, and water that left a permanent film on my lips, eyes, and skin" (91). Able to produce his own sexual secretions as an adolescent, Bernard rescripts his earlier sexual abuse by imagining a mysterious man, whose identity is specified only through his "dark arms." Whereas the bathroom had initially been described as a place where the narrator "shivered" and "cried," his fictive lover appears from a "glistening wet wall," suggesting a pleasurable locale for the pursuit of queer yearnings. Bernard's sexual arousal is predicated on his suffocation, once again reinforcing the bridge between queer desire and the threat of death. Even as he is able to begin a path toward sexual self-authorship in his psychosexual life, he comes to terms with a larger public spectacle of shame and ostracism. The imagery at this passage's conclusion recalls his desire for "camouflage," as he is unable to scrape away the psychic layers of sexual abuse that he literalizes as a combination of "lye, sperm, and water." His entire exterior is covered in this "film" such that "camouflage" is rendered impossible, and he is set apart from the heterosexual realm. For Bernard to continue through his survival plot, he must find a way to embrace a queer sexuality that extends beyond its traumatic connections to assault and incest. Fortunately, the realm of the imagination, which reconstructs the meaning of desire, water, bodily fluids, and the bathroom, offers him a tool to deal with sexual traumas.

In one final scene depicting childhood erotic development, Bernard recalls his experience of becoming sexually aroused at an inopportune moment. He explains, "When I mixed up my catechism one day Father Lem took out his bamboo rod. He pulled down my pants in front of the boys. As he began to whip me, tears welled in my eyes. As the thin bamboo danced on my flesh, a warm feeling slowly arose and took over the pain. Maybe it was blood. I had an erection" (91). In a very offhand way, this passage reveals the main character's postcolonial upbringing as his boarding school education occurs at a Catholic school. As a site not only of edification but also of spiritual indoctrination, this institution forces the narrator to learn that, to avoid punishment, he must not deviate from his religious studies. At the same time, in the classroom's public space, he becomes sexually excited only after being beaten, underlining again the ways in which his arousal is often contingent on sadism and violence. The passage illustrates how the lines between pain and pleasure cross in a dynamic equilibrium. Whereas the pain initially results in tears, soon Bernard narrates that the bamboo rod "dances" on his "flesh," and he cannot hide his erection from his classmates. This performance-based metaphor foreshadows his later work at the bathhouse where he will "dance" for the anonymous voyeurs, exposing the critical importance of the body's movement in relation to queer sexuality.

Bernard's initial molestation, his subsequent sexual fantasy, and his boarding school punishment all help illuminate how he is able to move through an extended survival plot, one that lasts well into his adulthood. Despite the traumas of his childhood and the fact that he endured the sexual abuse perpetrated by a family member, he comes to reorient and revise his understanding of particular spaces and actions. The bathroom functions on multiple levels here: a waste disposal location, a place to clean one's body, and a potential site of sexual violence and molestation. And once Bernard has settled in the United States and makes a life in Los Angeles as a bathhouse performer, the significance of his occupation deepens. During the proverbial climax of his show, Bernard "let[s] [his] spunk spill over the red cloth on the floor. Like a wave, [his] energy gathers force and moves over the passive waiting men. Uncle Apostol is drowning in [his] river" (93). Here the queer Asian North American storyteller experiences an orgasm that is symbolically significant in its imagery. Bernard revises the power dynamics of his childhood molestation by imagining his sexual secretions blasting his uncle, so much so he is "flailing with his arms and his mouth opens and closes without a word" (93). This vision clearly upends the degradation and brutality that he faced when being subjected to his uncle's sexual appetite. Whereas earlier Apostol "tightened his grip around [Bernard's] throat" to silence him as a child and then forcibly gagged him through oral sex, Apostol is now rendered voiceless by Bernard's sexual power. Notably, Apostol's figurative death occurs by drowning because it also reorients Bernard's relationship to water, marking it as a substance that can renew. Apostol undergoes an imagined death that Bernard can orchestrate, a death that produces sexual excitement. This intermixing of bodily pleasure and violence sheds light on Bernard's continual attraction and repulsion to dangerous encounters such as anonymous sex acts.

The bathhouse performance also serves to rewrite the perversion of the private bathroom in which his queer sexual acts were themselves coded in shame, to be left in an enclosed space with no one to witness. Here I posit that Bernard's participation in public sex derives not simply from economic necessity (we know at this point in the text that his sex work gives him money to supply his drug habits), but also from an understated politic, though one that would not likely be acknowledged as such (by Bernard) and certainly not easily perceptible by the bathhouse patrons (such as Chino). Documentary filmmaker Celine Parreñas Shimizu undertakes vigorous readings of the overtly sexualized actresses who take on roles as prostitutes in the Broadway musical *Miss Saigon*. Shimizu goes on to argue that these actresses deploy productive perversities. Through subtle reconstructions and resistances, these actresses demonstrate that there is much more to be seen than the crotch grab or the pelvic thrust that occurs on stage. As Shimizu elaborates, "To understand acting as simply re-presentation of corresponding phenotypes and national identities is to say that actors play roles as noncreating beings. The way actors occupy their roles and fill them with specific choices helps to determine the roles they play" (*Hypersexuality* 257). Her argument makes clear how even within limited roles, the actresses possess their own agendas, which deviate from the "absolute" (257) nature of what a performative act might be designed to signify. As Shimizu maintains, in the admittedly confined space of such performances, Asian North American actresses complicate how to understand erotically suggestive and explicit gestures that seem to reify racial and sexual stereotypes. I borrow from her analytical interventions to align Bernard more firmly with the political aspect of his bathhouse performance, one that simultaneously caters to the scopophiliac desires of the audience and recasts his own tortured sexual history. His climax is not merely seen then as a functionality of sex work. Instead, his act addresses a more nuanced physical and psychic terrain of displacement, sexual abuse, and pleasure. By performing his queer sexuality in the bathhouse, he takes hold of a privately configured shame and transfigures it in a public space, for others to consume through bodily enjoyment and mutual consent.

If anything, Bernard camouflages the political undertones to his performativity. This masking is made most clear when we revisit the earlier encounter between Bernard and Chino. Chino's negative reaction to Bernard's association with the bathhouse cannot encapsulate the potential psychic complexities of Bernard's performance, nor does Bernard himself consider how his sex work engages a personal history that could ameliorate the traumas stemming from his molestation. When Chino points out the hypocrisy of Bernard's life, Bernard must address his seemingly incongruous acts: he works in a bathhouse that might contribute to HIV caseloads on the one hand and volunteers for an AIDS clinic on the other. We remember his bodily reactions to this conflict as he throws up his breakfast. But, once again, both the location of this event and the mode of regurgitation require careful analysis. As the primal site of sexual abuse, the bathroom is the location where this bodily revolt takes place. Leong's narrative returns here to show its importance in the main character's psychosexual development. Coming to the bathroom to escape his public confrontation with Chino, Bernard employs its isolation as a refuge, if only momentarily, but his vomiting signals his conflicted psychic state. His voice is stifled, as his throat is covered in a sticky film that echoes the layer of lye, sperm, and water that marked him as a sexual deviant at the boarding school. Consequently, readers must mull over how the story itself continually calls attention to the past and the ways in which Bernard's present actions come to be determined, at least in part, by the struggle and the nature of his survival plot in the aftermath of sexual abuse and queer desire.

Inscrutable Belongings: Queer Asian North American Activism Versus Bathhouse Patrons

Bernard's survival plot does not end merely because he has escaped from the conditions that left him prey as a child to his uncle's advances. Some critical issues remain that undermine any simple resolution to the story. For instance, "Camouflage" underscores the larger structural forces that oppress the queer Asian North American and that target him for continued physical violence and social death. The story makes clear that someone like Bernard can still be killed for expressing his desire, a fact made evident when his friend is "tracked . . . down to his studio" and "bludgeoned . . . to death" by two individuals who were angry for having their photographs taken and later published in a "gay porn mag" (98). This revenge killing is coded as a hate crime, because these two individuals mutilate his body in such a way as to brand him as a sexual deviant; these murderers "thrust an icepick up his ass and a vibrator down his throat. It was still buzzing when they found him" (98). Attempting to assert their masculine, heterosexual superiority over Bernard's friend, these murderers incite homicidal penetrative acts that serve as a warning to anyone who deviates from heteronormativity.

While this event focuses on the severest possible physical consequences for the queer Asian North American, Bernard also provides us with indications that violence occurs in more subtle ways. While sitting in a common area of a gay community center, Bernard "flip[s] through the gay mags that are distributed free to the agencies. Airbrushed White men dominate the pages of ads for everything your body ever lacked: abs, nose, thighs, teeth, hair, and amino acids and enzymes coursing through your system" (96). Bernard's observations unmask a subtle form of social death in which the queer Asian North American cannot find visibility and recognition as a subject of desire. He is eliminated even in the symbolic terrain of queer cultural production, a ghostly figure who exists only in the space of lack. Bernard's adult life reveals how the survival plot remains ongoing and that his endurance is reliant upon inscrutable belongings.

Bernard's survival plot as an adult is tied to his commitment to the AIDS clinic, a location that offers him a space to generate bonds with other queer Asian North Americans and to honor those who have died. The clinic is precisely the location that mirrors the ambivalence of their collective lives. Though Bernard himself is not seropositive, he feels a deep enough affinity for the individuals who frequent the clinic that these men form his most obvious inscrutable belonging. He is biologically unrelated to them yet finds himself continually drawn back to their community. When Li-Li passes away, the news possesses an incredible charge for Bernard, who had remained close to Li-Li in his final days: "After his last bout with pneumonia no one except his family, his caseworker, and I had seen him" (94). Given his lack of contact with any biological family members, Bernard finds companions at the AIDS clinic with whom he can connect on a deeper level. These individuals include "Nestor, a Filipino rapper with a shaved pate; Lee, a Taiwanese who lived with his rich White doctor lover in the Los Feliz Hills; Ricardo, a transsexual mixed-blood hairstylist; Hoang, a former jewelry designer from Saigon; Rahu, an economics teacher from Thailand; and Chino, an aspiring Japanese American actor" (94). This panethnic fellowship comes together to honor one of their dead: "Candles, colored construction paper, and flowers are already heaped on the table. We would write good-bye notes to Li-Li, as we had done for the others. His photograph is propped up on one corner of the table" (94). So even as the clinic affords Bernard a place to feel at home, it is a place involved in the persistent process of mourning. Here the storyteller cannot escape the presence of physical degradation, in the form of Li-Li's passing, or social death that emerges in relation to the larger disavowal of the many individuals who have died of complications from AIDS/HIV. The mourning rituals model their defiance against the possible erasure from heteronuclear family structures and other associated social institutions.

Bernard's endurance hence must be considered alongside his devotion to the AIDS/HIV clinic patients and the associated intimacies he develops. But still, we must recall the fact that Bernard's survival plot involves his occupation as a performer at the bathhouse. Even as he embraces a form of activism through his volunteer work at the clinic, Bernard is critiqued by Chino as someone who may actually be hastening the deaths of others through his bathhouse work. When he performs as Sakoi, Bernard is forced to digest—to pun here briefly—whether or not bathhouse patrons may be engaging in unsafe sex practices, and that therefore he may indirectly be contributing to the population that would need the services of that very same clinic. But Bernard's labor at the bathhouse takes on multiple significations.

Confronting sexual traumas as a child, his performance enables him to continue to work through these events, and he employs his time on stage as a tool to take control over his body, his pleasure, and his livelihood in the process. In addition, Bernard's ability to showcase his body rhythmically in space enables another subtle, but no less important inscrutable belonging to surface, one that extends to the patrons who frequent the spa and bathhouse. Bernard manages to act as a nexus point for these customers: he takes center stage in a queer community intent on both individual and collectively experienced sexual release. Here the inscrutable belonging comprises a diverse set of individuals. As Bernard points out, "The spa caters to Whites and Latinos, mainly, with a few Blacks and Asians. There could be from twenty to forty guys on a given night" (93). The short story depicts the murkiness of this aggregation because the very existence of the spa is necessitated by the problems related to queer visibility. Spas and bathhouses provide the queer men an outlet—and for some, possibly the only outlet—to explore sex acts. My point is not to glorify this location as a transcendent space for sexual liberation but rather to emphasize the multipronged contours of Bernard's inscrutable belongings. The spa-bathhouse affords this group of men an opportunity to display their sexual desire in a visible domain without a sense that such acts will be denigrated.

In essence, this space, however small in scale and potentially ephemeral in its construct, allows queers social recognition even amid structural forces (such as the legal policies and cultural norms) that presuppose their status as pariahs.[27] At the same time, their actions in the bathhouse could hasten physical death, especially for those who may contract AIDS/HIV during Bernard's performances.[28] In this sense, the move toward giving metaphorical life to queer sexuality in a public space is tempered by the potential proliferation of disease and physical death that such sex acts might cause. I follow Richard Hornsey's point that critiques of bathhouses cannot assume a unitary rhetorical position.

Therefore, I consider such sites as "variant in their location, dynamics, cost, and clientele and . . . in turn experienced, used, enjoyed, and abhorred by many different men. Status, income, ethnicity, and politics may greatly influence one's access to and perception of these spaces, but they never fully determine it. Such sites, in practice, are surely the setting for both revelations of social connectivity and unwelcome moments of profound alienation for different people and at different times" (51). Hornsey's remarks also clarify how we can understand the short story's construction of the inscrutable belongings that come to constitute both the promise and the peril of Bernard's survival plot. But, crucially, the communion that Bernard helps to foment in the bathhouse is one based on pleasure and agency. Further still, he cannot be held solely responsible for how the patrons themselves choose to engage in sex practices, nor is there any explicit revelation that any customers actually do contract HIV during Bernard's performance. Ultimately, the bathhouse is a place that enables mutually consenting adults the choice to initiate sexual activities on their own terms.

In the story's conclusion, Bernard goes to the park to cruise. Bernard deems his own sexual act with Chino, the Japanese American actor and bathhouse patron, as "crazy." But the story's fragmented and anachronic narrative encourages an alternative reading, one that contextualizes the act as deriving from Bernard's personal experiences, history, and attempt to take control and to revise the nature of queer racialized desires. In Michael Warner's contention, "Sex has long been associated with death, in part because of its sublimity. There is no sublimity without danger, without the scary ability to imagine ourselves and everything we hold dear, at least for a moment, as relatively valueless. In this instance, the pursuit of dangerous sex is not as simple as mere thrill seeking or self-destructiveness. In many cases, it may represent deep and mostly unconscious thinking, about desire and the conditions that make life a value" (213). I take Warner's position very seriously because it underscores a more complex mode of queer racialized sexuality at play in this short story. On the surface level, Bernard does recognize the potential self-destructiveness in his bathhouse sexual performance and in his cruising. In the case of the bathhouse, his acts can serve to impede the progressive politics behind his AIDS volunteer work, and his understanding of this possibility is indexed by his vomiting. With cruising, the relative anonymity of the sex act can leave him vulnerable to sexually transmitted diseases as well as bodily violence. Though Bernard's life is at risk, Warner would read sublimity here because Bernard's acts can still "make life a value." For Bernard, sublimity can flourish in a sexual terrain that derives from the body's confrontation with mortality and the pleasure that is produced even with the possibility of self-destruction. Moments like this one hallmark how the queer Asian North American exists in a state of living death.

Like Bernard, Chino functions as a bridge between both the group that attends the clinic and the patrons who come to Camouflage in search of sexual release. Both communities, however divergent in their motivations for meeting, establish the ambivalent grounds on which the storyteller enters into inscrutable belongings. These social formations do not disavow the presence and possibility of death, but offer this narrator-protagonist a potential place to feel and even to live, however transitorily, at home. Bernard's inscrutable belongings are elective and exist beside any traditional conceptions of the heteronuclear family. He is not bound by law or by biology to either the bathhouse patrons or the AIDS clinic patients, but both communities are indispensable to his vitality.

In the concluding sex act between Bernard and Chino, we see how their sexual pairing unequivocally brings together the two communities that Bernard has attempted to separate prior to this point. The overlap among the political views of queer Asian North Americans and the desire for pleasure, even amid the possibility of disease proliferation, all coalesce in this final narrative sequence. Bernard survives to tell his story, one that finds its apex in the dance between life and death, activism and hedonism, the individual and the collective, personal experience and history. To exist in the state of living death, then, means to acknowledge the contradictions of survival and the need for a refuge beyond the home space.

Before closing this chapter, I want to discourage making a causal connection between Apostol's incestuous relationship with Bernard and the boy's developing sexuality. I have aimed to show how Bernard's queer orientations are certainly informed by a history of sexual trauma, but cannot be seen as originating from Apostol's abusive actions. Indeed, such a conclusion would be shortsighted and reductively speculative. As the story ends with the act of cruising and anonymous sex, we see how far the narrative goes in terms of writing away from both the bildungsroman and the marriage plot. Bernard is aggressively unattached; he seeks no sort of integration into a national citizenry. He is a tactician who lives in the shadow of social death. There is no transcendence here and no closure. He has survived, but certainly at great cost.

As my reading of "Camouflage" reveals, social death and the threat of physical harm endanger the queer Asian North American's survival plot. Bernard generates variations on inscrutable belongings in order to navigate this ominous representational terrain. His endurance is revolutionary because his ability to survive to the very last page is a kind of narrative sequencing that has just become fully imaginable in fictional worlds. He finds a way to persist against such debilitating forces while daring to create communities of refuge, however temporary, among outcasts, pariahs, eccentrics, and strangers. Queer diasporic and queer of color reading practices are paramount precisely because Bernard is a transnational subject who must confront the dynamics of his racial and sexual backgrounds in the United States.

In this extended reading of Leong's "Camouflage," I provided a general analytical template for the following chapters. I attended to the formal and thematic aspects of queer Asian North American fictions in relation to the survival plot and the storyteller's movement through the narrative. Further, I established the critical importance of the storyteller's emergence alongside inscrutable belongings, which are informed by the protagonist's past experiences as well as the larger and often violent social, cultural, legislative, and historical forces that bear on particular bodies and lives.

At the same time, I have emphasized the longer critical arc in this book. As the Introduction mentions, *Inscrutable Belongings* moves forward with a rough historical trajectory in mind. The analyses driving this book are grounded in social contexts connected to politically charged moments involving queers and/or Asian North Americans that are then imagined in fictional worlds, including the rise of the civil rights movement, the AIDS/HIV epidemic, and postcolonial independence movements. The chapters accrue critical textures, which punctuate the need to consider these cultural productions as a collective grouping. Together, as racialized queer forms, these fictions telescope the trying conditions that produce the narrative test of endurance for the storyteller, and that prescribe the critical necessity of dynamic social formations.

CHAPTER 3

INSCRUTABLE BELONGINGS IN PATHOLOGY

INFECTIOUS GENEALOGIES

IN ALEXANDER CHEE'S *EDINBURGH*

IT IS NO ACCIDENT that queer Asian North American fiction writers are so invested in conceptions of the child. A youth is imbued with a fragility that can be said to prefigure the precariousness that might come to mark his or her adult life. As the first chapter already has shown through its assessment of three narrative patterns that I call tactical diversions, the larger corpus of these fictions contains many examples of such characters. The second form of tactical diversion involves narratives that position an Asian North American child (or teenager) at the center, but he or she does not grow into legal adulthood. Any explorations of sexuality are therefore complicated and potentially undercut by the child's age.

Consequently, I have labeled these young Asian North American characters protoqueer as a nod to their fledgling and often still-conflicted understandings of sexual desire. The focus on this period is notable because such works do not offer a longer trajectory in which such youths come to grips with more explicit manifestations of their sexualities. Hence, these fictions only begin to stage the many dangers these youths confront. Such children (and teenagers) must often find a way to take care of themselves, because their adult counterparts either do not provide them with adequate guardianship or are generally ignorant of the many problems they face.

Chapter 2 provided us with another glimpse into the life of the protoqueer Asian North American child. Recall that my reading of "Camouflage" examined how the narrator, Bernard, appears as part of a survival plot in which he is molested and sexually assaulted by a family member as a child, although this short story diverges from the second form of tactical diversion, as our narrator matures to adulthood. Coming of age, he must come to terms with his life as a queer Asian North American. Given the story's length, we do not get an extensive arc of Bernard's childhood, though we understand it to be a time of great uncertainty, such that we can rationalize the decisions he will make later, especially with respect to his choices to work as a bathhouse performer and to volunteer at the AIDS clinic. The propagation of his inscrutable belongings, based on the bathhouse community and the queer Asian Americans who populate the clinic, enables him to find metaphorical, yet transitory homes.

In this chapter, the critical conversation concerning retrospective storytelling, childhood, the survival plot, and the momentous part played by inscrutable belongings will continue with an extended analysis of Alexander Chee's debut novel, *Edinburgh*. In contrast to "Camouflage," *Edinburgh*, imbued with the expansiveness of the novel's length, offers a more detailed depiction of the protoqueer Asian North American childhood. Here our storyteller, looking back on his youthful past, charges his younger self with a kind of criminality and perversity. These darker conceptions of childhood invite us to engage larger discourses involving the period connected with one's youth. I accordingly turn to major developments in queer studies and Asian North American studies in order to cast a stronger light on *Edinburgh*'s depiction of children.

As briefly outlined in the Introduction, Lee Edelman issues a call to arms related to the embrace of queer pessimism. He encourages a stand against normative family values: "It is we who must bury the subject in the tomb-like hollow of the signifier, pronouncing at last the words for which we're condemned should we speak them or not: that *we* are the advocates of abortion; that the Child as futurity's emblem must die; that the future is mere repetition and just as lethal as the past" (31, emphasis original). For Edelman, the Child is the logic of a reproductive future in which queers have no part—we are precisely that which is against the Child.[1] Of course, Edelman cannot be taken too literally. He advocates for a worldview that complicates the primacy of linear progression in the realm of both politics and aesthetics. Edelman's Child—who must be denoted with a capital *C*—is certainly not some proto-LGBTQI child.[2] The Child is going to grow up, marry, and raise a very heteronormative, nuclear family. The Child is also deracinated, devoid of difference largely because this entity is torqued by the demands of hegemony, finding shape in its promising heterosexual normativity (66).[3] Indeed, social difference of any kind cannot be tolerated in this vision of the future. The Child also casts the pall of a reproductive logic that blots out the place of all queers (both young and old) in the larger social order. Further still, the Child needs to be protected because he or she is innocent, powerless, and the sacred symbol of the reproductively heterosexual future.[4]

Though seemingly different in form and context from Edelman's *No Future*, the already infamous memoir by Amy Chua, *Battle Hymn of the Tiger Mother*, offers another provocative consideration of the child. As I previously examined in Chapter 1, Chua's creative nonfictional work has been a lightning rod for controversy because it can be read as a reinscription of the model minority myth. Further still, Chua's memoir is invested in a form of the reproductive future, one located in the potential and the obedience of the child. This child must follow a predestined path and accrue certain forms of social, cultural, and symbolic capital as he or she advances to gain educational degrees and prominent career posts. This racialized progression comes with a cost: the parents' strict regulation of this child's life leverages him or her with a debt that cannot be repaid, a fact made alarmingly apparent in recent scholarly studies concerning similar issues, including erin Khuê Ninh's *Ingratitude* and Min Hyoung Song's *The Children of 1965*.[5] While loyalty and ambition are expected in this child, the future is already premapped and predestined, at least according to the tiger mom.

Providing a counterpoint to these conceptions of the (Asian North American) Child, Chee's *Edinburgh* invites readers to differentiate between sexual assault and sexual consent, and to contend with the discourse of queerness, especially as it might arise in childhood. *Edinburgh*'s plot details the contentious journey for its protagonist, a biracial Korean American queer named Aphias Zhe who comes of age in suburban Maine. Nicknamed Fee, he is twelve years old and auditioning for a choir when the novel begins. Later, he is one of many boys who are sexually assaulted by their choir director, Big Eric. The novel follows how these choirboys deal with—or, in some cases, cannot deal with—their traumatic experiences as they reach adulthood.

Edinburgh's present-tense, first-person narration creates a strong sense of immediacy, as if the story unfolds as it is told. But we begin to see some obvious ways in which the narrator appears in split time frames. In one is the child who eventually grows up to be an adult; in the other is the adult who reframes his childhood experiences and filters this period with his otherwise enlightened perspective. In the novel's earlier sections, this adult narrator materializes only a couple of times. One of the most striking moments transpires just before another one of the choirboys kills himself. The narrator mysteriously interrupts to say, "The survivor gets to tell the story. Have you figured out who survives yet?" (88). This statement and the subsequent question reveal the shadow and overlay of the adult narrator, our queer Asian North American protagonist. The rhetorical question seems to have a slightly confrontational tone, but this retrospective position immediately emphasizes that this story is important to understand through its sequencing: that is, Fee's movement through the narrative is a survival plot. In this case, Fee's ability to endure to the conclusion comes with it the power to construct this narrative, but the story is not solely concerned with Fee's triumph over his many demons. Instead, *Edinburgh* revels in the murkiness that comes with growing up and pushes us to reevaluate the ways in which the child and his later maturation are represented.

The novel hence enables us to revisit discourses of childhood offered by Edelman and Chua. Edelman's Child exists only as a condition of an idealized future, perfectly preserved in his or her preheterosexual innocence. Chua makes apparent the ways that the child is the locus of certain expectations that take on racialized characteristics: the child is the emblem of progress, the paragon of minority achievement. These various figurations contrast sharply with Chee's realist representation of Fee: *Edinburgh* conjures up a protoqueer Asian North American child, who eventually grows up to embrace his queerness and his manifold ancestries. In its depiction of this process, *Edinburgh* explodes the structure that upholds the protoheterosexual innocence of the Child. In Edelman's conception of the reproductive future, the queer is always the third party, threatening the inexorable linearity in which the Child eventually becomes the heterosexual Adult. As the indisputable villain of the story, the queer must be written out. For Chua, heterosexuality looms as the precondition of reproductive futures, the ones in which her perfectly groomed children can take part. As with Edelman's version of the Child, there can be no deviation from a predetermined, progressive path.

Diverging from the discourses of youth presented in *No Future* and *Battle Hymn of the Tiger Mother*, *Edinburgh* places the Asian North American protoqueer child at the narrative center and finally illustrates how fragile the illusion of innocence can be. Despite inhabiting the most prominent position in the narrative space, this child cannot take his survival for granted, nor can he expect protection from those adults (heterosexual or not) who oversee him. Whereas Edelman's theory of the reproductive future helps draw a strict line between who should live (the Child) and who should die (the queer), *Edinburgh* reveals a far more tortuous terrain in which the protagonist must continually reconfigure his understanding of mortality and heroism, what it means to be charged with the power to do harm, and what it means to command the narrative discourse rather than to be killed, marginalized, or terminated from the plot.[6] While Chua's memoir touches on a strict genealogy of the reproductive future in which her ferocious parenting operates to ensure the ideal outcome, *Edinburgh* imagines metaphorical inheritances that widen the pool of progenitors the child can draw from to reimagine conceptions of family and kinship.

This chapter is structured in three basic parts. In the first, I explore Chee's depiction of the protoqueer Asian North American childhood, one that involves the protagonist's ability to employ the Eastern folktale of the fox-demon to understand a history of trauma and to negotiate his own social difference, particularly of his biracial background. In the second, I move to the ways that this child is forced to mature in the face of an antagonist who exercises potentially deadly force over him. Here the folkloric figure of the fox-demon continues to exert an important influence over the protagonist, as he must contend with whether he models the heroic or the most malevolent qualities associated with this cunning shape-shifter. Though the child endures, his survival plot remains unstable because he still carries the traumas that derive from sexual abuse.

In the final section, I trace the developmental process shaped by the protagonist's retrospective narration, which speaks to his ability to place his own traumas in comparison to other individuals who are destined for discursive termination and even death. I am interested not so much in the reproductive future, then, but in forms of the reproductive past engendered by *Edinburgh*. The past—as it relates to Fee's life and the lives of others—is reconstructed in this narrative as a way to bear witness to multiple forms of intergenerational trauma. The point here is that if the unidirectional, reproductive future is always already foreclosed to the protoqueer Asian North American child (or, by extension, to similarly marginalized figures), then the reproductive past offers him a way to imagine alternative social formations that provide the basis of his inscrutable belongings.

What seem to be, then, narrative digressions—related to individuals marked as diseased or deviant—that move us away from Fee's personal battles instead actually enable the survival plot to come into its most crystalline form: readers are led to make sense of his incredible fortitude through what I denote as *infectious genealogies*. These metaphorical and biological kinships based on disease, infection, and associated discourses of monstrosity and exclusion bring together various forms of intergenerational and communal trauma depicted in the novel, which are related to the AIDS/HIV epidemic, the bubonic plague, colonial atrocities, and childhood sexual abuse. By no means transcendent or triumphant, this narrative is the one in which Fee must find a way to navigate his survival plot without subjecting others to the harm he has experienced. To close this chapter, I return to the discourse of the Child in order to emphasize the importance of *Edinburgh* as a novel that models what other narratives can exist, what other life paths can be made possible.

Revising Fox-Demons

The novel's prologue spotlights a model of intergenerational transmission that involves confronting a traumatic past in order to repurpose it for the benefit of the protoqueer Asian North American child's survival. Fee narrates, "My grandfather lost his six older sisters to the Japanese during World War II," and adds that these sisters were "[g]one and never heard from again. Comfort women was what the Japanese called those they stole for their soldiers. They were girls though" (1). As Kandice Chuh contends, allusions to "comfort women" in Asian North American literature inhabit a complex narrative function through a "reconceptualized form" that is "reconstituted to work as a reference to multiple ideological and institutional discursive practices that materialize bodies" (8). Comfort women were forcibly taken from their homes and conscripted as sex workers for the Japanese military during the colonial occupation of Korea.[7] But, following Chuh's contention, the representational function of comfort women alters in the context of a given narrative. In this case, the grandfather's admission situates Fee's life as one already influenced by a lineage of trauma and postcolonial history.

As Grace Cho notes, the figure of the comfort woman exists at a complicated nexus in Korean American culture. Her sexual servitude functions as a site of personal and national shame, which in part explains the long history of silence regarding such colonial atrocities. At the same time, despite the desire by some comfort women to demand public recognition for their traumas, the Japanese government has refused (and still refuses) to offer an official apology for these and other injustices. Cho's argument riffs off Abraham and Torok's theory of the transgenerational phantom, contending that "[d]uring those fifty years when the Korean comfort women tried to maintain silence about their sexual enslavement, their secrets were already being transmitted to the next generation of women, some of whom would follow (or be led into) the same path of sexual servitude" (6). The interventions offered by Cho's study are applicable to Chee's *Edinburgh* due to the invocation of comfort women as part of Fee's ancestral genealogy. In this novel's case, the transgenerational phantom appears at least partially appeased because the secret history of sexual servitude is unveiled, suggesting then that Fee may be able to avoid a fate similar to that of his great-aunts. Through the grandfather's willingness to share this family history and to claim his sisters as victimized subjects, such traumas transform into a productive inheritance rather than a secret through which the psyche acts out unconsciously. Fee's connection to comfort women also dramatically encapsulates how the novel can be read through queer diasporic and queer of color critical approaches. The genealogy that links Fee as a mixed-race, queer Asian North American to comfort women is based on the asymmetrical but shared lineage of tortured sexual backgrounds. For Fee to get a stronger sense of his ancestral past, the fact of his great-aunts having been comfort women must be made known; their experiences come out of what might be called a postcolonial closet.

As the grandfather tells the story of his family and its harrowing disintegration, that event is passed down orally and across generations to Fee. As Fee recounts about his grandfather, "After his sisters were taken away, the Japanese occupying force sent my grandfather to Imperial Schools. My first language is Japanese, he tells me. English far away. But okay. Be like a fox, he says. Okay" (2). Fee's grandfather tells him to "be like a fox," as if to suggest that one must be willing to outwit a perceived enemy in a tactical manner, despite the fact of incredible losses. In some ways, the grandfather's advice seems prescient given the kinds of struggles that Fee eventually faces.

The phrase "be like a fox" also references the fox-demon myth that originates in many Asian folktales. *Edinburgh* includes such elements of myth, folktale, and fantasy to help convey the whimsy as well as the terror of the protoqueer Asian North American childhood.[8] Fee must use these speculative narrative forms as cultural tools to make sense of a chaotic and dangerous world.[9] Because the folktale and fairy tale so often conjure up issues related to morality and mortality, it is not surprising to see these forms at play in works that deconstruct the innocence associated with childhood. Fee's father tells him the story of Lady Tammamo. In the novel, Lady Tammamo's name is spelled with one more "m" than in established versions. This fox-demon changes into human form so she can marry the man she loves. Because people fear her, Lady Tammamo and her husband live on an island somewhere between Japan and Korea. After years of happy marriage and the birth of many sons, the husband dies. In response, the fox woman immolates herself on his funeral pyre and sacrifices her immortality, ostensibly because she prefers death over a life without her love by her side. Due to her untimely demise, her children grow up without understanding how to live as foxes, and "so her descendants have lived as ordinary men and women since" (3). Fee's father tells him this story not simply as an extraordinary tale of love, but also to detail a supernatural ancestry. Like the mixed-species fox children who had "red in their hair" that could be seen only when "the sun shone right on it," both Fee's father and Fee have strands of errant red hairs that grow on their scalps (3).

Intriguingly, the father's version of the fox-demon folktale contradicts traditional accounts. One of the more established tales of Lady Tamamo-no-ae involves the fox-demon employing her shape-shifting abilities to infiltrate the emperor's (Toba's) court.[10] When the emperor falls ill, a mystic is called to help diagnose the problem, and his efforts reveal Lady Tamamo's malevolent influence. She flees and is eventually hunted down and vanquished, though her spirit then enters a stone that kills anyone who touches it. A religious figure is able to perform rituals to appease the spirit, and Lady Tamamo "was eventually enshrined as a tutelary deity, venerated in Nasuno as Sasahara Inari, where the deadly stone remains today" (Bathgate 3). Michael Bathgate goes on to explain that "Tamamo's seduction of Toba was in fact only one episode in a malevolent career that spanned millennia" (3). Many of her misadventures have involved toppling political regimes in various countries including India and China.[11] In an interview with creative writer Matthew Salesses, Chee notes one of his intentions in revising the Lady Tamamo myth: "I looked up where it took place, and it was easy for me to imagine her flying through the air and landing on an island off the coast of Korea. This was one of those third things—a 'if this and this then this' moment. She didn't strike me as the self-destructive type. She struck me as an enormously resourceful character." Indeed, in the novel's version, Lady Tammamo is a revered figure as well as a feared one, especially from the perspective of Fee's paternal Korean immigrant forebears.[12]

The fox-demon folktale offers a different intergenerational inheritance than the one passed down through the postcolonial trauma suffered by Fee's great-aunts. Though the fox-demon ends up killing herself, her legacy cannot be reduced to her suicide. Instead what she bestows on her descendants is the potential capacity to outwit and to challenge antagonists. As a result, Fee's grandfather tells him to "be like a fox" as a testament to the fox-demon's adaptive capabilities, the sense that Fee can access the same kind of skills that will be necessary given the many challenges he comes to withstand. Chee's alteration of the folktale source material is significant insofar as the fox-demon's suicide reminds us that even the most powerful individuals have their vulnerabilities and that Fee cannot simply assume he will come out of his childhood unscathed and free of any psychic injuries.

During Fee's childhood, references to the fox-demon appear at important moments, which correspond to the identity crises that arise from his ethnoracial background. At one point, Fee starts to read the dictionary to increase his English vocabulary at the expense of learning Korean. He is so engrossed in his study that he "can only hear inside me, a voice, reading to me from the book, lower than my own. This voice hints at directions, possibilities, even as it presses forward, inexorable, to the next word in line. Defect, Defection, Defective. Define. Definition, Definitive. On the next page, I peek. Demon" (10). This other vocal register recalls the fox-demon who can "speak through you in a second voice" (2), but rather than being a source of anxiety, the fox-demon provides Fee with a sense of the world opening up. As a result, even as his father instills in him the importance of English-language fluency, the fox-demon figure still retains her influence. It is a "second voice" from which Fee can draw the powers that might come with being a little bit different from his many classmates and fellow choirboys. Language itself, the text suggests, is the site of transformation, and the sequencing of these words, far from only alphabetical, models a kind of revisionist aesthetic, as the words themselves yield slightly different connotations, what Fee calls "possibilities." The site of language and culture becomes a place where Fee can reconstruct his experiences, elaborating on everything from the "defects" to the "definitions" that come to constitute the contours of his protoqueer Asian North American boyhood.

Fee finds the fox-demon figure can help him negotiate his conflicted feelings concerning his mixed-race ancestry; in relation to his pastime of sketching, he admits that he can "never decide easily whether to draw the eyes as white eyes or Asian ones" (23). But soon after he muses on this troubling issue, he begins to draw his favorite character from *Dungeons & Dragons*, "a sorceress I've named Tammamo, for my long-ago great-grandmother. I draw a heart-shaped face atop a beautiful body, with flowing red hair past her waist that rises behind her like fire in a storm wind. I try to make her look like one of my grandfather's missing sisters" (23). This scene is fundamental for a number of reasons. First, it shows Fee's personal artistic revision of the fox-demon. Fee's version, drawn from his sudden inspiration, is entirely different from the menacing figure he receives from his cousin, who sends him a comic from Korea: "FOX-DEMON MUST EAT THOUSAND LIVERS, YOUNG MEN VIRGINS, TO BECOME HUMAN. This fox has been drawn ugly, but she wears a beautiful mask, made from the face of a victim, to hide her ugliness" (24). Fee's approach toward re-creating the fox-demon is important enough to him that he mails his cousin his version of Lady Tammamo that is replete with her in a "buckskin bikini" and a "power gem" that "rests on a headdress ... atop her hair" (24). Second, Fee's mention of the cousin's version calls attention to the fact that Fee redraws Lady Tammamo from his protoqueer Asian North American perspective. By directly connecting foxes to his grandfather's sisters, Fee provides his lost great-aunts a representational afterlife. In this testament to their having survived in some form, their spirits live on through Fee's renderings. Lady Tammamo undergoes another transformation in this context, as she casts more light on a history of sexual conscription and postcolonial trauma.

Fee's childhood directly engages the shape-shifting powers of the fox-demon, and he often compares this figure to other folktales, myths, cultural depictions, and legends. At one point, she is measured against "Greek gods and goddesses," but Fee decides that Tammamo is "mightier. For the man she loves lived to die a natural death, and the Greeks always kill the mortals they love, through design or accident. None of these gods would renounce their godhood" (25). Again, the fox-demon emerges as a heroine, and in this case her powers are evident not only in her ability to "conjure a storm" (25) but also because she does not use her powers to destroy humans. Rather, she emulates and desires the very mortality that would weaken her. This viewpoint reminds us of the extreme divergence from the cousin's declarations that the fox-demon must consume one thousand human livers, preferably those of young male virgins. Especially given Fee's emerging queer sexuality, Lady Tammamo's transgressive love for a mortal seems relevant to his growing attachment to his friend and fellow choirboy, Peter. In relation to William Shakespeare's *The Tempest*, Fee opines that Ariel "was perhaps a fox, far away from home and lost" (35) after Big Eric tells him that Ariel was a "magical servant" and a "shape changer. Could ride lightning, stand at the bottom of the sea, or impersonate a storm" (35). The reference to Ariel is pivotal insofar as it reveals another instance whereby Fee reconfigures the fox-demon folktale. As "magical servant" and Prospero's underling, Ariel becomes an imaginary figure who is elliptically associated with Fee's great-aunts. Like them, he is forced to work in the service of a domineering entity.

Childhood Sexual Trauma and the Survival Plot

Using the figure of the fox-demon as a malleable template, Fee reconsiders the nature of his racial and ethnic differences and reorients some of the troubling significations of his emerging sexuality. Fee, as the so-called descendant of Lady Tammamo, thus attempts to accept his own transformative capacities. The novel introduces the first variation of an inscrutable belonging based on this powerful demonic progenitor. As Fee recognizes his fox-demon ancestry, a folkloric past becomes reproductive. But if the fox-demon is able to provide Fee with a stabilizing cultural platform to navigate his protoqueer Asian North American boyhood, then his adaptability and his creativity are tested once Big Eric initiates his sexual predation. Fee's survival plot begins in earnest when he meets Big Eric and must contend with the fallout stemming from childhood sexual abuse.

Big Eric is a choir director, charged with mentoring young children to train their voices and to perform musical pieces. In this caretaker role, he holds tremendous influence over many children. According to Judith Butler, sexual abuse is treacherous because a bond between a child and an adult is integral for the child's security: "[D]ebates about the reality of sexual abuse of children tend to misstate the character of the exploitation. It is not simply that a sexuality is unilaterally imposed by the adult, nor that a sexuality is unilaterally fantasized by the child, but that the child's love, a love that is necessary for its existence, is exploited and a passionate attachment is abused" (*Psychic* 8). For the child, the "passionate attachment" is necessary because the child needs multiple types of support from an adult, ranging from foodstuffs to shelter, education, and guidance that will allow the child to one day survive on his or her own. Love becomes the method through which the child can enable his or her own "existence," but it can come only through a relationship of dependence. In the case of *Edinburgh*, the "passionate attachment" encapsulates Big Eric's enthralling power over the children. Extending their love, the choirboys seek the approval and attention of Big Eric, who controls admittance into the choir and effectively creates the rules that bind the choirboys. And as choir "subjects," they achieve a sense of imagined agency under Big Eric's tutelage. They learn about the range of their voices and master difficult notes and pieces. But his position as an instructor and as a trusted elder masks other, more violent impulses.

For Fee, this danger of the passionate attachment is framed within the logic of magical and metaphorical transformations, though Big Eric is not associated with the fox-demon. Fee likens him to a different creature: "I look up at him. He is a tall man, he does carpentry. His round-rimmed gold-framed glasses give him an owlish demeanor, though not the wise owl but the startled one. When the owl blinks around trying to see" (23). The owl metaphor is apt insofar as Big Eric is consistently linked with predatory animals and other monstrous beings. Fee also connects Big Eric with the Roman myth of Saturn, who feasted on his children after it was foretold that one of them would terminate his reign. At one point, Big Eric shows Fee a book he bought while in Sweden, which depicts naked grown men working out with young boys. They happen to be looking over this book while they are listening to Gustav Holst's *The Planets*. Fee recounts that "I recall a painting I saw printed once, in a book, called *Saturn Eats His Children*. To prevent the new race of gods from overtaking him, Saturn ate his children whole. They cut themselves out of his stomach, and went on to rule the world. These boys on the carpet look like they are trying to escape being eaten" (40). Here Fee refers to the painting Peter Paul Rubens completed in 1693, which depicts Saturn consuming one of his children, who looks to be just an infant. Though Big Eric is not directly compared to Saturn here, Fee later makes this mythic association explicit, especially after Big Eric has been charged with twelve counts of child sexual abuse:

> I saw us then in a dim procession, Big Eric *was* Saturn, he had swallowed us, out of fear and gluttony, and now we marched out of him as out of a cave, and overhead, a now-happy Ralph, winged not like angels but with tiny brown wings of a sparrow or a phoebe. He would perch, hold the walls tight, as if he didn't trust his wings to hold him up. When nothing else had. (66)

In this passage, Fee refers to himself and his fellow choirboys as the survivors of Big Eric's cannibalistic practice. Fee also refers to Ralph, who was Big Eric's adopted son and who had drowned at the choir camp that Fee had attended. That Ralph is likened to "a sparrow or a phoebe" reminds us again that Big Eric is approximated to an owl, a bird of prey known to eat other flying creatures. These significations pile on top of one another to present readers with Fee's clear antagonist from his childhood, a man who undergoes a metaphorical transformation from benign choir director to voracious cannibalistic monster.

Exploiting his position as a choir director, Big Eric seduces the boys by luring them into camping trips and retreats, replete with the promise of diversion and recreation. In these isolated locations, Big Eric manipulates power dynamics and, in the process, transforms the world around the young boys into a landscape of equivocation.[13] In particular, Fee and two other choirboys, Little Eric and Zach, are taken on a "section-leader camping trip" (12), during which Fee and the other boys are molested. As Fee narrates, "[T]hen we take off our clothes, Big Eric first, and he removes all of his and stands, looking at us waiting. Swimming nude, he says, is one of God's greatest gifts to us" (13). By invoking God, Big Eric rationalizes their nudity within a moral framework, and because he does not physically force them to undress, their actions seem to be cast in the logic of their voluntary participation. Once the boys are nude, they decide to go swimming. While the boys enjoy themselves, "Big Eric holds his camera across his broad hairy chest. He aims at Little Eric and shoots. Krick. Slower, that time, his finger lingers at the sight in the frame" (13). In this case, the children are having fun, but they do not fully realize the unprincipled ramifications of Big Eric's photography: he uses this occasion to document and to archive their naked forms. As noted previously, Big Eric is constantly associated with the owl (23), a bird of prey, and never does that seem more relevant as in these photographic sequences.

Child sexual abuse traumatizes children not only because they lose their sexual agency, but also because they cannot fully understand the nature of the power dynamics. As Susan A. Clancy notes, "[I]t should not be surprising that young people 'allow' abuse. Not only do children not understand the full meaning or consequences of their actions, but they are conditioned biologically and psychologically to want and need very basic things: love, attention, positive feedback, and rewards. And it is precisely what perpetrators are offering them" (70).[14] Clancy's perspectives are obviously at play in *Edinburgh*. In the novel's case, exploitation and sexual abuse take on a subtle undercurrent that can be unmasked only from a retrospective location—the site of Fee's adult perspective, which reveals key ambivalences in these sequences. The children desire Big Eric's approval, but Fee's storytelling unveils Big Eric's predatory nature and how he takes advantage of the camp's secluded location to initiate his sexual abuse.[15]

The extent of their trauma manifests most acutely during and after their experiences inside their tent. As Fee divulges, "[T]here is a quiet in which I pretend I don't know what all of this means, Big Eric's talks on the drive up here about libertarianism, nudism, child rights. And then I don't pretend. The mosquito-screen zipper sizzles shut" (14). The slippery phrasing suggests that Fee is completely aware of what is going on, but what he cannot understand at that time is how this moment will reverberate for many years and even decades later. Again, Big Eric's discussions, especially of "child rights," are related to a form of seduction in which he grants full agency to the children on the camping trip, though we know, of course, that the boys have nowhere to go, given their spatial isolation and their emotional attachment to the choir director. The image of the zipper as it "sizzles shut" reminds us of the ways that these boys are metaphorically imprisoned and will be burned by Big Eric's actions. Once inside the tent, Big Eric is described by Fee as "huge. Covered in hair. His penis looks comical, enormous, a cartoon. His age renders him like another gender, or a species apart from us. Our bodies are small, bones are small" (14). The physical difference reveals the unequal power gradient here. Further still, Fee's description denotes Big Eric's monstrous metamorphosis from owl to hairy, oversized beast.

In the morning after the abuse, Fee begins to piece together the nature of what has occurred. He recollects,

> And then the trees, the prismatic air presses on everything that needs it here on earth, the sun fires itself on the stream and spreads light through the under brush where we are camped, spangling our faces. Vertigo. The night before scatters away. I press the hot coffee to my face. I look at my face in his shaving mirror and don't recognize myself. My hair is streaking from the sun. My pupils are huge. I want to say, Take me apart. Leave me here for dead, if you can.
> Zach gets out of the tent and stands in front of me and when I meet his eyes he winks. He puts a finger on my lips and smiles. Hey, he says. Nice tan. (14)

In this passage, Fee experiences what Cathy Caruth might call a "delayed" and "uncontrolled repetitive occurrence" of sexual trauma ("Unclaimed Experience" 181).[16] While he is sitting up on the morning after his molestation, Fee desperately seeks to make sense of the past night in which the children took turns in the sleeping bag with Big Eric. But Fee is soon shunted back into the present where the "prismatic air presses on everything" and the "sun fires itself on the stream." The shock of the present exists to produce a tension with the past, such that the sexual trauma is understood to have made a "wound of the mind" (Caruth, *Unclaimed Experience* 623). Hence, Fee implores, "take me apart," in response to the sexual trauma he has felt, in order to provide some way of avoiding the flashbacks that his molestation triggers. Although descriptions of both boys hint at their complicity in the sexual acts through Little Eric's "giggles" (14) and Zach's "wink," the narrative arc continually underscores that the outward performative acts of these boys (and later young adults) fail to encapsulate the complexities of their psychically damaged interiorities. Insidiously, Big Eric convinces these young boys to engage in sex acts, while still rendering them as objects through his photographic documentation and his ability to manipulate their actions. Again this sequence reveals how Big Eric abuses the passionate attachment the children hold for him; the boys lose their sexual agency to a trusted adult figure and believe that they have freely participated. Fee, Zach, and Little Eric enter into a fragile queer community wherein sexual desires are based on secrecy and shame. Zach knows to put a "finger on [Fee's] lips," precisely because he realizes that their acts have a forbidden element to them. When Fee fails to recognize himself in Big Eric's shaving mirror, he begins to confront the violence that has been perpetrated on them. In essence, the shaving mirror symbolizes how Fee has precociously come of age, faced with traumatic sexual knowledge.

As an adult, Fee struggles to work through his deep sense of loss. Fortunately, his grandfather provides Fee with the fox-demon figure as a tool that he can reformulate as part of a mythical lineage, especially as he faces incredible trials as a protoqueer Asian North American boy. The fox-demon becomes the basis of Fee's primary inscrutable belonging, a magical progenitor who provides him with a measure of inspiration in a dangerous childhood. At the same time, his inscrutable belonging appears troubled by its association with Big Eric, a figure who also possesses transformative capacities. By the time Big Eric has finally been prosecuted, Fee believes that he is partially to blame for not protecting the other boys, for not speaking up about what was going on. As Fee divulges, "the criminal is still here. Story, here" (67). In the aftermath of Big Eric's imprisonment, Fee harbors a tremendous sense of guilt, especially in relation to Peter: "Sometimes I wonder if [Peter] knew why I always asked him to never tell. Why I helped Big Eric hide in plain sight. I didn't have an answer for Peter then but he never asked. I have an answer, *now*. Hiding [Big Eric] hid me" (69, emphasis added). In this passage, Fee ponders over the many parallels he might possess with his former choir director. The key word *now* suggests that Fee's adult retrospective self is able to revisit his potential complicity in the sexual molestations. And if Fee is a descendant of the fox-demon, then there exists the possibility that he may have inherited other more malevolent traits. The duality undergirding Fee's genealogical tie to the fox-demon finds its darkest signification in this moment due to this entity's ravenous appetite, as we recall that Fee's cousin notes how this figure exhibits a predatory hunger for human livers. The links between Big Eric, the fox-demon, and Fee constitute a new triangulated social formation based on shape-shifting, rapaciousness, and destruction.

Fee's maturation to adulthood requires him to reconsider the nature of this evolving inscrutable belonging and to face how earlier traumas can take other morphologies and shape the lives of those who hail from following generations. In this case, Fee begins to realize how he has not fully dealt with the psychic wounds from his childhood years, and interestingly enough his view of Big Eric undergoes a radical conversion. I thus move to explore how *Edinburgh* stages Fee's progression to adulthood, a process that pushes him to evaluate traumas in relation to one other. Fee must ponder over whether he, too, should be held responsible for a process in which brutality continues to extend intergenerationally. In this sense, Fee must accept how even someone as destructive as Big Eric can potentially inform his elective associations to others and how he must still find a way to separate himself from the violent models of attachment first perpetrated by Big Eric. This later period hence denotes how Fee's survival plot remains unresolved.

Having left Maine for college and then lived for some years in New York following the completion of his degree, Fee subsequently returns to his home state and works as an interim high school swim coach. One student swimmer named Warden develops a romantic obsession with Fee. Eventually, they embark on an illicit relationship. Readers are meant to understand that Fee succumbs to Warden's pursuits because Warden uncannily resembles a choirboy named Peter whom Fee had once held strong feelings for when both were young adolescents. Significantly, Peter kills himself in his teenage years. Before the novel ends, Fee discovers that Warden is actually Big Eric's son and that Warden—learning that his own father had once sexually assaulted young boys and finding out that one of those boys was Fee—has murdered his father. Though Big Eric has already been legally punished for his actions by being imprisoned, the novel offers him this violent—and perhaps Oedipal—mode of retribution.[17] Warden, of course, perceives his homicidal act as one of gallantry, but as Fee goes on to note, "You want to tell this boy next to you, how his father isn't dead. Not the part he wanted to kill. Not as long as you are there. He's hiding inside us now, you want to say, but you drive him away from the fire instead" (205). Big Eric finds a way to "hide" inside Fee and Warden precisely because their own relationship has become a skewed refraction of Big Eric's abuse of the choirboys. Though Warden aggressively pursues Fee, it is Fee, as a high school swim coach, who retains a position of exploitative power in this relationship. This very dynamic leads Fee to view Big Eric as someone who

> searched us like a pannier looking the creek bed over, searched every flash of gold for the sight of a lost love. Burning hides what it burns there. Somewhere deep in him was a memory of light that pierced him from end to end like a spit. He couldn't see that he was large and we were not. His body to him felt outsized, a bear costume borrowed for a party, and then it vanished. In the moment he touched us, he was a boy again. And in the moment he touched us we were run through also. The pain reached out, passed, like fire does, from the burned to the burning. Burning hides what burns. (199)

In this fascinating rendering, Big Eric transforms from a pannier in a "bear costume" to a boy, but this process is imbued with a pain that spreads out in a metaphorical conflagration. Here Fee revises Big Eric's voracious monstrosity as one that comes from a specific place and time. Big Eric is not only a mythic being out to consume young children, but also a boy himself who suffers from a "lost love." The pathology of this "lost love" is marked by the way it rapidly radiates harm, so much so that Big Eric cannot fully control how it proliferates and extends intergenerationally. The problem with Big Eric's delusional transition from adult to boy is that this alteration cannot recover the love he has lost. His raptorial pursuit of boys is but a palliative, an attempt to ameliorate a painful rupture that cannot heal. He is, in fact, not a young boy, and none of the boys he abuses can take the place of whomever he has lost. This pathological melancholia is the grounding point of Fee's new understanding of Big Eric: he is a monster now tamed, and the source of his insatiable hunger is exposed. The novel follows established studies that show the ways in which sexual abuse is cyclical, especially as childhood victims can later become adult perpetrators. In this respect, the novel foregrounds a larger context that ultimately resists the thesis that perpetrators of sexual abuse are purely and unequivocally "irredeemable and even subhuman" (Schultz 200).

Caught in the wake of Big Eric's infernal search is Fee, who even as a being supposedly capable of metaphorical transformation is "run through" with the fire. So too are the other choirboys. For Fee, the fire that originates first from Big Eric's search for lost love and his impossible desire to be a young boy informs Fee's own shape-shifting capacities, as Fee attempts to deceive himself into believing that Peter can be found in some other body. In this sense, Fee's relationship with Warden finds some parallels with Big Eric's futile recovery effort. Fee seeks through Warden to replicate the relationship he once had with Peter, but in that process he, however tangentially, violates the proprietary and professional boundaries that separate students from teachers, coaches from athletes. In this sense, Fee might be identified as a "criminal," but we are pushed to differentiate between Fee's shape-shifting and Big Eric's.

To address this concern, we can turn back to Chee's revision of the Lady Tamamo-no-ae tale: we recall that the fox-demon is an object of scorn and fear. At one point, the fox-demon and her husband have to move: "After some trouble in their village for which she was blamed, they left and moved to a tiny island where they settled and were accepted by the fisherman there, who had seen many things and were not afraid of her" (2). Lady Tammamo is bound by her fidelity and love to her human husband. While a tale of deep romance is itself seemingly quaint, it is intended to be a revolutionary form of love, one that crosses the boundaries of beings—certainly a queerish kind of desire—and challenges any blanket categorization of the fox-demon solely as troublemaker and agent of destruction.

In addition, we recall that as a child Fee had sketched Lady Tammamo to make her look like his great-aunts. This redrawing of the fox-demon reminds us of the importance of this magical lineage, especially in relation to postcolonial trauma. In the final section of the novel, narrated at the point of Fee's movement into adulthood, he imagines his great-aunts again as fox figures: "They would be like my grandfather, of course, thin and tall and silver. Their hair would be wrapped into modest buns, let down only at night, when some daughter might help them brush it. The red hair would be gone, turned silver now. The white fox, very rare, is the good fox, the most holy one. Helper to the rice god" (171). Departing from the traditional understanding of the fox-demon as a powerful villainess, this passage shows how Fee's great-aunts have aged and exhibit frailty with their "thin" bodies. Fee sees his great-aunts somehow magically surviving their tenures as comfort women, but this possibility is itself a source of more questions: "If they were still alive, though, they would have come home. Could they be alive out there, somehow unable to have found their way home?" (171). Despite such uncertainties, Fee continues to "see them: old women, vigorous as teenagers, stepping across the night in a rush of wind, their hair turning to fire. When the fox flies her hair is a fiery tail behind her. Watch them come. They dodge church spires and office towers in their pell-mell, sow sparks, set mysterious fires at the homes of their now-elderly tormentors, who emerge to put them out, a little afraid, they laugh as they go" (171). He muses that his great-aunts would proclaim their love for his grandfather, "their words scattering across the roof of sky. We miss him. But we can't come home" (171). This sequence interrupts the novel and does not link up in any direct way to the plotting that directly precedes or follows it. At the same time, this whimsical vision provides another layer to the fox-demon mythology that Fee engages, first as a child and now as an adult. In this version, the great-aunts, as fox figures, employ their powers to cause mischief and trouble for the Japanese colonials who were once their tormentors. These foxes do not harm their tormentors, and the limits of their abilities are revealed when they cannot be reunited with their brother, Fee's grandfather. In this respect, the awe-inspiring command of the weather that epitomized Lady Tammamo's abilities diverges from the subdued misadventures of Fee's great-aunts, who transform the sky into a canvas to communicate their sadness, but cannot transport themselves to their sibling.

This passage concerning the great-aunts is relevant to the ways in which Fee repositions the vast powers of the fox-demon from his adult perspective. Though Fee cannot bring his great-aunts back to his grandfather, he can at least provide narrative resurrections. But this tale accrues another level of resonance with respect to Big Eric. Fee cannot repair the rupture of postcolonial trauma, but he can still honor the abyssal loss faced by his grandfather during the Japanese imperial era and simultaneously imagine his great-aunts as figures who do not become swallowed up in a quest for vengeance. These considerations of the fox-demon provide templates that Fee must eventually follow as an adult. For Fee to put into action the productive capacity of the fox-demon, he needs to honor his own melancholic love without having to harm another unjustly. In other words, he endeavors to contain the ways in which Big Eric's inferno-like melancholia continues to spread and to proliferate into more acts of brutality.

As the novel concludes, Fee faces a choice about whether to run away with Warden, a decision complicated by Warden's belief that he has enacted a form of retributive justice for Fee. They arrive at a hotel, seemingly to decide on their next move, and Warden falls asleep. Fee muses, "I want to wake him and tell him, that we need to escape this, that what he's done has trapped us and not freed us, but the planes of his sleeping face rebuke me, which is when I see myself in the mirror above the bed: tired, lonely, him stretched out below me, looking for all the world like I've knocked him out or worse" (208). This striking scene recalls a similarly structured and equally pivotal occasion much earlier in the novel: the horrifying lead-up to Big Eric's actual arrest when Fee is just a young choirboy. In this scene, one of the other choirboys, Freddy Moran, goes to Big Eric's hotel room, where he finds Big Eric naked and Little Eric immobile on the floor. He fears that Little Eric may be dead, but readers discover that "Eric Johannsen was later confirmed to have been asleep, as the result of a sleeping pill dosed to him by Mr. Gorendt so that he would not interfere with the seduction of either Peter or Freddy" (65). Freddy's fear that Big Eric has injured or killed Little Eric leads him to run out of the room and seek refuge in the locked hotel room of another choirboy: "At this point, Big Eric was pounding the door, now locked against him, bellowing various threats" (66). This scene is pivotal in that it presents indisputable evidence that Big Eric not only molests children but also physically endangers them. (Fee early on discloses that Ralph, Big Eric's adoptive son, accidentally drowned while camping with his father and the choirboys. But Fee believes that the death was no accident and that the boy might have killed himself, desperate to escape Big Eric's sexual assaults; or perhaps, more gravely, Big Eric killed him.) As Fee recalls this moment involving Big Eric's arrest at the hotel, "I know that if Big Eric had been photographed in that hour he wouldn't have recognized himself at all" (65). Big Eric's aggression unveils the addled mind of a man who cannot confront his status as a child abuser. The police are called in by Freddy Moran's mother and the "owners of the hotel, frightened into thinking Big Eric was a stranger. They didn't, they said, recognize him as being the kind man who had checked in" (66).

Whereas Big Eric cannot acknowledge that his desire to transform into a child has failed, Fee's vision is not so limited. In the hotel mirror, Fee can see himself as a potential abuser and an accomplice to Warden's murderous act. He accordingly seeks to end any association, sexual and homicidal, with Warden—and by extension Big Eric—and he goes on to speculate on his options: "I don't want to be the one to turn [Warden] in to the police. I want him to do that or not. I want him to have the choice, to say he did it or not, but I want him to choose what happens next even as I do, as I walk toward the door and, leaving the key inside on the carpet, close it. From a pay phone I call the hospital and say I need an ambulance for room 322, that my friend has closed the door and won't answer and I think it's an emergency" (208). Fee chooses to exit the room, symbolizing his attempt to end his participation in the cycle of sexual abuse and violence that continued when Warden and Fee began their relationship and when Warden murdered Big Eric. As Fee contemplates his actions, he reflects, "I stopped it, I tell myself, not sure where I am walking. I stopped it. He didn't die" (208). Fee associates Warden with the many choirboys and children who eventually came to tragic ends under the hawkish gaze of Big Eric. Here Fee's survival plot comes full circle, as he must place his life alongside that of Warden's: he cannot stay with this teenager, if either of them are to be able to break fully from Big Eric's destructive hold upon both of their lives.

Fee's decision to leave Warden behind reveals how he finally confronts his ambivalent position as the fox-demon's descendant; he might be seen as a hero or villain, depending on the context. Although Fee participates in an inappropriate relationship with his student, ultimately he ends that relationship, evidencing his willingness to face the consequences related to Warden's murder of Big Eric and to his affair with Warden. This conclusion outlines the gray zones Fee must inhabit wherein he cannot fully absolve himself from blame; nor can he simply ignore that he, too, had been victimized. Curiously enough, after he decides to leave Warden, he experiences a rapprochement with his fox-demon self, whom he sees in the water's reflection: "I say nothing. I want him gone, even as I know, my standing here is the only way he can speak to me" (208). This strange meditation conveys how Fee resolves his own survival plot: he must take responsibility for his life and the fact of his power to take care of and to damage others. This moment is as much about Fee's maturation as it is about a revision of the fox-demon mythology. He tells his fox self to "stay" (209), assenting to embrace his inscrutable belonging, one in which he can resolutely claim the fox-demon as a magical ancestor, while understanding that even someone as baleful as Big Eric could help him to work through his own melancholic attachment.

Retrospective Storytelling, Expanding the Survival Plot, and Infectious Genealogies

By the novel's conclusion, the fox-demon can be situated from multiple angles, not only as a heartbroken heroine who sacrifices her immortality for love, but also as a villainess with the ability to wreak havoc on others. Fee, too, assumes the burden that comes with the capacity to do harm, while at the same time reconciling the fact that, as a child, his options to resist Big Eric were limited. We of course must recall the centrality of the novel's retrospective narration, that it is an adult Fee casting back into the past and reconstructing the narrative, even as it is told in the present-tense, first-person mode. The resolution of his survival plot and the maturation of the protoqueer Asian North American child are partly evidenced through this storytelling perspective.

As a sequence, Fee's survival plot is retrospective in its formation. As an adult Fee recounts in this basic order: (1) as a child, Fee endures sexual abuse at the hands of Big Eric, (2) later he returns to Maine as an adult and engages in a controversial relationship with the teenager Warden, but (3) he ends his attachment to Warden, especially in light of Warden's divulgence that Warden has killed his father, Big Eric, as a form of retributive justice. At the same time, the novel's depiction of other character trajectories begins to undercut the seemingly linear nature of the survival plot. If Fee is able to endure, then what about other figures who do not last until the novel's conclusion? As we recall, a number of children in the choir end up killing themselves, gesturing to the fact that Fee's livelihood is obscured by the shadow of these suicides. His durability in the face of his traumas accordingly finds more texture in relation to others who have passed before him. To further investigate this issue, I consider the broader power of Fee's retrospective storytelling as a way to confront how his survival plot becomes more expansive.

Fee experiences one key moment during his childhood that leads us to see the inconsistency of his narrative perspective. As he goes through puberty, his voice changes, and he cannot maintain the upper registers that he once did as a young child. He feels this alteration acutely because his singing ability is what gave him power: "whatever there was about me that was fragile disappeared when my mouth opened and I let the voice out" (68). So when he turns fifteen, he notes of his new vocal register, "When my voice changes I know this new creature is capable of no significant touch, no transformations. This voice cannot erase me, take me over and set me aside. This new voice has no light" (68). In the process of getting older and undergoing physical changes, Fee perceives he has less agency than ever. But these lines simultaneously speak to a new voice that emerges as he advances in age, one that can, in its own way, enable dynamic metamorphoses. Though Fee feels he had more power as a child through his singing voice, his youthful talent also happened to make him a target for someone like Big Eric. Even as he loses that vocal skill, he comes to learn the productive command he attains in re-creating, revising, and altering folktales to make sense of his losses and to work toward breaking a cycle of sexual abuse, violence, and brutality.

At another pivotal point during Fee's protoqueer Asian North American boyhood, he and his fellow choirboys attend camp. The choirboys often spend their spare time participating in fantasy role-playing games. Gifted with the ability to tell fanciful tales, Fee is deemed a dungeon master, the individual tasked with creating quests that the other choirboys use to guide their heroes through to fight monsters and villains. This leadership position is important enough that Big Eric takes an active interest in making sure that Fee allows any camp attendee to play. Fee provides an apparatus for the children to see the drama between good and evil play out, to understand that there is a world in which evil forces can be vanquished and magical items found. What small comfort these stories might have been in such a troubled time—a small but necessary measure of imaginary resistance in a world dominated by Big Eric's predatory advances. But maturation requires a different form of storytelling: Fee's adult retrospective narration is a revision of this dungeon master position, in which he has the opportunity to shape the nature of particular characters as survivors.

Earlier in the chapter, I analyzed Big Eric's melancholic desire from the framework of its fiery expansion. His pathological attachment to loss is rendered as a metaphorical conflagration that spreads in a manner that can correspond with pathogenic infection. As Big Eric's melancholia consumes Fee and the other choirboys in its path, they too become diseased. This burning infection, though deleterious in its many manifestations, also links Fee to a larger community of choirboys who, together, form an admittedly fragile and afflicted inscrutable belonging. In this way Fee's survival plot involves other figures who coalesce as part of interlocking infectious genealogies.

These unexpected aggregations help situate why the novel deviates from Fee's experiences as a choirboy and moves into other realms, such as when he is hired as a young teen to be the research assistant for a historian named Edward Speck. The import of the novel's title comes from Fee's time providing support for Speck's scholarly pursuits. The historian seeks more information about Edinburgh, the capital of Scotland, in relation to the Black Death. This location is important to Fee for a number of reasons. On the most basic level, Fee identifies with the site ethnically, as he is half Scottish Irish on his mother's side. His work with Speck further gives him the opportunity to read an old manuscript, purportedly written by Andrew Norman, a bubonic plague survivor who had been entombed alive.[18] Fee is expressly attuned to this research assistantship because he had already gained some knowledge about the Black Death through a school reading assignment on *The Decameron*. As Fee recalls, "*The Decameron* was a collection of love stories told by ten people running from Florence during the time of the Black Plague. They told stories to pass the time rather than playing games, at the direction of the Queen, traveling with them. Seven women, three men. Everywhere they looked, people dying. What a pleasure it must have been, I think, as the story flies up the screen in front of me in sections. To survive" (44–45). His response to *The Decameron* is noteworthy precisely because he understands that outlasting such a plague is never assured. One element to note from Fee's response to this cultural production is his focus on storytelling: these narratives offer a community of men and women a form of entertainment in a time of great peril. This activity reminds us of Fee's work as a dungeon master, telling tales to the boys in the midst of Big Eric's predatory company.

Fee's research for Speck naturally offers him more opportunities to ponder over the nature of life and death. Fee reads directly from Andrew's account concerning the period after he recovers from the ill effects of the plague; Andrew proclaims, "Surely it is Heaven's own intent that I be here, alive, to record what has been done" (84). Though no apparent biological genealogy links Fee to Andrew, Andrew's experiences obviously resonate with him. Andrew is a figure who recovers from a virulent infection and who chronicles his circumstances. Andrew exists as a symbolic progenitor for Fee, who survives a figurative plague, one generated in part by Big Eric's melancholic desire that spreads harm to so many others. Through Fee's retrospective narration, we begin to see that Andrew's desire to "record what has been done" parallels what Fee accomplishes in recounting his fortitude and detailing the untimely deaths of the other choirboys.

In another instance of intergenerational transmission related to disease and death, Fee aligns artistic production with the bubonic plague. Just before being hired by Speck, Fee "had been doing an English paper on the pantoum, a literary form, originally Sri Lankan, that came to Italy in pages wrapped in silks. The same silks that perhaps had arrived with the infected fleas of the Plague. I think of the elegant horses, stung as they ride, carrying the death of nations" (78). Here the pantoum is itself involved in the process of transmission; an artistic form is implicated in an epidemic's propagation. At the same time, the form persists across time, gesturing to the power of art to withstand the plague. For someone like Fee, the pantoum's durability acts analogically with respect to his own excruciating experiences, offering him evidence that he too can outlast the spread of infection.

References to plagues and infectious diseases crop up throughout the novel, which together coalesce into an inscrutable belonging based on pathogenic transmission. References to the bubonic plague remain primarily centralized in the early part of the novel, when Fee is just a teenager. As an adult, Fee must confront another catastrophic pathogenic context: the HIV/AIDS epidemic, especially as it affects Freddy Moran, once a fellow choirboy but at that narrative point in the final stages of AIDS infection. At this point, *Edinburgh* reminds us of Leong's "Camouflage," as the novel directly bridges the queer Asian North American storyteller to individuals who seroconverted during the darkest years of the AIDS/HIV epidemic. Whereas Bernard in "Camouflage" immediately details an inscrutable belonging based on his volunteer work and the patients who frequent an AIDS clinic, Fee's own association to Freddy once they are adults is at first flimsy. Nevertheless, over time, Fee's devotion to Freddy strengthens, situating *Edinburgh* as a narrative that must be read through its connection to the subgenre of AIDS narratives.

The discourse on the representation of AIDS in literature has been of course quite controversial, especially since early scholars on the topic such as Douglas Crimp and Michael Denneny have been adamant that cultural representations should operate with an activist rhetoric.[19] This viewpoint has been energized by a desire to combat a generalized fear that AIDS is a gay disease. As Emmanuel S. Nelson puts it, this stance concerning the queer man's relation to AIDS "has doubled the burdens of the American homosexual male: in the pre-AIDS era, for example, his sexuality was the target of social stigma; now he is additionally stigmatized because he is also assumed to be an agent of an infectious, fatal disease. This perceived connection between his sexuality and an incurable illness has helped reinforce traditional anti-gay hostility" (48).[20] The danger of aestheticizing AIDS is made apparent in James Dawes's reading of Randy Shilts's *And the Band Played On*: "[W]hile narrative certainly does evoke sentiment, it evokes a specifically *narrative* sentiment—*mere* sentiment—an emotion not necessarily convertible into the statistical compassion needed to move the individual from the local example toward broader social action. Narration *closes* histories; and for the activist, histories must always remain open, like a wound" (31). Dawes's point is that narrative constructs can have a superficial effect on the reader, who may approach depictions of the AIDS crisis as dramatic and even entertaining, something entirely removed from actual lives. Dawes argues that Shilts's journalistic approach minimizes cursory consumption through a particular technique and emphasis on the material: "[Shilts] continually makes visible the damaged body. His text thus alternates between the medical report and the melodrama, balancing one against the other. His strategy is self-defensively comprehensive, inflecting the brute fact of the body with narrative sentiment, while also attempting to substantiate narrative emotion by borrowing from the vividness of the corporeal" (31). The "damaged body" is more difficult to behold in a passive way because it points to the graphic reality faced by AIDS sufferers in the pre-retroviral-therapy era. For Ross Chambers, the emphasis on such stark degradation is vital to any writer who seeks to approach this topic with the intent to witness. Chambers argues that a writer should punctuate what might be understood as "*obscene*" (22, emphasis original) by focusing on the progress of an infection in all of its grotesquerie.[21]

I turn to reading *Edinburgh* from the frame of its representations of AIDS, focusing on Fee's role as the witness to Freddy Moran's swift decline and death. Following Dawes's point about the emphasis on the material and Chambers's argument that witnessing functions by affirming the complexities of disease progression, I argue that the novel engages a depiction of AIDS and illness that moves beyond "mere sentiment" with its focus on Freddy's limited social contacts, his isolation, and his terminal bodily disintegration.[22] Fee is called to action by observing and recording what has gone on with Freddy and in this process also highlights his own commitment to alternative social formations. The pathogenic kinship extending from Fee to Andrew Norman hence incorporates those suffering from and affected by the AIDS virus. Though the novel's depiction of Freddy may not be considered explicitly activist, I also am influenced by Timothy F. Murphy's point concerning AIDS narratives in relation to genre and form: "Elegy, or testimony, as I prefer to call it, belongs to the continuum of moral and political conscience which fuels activism in the epidemic and has an important function in the protection of the individual. Such testimony also offers the opportunity for resisting the infantilizing of the dying and the dead which often occurs in the context of their health care" (53). In keeping with Murphy's perspective, *Edinburgh*'s representation of Freddy can be understood as a fictionalized elegy: Fee acts as a witness to the events that continue to show how diseases and pathogens both destabilize and reconfigure the bounds of inscrutable belongings.[23]

Before Fee moves back to Maine, he receives a letter from his mother detailing that one of his fellow surviving choir members, Freddy Moran, is suffering from the devastating later stages of AIDS. As Fee's mother explains it, "You see, Freddy's been HIV-positive for a few years now, and recently his health took a turn for the worse. And now [his mother's] been frantic caring for him. She doesn't feel up to the job, now that she's buried her husband, to now bury her son. It doesn't look good" (175–176). Though the letter's content is straightforward enough, its form takes on increased significance because it is a document that operates with an appeal to a specified audience. We recall that Andrew Norman's record of his living entombment functions as a testimony of what survivors of the Black Plague had to endure. Edward Speck will eventually publish a book that could be read as a scholarly confirmation of Andrew's testimony, a book titled "*A Letter to the Digger: A History of Edinburgh During the Plague*." The reference to the "digger" gestures to Andrew's situation of being buried alive, and the book then a kind of "letter" of response to the one who had been entombed prematurely and who still tried to find a way out. In a similar fashion, Fee's mother encourages Fee to take the responsibility of helping care for Freddy, especially given their overlaps: as choirboys under Big Eric's destructive tutelage and, later, as adults who have gone on to explore their queer sexualities. But Fee's relationship to Freddy is a tortured one precisely because Freddy reminds him of the courage he believes he did not have, since it is Freddy who first alerted police to the fact that Big Eric was perpetrating physical violence upon the other choirboys. Given these sentiments, it is not entirely surprising that Fee does not respond to this letter and does not bother to visit Freddy until moving back to Maine three years later.

By the time Fee does move back to his home state, Freddy is bedridden, unconscious, and close to death, a fact that is sobering given Fee's memory of running into him three years prior. As Fee recalls of that earlier meeting, "Freddy glowed, rosy-cheeked, smooth-faced, he smelled clean from where I stood, and was dressed in a red polo shirt and khaki pants, brand-new running shoes on his feet. He looked protected from germs, depressions, extremes of poverty and misfortune. None of this was true, though, just a marvelous show. Marvelous even as mine was drab" (180). Though Fee is the one who might be presumed to be sick, given his penchant for smoking and his "drab" attire, it is actually Freddy whose health has been deteriorating. Fee presents this more salubrious depiction of Freddy to accentuate the drastic changes that later take place, especially as Freddy exhibits signs of dementia: "He'd been wandering the streets in his coat, no pants. In his apartment, his clothes were found, all of them soiled. He was wearing only the coat because it was his only clean thing to wear—he hadn't lost all of his mind. His mother came and burned the clothes, packed up his things and tried to clean the apartment" (180–181). Whereas the previous passage emphasizes Freddy's preppy attire, the latter directly confronts the grim reality of Freddy's mental and physical regression. But Fee's decision to stay seems to hinge in part on the fact that he meets Freddy's mother at her home to get an update on his condition. It is there that Freddy's mother takes out an old photo album, and then later, obituaries of Peter and Zach, fellow choirboys and links to a traumatic past that still ties Freddy and Fee, however tragically, together.

At this point, Fee exhibits a change in his attitude and realizes that he must attend to his old friend, a process that requires him to confront Freddy's decline. As Fee notes during one visit, "In his bed at the hospital, he's a tiny map of himself. A reduction. The dementia is now the least of it. I recalled a friend telling me how either his meds or his virus caused his face to hollow as it went for the fat under the skin. Freddy's face has hollowed, and the bed rises a little in a way that is meant to be his body" (181). Here Fee refers to the process of lipodystrophy, which in late-stage HIV and full-blown AIDS results in facial wasting. Per the earlier discussion, this moment disrupts any sentimentalized view of disease and tragedy by referring to the material nature of viral infections and their inexorable progressions. Freddy's frailty is emphasized in the way that his body has become so tiny that the bed takes the place of his torso. Fee's witnessing is paramount given Freddy's inability to articulate speech: "I bring flowers to Freddy, cut them down and set them in a water glass by his bed. I straighten the edge of his sheet, check his vital signs. He never makes a noise while I'm there. I understand he sometimes sings. I don't know what I'd do, if he started singing" (189). This passage continues to couple Fee to Freddy on the basis not only of their shared queerness but also their past as choirboys. Fee's anxiety over the fact that Freddy might sing obviously signals how the traumas sustained in their youth remain at the forefront of his mind.

But Fee's witnessing to Freddy's enfeeblement also takes on multiple dimensions, because it provides him a gateway to discuss the disease as a larger phenomenon. Fee's narrating arcs out to enfold a wider community devastated by AIDS: "I think of some of the stories I know to fill the silences of being with Freddy: a man who found out he was positive and shot himself in the head, his house rigged to burn to the ground. Another who found out his status when he collapsed from walking pneumonia, and died a few days later" (189). Fee's storytelling moves Freddy's disease into a collective narrative framework, with these musings that detail the abrupt endings to these lives. In this sense, the modern-day plague of AIDS is another kind of legacy that Fee must eventually embrace, both on an individual level with respect to Freddy and as a social phenomenon, which especially affected a generation of queers in the 1980s and early 1990s. According to Michael Denneny, the AIDS epidemic was a "shared social disaster" (37), and he adds, "When death becomes a social event, the individual death is both robbed of its utter privacy and uniquely individual meaning and simultaneously amplified with the resonance of social significance and historical consequence. When death is a social event, both the individual *and the community* are threatened with irreparable loss" (37, emphasis original). Thus the task of the AIDS narrative is at once to counter "irreparable loss" through representational resurrections at both individual and communal levels. In the case of *Edinburgh*, Freddy's individual death is also placed into conversation with other queer men who have passed, revealing the devastating reach of AIDS.

Freddy's sickness appears tangential to the main plotting, but its import relates to issues of contagion and intergenerational transmission that manifest in so many different forms. Fee's storytelling encourages us to consider the radical reconfiguration of family and kinship that can occur in light of disease and impurity, especially with respect to the Black Plague and to the HIV/AIDS epidemic. I follow Sam Coale's point that "[i]t is perhaps a bit facile to draw connections between the Black Death and AIDS, but the connections still stare out at us as if they demand obeisance. In both instances, the public demands its scapegoats" (98). Both plagues—if we might call them that—are defined by their broad global impact and generated a culture of fear in which individuals who fell ill were marked as pariahs.[24] For Andrew Norman, this social exclusion is dramatically depicted in his living entombment, an aggressive mode of quarantine that did not address the actual nature of pathogenic transmission. His experience is of course not so singular, as other scholars have noted the shunning that occurred to plague survivors,[25] but his isolation and alienation call attention to the fact that he was far from his ancestral home, left to die among strangers. Andrew's situation is somewhat mirrored by Freddy's, since Freddy's mother at first seems to be the only one who is willing to take care of him and is overwhelmed by the responsibility. The lack of support that Freddy's mother receives in light of her son's condition is never fully explained in the novel, but nevertheless conjures up the hysteria and fear that first erupted during the early years of the HIV/AIDS epidemic. Though Fee cannot directly intervene in Andrew's case, his comforting presence and loyal vigil to Freddy cement an inscrutable belonging based on their association with the HIV/AIDS virus and its impact upon queer men. Both Andrew and Freddy further function to cast light on the many lives lost in the shared social disasters of global epidemics. These various viral references tie Fee to histories and communities facing marginality and erasure. In recounting his research on Andrew Norman and Freddy Moran's eventual death from the AIDS virus, Fee understands that his traumas must be put alongside the struggles of others. Imbued by these infectious genealogies, Fee's retrospective narration becomes enriched.

The novel's link between the Black Death and the AIDS virus extends to the way that Fee attempts to construct special spaces to honor the dead. At one point, Fee—at the time just a young teenager—is so affected by the account provided by Andrew Norman that he decides he will build his own underground memorial, one that cannot be seen by those walking above him. His impetus is to create his own version of Norman's vivisepulture: "The first tunnel went by in two months of digging. The second had to wander around submerged deposits of bedrock. I pushed the last dirt aside and walked all the way through, end to end to end to end. Four corners here. I had read about the pyramids, burial mounds, but nothing matched my Edinburgh, my streets paved over, my city under a city" (86). Fee's strong identification with Norman emerges most forcefully in the way that Fee understands himself as only a partial survivor. That is, he experiences a metaphorical living entombment: he must endure the deaths of Peter and other choirboys, while being unable to express fully his desire to be free of the melancholic effects of his sexual trauma. Fee goes on to elaborate about this secret "city under a city": "Down below, in the hill, I have set sconces in the walls, for torches, citronella to keep out the mosquitoes. The floor is slate. I go down. The secret of the king of the hill is that he rules it from underneath. In the dark, I smoke. I sing, sometimes, pretending it is the Plague years, and that I have been left here to die in the buried city, to sing songs for the dead" (87). Here Fee makes explicit his association to those who managed to endure a period of illness, only to discover that they have been buried alive.

The underground city that Fee builds does not warrant a mention in the novel until the period in which he is caretaking for Freddy, and the novel sees fit to converge Fee's response to Andrew Norman's letter with this adult period of his life. After one hospital visit with Freddy, Fee takes his boyfriend Bridey to his underground city; the remains of the tunnels are still there, and Fee decides he must "fill it in" because "[w]hat I felt about wanting to die, that's not right. Look at Freddy. He wants to live" (191). Fee's caretaking of Freddy makes him realize he is being myopic. As a survivor who is seronegative, Fee cannot simply take his life for granted, and he cannot romanticize a living entombment.

Bridey convinces Fee that he should not destroy the tunnels, but instead should "[b]uild something else" (191).

Agreeing with Bridey's advice, Fee decides to build a chapel, one with an interesting structural feature, a foundation made up of rocks that are "set" so "that gravity holds them in place" (137). Fee bases "the construction on designs" he observes "of Roman bridges and also things made in South America, by the Incas" (193), but he never divulges the fact that this idea probably came from his time researching for Speck. Indeed, in Andrew Norman's account of the plague, he explains the reason why he traveled to Edinburgh: "In particular, I had been interested in a Roman bridge, back in Normandy, where my family is from, made of coursed stones, and made so that the water passing could pass through the stones, even as the bridge stood. Many days I spent looking at the bridge, studying the construction" (83–84). Fee's decision to erect this chapel, then, originates in part from Andrew Norman's own architectural interests. Though Fee hardly seems to ascribe to any religious denomination, the chapel's completion is appropriately symbolic; it stands as a testament to those who had been afflicted by plagues and who have passed on. The chapel is a spatial location that helps to cohere the infectious genealogies that bind Fee to both Andrew Norman and Freddy Moran.

The novel poignantly presents the possibility and the fragility of these pathogenic ancestries, which appear through a reenvisioning of disease and monstrosity, social difference, and marginality. Fee first employs the fox-demon myth to navigate a perilous Asian North American childhood. Embracing an ancestral lineage with Lady Tammamo, Fee overturns simplistic binaries that demarcate the divide between good and evil, champions and blackguards. Fee also confronts a virulent inheritance wrought by Big Eric's inferno-like melancholia, which enfeebles him and the other choirboys. Inasmuch as the fox-demon cannot be seen as categorically evil, Fee's recounting reveals how disease, infection, and the intergenerational transmission of trauma can offer productive rather than only deleterious outcomes and even provide the grounds for community. He finds storytelling artifacts that persist through catastrophic plagues—such as Andrew Norman's account and the pantoum—and comes to realize that he must tell his tale. In doing so, he helps document those who perhaps cannot live to do the same. Plague survivors, HIV/AIDS sufferers, the descendants of fox-demons, and the victims of childhood sexual abuse all come to be related through Fee's retrospective narration, generating an idiosyncratic community whose struggles and traumas will not remain buried.

Other Kinds of Children, Other Kinds of Families

My reading of Chee's *Edinburgh* demonstrates the ways in which the queer Asian North American's survival plot is made unstable by the forces of social death and the brutalities that arise out of sexual trauma. Fee acts as a witness to comfort women, bubonic plague sufferers, and AIDS victims and resists the social disavowals of their deaths. Yet he also works through his personal demons, ones that require him to terminate cycles of abuse that traffic across generations. Ultimately, Fee endures through and by the evolution of his inscrutable belongings, which help constitute a community beyond the bounds of the heteronuclear family. Queer of color and queer diasporic critiques help clarify both the racialized and transnational stakes of these dynamic kinships and highlight the crucial need for the kind of fortitude modeled by this retrospective storyteller.

Edinburgh leaves one plot issue tantalizingly unclosed, involving Fee's relationship to a woman named Penny. Penny is one of the first individuals he befriends while attending Wesleyan University as a college student. Penny is indispensable for Fee because she is one of the first individuals with whom he can share his melancholic attachment to Peter: "Romantic, to the point of putrefaction, I wrote long terrible poems about whoever it was I was infatuated with. Penny laughed at it all, and came to ask always, which one is it now? She knew there was a way in which these boys were all the same" (107). Here Fee notes how Penny comes to understand that Fee never quite got over Peter's death and that his attempts at dating are a partial palliative directed at trying to find his lost love somewhere in these other men who possess some passing physical resemblance to Peter. Given Fee's ability to confide in Penny, it is fitting that she becomes one of the few friends with whom he maintains a very strong relationship long after he has graduated. Penny also comes to be a focal point of triangulation with respect to Fee's relationship to his boyfriend Bridey. On the day that Fee discovers that Edward Speck has died, he is with Bridey and Penny at the beach, describing these other two as "[t]hick as thieves" (177). As Fee goes on to note, "My oldest friend and my best one, together. Who knew what they might come back with? Some days they returned with a new friend, usually for Penny" (177). For Fee, Penny comes to stand in as a potential member of an alternative kinship, one based on their elective choices to remain affiliated with each other.

Penny is also able to convince Fee to take on her position as a swim coach at a high school in Maine. In this case, she would be on maternity leave, presumably pregnant through artificial insemination, the sperm having been donated by Fee. As Penny explains it, "Fee. I want to have a child, and when I think about what man I want the child to resemble, considering the amount of time I'll be with him or her, I thought of my oldest friends. I've not known anyone as long as I've known you, besides my family. . . . I'll be with the child so long, and it only gets harder as I get older. I don't want to wait to meet some guy I've not yet met" (182). Penny's impassioned plea is enough to get Fee to agree, but her rhetoric is important to break down. Certainly Penny places Fee in line with her biological family, marking Fee not only as a suitable sperm donor, but also an active co-parent. In the novel's case, Penny chooses what is called a "directed donor," an individual who is drawn from a known social network (Mamo 97).[26] Through this child, Penny and Fee establish the potential grounds of a kinship system that moves outside of the traditional North American heteronuclear family.

The novel's inclusion of this storyline dovetails with the social contexts of the late 1990s and that continue today with respect to the use of assisted reproductive technologies, such as in vitro fertilization, and the increasingly commonplace practice of employing surrogates, gamete, egg, and sperm donors to reconstruct the bounds of social structures.[27] But because such technologies and methods of reproduction offer radical reconfigurations of interpersonal networks, "concerns arise over how to balance the state's right and responsibility to legislate family and reproductive relations with its duty to protect people's reproductive freedom" (Markens 16). In the case of Maine, where the novel is set, Fee's legal status as co-parent would be questioned insofar as he is not married to Penny.[28] Further still, if Penny chooses to use a medical intermediary for the process of artificial insemination, Fee would automatically relinquish all legal rights to being the child's father (Mamo 111). Penny's request to Fee is thus not without a number of possible complications.

Penny does become pregnant, but Fee's relationship to the child remains unclear, especially as the novel hurtles toward its murderous climax. Of Penny's pregnancy, Fee relates, "I have no sense of her carrying our child. I think of it as hers. Entirely. Every now and then she cracks a smile, pats her tummy and says, Hey, Daddy. But I don't know what to make of it" (192–193). Interestingly enough, this passage is the last mention that Penny receives in the novel, so readers are unsure about the status of Fee's rapport with this child by the time the narrative is over. Though Penny obviously hopes that Fee will take a visible role in the child's life, regarding him as more than just a source for genetic materials, Fee seems nonplussed when referenced as a "Daddy." When offered an invitation to what could be termed another inscrutable belonging—especially since Penny and Fee are not related, nor can they be understood within the framework of a heterosexual, romantic partnership—Fee's rather ambivalent response reveals how the novel continually overturns the centrality of any reproductive future.[29]

In sum, Fee's retrospective telling accomplishes many admirable feats. First, it details the thorny progression of a protoqueer Asian North American child to adulthood. Second, the narrative undermines any simplistic categorization of antagonistic entities, especially as Fee comes to reevaluate the dissemination of trauma as it extends across time. The protagonist's maturation recasts trauma from a widened lens, as he not only narrates his survival plot but also chronicles the lives of those lost across a variety of sociocultural circumstances. As I have argued, individuals associated with childhood sexual abuse, AIDS/HIV, intergenerational trauma, Black Plague, and postcolonial sexual subjection are brought together as part of infectious genealogies that form the core of this novel's inscrutable belongings. As the negative connotations of disease are repurposed in this community-oriented way, the queer Asian North American storyteller navigates and resolves his survival plot. But *Edinburgh* brings up another critical problem precisely because the discourse of disease appears alongside the treacherous narrative journey first made by the queer Asian North American child.

The novel's representation invites us to return to the conceptions of the child as offered by Edelman and Chua, a youthful figure associated with a linear, unidirectional maturation process. As Edelman reminds us, the logic of the reproductive future ensures the survival of one kind of Child: the promising protoheterosexual youth who matures to adulthood and goes on to have his or her own protoheterosexual children. Racial difference and protoqueer difference—indeed, social difference of any kind—cannot be attached remotely to this Child because he or she instead models the perfectly deracinated, homogenized tomorrow filled with heteronuclear families, then replicated in perpetuity. Chua's depiction of the model minority youth traffics in a racialized formulation of the reproductive future reliant on the strict obedience of the child, one who seeks to garner the approval only of his or her biological parents. Familial recognition is seemingly conditional on success and achievement, a narrative of upward progression that demands unwavering loyalty under an assumed biologically determined aegis that he or she will grow up and likewise become a tiger parent.³⁰ In contrast to the tiger mom, *Edinburgh*'s fox-demon operates as a symbolic progenitor, inspiring Fee to welcome an expansive network made up of supernatural forebears and disease-based genealogies. It is hence not the future but a reproductive past that provides the grounds for a possible journey through a danger-filled narrative. As these transformational and cross-generational alternative kinships converge in his retrospective storytelling, Fee can reframe his traumatic childhood and move beyond it.

Edinburgh reminds us that we must also wonder about many other kinds of children, including those perhaps not ensured the type of attention offered by society's unconscious and sometimes not-so-unconscious project to value certain developmental trajectories over others. In imagining the life—however challenging in its progression—of the protoqueer Asian North American child who grows up to recognize an inscrutable belonging comprising the diseased, the deviant, the demonic, and the dying, the novel encourages us to keep looking backward instead of categorically embracing a future in which only a hallowed, healthful few find a place.

CHAPTER 4

INSCRUTABLE BELONGINGS IN CINEMA

FILMIC LINEAGES IN NOËL ALUMIT'S

LETTERS TO MONTGOMERY CLIFT

WHAT DOES IT MEAN TO ENDURE? For the queer Asian North Americans who are depicted in the fictional world, their livelihoods and their places in the narrative are certainly not predestined. As figures marked as deviant, branded by social death and subject to various forms of physical harm, their narrative positions are tenuous. As these figures journey through what I have called a survival plot, they find a way to reconsider their pasts. Through these recollections, it becomes apparent that their ability to make it to the narrative's conclusion relies on the construction of inscrutable belongings, alternative social formations that move beside biological affiliations or legal ties and that provide the storytellers with indispensable, however often ephemeral, support systems.

In Chapter 2, I employed Russell Leong's "Camouflage" as a template through which survival plots and associated inscrutable belongings could be analytically engaged. *Edinburgh*, which was the focus of Chapter 3, expanded how we understand both the survival plot and associated inscrutable belongings in its focus on a storyteller named Fee, who must contend with childhood sexual abuse and the corresponding traumas that remain to be worked through.

As I bridge "Camouflage" and *Edinburgh* to Noël Alumit's *Letters to Montgomery Clift*, similar issues will influence my analyses.[1] For instance, I remain in a similar historical arc: *Letters*, like the two previous publications, moves through the 1980s AIDS crisis era and beyond. All three works are also joined by survival plots that begin in the queer Asian North American storytellers' youth, a time in which their lives are endangered by adults, who should function as guardians but fail in this task. But *Letters to Montgomery Clift* develops the broader narrative of my book through its exploration of a lengthier survival plot. The short length of "Camouflage" provides us with only a brief glimpse of Bernard's life, however harrowing it might be. *Edinburgh*, though offering up a more comprehensive sequencing of a storyteller's journey through the narrative, nevertheless cedes ample space in the middle of the novel to another character's voice. Although an understandable choice given that the other storyteller is Warden, the high school student with whom Fee has a brief affair, this move does limit the amount of storytelling narrative space given to Fee. In contrast, *Letters to Montgomery Clift* presents us with a narrative in which a queer Asian North American storyteller's perspective predominates over two hundred pages.

Letters to Montgomery Clift, in fact, imagines variations of the same storyteller in two different voices. First, the novel is narrated retrospectively through the autodiegetic voice of Bong Bong Luwad. As the novel opens, an adult Bong is about to fly to the Philippines to look for his mother. He is commenting on the various letters he has written over the years to movie actor Montgomery Clift. The novel's opening frame then moves us back to when Bong first arrived in the United States to live with his mother's sister, Auntie Yuna. But the preface of most chapters is a verbatim excerpt or reprinting of the titular letters he writes to Montgomery Clift. Hence, these letters form the second storytelling voice.

Though most chapters begin with a letter that Bong addresses to Clift, we know that Clift cannot respond—he is dead. Bong's own belief that Clift will eventually return some sort of missive is no doubt inspired by his sense of childlike wonder and imagination. The retrospective narration that follows the letters provides us with more context concerning the letters' contents. At the same time, the survival plot emerges as a result of the sequencing of the letters preceding the blocks of retrospective narration: we are tasked to gain further understanding about why the tones of the letters are so plaintive, which becomes clear only through comparing one discursive mode to the other.

The circumstances around Bong's arrival are murky until we discover that his mother, worried for Bong's safety, sent him to the United States after Marcos government officials forcibly took away his father. Though his mother was to follow him, she never arrives, and Bong wonders obsessively about the status of his parents, especially whether they are even alive. Bong eventually moves into the foster care system after his Auntie Yuna unexpectedly vanishes; bouncing around from one foster home to another, he eventually settles with the Arangans. The Arangans are a Filipino American family with one daughter named Amada, who is one of Bong's most trusted confidantes. Bong begins to research what might have happened to his parents; he eventually connects with Mrs. Billaruz, a woman living in Hawai'i who reveals that his father was tortured and killed. She does not know the status and whereabouts of his mother.

Tensions arise when Bong discovers that Mr. Arangan worked for and benefited from the Marcos government. Bong, believing the Arangans to be partially responsible for his father's death, his mother's disappearance, and his ruptured family, distances himself from them. After revealing to Amada that he is in an imagined relationship with Montgomery Clift, one that we, as the readers, know is partially mediated through the letters he writes to him, Amada's unsupportive reaction leads Bong to drive his motorcycle recklessly through the hills of Los Angeles. Not surprisingly, he crashes; he then ends up in the hospital and later is psychiatrically evaluated, at which point his relationship to Montgomery Clift is more thoroughly addressed and analyzed. The concluding arc of the novel sees him leave the psychiatric facility, enter a tentative relationship with a mixed-race Asian North American named Logan, and discover that his mother may, in fact, be alive. To determine what has happened to his mother, Bong travels to the Philippines with the hope of finding her. While he faces some difficulties tracking her down, mother and son are eventually reunited. The last posted letter to Montgomery Clift in 1998 reveals that Mrs. Luwad will be moving to the United States. Though I have explained the narrative in a chronological sequence, the letters interrupt this general flow, forcing us to consider why certain moments are emphasized doubly: first, through the present-tense narration of the letters, and second, through the associated blocks of retrospective storytelling that tread similar ground.

This chapter comprises four major sections. In the first three, I focus on how this novel poses an inscrutable belonging that originates from Bong's interest in Clift and in Hollywood cinema. As a child, Bong sees Clift as a fairy godfather who protects him and restores order in a chaotic period during which Bong is abused and abandoned by his Auntie Yuna. This inscrutable belonging, and the associated process of constructing this social formation, is made necessary because, from the beginning of the story, the protagonist's life is in peril. In this case, Bong's primary antagonist and obstacle to the navigation of his childhood survival plot is none other than his own blood relative. In this sense, we are not surprised to see why Bong must go beyond the bounds of biological family to create a sense of safety and stability. As we have already seen with "Camouflage," the biological family cannot always be expected to provide a supportive and nurturing environment for the child's upbringing.

Bong's narrative position as an adult looking back on his childhood clarifies how we can read Clift first as a parental surrogate and how he later transforms over the course of an extended survival plot. While initially marked as a filmic patron saint, Clift shifts in his importance to Bong, as he becomes Bong's imagined lover. But his movement into this eroticized position is troubled by Bong's acculturation and entrance into the Hollywood film industry as an actor. Given Bong's struggle to land jobs, his relationship to Clift evolves, and the survival plot accordingly changes course.

The fourth section of this chapter tracks how Bong must confront his invisibility in a cinematic imaginary populated by so many white movie stars. Clift, known for his many films and starring roles, stands as a polar opposite to Bong, who subsists in the movie industry as an extra. Clift elliptically calls attention to the biases in Hollywood casting, inviting a critique that recasts the novel through the lens of race and cinema. If Clift signals the individual who is awarded the starring role, then Bong's narration undercuts Clift's place in the story. As the novel ends, the letters written to Clift reduce in their frequency, resulting in a structural shift in the narrative recounting process. As Bong places himself centrally in his own romance plot and comes to a larger consciousness about the status of his marginality and that of other Asian North American actors and film industry workers, another inscrutable belonging coalesces. By making his voice and other voices like his indispensable to the story, Bong's first-person narration embodies nothing less than a revolutionary form of representational survival.

I end this chapter by bridging Bong and Clift through their shared queerness, which is not disavowed, especially as evidenced through the epilogue. Bong's trajectory grants him an inscrutable belonging informed by queer sexuality, Hollywood cinema, and racial marginality in the film industry.

Of Saints and Witches

Letters to Montgomery Clift depicts the progression of a Filipino American youth who will grow up and enter into a relationship with a same-sex partner. As briefly mentioned in the chapter's summary, the novel engages a dynamic narrative discourse through the use of first-person retrospective narration and epistolary forms. The first letter addressed to Montgomery Clift and signed "Bong Bong Luwad" is dated 1976. In the letter, Bong reveals his central desire to have his "mama back" and promises that "if nothing bad happens" he will continue to write to Montgomery Clift (2). But what this missive means is a mystery until we read the accompanying retrospective first-person narration. It reveals that Bong is now an adult, about to board a plane to look for his mother; he is rereading earlier correspondences to Clift (2). The letters, then, provide a sense of Bong's life directly as it unfolded, giving us unmediated access to the child's voice, while they simultaneously offer Bong a chance to review his past, to "see who [he] was" (2). These missives, in their many grammatical and typographical errors, spotlight the challenges of his American acculturation and rudimentary understanding of English. The retrospective narration that accompanies these letters details the harassment he experiences at school for his inability to speak English fluently (6) and helps establish how to read beyond these missives to situate some of the traumas associated with his upbringing. And crucially, this backward-glancing narration persistently reminds us that our narrator has survived to tell his tale, leaving us with the question, how did he manage to endure?

This question is especially palpable in the novel's first part, which offers a gothic rendering of a childhood, replete with heroes and villains, references to visions that come from smoke, undead beings, and mythical monsters. It is, in essence, a kind of world turned upside down, a warping of reality. Though Part 1 does not refer to a specific myth or surreal genre, the novel's representation of childhood does invoke particular cultural contexts and supernatural elements that can be found in many folk and fairy tales. Concerning fairy tales and their oral counterparts, Jack Zipes notes that such narratives and stories often include magical components, such as "spells, enchantments, disenchantments, resurrections, recreations" ("Changing Function" 7). These various chimerical elements are essential because they enable Bong to reframe the many traumas he is enduring through the realm of his active childhood imagination. As Bruno Bettelheim notes, "The figures in fairy tales are not ambivalent—not good and bad at the same time, as we all are in reality. But since polarization dominates the child's mind, it also dominates fairy tales. A person is either good or bad, nothing in between" (9). Bettelheim's point is certainly applicable to Bong's life and how it benefits from the "polarization" found in fairy tales. To make sense of the world around him—that is, to survive in this austere environment—Bong cannot employ ambivalent frames but must instead locate stable boundary points that provide order in a chaotic, brutalizing childhood. Consequently, as his harrowing tale of endurance begins, Bong attempts to fix individuals within binaristic paradigms, locating his Auntie Yuna as the primary antagonist while Montgomery Clift functions as his imaginary and unassailable protector. In this world turned upside down, Auntie Yuna, as a blood relation, signifies as an oppressive force of supernatural destruction, while a long-dead film star becomes a paternal, enchanted fairy godfather and the initial basis for Bong's inscrutable belonging.[2]

Bong's survival plot originates in his relationship with Auntie Yuna, the family member presumed to be overseeing him while his family remains in the Philippines under murky circumstances. As Bong's guardian, she configures and contorts the boundaries of his daily reality, especially through a focus on mystical and spiritual belief systems. Auntie Yuna "prayed all the time" and "looked at pictures of saints and dead relatives on the shelf" (3). As Bong further explains, "Auntie Yuna and I would eat the food she left for the spirits. She said the spirits touched the food and made it lucky. By eating the food, we became lucky, too" (3–4).[3] Bong's reflections here reveal a Filipino American transnational culture in which ancestor worship, animistic belief systems, and Catholicism syncretically combine.[4] According to the historian Filomeno V. Aguilar, the animist belief system appeared prior to colonial contact with the Spanish in the sixteenth century (27).[5] Though Christian indoctrination sought to wipe out animistic and precolonial belief systems, such practices persisted over time (Bankoff 40–41).[6] The scholar Fe Susan Go notes, "Few Christian Filipinos, whether educated or not, perceive any serious contradictions between indigenous and Christian beliefs and practices. Rarely do these two 'traditions' come into open conflict and rarely do Catholic Filipino priests point out or directly oppose the contradictions existing in the religious practices of their parishioners" (188).[7] Auntie Yuna's ritualistic activities follow the mixture of various religious and spiritual traditions, as elucidated by these scholars, and gestures to the cultural hybridity of this household.

Auntie Yuna serves to instill a foundational worldview for the protoqueer Asian North American child: the afterlife must be honored, angels and demons exist, and humans can benefit from association with those who have passed on. At the same time, with Auntie Yuna's guardianship comes constant physical abuse, though Bong does not reveal the extent of his beatings to anyone. Instead, he confides only in his imaginary friend, Montgomery Clift. In one of his letters, he pens, "At school my teacher wanted to know how I got my fat lip. I told her that my next-door neighbor hit me. I didn't tell her that Auntie Yuna did it. I didn't tell her that Auntie Yuna drinks. I didn't tell her that Auntie Yuna wakes up in the middle of the night and tells me to clean up. I didn't tell her that Auntie Yuna hits me with her witch's broom" (33). Though Auntie Yuna is supposed to take care of Bong, she is more akin to the evil stepmother of the Cinderella fairy tale—and scholars do note both Western and Eastern versions of this popular narrative—with Bong as the symbolically orphaned child.[8] Further still, the novel's ethnic context reminds us that Auntie Yuna's association with the "witch" could elliptically reference the *aswang*, a catchall phrase for a malevolent being popular in many Filipino folk narratives.[9] According to Michael T. Tan, "Obviously, the *aswang* does not really exist in the sense of a ghoul cannibalizing the sick and the dead. Rather the label is a social construct serving a particular social purpose, that of stigmatizing and excommunicating asocial or 'different' individuals, often within one's own community" (73, emphasis original). Tan's point clarifies how we can read Auntie Yuna. Her status as a witch, perhaps a variation here on the aswang, is more largely suggestive of the way that Bong constructs her to fit a gothic paradigm. As the antagonistic center, the indisputable villain of his youth, Auntie Yuna signals danger and inspires awe because she transforms Bong's childhood landscape, radically altering his relationship to everyday objects and items. In this case, the broom functions as a tool involved in his beating and as a cleaning instrument in forced labor.[10] The violence of the broom takes on extended significance, as he uses it at one point to describe it in relation to Auntie Yuna's hair: "It stayed in one place like the head of a broom" (21). The negative connotations associated with that object are repetitively invoked, reminding us of the way that Bong's world stands irrevocably altered.

Auntie Yuna's preternatural beliefs also encourage Bong to render her through grotesque metaphors. To Bong, Auntie Yuna looks increasingly monstrous, with eyes that were "Cave empty. Cave cold" (21); she is later described as "a wave going back into a dark sea" (35). Bong likens his subjection under Auntie Yuna's assaults as a form of mystical manipulation: "Auntie Yuna somehow cast a voodoo spell on me. I become a zombie when Auntie Yuna comes at me like a tiger" (33). Later, Bong relays that the "light from the kitchen would cast her shadow upon me: a big black shape of ugly. I'd see the shadow of her head in front of me. Her hair messed up like frozen snakes. That's how she mesmerized me, made me her victim. She was Medusa" (35). If Auntie Yuna alters into other dangerous beings and mythical monsters—a tiger, a witch, and Medusa—Bong likewise transforms. Either as a stone "victim" or as a zombie, he dissociates from his body to endure the traumas of her beatings, forced labor, and tasteless food. Most acutely, cultural hybridity manifests in its baleful complexity here, as Bong employs Greek myth (Medusa) and a Haitian religious element (voodoo) to pinpoint the frightful conditions of the home.[11] Appropriately, Bong often mentions the brand of the alcohol, King Cobra, that Auntie Yuna prefers (25, 32, 35) and at one point describes Auntie Yuna during one of her many drunken stupors as a woman who "hissed, got up and wobbled toward the bathroom. She swayed from side to side, leaning against a wall, then against a chair, then against a wall again" (32). Auntie Yuna's fearsome presence dominates Bong's understanding of his childhood world, as she is associated repeatedly with a venomous being.[12]

It is not surprising, then, that Bong creates such a strong attachment to Montgomery Clift, the fantasy guardian angel of his impoverished youth. Clift exists in opposition to Auntie Yuna, who functions as an antithesis to the caretaking role expected of her. Certainly, in Bong's head, Clift is presented "not as a hallucinatory symptom of his psychological problems but as an internal component of his survival strategies" (Ponce 174). While Martin Joseph Ponce reads Montgomery Clift as a "maternal surrogate" during the period of Bong's youth and later as an "embodied queer lover" (173), I diverge by arguing that Clift also functions as the heroic and *masculine* construct called forth to help Bong battle Auntie Yuna and replace her as a familial support. In Bong's youth, Clift plays the role of a knight in shining armor, protecting the powerless and vanquishing malevolent forces. For Bong, Clift is the foundation of the inscrutable belonging: a figure who helps him to endure physical abuse and psychological torment, even if the film star may not even exist in the same time and space as our queer Asian North American storyteller.

Bong's attachment to Clift solidifies after he watches *The Search* (1948), a film in which "Monty Clift plays a soldier. He finds and cares for a small boy whose mother was taken away by bad people. He takes the boy home. He gives him candy. He buys him shoes. He teaches him English. He keeps him safe. He guards the boy till his mama comes" (4–5). *The Search* is the first reference in the novel to any movies starring Montgomery Clift, and it also happens to be his debut. *The Search* relates to Alumit's novel in a number of ways. The Jewish boy from the movie, Karel, with whom Bong identifies, is a concentration camp survivor of Czech descent with only a rudimentary understanding of English. In the postwar reconstruction of Germany, Clift's character, Steve, develops an attachment to the young boy and decides to adopt him. Far from a maternal surrogate here, Steve epitomizes the quintessential masculine American patron. Bong's summation of the movie entirely glosses over the historical context of the boy's trauma, focusing on the more immediate and universal themes that relate to familial estrangement. This moment reveals how a film becomes a tool used by the protoqueer Asian North American child to make sense of his own traumas. Of course, if we think in more metaphorical terms, Steve epitomizes the moral center of the film, embodying the unadulterated sense of human compassion and selflessness that draws a clear dividing line between the villains and heroes. *The Search* is a kind of fairy tale narrative, in which the innocent (Karel) and the good (Karel's mother) can survive, and evil, in the form of abandonment, is defeated.

Inasmuch as Bong selectively identifies with the film, Clift's character, Steve, never signifies in any way that might connect him to the American military incursions, which include its colonial occupation of the Philippines. Further still, Karel, who is later renamed Jim, acts as the appropriate foil to Steve in that he offers himself up through what I would call a digestible difference, as this character attains an acceptable level of eccentricity. That is, Karel/Jim is foreign, but his implied racial background—he is undoubtedly fair-haired—relays the possibility of claiming a future whiteness in the event that he actually moves to the United States. Steve's attachment to Karel/Jim is interesting insofar as it presents this child as a figure who potentially can be saved and reconstructed as a new American. And all is seemingly set right by the film's conclusion, as Karel is reunited with his mother.[13] Steve's unwavering, good-natured guardianship is a totally seductive depiction because it easily overpowers other, more morally complicated readings that the film could welcome.

The significance of Clift's movie role and the possibility of his spiritual presence help to restore a binary logic to Bong's childhood, and, we could say, Clift acts metaphorically as his fairy godfather. I use the phrase "fairy godfather" here in a doubled sense since Clift purportedly was bisexual, though some have claimed that he was gay; he operates to help Bong survive the evil machinations of Auntie Yuna, the evil quasi-stepmother.[14] In this inscrutable belonging, Bong creates a metaphorical lineage through filmic spectatorship and imaginary identification: he sees himself in Karel and reconfigures Clift as his (however fanciful) version of Steve. Indeed Bong's deep connection to this film brings to mind the foundational scholarship of Nick Browne, Jean-Pierre Oudart, and Stephen Heath, who reveal the ways in which the spectator is seamlessly brought into the cinematic world, so much so that the camera's mediating presence becomes obscured. Though *The Search*'s war-torn landscape might seem a crude metaphorical parallel to Bong's time in Auntie Yuna's residence, the locations exhibit some parallels. As Bong sees it from his childhood perspective, he's an embattled subject whose existence is rendered unstable and whose endurance is made possible only through the intervention of a heroic father figure. With Clift as his magical protector, there is a chance he will be able to withstand Auntie Yuna's brutal guardianship.

Of Psychosis and Spirituality

Bong's childhood is marked by social turbulence: a film star becomes a metaphorical father and an actual blood relative is associated with the mystical and the horrible, a person to cast out from one's kinship. To cope, Bong must navigate this estranging world, one in which he confronts the destructive powers of the occult and his aunt's physical abuse. At one point, Auntie Yuna enlists Bong to steal an item of clothing owned by their neighbor, J, so that she can create a love spell and force J to fall in love with her. The love spell is a necessity in her mind because J seems to be fully engaged in a romantic relationship with a young woman named Baby Bounce. Hence, Auntie Yuna's quest to find true love involves Bong in the use of witchcraft. Though Bong is clearly fond of J, Bong agrees because he believes he will receive a letter from his mother that Auntie Yuna has been withholding; this letter would be the first correspondence from her since he arrived in the United States. Bong further believes that this request "proved Auntie Yuna was a witch. She didn't have to say what she was going to do with that sock or that shirt. There was a guy who walked the streets of Baguio City. He talked to himself and waved at no one in particular. A love spell that went bad, people told me" (25–26). Here Bong directly references the ethnic context for the love spell and again reveals the importance of Filipino folk culture to his life. Bong speaks both Ilocano and Tagalog, linguistic backgrounds that suggest his familiarity with something like the *gayuma*, otherwise translated from Tagalog as a "love charm" (Madale 63) and a potion "made from herbs and roots or spells that would induce feelings of love" (R. A. Reyes 17).[15] According to Fermin Dichoso, "the use of [a] love charm, love potion (gayuma) is quite often resorted to if a girl spurns her lover" (62). Bong's fear of Auntie Yuna's occult powers transforms his life into a grotesque nightmare in which he and others are subjected to Auntie Yuna's schemes.

For Bong, the apotheosis of the survival plot emerges here, as he believes Auntie Yuna has the power not only to redirect people's love but also to alter their entire being in the process. In other words, the power of the love spell is the absolute dominion over an individual's desire and therefore unmakes a person in that process. Auntie Yuna's mystical witchcraft can also be read as a force annihilating any outlawed sexualities, even heterosexual desires in this case, as J's romance with Baby Bounce is couched as expendable. In this sense, Bong's nascent understanding of his own same-sex desires, which is evident in his orientation toward other men early on in the novel, renders them as illicit by association; his feelings could be targeted by Auntie Yuna for occult-based regulation.

The novel's plot is thus sequenced to show how Bong's childhood pits two figures against each other in a binaristic world akin to many fairy tales and folktales: Auntie Yuna, as a malevolent witch-figure, and Montgomery Clift, as a heroic knight in shining armor. Though Bong develops some coping skills, as evidenced by the letters he composes to Clift, he does reach a breaking point—a trauma that manifests itself in a temporary rupture from reality. This event is not very surprising, as his childhood is spent in an environment in which zombies, snakes, and love spells loom large. In other words, reality and fantasy collide, creating the grounds on which Bong's psychic visions proliferate. This event is crucial to the survival plot's sequencing because it emphasizes Bong's wounded internal psyche and that such mental injuries will bear a lasting imprint on his adult life.

Given the incredible burdens Bong shoulders in his time with Auntie Yuna, it is understandable that he attempts to preserve his own life by harming her. Bong's rage over Auntie Yuna's repeated abuse appears most prevalent in the ideation of violent acts he would commit on her sleeping body: "I wanted to smother Auntie Yuna, place a cushion over her face and snuff her out. I wanted to set her hair on fire, stick needles into the bottoms of her feet. I wanted to bite her, rip some of her flesh away from her bones" (30). Not only desiring to kill his aunt, Bong reveals his wish to extend Yuna's pain in ways that would transform him into a torturer. He now revels in an occult mysticism, replete with the voodoo imagery of sticking pins in her feet. Further still, we recall that Bong once called Auntie Yuna a tiger. We see him taking on a similar role by taking a "bite" out of her. He then goes "into the kitchen and stare[s] at the dirty dishes in the sink. From the sink, [he pulls] out a knife still covered with peanut butter" (30); Bong "just wanted to hurt her a little, leave a small cut or jab her a bit" (30–31). But before he is able to inflict any pain on Auntie Yuna, Bong feels Montgomery Clift's presence and a distinct impression that Clift does not approve of his plan to harm her, leading him to drop "the knife, hearing a small thud as it fell onto the shag carpet, the green shag carpet. [He] saw the brown peanut butter on the knife look somehow peaceful against the green. It reminded [him] of dirt and grass" (31). The reference to the peanut butter is important in the way it showcases how Bong's world is made and remade as the traumas of his childhood abuse begin to affect him in more conspicuous ways. A knife originally used to spread peanut butter transforms into an object that can harm, perhaps even kill. These alterations take on an almost magical quality, so much so that the color combinations before him are compared to "dirt and grass."

The cultures of the occult and the afterlife that infuse Auntie Yuna's home come to be reflected in the ways in which Bong reformulates the world around him to make sense of the physical and emotional abuse he is suffering. In a ring of smoke he believes comes from Clift's cigarette behind him (he does not look directly at Clift, stating that he "knew he was there"), Bong sees a "cloud of smoke balled together then parted like waves, creating images above me. I saw a tree, a fig tree I used to sit under in the Philippines. I waited for Mama there sometimes. While she cleaned houses and I was bored, I waited for her under that tree, choosing the ripest figs. I'd bite into one and watch the pink insides ooze out, tasting the sweetness." The cloud of smoke then takes the shape of "Mama's face." The visions end only at sunrise: "I was returned to an ordinary apartment, a ceiling void of Mama's image, made merely of plaster" (31). This signifying chain portrays an addled mind and powerfully demonstrates the level of distress that Bong faces in his protoqueer Asian North American childhood. Besides a fleeting moment when he believes he sees Clift in the flesh at Echo Park, these visions extensively detail the most flagrant warping of Bong's reality. The smoke in addition possesses enough agency to direct its own movement, interacting with objects in the apartment: "It wafted through the legs of the coffee table, skimming the magazines resting on it. It hovered above Auntie Yuna and blew away from her face when she exhaled. The blue smoke created a cloud near the ceiling. I watched it move and roll, bumping into walls" (31). If we take into account philosophical and psychiatric approaches to mental illness, discourses that are welcomed by the novel when Bong ends up in a mental ward later in his life, this moment helps place into context these fanciful perceptions and his other interactions with Clift throughout the novel. Paramjit T. Joshi and Kenneth E. Towbin remind us of the challenges of diagnosing psychoses in children: "Immaturity makes children more susceptible to environmental stressors and cognitive distortions. Children routinely have intrusions of fantasy into ordinary mental life; determining when this becomes pathologic can be a matter of degree" (613). Joshi and Towbin go on to note that the clinician must be able to distinguish between a child who experiences a true psychotic break—one in which the child's thoughts are impaired and hallucinations and delusions occur—from a child who is aware that he or she is simply in a realm of make-believe (614). On the basis of this distinction, Bong's recounting of the smoke and its many transformations suggests an extensive break from reality.

But one issue that Bong's visions bring up relates to the way he narrates the event as a spiritual experience. Here his visions take on a religious quality, as he stares at the smoke transforming into his mother's face as if he was "peering upward like the children of Fatima witnessing the appearance of the Blessed Lady" (31). In one of the classic articles exploring the relationship between spirituality and psychopathology, K. W. M. Fulford and Mike Jackson conclude that "the question remains whether in an individual case the distinction between spiritual experience and psychopathology can be made solely in terms of traditional diagnostic methods as set out in standard psychiatric texts" (44). For Fulford and Jackson, the challenge is determining whether or not a break in reality is psychotic (and thus evidence of a harmful mental illness) or evidence of a spiritual experience. For Caroline Brett, the distinction between a psychotic break and something like a spiritual epiphany is not always easy to delineate, but she argues that "an experience of an altered state that leads to a positive outcome, or can be interpreted and integrated in a positive light, will be a spiritual experience, and psychotic experiences by definition are those altered states that lead to a negative outcome" (322). But, as Marek Marzanski and Mark Bratton contend, spiritual experiences are not uniformly positive, especially as many such episodes include forms of asceticism and "purgative suffering" to attain enlightenment (370).[16] I take the time to rehearse the different perspectives regarding the definition of pathological or harmful psychotic breaks because it helps to situate what Bong experiences as a child observing images, forms, and faces that take shape from the smoke surrounding him.[17]

If we think of Bong's childhood as a surreal landscape in which fairy tale villains and folk monsters loom oppressively large and heroes remain elusive, then his strange visions seem more rational. On the surface, Bong's visions might be termed make-believe by Joshi and Towbin, especially since he eventually "falls out of delusion" as his mother's face gets replaced with the apartment ceiling. But Bong's trance-like state ultimately leads to a "positive outcome" (as Brett would call it) and finds many resonances with a moment of spiritual enlightenment. Clift's fantastical materialization by way of the smoke from a cigarette punctuates his function as a pivotal part of Bong's construction of an inscrutable belonging: Clift is the paternal figure and moral center who will protect him. Hence, it is not surprising that Bong feels his presence just before he is about to stab Auntie Yuna. Clift's presence moves temporarily outside of the cinematic terrain to influence Bong's reality. In addition, for Bong the peanut butter and shag carpeting initially become "dirt and grass," which later change into a fig tree, one that Bong remembers from the Philippines. Here the fig tree from the Philippines presents itself as both a counterpoint to the foods that Bong is forced to eat and evidence of an ethnic past in which he did not have to worry about his physical difference or love from a parental figure. Finally, the emergence of his mother's face from the smoke provided by Clift's cigarette implies the possibility that Bong's mother is still alive and that there is hope she will be found. It is pivotal to note that access to these visions of the Philippines and Bong's mother manifest only through Clift's presence. That is, Clift provides Bong with a vision that helps him to endure in a dangerous time.

Bong's psychotic break, then, seems to comfort rather than to harm, and the religious connotations of his visions function reparatively. As Bong's experience is likened to seeing the Virgin Mary, the vision is imbued with a divine virtue that restores order. In the context of fairy tale narratives such as "Hansel and Gretel," Donald Haase notes that "home itself becomes an ambiguous location, embodying both the danger of violence and ultimate security" for youthful characters. He writes, "When violence upsets their familiar environment, the children [from the fairy tale] are physically dislocated and forced into exile, into a defamiliarized perception of home. In typical fashion, their displacement is followed by relocation to a secure or familiar environment—that is, home reconstituted on a new plane" (364). In a similar manner, Bong's home must be "reconstituted." For him, this transformation, a psychic "relocation," happens only when a dead film star provides the foundations for an inscrutable belonging. This dynamic social formation functions in obvious contrast to his actual living situation, which exists as an uninhabitable wasteland in which his blood relative takes on the guise of a malevolent force, intent on serious harm. The spiritual—even in occurrences that seem to border on psychotic breaks—and the fantastical offer him tools to confront these forces of evil, as he attempts to refashion his life into one filled with long-term sustainability.

Beyond Protoqueer Asian North American Childhood: Revising Heroism and Villainy

I have focused only on select events early in Bong's protoqueer Asian North American childhood to spotlight how the survival plot unfolds and the ways that an inscrutable belonging, based on the storyteller's adoption of a dead film star as a metaphorical father, offers him a measure of comfort in a dangerous period. As an angelic guardian, Clift is granted religious significance: Bong prays to him, requests advice, and writes constantly to him. Bong further reconfigures Clift as part of a filmic lineage, in which Bong might play a role not so dissimilar to Karel from *The Search*, a lost child in a violent environment in need of a savior, played of course by the Hollywood legend. Auntie Yuna, though a blood relative, exercises brutality rather than protection. But when she is eventually deported, Bong is left even more alone and is forced to find ways to feed himself. This period clarifies how Bong's life has been critically endangered, but as with earlier hardships, Bong turns to his letters to Clift for hope. This difficult period ends only when he is adopted by a Filipino American family, the Arangans.

While his new life with the Arangans is rather idyllic in contrast to his time with Auntie Yuna, perhaps signaling the end of the survival plot, Auntie Yuna's reappearance toward the novel's conclusion reminds us that Bong's fortitude must be reexamined. Bong's passionate attachment to Clift and his equally passionate hatred of Auntie Yuna are reductive in that they reinstitute the inviolate binary between good and evil, heroes and villains, truth and fiction. Therefore, Bong's maturation becomes evident through the development of a critical self-consciousness that is unveiled in the novel's concluding sequence. While searching for his mother in the Philippines, he happens to bump into Auntie Yuna, which is her only other major interaction with Bong in the novel. She is working in a Philippine church as a domestic. They come to a sort of rapprochement. As Auntie Yuna admits, "I spent a lot of years being awful. This is what I get—a rundown apartment with nobody" (224). A gothic sentiment returns briefly, as Bong describes her apartment, in which its "white curtains grappled with the wind, resembling ghosts begging to be set free" (224). Bong allows

Auntie Yuna to tell others that Bong is her nephew; he even considers the possibility of writing letters to her, but the evidence of a sturdy reconciliation seems flimsy, especially since she recedes from the narrative following this point.

The "ghost curtains" of Auntie Yuna's apartment in the Philippines remind us of the horrors Bong endured as a child with her in Los Angeles, in a domestic space filled with her monstrous presence. It is fitting that Bong finds her working in a service position given the forced labor he himself endured, but this fact also recalls the many times Bong was awoken in the middle of the night to clean Auntie Yuna's apartment. During those nights Auntie Yuna would tell him the "When I was Young Stories" (35). Though Bong clearly disdains having to listen, he still tells his imagined audience the content of these stories, which engage a different social context for Auntie Yuna's life: "When I was young, I worked in bars in Manila. Near Subic Bay. American sailors would want only me to serve them. No one else" (35). Concerning Bong's mother, Auntie Yuna explains that "she didn't have what it took to work in a bar. She didn't know how to play up to the men. She didn't know it was OK to let them touch you. Kiss you" (35). Reading the novel in its initial iteration or without keeping in mind Auntie Yuna's final character trajectory, these earliest moments might be read solely through her vanity, the desire to recapture her lost youthful beauty. Further still, Auntie Yuna's critique of Bong's mother conveys her belief that her sister did not possess enough mettle to employ her beauty to extract monies from the soldiers stationed at Subic Bay. Yet this later reunion forces a strong rereading of the earlier scene, as Auntie Yuna emphasizes the circularity of her life: "I found myself back in Manila. I worked in bars again. I got tired of that. Or they got tired of me. I wasn't pretty like before" (224). Auntie Yuna's experiences speak to the postcolonial construction of gendered sexuality, as her experience as a bar girl gestures to the larger group of women who sought economic opportunities in the shadow of military bases located in the Philippines.[18] While Auntie Yuna never directly admits to sex work, her flirtatious use of her body suggests that she participated in such activities to garner more monies from military officers.

Auntie Yuna's character trajectory encourages us to revisit her monstrous characterization from Part 1, especially in conjunction with her sexual agency. Her attempts to lure J into a romance using an occult love spell link her with witchcraft. According to the cultural critic Sheldon Cashdan, "Of the many figures who make their presence felt in a fairy tale, the witch is the most compelling. She is the diva of the piece, the dominant character who frames the battle between good and evil" (3). Cashdan later clarifies that "for a fairy tale to succeed—for it to accomplish its psychological purpose—the witch must die because it is the witch who embodies the sinful parts of the self" (30). For Bong, the witch's death is far more metaphorical because it involves reframing Auntie Yuna and her actions.[19] For instance, Auntie Yuna's unorthodox approach to inciting a relationship with J appears ineffectively aimed to reverse the power dynamic that left her as a sexual object for U.S. military men in the Philippines. In the United States, as Auntie Yuna's alcoholism deepens and her financial troubles persist, she turns (once again) to prostitution to help pay the rent (38). This move to America introduces what would seem to be a general improvement from her prostituting background that instead ends in her ruin and her deportation. One of the last images of Auntie Yuna prior to her deportation that Bong describes is seeing her throw up after a prostitutive act: "I went back upstairs to Auntie Yuna's apartment. Mr. Boteng was leaving. A smile across his sagging face. Auntie Yuna was spitting into the sink, spitting her insides out it seemed" (39). This scene of defeat reminds us of Auntie Yuna's continued sexual subjection. Bong's phrasing, that she seemed to be "spitting her insides out," helps clarify Auntie Yuna's desperate desire to retain control of what goes into her body and how her body is used.

Ultimately, Bong's ambivalent reunion with Auntie Yuna at the novel's conclusion helps signal the need to review her character's fuller trajectory: she is not so simply made out to be an evil villainess, then, but instead can be seen as a flawed woman whose frequent abuse of Bong signals a transference of her own traumas sustained through her former status as a postcolonial bar worker. Certainly my reading is not meant to absolve the obvious danger that Bong is placed in or the fact that his life is rendered so precariously due to her lack of guardianship. At the same time, the survival plot can only find some resolution through this reconnection, precisely because this moment shows Bong's maturation to adulthood and his ability to forgive.

So too might we revisit Bong's relationship with Montgomery Clift. Though Bong's letters showcase an obvious great esteem for Montgomery Clift, at no point do they trigger a letter back from him. On the most literal level, the letters reveal the futility of Bong's multiple hailings. For instance, in his first letter he asks Clift to "bring [his] mama back to [him]" (1), a request that goes unfulfilled. Bong must go to the Philippines himself to find her. When Auntie Yuna requests that Bong steal an object from J, their neighbor, Bong asks Clift what he "should do" (26) because he has formed a friendly attachment to J. Bong requests that Clift "give [him] an answer by morning" (26), but of course, no direct answer comes. When the Arangans take Bong out of foster care, he attributes this fortunate change to Clift. In Bong's fantasies, Clift never fails him, but this perfection is required because without it, Bong's world would be dominated by the frequent ways he is disavowed, abandoned, or mistreated, especially by Auntie Yuna. Clift is the symbol that holds together a fragile fantasy—that is, his own version of a childhood fairy tale—in which Bong, too, can be someone special, someone worth loving, both as a son and later as a queer sexual being and a racial minority.

If Clift is the hero of Bong's personal fairy tale, then Auntie Yuna is undoubtedly the villain. But Auntie Yuna is ultimately given a character trajectory that challenges her original position as evil quasi-stepmother; that redefines her life within the context of U.S. imperialism, transnational sex work, and service economies; and that finally encourages us to reconsider all depictions within the novel from a retrospective position. Clift, we might say, has the opposing narrative evolution in that he moves from being seen as an unadulterated protector to being envisaged as a screen icon with limited power to change Bong's life. The literary critic Martin Joseph Ponce reads the concluding letter as evidence of Bong's continuing "queer melancholic attachment" to Clift, but in my opinion, this last letter is more productively read through its intertextual referentiality. We recall Bong's first mention of Clift in a movie is *The Search*. Bong's plot summary of the film reduces the film to a seemingly enchanted triangular relationship. The angelic boy Karel is not only protected by Steve, his heroic American hero (played by Clift), but also reunited with his mother, who never stopped believing he was alive. In perfect parallel fashion, Steve never formally meets Karel's mother, though the two are within each other's presence by the conclusion. Karel acts as the bridge, much like Bong, between his imaginary guardian and his own mother.

In his final letter to Clift, Bong refers to one of Clift's most problematic films, *Terminal Station*, which was later rereleased in a different form in the United States as *Indiscretion of an American Wife*. The main triangular relationship in this film occurs between a married American housewife, Mary Forbes (played by Jennifer Jones), her Italian lover, Giovanni Doria (played by Clift), and her nephew, Paul (played by Richard Beymer). The main action takes place inside a train station, where Mary decides to see her lover one last time before breaking off the affair. Bong explains the plot as such: "You [Clift] played an Italian pursuing Jennifer Jones, a wife with a husband in America. You rendezvous with her, meeting her. Both of you love each other, but know a life together could never be. She has her life in the states with her family, and you have another life to tend to" (244). The nephew receives little screen time, so it is no surprise that Bong completely omits this character's role in his plot summary. But the nephew serves as an important corporeal reminder of Mary's commitment to her family. Bong identifies most strongly with Mary, suggesting both his maturation into adulthood and the ill-fated nature of his imaginary relationship with Clift. Despite the deep love Mary and Giovanni share for each other, their relationship can never be made public or legitimate. The film's outcome reorders the American wife's world according to the logic of marital fidelity. Far from the fairy tale ending of *The Search*, which spoke to Bong's most deeply held yearnings during his protoqueer Asian North American childhood, *Indiscretion of an American Wife* concludes with a painful rupture. This outcome refracts how Bong must reconsider or even sever his own imaginary attachments to Clift. Giovanni, as Mary's extramarital lover, is far from the heroic guardian that Clift portrays in *The Search*. Instead, his role is imbued by ambiguities and failures. Consequently, Bong's final letter speaks to his attempt to deconstruct the perfection of his fairy filmic godfather in his talismanic abilities to protect and to function as an object of romantic sublimation. At the same time, the fact that Bong's last discursive act is to address Clift reveals that the actor cannot be cast off as an entirely inappropriate part of Bong's inscrutable belonging. Instead, what the ending demonstrates is a more measured understanding of what cinematic heroes can provide as a mode of support.

Perhaps the most startling comparison point between the happy ending of *The Search* and Bong's quest to find his mother as an adult is that his mother never actively looks for him, despite knowing that he is in the United States. Whereas Karel's mother aggressively pursues all leads to find him, Bong's mother struggles under the weight of her own traumas; at one point, she actually runs away from Bong. Though they eventually reunite, the degree of torture that Bong's mother had experienced implies that her move to the United States will not be an easy one. As Bong describes after first finding her: "I didn't realize how small she was. As a child, my head reached her chest, easily falling between her breasts when I hugged her. Now her head fell below my shoulders. It used to take both my arms for me to embrace her. Now I was sure I could encompass her with just one" (234). In an incredible role reversal, it is Bong who rescues his mother. As she admits, "Forgive me for not finding you. I thought you would have more to lose if I did" (240). His mother's statement sounds rather odd, when accounting for Bong's single-minded focus to find her. She rationalizes her sentiments through the presumption that life in America would be better, but his childhood experiences suggest a far more complicated conception of refuge and safety. In some sense, it is only by luck that Bong is settled with the well-to-do Arangans, so we begin to see how Bong's vision of his mother as a kind of Virgin Mary figure is a fantasy. If we think back to Bong's parallel with Mary in *Indiscretion of an American Wife*, then his move to return to the fold of the nuclear family comes with an alteration of traditional North American kinship structures. The mother must take part in a familial metamorphosis to make room for Bong's ever-evolving inscrutable belongings.

One Survival Plot to Another:
Clift as Narrative and Cinematic Competitor

As a child, Bong enters a gothic world, one filled with witches, snakes, saints, and saviors. Auntie Yuna and Montgomery Clift function as polar opposites, but it is Clift whom Bong embraces as part of an essential inscrutable belonging that first develops when he is young. As Bong matures, the novel reveals a shift in his understanding: he moves beyond the binaries that are inspired in part by the folktale and fairy tale constructs that enable a child to polarize the positions of hero and villain and, in this case, fairy godfather and evil witch. Bong's retrospective narration offers the readers a way to understand how he must revisit the past to give it new meanings and to reveal how both Clift and Auntie Yuna are finally constituted as part of a dynamic but interconnected lineage of flawed guardian figures. In this way, Auntie Yuna can be conditionally included in Bong's conception of a larger tapestry of loss, trauma, and postcolonial subjection. So, too, does Bong come to see that his idealization of his mother as an infallible protector figure requires revision. For Bong, the inscrutable belonging encapsulates both biological and metaphorical relations, redefining the bounds of the heteronuclear family.

The other element that we must return to in order to situate the protoqueer Asian North American's survival is Clift's relationship to Bong's notions of kinship and family as a legal adult. In Part 1, as a young child, Bong comes to see himself as selectively positioned within a filmic lineage. As already mentioned, in *The Search*, Bong identifies with the young boy Karel, who is saved by Clift's American military serviceman, Steve. But Bong's identification with Karel is in some sense a mode of deracination, one that hints at the fact that his attachment to these films evidences a form of racial melancholia. As espoused by Anne Anlin Cheng and others, racial melancholia surfaces when the Asian North American must confront his or her position as a not-fully-integrated Other.[20] In this novel, racial melancholia manifests precisely because Bong must confront how the Asian North American is presented in the cinematic imaginary as a ghostly figure, one who is alluded to but is not directly acknowledged. Bong's obsession with and strong attachment to Clift as a surrogate father figure requires him at first to look past the ways in which Clift's movies might be read through the social context of Hollywood's white supremacy. During the era in which Clift reached stardom, only a handful of Asian North American actors achieved any sort of mainstream visibility.[21] The novel invites us to acknowledge the discourse of Asian North American presence in Hollywood precisely because both Amada and Bong attempt to find work in the movie industry, as they make lives as independent adults. Later, Bong's first long-term and significant queer relationship occurs with a mixed-race Asian North American man, Logan, who is an aspiring screenwriter. Their occupations within the Hollywood film industry provide the grounds for another branch of an inscrutable belonging.

As a consequence of these issues of racial melancholia and filmic representation, I shift to the ways in which Bong begins to confront racialized ghostliness in cinema and other associated media such as television and photography. His desire to make legible the struggles of Asian North Americans in this line of work offers us another explanation to the problem that arises in light of Bong's many attachments to Montgomery Clift. As I make evident, Montgomery Clift's relative success in the movie industry serves as an obvious contrast to the struggles of all Asian North American characters in this novel seeking stardom and fame. Thus Clift also signifies as a representational adversary; he becomes the key antagonist in Bong's evolving survival plot. That is, as his movies bear the imprint of his lasting impact even beyond his death, Clift's prominent legacy threatens to overshadow other performances and other stories that can be told. In this sense, as Clift threatens rather than protects Bong, the filmic lineage that initially composed the inscrutable belonging alters in order to make room for a more expansive social formation informed by the racial politics of visual representation.

By the time Auntie Yuna is deported, the novel has completed only about a third of its arc. In this sense, the novel slowly shifts the focus of antagonism from Auntie Yuna to Montgomery Clift himself. It is also here that queer of color and queer diasporic reading practices are most relevant. Our narrator must not only affirm his genealogical connection to his aunt through their blood relationship but also interpret her experiences as ones that might help inform his adult life. Indeed, her sexual subjection at the hands of U.S. military servicemen appears as an unacknowledged form of exploitative bodily labor. Auntie Yuna's life takes on increased complexity as Bong matures to adulthood, and he must also reevaluate both his racial and sexual subjection within the Hollywood film industry. Queer of color and queer diasporic reading practices thus respectively help bridge the ways in which Bong's many trials and tribulations involve both national and international dimensions.

Notably, the survival plot's evolution is necessary, as it reveals how our storyteller's life remains, as always, in peril. This sequencing of one threat to another reminds us of the ways that our protagonist must remain ever vigilant, even as he attempts to refigure how antagonistic figures are crucial to his endurance, that they cannot be categorically expunged from his inscrutable belongings. For his part, Bong's association with the film industry is best characterized as ambivalent. Though he is invested in the culture of film production and movie making, he is not necessarily dedicated to becoming an actor. He does exhibit some ambition through his work as an extra: "I've been doing as many extra gigs as I can find to make ends meet. I go from job to job, wherever I'm needed. I spent last week, every day, eight hours a day pretending to be an Indian for a new western. They put a long wig on me while I stood around in a loincloth. Yesterday, I wore a suit and pretended to be a businessman for a commercial pushing a construction company in Santa Monica" (156). The roles Bong must play are limited, parts of an extra's task to help generate authenticity in a given film. But we cannot overlook the importance of the extra as a site of critical analysis. Here I follow Will Straw's point that "character actors, extras, bit players, ensemble casts and stock companies are a persistent focus of the devotional and connoisseurist dispositions people bring to the practice of film viewing, but they have received little attention in academic writing on the cinema" (79). As Straw goes on to note, these more marginalized roles are "typically unheralded," and because they are "reduced, much of the time, to fleeting moments or undeveloped functions," it is a challenge to move beyond reading such roles as forms of "stereotypification" (79). One way to tackle the nature of extras and the propagation of stereotyping through such limited roles is to engage the politics of film and television production and casting considerations. For instance, the racial barriers Bong faces as an extra are overt. Bong's reference to his work as an "Indian" is more largely emblematic of the ways in which minority characters are so often forced into roles based on superficial phenotypic specifications, which often results in the use of cross-racial and cross-ethnic casting.[22]

To be sure, the progression of the civil rights movement helped usher in a period that saw cross-racial and cross-ethnic casting (Pao 16) as a means to expand the ways in which theatrical productions could be staged. As Josephine Lee has also noted, Asian American theater companies have employed cross-ethnic casting to create a sense of racialized solidarity (*Performing* 17).[23] But with respect to the novel, Bong's casting as an Indian more largely follows how the film and television industry so often delineates racial and ethnic minorities as inherently indistinguishable, as a means to render them as part of an insignificant background.[24]

The problems related to racialized casting of extras manifests again in the novel when Bong works on a Vietnam War–era film. Although he is ethnically Filipino, he is hired to play a Vietnamese character: "I called up the place that used to get me jobs as an extra. I got a gig working on a movie. It was about the Vietnam war. I thought they would stick me in a crowd, my face buried among the masses" (189). Bong is correct about his rather limited position, as the "movie was about battered American soldiers and Vietnamese villagers" who are "put in a prison camp" (189). In one scene, the director wants to generate a sense of pathos for those subsisting in the prison camp: "She did a series of closeups of all the Asian extras looking sad and pathetic. I thought about my parents. I found myself crying, wondering about them—how their lives were, and how I wasn't a part of it" (190). Though the film in the novel is being directed in 1993, this moment reminds us of the casting and location controversies related to *Apocalypse Now*, a film that was shot in the Philippines. Famously read by Jean Baudrillard as a form of simulacrum, the movie's depiction of Asian locations and faces as interchangeable functions as a mode by which certain ethnic backgrounds generate Orientalist authenticity.[25] In Bong's case, his Filipinoness is deemed Asian-looking enough to stand in for a Vietnamese face. At the same time, Bong's status as a marginal character in the film calls attention to the ways in which Asian figures are continually marked as decorative rather than integral to the cinematic experience.[26]

Bong's experiences in the film industry are obviously not unlike the fates of many Asian North American actors.[27] As Teresa Mok notes, "Asians often are used as 'background color'—assigned to such minor roles as waiters, cooks, servants, laundry workers, peasants, or gardeners. When they are cast in more prominent roles, these roles often lack depth, portraying Asians as villains, warmongers, geishas, karate experts, dragon ladies, or prostitutes" (186).[28] Helen Zia further reminds us that "ever since the silent screen days, portrayals of Asians on stage, screen, and TV have fit into a narrow band of selections. Some, like the sinister alien spy, have become archetypal straitjackets for Asian American actors and audiences" (112). As detailed by a number of scholars, the problem of diversity in Hollywood casting with respect to Asian North Americans has been evident for more than a century, especially given the continued use of yellowface and the persistence of racial stereotypes on screen.[29] Though some actors achieved widespread cinematic prominence, including the aforementioned Anna May Wong and Sessue Hayakawa, and others such as Bruce Lee, James Shigeta, Lucy Liu, and Jamie Chung, the challenges in finding starring roles remain numerous.[30] With the more recent successes of both mainstream and independent films involving Asian North American themes and casts,[31] the future for minority actors in Hollywood seems far brighter. But questions remain as to whether these changes are sustainable or will ultimately result in more lead acting roles. In critical readings related to the films *Rush Hour* and *Crouching Tiger Hidden Dragon*, Minh-ha T. Pham cautions that "Asian actors and filmmakers are not invading Hollywood as much as they are finally being admitted into Hollywood—under very specific conditions and for very specific roles" (122). With respect to the problems facing actors in Hollywood as detailed by Pham, *Letters to Montgomery Clift* would seem to tread some repetitive ground. At the same time, the novel is gesturing to a larger issue related to representational survival: that is, what kind of Asian North American lives can be imagined or depicted if there are so few roles available at all?

This quandary is further compounded in Bong's case because he seeks roles both as an Asian North American actor and as a queer one. In this sense, this variation on the survival plot appears in concert with the need to give life to other oft-ignored representational trajectories and stories portrayed on screen. We can return to Bong's experiences as an extra to scrutinize his status as a queer Asian North American actor.[32] Bong characterizes the desultory nature of extra work in this way: "I spend most of my time waiting. I wait for the cameras and lights to be set. I wait while the actors rehearse. I wait for those few precious moments when the camera rolls, and the director says, 'Action.'" (156–157). He adds that "being an extra can be a mind-numbing experience" (157) and muses that "I want an Elizabeth Taylor. I want someone to love" (157).

Here Bong exposes not only the boredom of his work as an extra but also his desire to exceed that position. Bong's reference to Elizabeth Taylor is one that a Montgomery Clift fan would understand as a nod to Taylor's and Clift's real-life relationship. Regarded as one of Hollywood's most glamorous couples, they were never actually romantically linked. Starring in multiple movies together, including *Raintree Country*, *A Place in the Sun*, and *Suddenly, Last Summer*, Taylor and Clift spent much time together off screen as well. Bong's desire to have his own Elizabeth Taylor is nothing less than an expression of discontent with his marginalized position within the cinematic landscape. He, too, would like a starring role in which the central romance plot directly involves him.

In this case, rather than idolize Clift or see him as part of an interconnected filmic lineage, however imaginary in scope, Bong attempts to substitute himself for Clift, revealing Clift's status as a cinematic competitor, someone who battles for the same kind of romantic leading role. Recasting this scene through the hypothetical possibility of Bong as the queer Asian North American leading man puts into perspective how revolutionary his star billing would be. When queer Asian North American actors have managed to land more substantive roles, especially ones that allot for the expression of sexuality, they are often relegated to peripheral positions, typically as comic, queenie sidekicks, such as Alec Mapa's Vern on *Desperate Housewives* or Rex Lee's Lloyd on *Entourage*. But these examples are restricted to the televisual landscape. Far more elusive is the queer Asian North American acting role in a mainstream Hollywood movie. For Bong to command the screen as a romantic lead—that is, to have his version of an "Elizabeth Taylor"—would mean becoming a pioneer in the movie industry, during the time period in which these sentiments are expressed (in 1989).

Not surprisingly, Bong never rises above his status as an extra in the movie industry, a nonprogressive arc more largely indicative of the severe hurdles for any minority seeking significant roles in Hollywood. While Bong struggles to make ends meet as an extra, his adoptive sister, Amada, experiences similar challenges. Her centrality to Bong's life and survival is especially vital given that she is the one who calls wider attention to Bong's imaginary relationship with Montgomery Clift, forcing him to deal with his traumatic attachments, which leads to his psychiatric institutionalization. Amada's intervention also helps enable him to receive professional counseling. As Martin Joseph Ponce further notes, "The novel presents Bong's relation to Monty not as a hallucinatory symptom of his psychological problems but as an integral component of his survival strategies (the other major part being his relationship with Amada)" (174). Clift and Amada are clearly "integral" to his fortitude, but what does Amada offer exactly in terms of survival strategies? On one level, Amada immediately signifies as a queer-ish character in relation to Bong because of one important subplot that marks her as a nonreproductive subject. As a teenager, Amada becomes pregnant, but decides to abort the fetus. It is during this sequence that Bong provides staunch support, helping to drive Amada to the medical clinic. Given her parents' religious beliefs, Amada realizes that her most likely supporter would be none other than Bong, whose own relationship to Amada's parents has been made tenuous in light of their support of the Marcos government. On another level, once Bong and Amada weather their various trials as adolescents, they both advocate for each other as adults who seek fully imagined film and television roles. Amada solidifies her place in a fledgling inscrutable belonging based on these two characters' negotiation of Hollywood as queer-ish Asian North American actors.[33]

Throughout the novel, Bong raves about Clift's performances in most of the films he starred in, but as Part 3 commences, he also begins to reveal Amada's path into the film industry. Amada's decision to be an actress comes with requirements. She, for instance, refuses to do extra work, but when she gets "her first real acting gig," she must confront the limits in the roles she will receive. As she tells Bong, "I play this foreign exchange student who falls in love with this American. I kill myself because he rejects me in the end" (145). After this admission, Bong states in interior monologue, "I was happy for her. I really was" (145). That he has to reiterate that he is happy for her relates, of course, to the fact that Amada's entry into the acting world draws on a long-standing stereotype concerning Asian women in popular representation: the tragic butterfly, or the Asian woman who kills herself because, for one reason or another, she cannot be with her (white) lover.

Unlike Clift, who achieves top billing in scores of movies, Amada must confront the meager roles available for an Asian North American woman, especially related to the character trajectories in tragic plots. Bong provides us with a frank account of the struggles that Amada faces. Not long after her role in that student film, Amada takes another job, this time portraying "a woman who had just been bombed in Hiroshima. It was an experimental play in Santa Monica. At the end, she killed herself because she couldn't stand her life after her home had been devastated" (157). Then, for an audition, Bong drives "Amada into Hollywood . . . [for a] callback actually. 'I play a hooker,' she said, 'who tries to straighten out her drugged-out life, but overdoses on Seconal and dies'" (158). As a bonding experience, Amada and Bong will later watch "some of the TV shows and movies she'd done. They were quick takes of her delivering a line here and a line there. In most of her scenes, she gets killed or commits suicide" (186). Regarding her part in *Blood Prom at Hell High*, Bong laughs when he sees "the shot of Amada with an ax in her head" (186). It is not surprising that Amada eventually laments to Bong, "Why do Asian women have to die all the time? And it's usually over some white guy. She dies in Madame Butterfly, and she dies in that musical about Saigon. Why do white guys feel that some Asian woman is willing to die for them? Fuck. If I knew an Asian chick who was willing to die for a white guy, over any guy, I'd kill her myself" (186–187). For Amada, the roles she must audition for and sometimes succeeds in attaining are ones in which she plays a bit part, a woman who is brutally written out of the story. As Amada also makes apparent, this death is so often staged in conjunction with a failed romance plot related to a Caucasian man. In this sense, the Asian North American woman's sexuality can be read as a kind of perversion that must be eliminated.

The novel showcases not only the challenges for the Asian North American actress, but also the representational paradigms through which the racialized, gendered, and sexualized body becomes most visible in cinema and popular culture. As Lynn Lu notes, "A parade of familiar stereotypes populates our cultural landscape: concubine, geisha girl, mail-order bride, dragon lady, lotus blossom, precious pearl. In this environment, Asian women thirst for realistic and three-dimensional images of ourselves that will not dissolve like mirages as we draw near" (17).[34] The celebrated author Jessica Hagedorn expresses a similar sentiment: "In many ways, as females and Asians, as audiences or performers, we have learned to settle for less—to accept the fact that we are either decorative, invisible, or one-dimensional. When there are characters who look like us represented in a movie, we have also learned to view between the lines, or to add what is missing" (79). Certainly *Letters to Montgomery Clift* offers us a character who does "thirst" for other images, ones that would enable her to take on more substantive roles, but what is so important about Amada's struggle, especially in light of its congruency with so many other Asian North American actresses over the course of multiple centuries?[35]

To answer this question fully, we must place Bong's acting roles in relation to Amada's. Both characters' roles so often require them to suffer, to die, and to remain marginal in the larger story. Further still, sexuality and desire, whenever referenced, typically involve the death of the Asian North American or the erasure of the romance plot involving this racialized female figure. But this kind of narrative delivers an imperative message about representational survival. That is, the story of the queerly positioned Asian North American only ever ends prematurely, either because this figure is not deemed worthy enough to be a central character of a romance plot or because she must be killed off because her desires are coded as perverse or unnatural.[36] Such a trajectory is then accentuated by the power and influence of media, especially in popularly disseminated forms such as Hollywood films. Sarah Eschholz explains, "Most viewers do not just consume the images and storylines in the media and walk away untouched. Although little evidence exists demonstrating a direct connection between the media and behavior, such as violence, contemporary studies are finding that media messages influence viewers' perceptions of reality in a systematic manner" (301). More insidiously, notes Bradley Gorham, certain representations can wield so much persuasive influence that "*[t]he way our brains process information may lead us to think things we don't even agree with.* That is, we may automatically make stereotype-congruent interpretations of news stories or film snippets even though we reject the stereotype in question" (100, emphasis original).[37] Gorham goes on to specify that "this [subconscious embrace of reductive representations] is especially troublesome given that stereotypes tend to be negative for all minority groups in society, and that the application of stereotypes to political issues tends to hurt minority groups and keep members of majority groups looking good" (100). Eschholz and Gorham, respectively, magnify the ways that we must critically consider what damaging messages media can transmit and how such images influence viewers' conceptualizations of racial and sexual differences and of whether or not minorities deserve to survive in the realm of cultural representations.

If media wield so much potential to alter how we think about a given minority population and how they are depicted on screen, then a novel such as *Letters to Montgomery Clift* highlights how performers like Amada and Bong could see their own lives as marginal, even deserving of premature termination and violent death. At one point, Amada jokes with Bong, "[I]f I die one more time, I'll kill myself" (186). Though said in jest, Amada's levity here also gravely speaks to the connection between representation and its influence on material realities. As Younghan Kim notes, "Stereotypical media images associated with Asians are likely to create doubts and ambivalence for some about themselves as well as about them among other racial groups" (45).[38] These "media images" coincide with the many roles that Bong and Amada take and could certainly contribute to the development of internalized racism. With respect to this issue, Helen Zia explains, "Asian American viewers absorbed the steady diet of demeaning caricatures with embarrassment and shame. Many wished, as youngsters, to be another race, to be anything but the images that dominated them" (115). The roles that Bong and Amada inhabit reinforce stereotypes, which take on amplified importance because there are fewer opportunities for any media representations of Asians to surface in the first place: "Representations thus become allegorical; within hegemonic discourse every subaltern performer role is seen as synecdochically summing up a vast but putatively homogenous community" (Shohat and Stam 183). If Amada's and Bong's performances function to "sum up" the Asian North American community, and there are so few other options for acting jobs, what ways does the novel offer for resisting the narrative in which the Asian North American is killed, written out of the plot especially in relation to his or her desire for romance, or made peripheral and decorative? How can Asian North American characters invested in the film industry find a way to resist a sense that their lives are fit to exist only on the very edges of a story?

To address these concerns, we can look to the novel's resolution of the career trajectories for these characters, who flounder so often in the film, television, and performance industries. Amada's arc leads first to theater and later to schooling. As Bong notes, Amada "worked almost full-time with an Asian American theatre troupe. They do shows around Southern California" (203), but later Amada is "still doing theater in town, but wants to go to school. She's thinking of getting a degree in arts education or something" (243). Amada's retreat from Hollywood cinema and into theater is not surprising given the roles she receives and her reactions to having to play so many Asian North American women who ultimately die (over their failed love affairs with Caucasian men). Of course, *Letters to Montgomery Clift* elliptically references the longer history of theater troupes such as East West Players that have offered Asian North Americans more opportunities for meatier, more nuanced roles.[39]

Bong's mixed-race, Asian North American boyfriend, Logan, seems to have the most promising career in Hollywood, but it is not in front of the camera: he focuses instead on screenwriting and directing. By the conclusion of the novel, readers discover that "Logan is still writing movies, and got hooked up with some grants. He's made some short films with the grant money, and started entering them into some film festivals" (243), but the content of such films is a question mark. Indeed, earlier in the novel, Bong relates Logan's interest in screenwriting that focuses on formula: "He wrote movies where the lovers managed to get together in the end, where the good guys always won, and no matter how poor or disheveled a family was, they managed to afford great gifts for the children at Christmas. He believed all that stuff. He believed in formula; it worked" (209). If Logan's interest exists only in writing formula films, then one wonders if his approach would offer any possible roles to Asian North American actors, especially since the narrative tropes that Bong mentions so often involve white or deracinated figures and contexts.

Formula scripts could hardly adapt the experiences Bong has faced up until this point. His father has been tortured and killed as a resistor to Marcos's governmental policies; his mother has gone missing; his closest relationship seems to be with a dead movie star; and his career as an actor never takes off. Even by the novel's ending, Bong cannot land any major roles and decides he will not work any more as an extra. If formula film and associated scripts and narratives cannot evolve to imagine the life of someone like Bong, what does the novel offer for queer Asian North Americans invested in the power and influence of the cinema, who desire a form of representational life beyond the margins? To examine this problem, I turn to the work of film critic Peter X. Feng, who in a rereading of *The World of Suzie Wong* attempts to revise the nature of his viewing experience, despite the stereotypes the film generates concerning the Asian North American woman as hypersexual. In Feng's argument, the racialized spectator can acknowledge the limits and even the racist nature of a film and still take pleasure in it by locating possible sites of resistance, ways in which the story can still exceed stereotypes and prejudicial representations ("Recuperating" 49–52). In the context of black cinema, Jacqueline Stewart notes the ways in which racialized viewers could engage in a "reconstructive spectatorship" (17) in order to reclaim a space for themselves beyond the limited (and often prejudiced) depictions offered in mainstreamed filmic representations.

In line with the arguments offered by Feng and by Stewart, I argue that Bong continually learns to be a more critical spectator, one who reads between the lines to understand the complicated position of the Asian or Asian North American in cinema, in television, and on screens in general. He begins to read racial representation with a more nuanced eye, especially when he sees Amada in a bit part. He acknowledges that her role at first seems insignificant: "She was on a show about detectives. She played a secretary in a monolithic downtown building, and told a detective to 'wait here' while she got her boss. She had about five seconds of screen time" (180). However, Bong also notes that "[s]he didn't look like a struggling actress or a woman who had an abortion at seventeen. She looked like an important woman with interesting people to meet and colorful places to go. It seemed she had another life, another world where she belonged, a world that wanted her there" (180). Bong's ability to root out the brilliance of her performance, though she appears for only five seconds, demonstrates his keen spectatorship as he concentrates his attention as a viewer on the bit player. Whereas his adoration of Clift's movies focuses on a leading actor with immense amounts of screen time, we begin to see that Bong understands that marginal roles deserve more critical scrutiny.

This exact skill of reading for the figures on the fringes is what enables him to discover that his mother is still alive. When Mrs. Billaruz—the person who had told Bong that his father was tortured and killed—contacts him again and tells him to play a videotape, he is unsure of the reason. The film is based on a "vigil in Manila to remember those who had disappeared during the Marcos regime" (206). As Bong goes on to note, "The camera rested for a moment on a woman who wore a sweater and a plain blue dress. She carried a photo across her chest. It was a photo of my dad. The woman holding the photo was old, her hair a little gray" (206). Presumably, Bong is unsure of who the woman is because she looked older than his mother did the last time he saw her, so he must rely on his ability to read this scene with more precision. As he details, "In the video, the woman did one thing that gave her away, that let me know she was my mother. She placed her hand over her mouth to stifle herself, to stop herself from crying" (207). This very gesture is the same one Bong recalls when he first "boarded the plane to come to the U.S." (207). Though Bong's mother materializes on screen for only "a moment," he captures the importance of this brief time. In a sense, his mother is one of many extras who are being filmed in light of a larger event, her own narrative potentially subsumed under collective traumas suffered by numerous individuals under the Marcos regime. But Bong affirms her place in this larger narrative and recognizes that she is actually alive.

Bong also takes one large step toward reconfiguring the marginality of Asians and Asian North Americans on screen: he spends less discursive space on his letters to Clift. Chapters 38 through 41, the final chapters, are the only ones in the entire novel that do not begin with at least one letter to Clift. Bong shifts his attention to the fact that his family extends beyond his biological mother and father and that his romantic life must move beyond an imaginary relationship to a dead Hollywood film star. In one telling sequence, he enthuses about a set of pictures. Bong's favorite is "of Logan, [him] and Amada at the opening night of a play she did" (203). He goes on to describe this photograph as "a family picture really—a semblance of a life" (203). Critically, these three figures, all peripheral to the Hollywood film industry, are the central subjects of the photograph. Their image is the basis of Bong's evolving understanding of another inscrutable belonging, one that comprises two individuals who are not tied to him biologically, an elective social formation that is about "life," rather than his suffering (at the hands of Auntie Yuna) or his representational negligibility in filmic representations (second to the starring roles of Montgomery Clift).

Logan, in particular, increasingly takes on the position of Bong's romantic foil and presents a conflict in relation to Bong's devotion to Montgomery Clift. In this triangle, Clift is eventually written out, as he must be sacrificed so Bong can engage in a romance that exists outside of the imaginary realm. The last letter to Clift, the epilogue of the novel, can also be reread in light of Bong's relinquishing of Clift as the appropriate and sole member of an inscrutable belonging. As I describe earlier in the chapter, in *Indiscretion of an American Wife*, Clift plays Giovanni, a character having an affair with a married woman. Clift's character does not end up with his female lead, and the storyline mirrors that Bong cannot promote Clift as his most important relationship, romantic or paternal. At the same time, the final letter to Clift must be critically analyzed for its many ambivalences, moving beyond the formula ending that a surface reading of the novel might offer. At this point, all seems wonderful: Bong is reunited at last with his mother; Bong has a great boyfriend, Logan; Bong tentatively reconciles with Auntie Yuna; Bong finally accepts that his adoptive family, the Arangans, worked for the Marcos regime, but does not necessarily see them as fully responsible for political corruption; and Bong no longer blames them unequivocally for the death of his father.

However, the novel charges us to reconsider this sort of ending, especially since the formula narrative so rarely involves a central racial minority, no less a queer one. Certainly Bong's reunification with his mother is felicitous, but recalling Bong's difficult acculturation to the United States, the last letter details the possible struggles Bong's mother will face as an immigrant. In relation to Logan, this novel posits the possible union of two queer Asian North American characters, a pioneering fact in and of itself, but one that must be read in light of the movie Bong references. In *Indiscretion of an American Wife*, the wife ends her affair with an Italian lover and returns to her husband and family. The survival of this marriage contrasts with the central romantic tensions in *Letters to Montgomery Clift*, not only between Bong and Clift but also between Bong and Logan. Indeed, marriage is not an option for any of these characters; in 1993, when the novel ends, no U.S. state had yet legalized same-sex unions. The novel's conclusion sees Bong writing to Clift that "I wept at the end of [*Indiscretion of an American Wife*]. I wept for us. I love you, Monty. I want the very best for you, too" (244). These final perplexing lines do not explain why Bong is weeping or what it would mean for "Monty" to have the "very best." A cursory reading might attribute Bong's tears to the understanding that he can never be with Clift, finally accepting that his love affair has always been imaginary. At the same time, the tears also signify that the inscrutable belonging Bong constructs with Clift has not been categorically severed just because Bong now has assumed the starring role in the story he himself tells. The present-tense verbs *love* and *want* gesture to an ongoing connection. In this sense, the novel retains its dynamic filmic lineage, reminding us that Bong, though occupying the central role and possessing an actual in-the-flesh leading man, cannot excise figures like Clift who still signify as sexual minorities who had been, or continue to be, subsumed in the shadow of social death. Bong's desire that Clift have the "very best" reminds us of the actor's fate as a Hollywood film star whose queer tendencies remained in the closet. Though he got to play so many different kinds of roles, suggesting an expansive representational freedom, his life outside of that cinematic landscape remained one in which queerness could be acknowledged only so much. The novel's ambivalent conclusion reveals the layered facets of Bong's inscrutable belongings.

Throughout his youth and adolescence, Bong employs Clift as a cinematic hero, a fairy godfather who exists as the basis of an alternative filmic lineage and provides him with a measure of inspiration in a dark and dangerous period during which Bong is abused and abandoned by his Auntie Yuna. Bong's inscrutable belonging first becomes evident through his reconfiguration of Clift's position as this cinematic father figure, who has the magical ability to intervene, so long as Bong's devotion remains steadfast. But Bong's maturation into adulthood is predicated on revising the polarization that divides hero from villain, and he views both Clift and Auntie Yuna from new perspectives that shed light on their limitations as two different forms of flawed guardians.

Our queer Asian North American storyteller faces down the antagonistic forces related to both physical harm and social death. On the one hand, Bong must endure emotional and physical abuse from Auntie Yuna during his childhood. On the other, Bong's journey to adulthood also comes with a greater knowledge of the contexts that helped to create Auntie Yuna's monstrosity, ones in part stemming from U.S. imperialism and military base proliferation. This parallel largely foreshadows the exploitative labor conditions he himself will suffer as a racialized queer actor attempting to make a living in the Hollywood film and television industries. For Bong to exist at the center of his survival plot, then, he must reconfigure the nature of his family and his kin.

Bong accordingly comes to a new understanding of Clift, especially in light of his experiences as a queer Asian North American actor working in Hollywood. These bit parts leave him subsisting, without his version of a suitable romantic lead. Clift becomes a cinematic competitor, one whose starring roles serve as a stark representational contrast to the marginal characters who Bong—and other Asian North American actors and actresses (such as Amada)—must play merely to find paid work in the Hollywood film industry. As Bong moves into a fully imagined romance plot, Clift must exit so that Logan can embody the proper, desirable, and tangible foil. The novel poses the aggregation of characters who collectively struggle as Asian North Americans in the film industry as another branch of an inscrutable belonging. Bong's affiliations with Amada and Logan enable him to confront the limits of his own representational peril as an Asian North American on film, television, screen, and elsewhere. We can think of the novel, then, as an ingenious formal reversal: that is, the novel's retrospective first-person narration is a kind of monologue that places Bong in the starring role. Though the form of this storytelling is far from cinematic given its emphasis on what is heard rather than what is seen, it is an apt choice: the narrative moves Bong out of the filmic realm to find queer racialized legibility through a performance and role all his own. And thus we come to understand another facet of Bong's retrospective storytelling: he looks back on his letters in order to place himself under scrutiny. This narrative spotlight models perfectly why the survival plot materializes as a facet of sequence. Only after Bong has managed to outlast so many antagonistic forces can he properly look back on his life.

Though Bong's relationship to Clift seems tenuous by the final pages, the fact that the epilogue is a letter still addressed to the movie star demonstrates how Bong retains him as part of a longer lineage of those queers who felt pressured to remain closeted and struggled to express their sexualities. For Bong, this history binds him to movie stars other than Clift, such as Rock Hudson. On the cusp of adulthood at age seventeen, and just prior to the ending of Part 1, Bong makes one of his more direct pleas to Montgomery Clift: that he save Rock Hudson from AIDS (109). Obviously, Clift cannot honor Bong's request, betraying how Bong continually seeks an impossible intervention. In this case, Bong directly confronts the ways in which his queerness is informed by the 1980s AIDS crisis, as Hudson's death clarified the devastating reach of the virus. Bong's sentiment that he "believed [he] would disappear, vanish like Rock Hudson, like so many men in that period" (109) is understandable given the little information provided about viral transmission early in the epidemic. The anxiety surrounding Bong's queer sexuality is so acute that he does not even allow himself to ejaculate: "I'd wake up hard and throbbing, but I didn't release myself. If I didn't think about sex, I thought I wouldn't get AIDS" (109–110). Bong's denial of his sexual feelings, of course, is not exceptional. He further rationalizes his sexual frustrations in relation to Clift: "I knew he hid his sexuality, too. I think that is one of the reasons why I liked seeing Monty in his movies: he was hiding. He was visible to millions of people, but he hid. He made a part of himself disappear. I understood the importance of hiding" (110). Here Bong finally makes a clear-cut queer identification with Clift, one that any reader familiar with Clift's murky sexual background would have been expecting.

But Bong's "hiding" obviously operates in a vastly different way than Clift's. Bong's queer desires are inextricably linked with the possibility of death, the fate of "so many men in that period" (109). To explore his romantic feelings with anyone living would be to introduce the potential for viral transmission. This sentiment clarifies yet another way that Clift functions as a surrogate for Bong, the ultimate form of the safe-sex partner. Bong inherits this genealogy of queer death, both in metaphorical and literal forms, as many queer actors (and performers) "hid" their feelings and later succumbed to the devastating effects of the AIDS virus.[40] By calling out to Clift in the epilogue, Bong honors the many contours of the inscrutable belongings that originate from his love of the cinema, cohering dead film stars such as Rock Hudson and Montgomery Clift with Asian North American film industry professionals such as Amada and Logan. Ultimately, in forming and bringing together these various inscrutable belongings, Bong resolves his survival plot.

CHAPTER 5

INSCRUTABLE BELONGINGS IN HUNTING

INTERRACIAL SURROGACIES

IN NINA REVOYR'S *WINGSHOOTERS*

THROUGHOUT THIS BOOK, I have focused on the queer Asian North American storyteller, who materializes through a form of discursive visibility that operates to defy his or her social standing as a sexual and racial outcast. The previous three chapters provided three complex, yet interconnected variations on this figure. One central question motivates me throughout all of my readings: What does it mean for this storyteller to last to the narrative's ending, even when that trajectory is undermined by his or her status as a character whose recognition is obscured by forms of social death and material violence? As I move further into the body of this book, the insidious ways in which the storyteller's life is endangered by both structural and material forces become increasingly apparent. To work through the traumas that arise from sexual predators and child abusers, while engaging their livelihoods as sexual and racial minorities, the protagonist-narrators from Leong's "Camouflage" (Chapter 2), Chee's *Edinburgh* (Chapter 3), and Alumit's *Letters to Montgomery Clift* (Chapter 4) needed to construct what I call inscrutable belongings, dynamic social formations that challenge the dominant imaginary of the racially homogenous, middle-class, North American heteronuclear family. These transitory but indispensable communities enabled these storytellers to forge elective affinities among bathhouse patrons, AIDS sufferers, and dead Hollywood icons, and therefore to endure to the final page. But survival is by no means a simple triumph. Indeed, all of my previous readings show how these fictional publications conclude with incredible ambivalence, reminding us that queer

Asian North Americans have only journeyed so far and that the road to comprehensive inclusion remains elusive.

This chapter offers an extended analysis of Nina Revoyr's *Wingshooters*, a novel that reveals how form and social contexts, race and queer sexuality, and familial dynamics and fortitude are intimately intertwined. Many of the most crucial events of the novel take place during a tumultuous historical period: 1973, a time which saw substantial change in North America due to legislation focusing on diversity and multiculturalism and incredible cultural shifts that illuminated the deep need for more social equality, especially for racial minorities. This chapter naturally progresses this book because the survival plots and associated narrative developments are getting longer. Because this novel involves a small midwestern town, it also requires a distinctive regionalist analysis, taking into account its agricultural industries and hunting cultures.

I am further interested in the novel's depiction of the protoqueer Asian North American girl and how her livelihood is at risk. As with previous primary texts, the child's life is in mortal danger, but the reverberations of this endangerment are felt for many decades after. Yet this novel prompts a major pivot in this study, with its focus on a queer Asian North American woman necessitating analyses that take into account the importance of gender to the construct of the survival plot and associated inscrutable belongings.

Indeed, those prior works under analytical consideration—Leong's "Camouflage," Chee's *Edinburgh*, and Alumit's *Letters to Montgomery Clift*—all have been told from the perspective of a queer Asian North American storyteller who is male. In addition, one of the strongest thematic undercurrents tracking through these chapters has involved the motif of disease: the respective protagonists confront the specter of the AIDS crisis in one way or another. As a number of scholars note, the transmission of HIV has disproportionately affected queer and bisexual men (in both the United States and Canada),[1] and this asymmetry in part explains why themes of contagion and disease proliferation do not necessarily extend to fictions penned by queer Asian North American women.

In the last two chapters of this book, queer Asian North American women find themselves more intimately connected to romance plots and reproductive politics that arise in the guise of nation-state paradigms and issues. My earlier analyses of SKY Lee's *Disappearing Moon Cafe* (in the Introduction and in Chapter 1) already make apparent that the queer racialized female body is the site of tensions related to the maintenance of the heteronuclear family. As

I noted in that reading, an issue immediately arises in the reproductive future if the Asian North American female character identifies as queer precisely because the propagation of succeeding generations is put into jeopardy. If the family's future cannot be ensured, then any form of symbolic national inclusion is obviously impossible because there will be no heirs who would struggle to establish their livelihoods. To a certain extent, Kae Ying Woo, one narrator of *Disappearing Moon Cafe*, sidesteps this issue because she bears a child, but her possible romance with Hermia Chow already makes unstable the nature of their future family formation. Pivotally, she leaves Canada in pursuit of Hermia, who resides in Hong Kong. This transnational movement generates a larger question about the sustainability of the Chinese family.

In other novels centering on queer Asian North American women, such as the ones penned by Revoyr, same-sex romances do not involve the bearing of any children through biological means. These fictions interrogate whether or not there will be any descendants who will necessarily stake claims as citizen-subjects. In this sense, it is not surprising that queer Asian North American female fiction writers are perhaps more attuned to the ways in which storytellers are enmeshed in discourses related to reproductive politics, race, and nation-state dynamics. Despite what might seem to be a strong thematic dichotomy existing between fictional worlds penned by queer Asian North American men and women, I pause to note that the themes of disease and reproductive politics still resonate in synchronicity. While pathogenic transmission immediately suggests possible death and the discontinuation of a specific lineage, reproductive dynamics exist as the opposite side of the same coin concerning the attenuated genealogy of the queer Asian North American. That is, if the queer Asian North American woman cannot be expected to or chooses not to procreate through biological means, then a family line might ultimately be eliminated.

Wingshooters shifts this study by focusing on the racial, gender, and sexual dynamics that entangle the queer Asian North American woman in her survival plot, linking her personal livelihood with discourses related to the nation-state and normative social formations. In this chapter, I begin by introducing Revoyr's larger publication history, which draws out the indelible overlaps between racial difference and queer sexuality. Here I am centrally concerned with Revoyr's novels *The Necessary Hunger* and *Southland*, and how twinned plots in each work involve interracial relationships and doomed same-sex romances. The remainder of the chapter is devoted to my extended reading of *Wingshooters*, revealing how the survival plot can be jeopardized when two variants of inscrutable belongings function antagonistically. The novel ends with the narrator's sense of failure and draws out the incredible ambivalence found in all three of Revoyr's fictions concerning the queer Asian North American woman and her frustrated desires for family and romance. But I read against this negative affect in order to emphasize how her reproductive power metaphorically surfaces in the act of discursive resurrections: she brings back to life the alternative social formations endangered by the prejudicial cultures of a small midwestern town in the 1970s and configures this moment as a microcosmic reflection of larger national concerns over the maintenance of a white, heteronuclear family.

Plots of Romance, Race, and Queer Sexuality in Nina Revoyr's Fictions

Revoyr's *Wingshooters* is groundbreaking for the fact that it depicts a queer Asian North American woman, one who holds great import in her discursive position. But the centrality of this character must be placed in a greater context in order to accentuate why Revoyr's novel is so innovative. In this regard, one broader issue that surfaces in relation to queer Asian North American women is that they face a form of social obscurity that likewise haunts them in representational terrains. To be sure, invisibility is hardly a new trope associated with queer and same-sex female, or lesbian, desire (Castle 2).[2] Renée C. Hoogland contends, "Rendered invisible, indeed, 'unthinkable' within dominant grids of cultural intelligibility, lesbianism belongs to the unconscious abject of the Western imagination" ("Swallow" 472).[3] If and when queer sexuality does emerge in female characters, cultural critics such as Sherrie Inness and Lynda Hart reveal in their book-length studies, *The Lesbian Menace* and *Fatal Women*, respectively, that these women are seen as a destructive and deviant force, fit to be terminated from the story.[4] In addition, many creative writers and activists in the late 1970s and 1980s—most famously Barbara Smith, Cherríe Moraga, Gloria Anzaldúa, and Audre Lorde—have directly addressed this issue, articulating the varied challenges faced by queer women of color. The struggle to grant more representational space to queer women of color continues, as evidenced by Jewelle Gomez's assertion that "[t]he shadow of repression has concealed the Black Lesbian in literature in direct proportion to her invisibility in American society. Women of color, as a whole, have long been perceived as the least valuable component in our social and economic system . . ." (110). Scholars such as Kara Keeling, Sandra K. Soto, Catrióna Rueda

Esquibel, Matt Richardson, Linda Garber, Gayatri Gopinath, and Laura L. Sullivan ("Chasing") take up this issue of invisibility, bringing queer women of color into the forefront of academic research and theorizing the intersections of race, gender, and queer sexuality.

At the same time, the figure of the Asian North American woman has tended to be overlooked even with this increased focus on queer women of color. According to JeeYeun Lee, Asian North American women are represented as "hyperfeminine, submissive, eroticized objects of white heterosexual male desire. This 'heterosexualization' and the forces of femme invisibility and devaluation work to exclude us from the dominant visual definition of lesbians as butch and converge to make femme and feminine-looking Asian women especially invisible" (122). In other words, Lee points out that the Asian North American woman cannot be anything other than heterosexual, precisely because she is inscribed in the dominant imaginary as feminine and compliant to male attention.[5] Concurrently, this presumption makes out the Asian North American woman who presents herself as butch to be a kind of impossible anomaly. In either case, the queer Asian North American female is, according to Lee, invisible.[6]

I take the time to bear out these discourses because they illuminate the central dilemma for the queer Asian North American fiction writer, who must contend with this ghostliness in her publications.[7] For Revoyr, this issue becomes immediately evident because in many of her novels queer racialized characters or issues initially seem secondary to other plotting, narrative, and associated social concerns. But recalling my exegesis of tactical diversions in Chapter 1, I argue that these publications model the relationship between queer racialized characters and other individuals branded as outcasts. I engage very short readings of Revoyr's first two novels, which prefigure some of the themes and formal issues that will arise in *Wingshooters*. These analyses show how Revoyr's fictions diagnose the imperiled state of the queer Asian North American female character in the fictional world. The novels share some obvious thematic concerns with *Wingshooters*, but diverge in one significant way: they do not provide an explicit survival plotting in which a retrospectively situated narrator sequences her own endurance from youth to adulthood. Nevertheless, these novels remind us that discourses of LGBTQI equality are productively embedded in the dynamics of racial equality.

In Revoyr's debut, *The Necessary Hunger*, the novel revolves around the unfulfilled same-sex desires of its protagonist, Nancy Takahiro. Though she is obviously queer, her inability to express her feelings for a close African American friend, Raina, ends up becoming the source of a deep-seated regret. While Nancy fails to communicate her ardor openly, the narrative moves to other issues: her success in basketball and the sports rivalry that ensues because Nancy and Raina attend high schools in the same district. In conjunction with these storylines, Nancy's father, Wendell, and Raina's mother, Claudia, are in a romantic relationship, a pairing not necessarily supported by those in the local community. Claudia's closest friends and confidantes, for instance, find it questionable that Claudia is dating someone who is not African American. Thus, on the level of events that take place at the diegetic level, the novel is far more concerned with other conflicts: the basketball competitions and Wendell and Claudia's relationship take up more narrative space than any explicit depiction of queer sexual desire. This novel falls under what I outlined in the first chapter as the second mode of tactical diversion (protoqueer narratives), in which the novel provides us with a shortened trajectory based on a character who is legally a minor. In *The Necessary Hunger*, queer desire remains entirely within the frame of the imagination and is never directly acted upon at any point.

In Revoyr's second novel, *Southland*, the main character, Jackie Ishida, investigates the mysterious bequest left by her grandfather for a young African American boy. Revoyr makes use of a third-person perspective that moves historically, with chapters set in different eras in the twentieth century, helping to illuminate the interracial and interethnic dynamics of Japanese American and African American communities. Though readers eventually discover that Jackie is queer, the novel's central mystery concerning the unclaimed inheritance takes up most of the narrative space. This novel, with its many perspectives and temporal periods, exemplifies the third mode of tactical diversion (ensemble narratives), in which the queer Asian North American's position in the narrative exists in an uneven relationship to other characters, who often are more central to driving the plot forward.

My brief engagement of Nina Revoyr's earlier novels draws upon a methodological approach first begun in the work of the literary critic Terry Castle, who explores the conception of counterplotting in lesbian narrative.[8] In *The Apparitional Lesbian*, Castle argues, "This work of counterplotting can best be figured . . . as a kind of dismantling or displacement of the male homosocial triangle itself" (82), because the male romantic lead is effectively written out of the story. The limits of this intervention, though, exist in relation to the consideration of multiple axes of difference. What occurs when the queer woman is a minority? Does queer female counterplotting still function in a similar way, or do we have to account for other narrative and discursive perspectives?

To answer these questions, let us review some of the patterns that emerge in Revoyr's first two novels. In both novels, racial tensions seem to be central to the main conflicts in each plot, despite the fact that each narrative also involves a prominent queer Asian North American female character. These novels foreground racial difference at the expense of queer sexuality, but not because one mode of social marginality is of greater importance. Instead, each novel is informed by a temporal sequencing involving two variations on courtship plots: the endurance of a heterosexual romance marked as racially deviant (from an earlier generation) later comes to affect the development of a same-sex relationship (from a descending generation). That is, in Revoyr's first novel, the tenuousness of the interracial, heterosexual relationship between Wendell and Claudia gestures to the obviously unstable grounds upon which a queer, interracial relationship between Nancy and Raina would be set. Though Nancy's retrospective narration reveals her deep feelings for Raina, it remains unmentioned whether or not Nancy would go on to have any same-sex romances as an adult. In this sense, queer desire remains a potential horizon that is gestured to, but not explicitly engaged.

In *Southland*, as Jackie eventually discovers, her grandfather once was embroiled in an interracial, heterosexual romance with an African American woman who bore him a son; that son tragically dies in the Watts Riots. The socially unacceptable nature of their interracial affair leads to its demise, and as Jackie determines, the bequest is an outdated inheritance that would have been given to a boy who has been long since dead. The impossibility of sustaining the romance between a Japanese American man and an African American woman in the years leading up to the Watts Riots again prefigures the challenges facing a similarly situated interracial and interethnic relationship from a queer perspective. Importantly, over the course of Jackie's unofficial investigation, her relationship with her white girlfriend, Laura, dissolves. The conclusion of this novel leaves Jackie unattached, even as another romance seems to be brewing between Jackie and a fellow law student named Rebecca Nakanishi. Even though queer relationships are not given the most attention in the narrative space, their importance unfolds in conjunction with racial tension and unrest. In both novels, the issue of racial disharmony as it occurs in the shadow of a heterosexual relationship is sequenced so that it appears as the unstable model by which a later queer relationship is compared. In addition, in both novels, the plot's resolution leaves the queer Asian North American woman without an explicit romantic partner. Such a conclusion, I argue, is evidence of the challenges still remaining for the queer Asian North American woman's integration at both local (for example, familial) and national levels. In this sense, Revoyr's fictions must be read not only with an attentive eye with respect to racial and sexual difference, but also with an awareness of the fragility of the queer Asian North American woman's ability to foment a sense of community beyond the home space.

Upon Retrospection

Nina Revoyr's earlier novels illuminate how racial and sexual difference are always linked and mutually informed in the fictional world and through generationally sequenced courtship plots. Following this representational genealogy aligning race and queerness, I read Revoyr's *Wingshooters*, the novel to which the rest of this chapter is devoted. To begin my extended analysis, I offer a brief plot description. The novel is told retrospectively through the first-person voice of Michelle LeBeau, nicknamed Mike, who tells a tale of her life as an eight-year-old child growing up in Wisconsin.[9] We do not know the age of the adult narrator at the time she recounts the story, nor do we know for certain what year this telling is taking place (the novel's conclusion suggests the year is somewhere close to 2011). We do know that Michelle is eight years old in 1974, and she has just been dropped off at her grandparents' place in Deerhorn, a small Wisconsin town, where her status as a biracial child, Asian and white, becomes a source of contention. Her paternal grandparents, Charlie and Helen, never really approved of the interracial romance between their son, Stewart, and his wife, Reiko Tanizaki. Stewart and Reiko raise Michelle for a number of years in Tokyo. Amid marital troubles, Reiko leaves alone for America, only to have Stewart and Michelle follow. Stewart leaves Michelle in Wisconsin with his parents while he travels to California in the hope of reconciling with Reiko. At that point the novel opens, and Michelle is making the difficult adjustment to small-town midwestern life.

When an African American couple moves to Deerhorn, racial tensions quickly mount. Mr. Garrett teaches at the local elementary school Michelle attends; Mrs. Garrett works as a nurse and also operates a free health clinic designated to help the area's rural poor. That the Garretts are the only black inhabitants of Deerhorn is trying enough for the townspeople, but they further incite controversy when they are suspected to have reported Earl Watson, a well-known resident, to the authorities for the physical abuse of his son, Kevin. Though the police question Earl, he is not arrested. Amid reports of more conflict in the home, Earl is taken to jail. Earl, harboring openly racist views, believes the Garretts are the impetus behind his arrest. Readers come to learn otherwise: the official booking occurs after a phone call from an undisclosed party. Earl's assumption leads to the climax of the novel: after he is bailed out of jail, a neighbor spots him taking Mrs. Garrett hostage. The town rallies to find out where Earl has gone with Mrs. Garrett. Michelle, helping her grandfather look for Earl, comes upon Earl in a rural clearing. Michelle had brought along the family dog, Brett, who Earl ends up killing. Later, when Charlie comes upon Michelle and Earl, he shoots Earl, fearing that Michelle may be in danger. Before his death, Earl reveals that he has killed Mrs. Garrett and that she had been pregnant. The novel's retrospective narration ends here, and the concluding chapter shifts toward Michelle's present life as an adult. At this point, she reveals her desire to reflect upon the events of her tumultuous childhood. It is also in these last pages that Michelle details her failed romantic relationship with a woman.

Upon first glance, *Wingshooters* is difficult to frame within a queer of color lens. The novel references Michelle's same-sex romance in only one paragraph at the story's conclusion, and much of the narrative is focused on the Garretts and their violent expulsion from Deerhorn. In this sense, as I mentioned earlier, the novel is not unlike Revoyr's earlier works *The Necessary Hunger* and *Southland*, in which the queerness of the Asian North American female protagonist seems secondary to other plotting and narrative issues. At the same time, the novel presents us with some unique elements, especially given the fact that the protagonist does indeed survive to reach adulthood and to tell her story in retrospective fashion, providing us with a chance to analyze what I have called a survival plot.

But what motivates Michelle to share her traumatic past? Certainly part of her desire to recount these events stems from guilt. In some ways, Michelle believes she had an indirect hand in the deaths of her dog, Brett, Mrs. Garrett, and her grandfather, who would later succumb to a heart condition that Michelle believes was brought on by what happened that fateful day in the woods. As the queer Asian North American storyteller, Michelle reveals that she suffers lasting psychic injuries despite her ability to move through a survival plot. She is hardened by her experiences and does not find complete absolution in her adult life, which takes her to Los Angeles to work with at-risk youth. As we discover, giving back to "troubled kids" (245) gives her only a brief respite from her pain. Despite Michelle's rather pessimistic viewpoint and the obvious sense of loss that pervades her daily life, I do not accept her defeatism precisely because the novel leaves me to wonder why the story would be even worth telling if it is so steeped in the narrator's sense of failure.[10] Here I read the narrative "reparatively" (Sedgwick 146) to make sense of Michelle's emotional state when she reaches adulthood and to reconsider the revolutionary import of her ability to disseminate this story in the first place.

Inscrutable Belongings in Hunting

Throughout this book, my conception of inscrutable belongings has been influenced by theories of alternative families and social formations. I rehearse some of the major strains here in order to emphasize how this chapter invokes these discourses and associated arguments. For example, classic studies by Sylvia Junko Yanagisako, on Japanese American communities, and Kath Weston, on gay and lesbian networks, demonstrate how American kinship can deviate from more normative conceptions of the white heteronuclear family.[11] In addition, scholars such as Eleana Kim ("Our Adoptee") and Kristi Brian reveal how the process of transracial adoption necessitates the formation of dynamic family structures.[12] Adoptees often create their own communities, as they work together to find birth families and provide each other with emotional and psychic support through the process of navigating both biological and adoptive family ties. One connecting element among these diverse studies is the attention to defining kin beyond genealogical models that privilege biology over elective social relationships. Further still, many of these scholars explore communities and minority groups that historically have faced systematic disempowerment. Collective experiences related to oppression and displacement can cement the affective and material bonds of these alternative kinships. But my work deepens these existing theories of alternative kinship by identifying variations on such aggregations, or inscrutable belongings, as they arise in queer Asian North American fictions.

This novel distinguishes itself from those studied in the previous chapters because *Wingshooters* focuses more firmly on generating a lineage between racialized queerness and racialized heterosexuality. At stake, then, is the way that Michelle's retrospection offers up a metaphorical form of kinship, one that effectively marks the Garretts as Michelle's symbolic progenitors. Michelle constructs what I call *interracial surrogacies* with the Garretts, not only instituting them as nonbiological parental figures but also more broadly linking racial oppressions experienced by minorities in America at that historical juncture. While the term *surrogate* has been most often understood in relation to modes of reproduction involving a third party (such as the use of a sperm donor for same-sex female couples), I broaden this word in order to convey nonbiological intergenerational affiliations that I would argue are still reproductive in the sense that they call for the construction of coalitions based on social difference. The unexpected bonds that Michelle holds with the Garretts provide her with the tools to later understand the conditions that made their collective endurance so precipitous.

The interracial surrogacies Michelle develops with the Garretts are juxtaposed with her attachments to her biological family, especially her affinity to Charlie LeBeau, her grandfather. Michelle's relationship with him enables her to claim a place, however shaky, within the Deerhorn community. This biologically based lineage is itself repositioned through Michelle's narrative with respect to the local agrarian community and a collective of sport hunters. Here Michelle understands that these outdoor enthusiasts offer another variation of an inscrutable belonging and a sense of companionship in which her mixed-race background does not seem to matter.[13] She in fact finds this fellowship one that upends traditional gender paradigms, while it simultaneously cultivates interspecies kinships. As Deerhorn experiences economic stagnation, the community of hunters also retains the small town's close-knit cultural ethos by attempting to preserve their claims to the land.

The germination of these idiosyncratic assemblages, of course, comes with potential risks, as those who violate social norms can be deemed threatening. In *Wingshooters*, Michelle participates in inscrutable belongings that bring together racial minorities who are sexually defined as deviant with white hunters who occasionally flout normative gender roles. In each of these ephemeral groupings, Michelle perceives the life of someone who arguably could be defined as a stranger to be intimately intertwined with and tied to her own survival plot, despite the lack of a traditional biological bond.

Wingshooters manifests two inscrutable belongings that conflict in ways that result in their dual destruction. Michelle's survival plot is so ambivalently portrayed precisely because it is brokered upon the categorical termination of these two dynamic yet transitory social formations. The novel's conclusion, in its heavy sense of resignation and loss, clearly situates the not-yet-possible union of these communities. Thinking of kinship beyond biological blood ties further allows us to see the protoqueer Asian North American child as part of a larger character-system in which family bonds are brutally refashioned through the effects of powerful social dynamics that render racial minorities—and by extension, queer subjects—as expendable from the narrative plotting.

But Michelle's narration establishes another achievement: as she is directed to look back at her life, to make sense of a tragic event and time period, the readers are invited to participate in the same process. In this respect, I follow Judith Butler's point that "a more radical social transformation is precisely at stake when we refuse, for instance, to allow kinship to become reducible to 'family,' or when we refuse to allow the field of sexuality to become gauged against the marriage form" ("Is Kinship" 39). My reading undercuts Michelle's melancholic sentiments only insofar as I argue that her narration, however belatedly and retrospectively, attempts to help us understand what "radical social transformation" could occur. Though the queer Asian North American woman's social death cannot be overcome, we see that Michelle's physical survival offers her a chance to tell a story concerning the past as a gesture to as-yet-unrealized futures. Accordingly, I now advance extended critiques of the novel's portrayal of Michelle's two inscrutable belongings and how her survival plot is destabilized once these divergent communities must come into contact with each other. In the final arc, I probe how, despite Michelle's sense of failure, we can reorient the novel's last pages through the subtle ways that our storyteller retains her investment in other inscrutable belongings.

Racial and Sexual Deviance

Looking back from her adult perspective, Michelle is disillusioned by her grandfather's inability to understand the value of the Garretts as members of the Deerhorn community. The novel itself is an incredible document that archives exactly how they were not "incidental" (241) to Michelle's life. In the process of focusing on this couple, Michelle's narration reminds us of the ways that sexuality and race must be read and analyzed intersectionally. In this sense, though her queer racialized desire does not initially seem a central concern, her adult perspectives as a queer Asian North American woman come to influence how we comprehend Michelle's experiences as an eight-year-old child. As a racial minority and a queer woman from an agrarian, rural upbringing, Michelle is a storyteller who imbues the fictional world with an attentiveness to the multidimensional nature of social inequality. Her retrospection immediately draws out how social differences of any kind—race and sexuality—become forces that destabilize the survival plot.

Not surprisingly, *Wingshooters* explores the tensions raised by interracial relationships. For example, the pairing between Michelle's parents is not supported by her paternal grandparents or by the Deerhorn populace at large. Helen attempts to talk Stewart out of marrying Reiko (4), and Charlie later refuses to attend Stewart's wedding (5). As Michelle puts it, "There was no way Charlie LeBeau would ever accept a foreigner into his family, and although he did finally meet my mother when my parents visited Deerhorn, he didn't smile for her or turn on his charm" (18). Michelle's presence in Deerhorn is not only received as unwelcome racial difference, but also situated as the product of a socially unacceptable sexual union: "And I was just as alien to the people of Deerhorn as they were to me. They'd been scandalized by my father's marriage—for many of them, my mother was the first non-Caucasian person they'd ever laid eyes on—and now, in their minds, by bringing me back, he was inflicting on them the terrible fruit of his sins" (22). That Michelle likens herself to an otherworldly being and a religious monstrosity reveals how interracial romance is regarded with open hostility. Michelle's observations are corroborated by the way she is treated by her classmates and by her grandparents' neighbors. At one point, two students call her father a "Jap-lover" (35) and her mother a "geisha whore," (35), and later, a neighbor calls her a "half-breed" who possesses "dirty yellow blood" (87). In these instances, her racial difference echoes alongside the transgressive sexuality epitomized by her parents' interracial relationship. In this sense, the novel follows the articulations of queer theorist Ian Barnard, who asserts, "[S]exuality is always racially marked, as every racial marking is always imbued with a specific sexuality (gender, class, and other classificatory inscriptions are equally determined and determining)" (2). If there is a form of queerness obliquely disclosed through Michelle's standpoint, then it manifests as racial difference coupled with sexual deviance.[14]

Queer of color and queer diasporic critical practices further enable us to unmask the intricacies of Michelle's childhood. On the one hand, her mother, Reiko, is rendered through a queer diasporic framework once she is considered "a geisha whore." Her sexuality functions through a transnational dynamic that must be demarcated as irreducibly foreign, despite the fact that she is fluent in English. The attraction and repulsion to the Japanese Other is made evident precisely because Reiko attains multiple significations. While she is in Japan, her language skills offer her a form of transnational capital, especially as tourists and American businessmen seek to employ her as a translator and tutor. But once she is married to an American man, she apparently then is imbued with sexual perversity. On the other hand, once Michelle's mixed-race background is unveiled, she cannot escape the possibility that she will be read as impure. In this sense, queer diasporic and queer of color reading practices attend to the way that race and sexuality mutually constitute Michelle's radical social difference through national and transnational frameworks.

Alongside the unwelcome hybridity that Michelle embodies, the presence of the Garretts generates more prejudicial perspectives. One of the first descriptions of the Garretts places them in a community configured on white racial homogeneity: "A black couple had moved to Deerhorn, a town that, before my own arrival the year before, had never been home to a soul who wasn't white. In that town, in 1974, this was as dramatic and inconceivable as deer starting to speak or a flock of ducks flying backwards" (38). Notably, the Garretts are immediately described as a "black couple," challenging normative conceptions of Deerhorn's nuclear family. Again, this marital union is characterized by its debasement, as their presence is made grotesque in its comparison to mutant animals. Michelle traces some of the townfolks' stereotypical understandings of African Americans soon after this point, observing that "blacks, they believed, were lazy and ignorant, and if any one Negro had not run afoul of the law, it would only be a matter of time before he succumbed to his basic nature and robbed a house or assaulted a woman" (38). Still later, Michelle relates that "the only black men who were respected were athletes—Dave May of the Brewers, MacArthur Lane of the Packers. But even they were only acceptable in their prescribed public roles—as sports heroes removed from everyday life" (39). In these examples, Michelle outlines the polarized sexual conceptions of the black man, who is seen to be either a rape threat or an athlete fit to entertain the American public as a sports professional. The queerness of the Garretts emerges in the very fact of their seemingly upper-middle-class marriage—their occupations as teacher and as nurse alongside their blackness strike anomalously, evidence of a transgressive heterosexual power base altering the racial makeup of Deerhorn domestic life. Their respectability undermines racial stereotypes, but this very shift in character affirms a different yet equally problematic abnormality: their marital stability and professional occupations together gesture to a mode of racial ascension that connote their status as usurpers.

The Garretts thus signal a union that is toxic to the verdant Deerhorn landscape. In this sense, Revoyr's novel is undoubtedly influenced by a regionalist impulse concerning both the cultural identity and the representation of the Midwest. According to William Barillas, the Midwest has been depicted through images of "farms, bucolic woods and streams, and small towns populated by plain-speaking upright citizens" (4). This paradigm, variously called the "pastoral myth" (Barillas 4) and "garden myth" (Weber 22), possesses a racial genealogy, as noted by Andrew R. L. Cayton and Peter S. Onuf: "At the beginning of the twentieth century, a great many people continued to insist that the typical American was the white, middle-class, Republican businessman in a small town in the Midwest" (122).[15] The attempt to cling to a racially homogenous, pastoral past is evident in Revoyr's novel, even despite the presence of industries such as meatpacking and food-processing plants essential to the Deerhorn economy.[16] The development of factory-type work, though certainly far from the agricultural foundations of the town, remains acceptable insofar as these occupations help support existing economic structures. As Michelle notes, the problem originates with the rise of large-scale commercial capitalism and other macroeconomic shifts that, for many of the residents, signal the end of Deerhorn's local roots: "Family farms that had existed for several generations were being squeezed out by the big industrial operations, or, more mundanely, losing their children to cities and towns and simply fading out" (63–64). This passage reveals Michelle's understanding of the small-town family ethos, one in which the future of the white heteronuclear family seems questionable given the apparent economic changes. As children leave the area, the implication is, of course, that undesirable figures are moving in to take their places, especially those of unwanted racial backgrounds. Furthermore, as Michelle narrates at the beginning of the novel, the expansion of the local clinic brings with it town resentments: "A big clinic meant outsiders coming through in order to get medical care. It also meant newcomers—clinic staff, technicians, tie-wearing administrators—who didn't fit with the town's blue-collar sensibilities. And it was the clinic that was responsible for what happened to the town and my family, that fall and winter of 1974. Had I been the only change the town had to adjust to, it would only have been me who paid the price" (25). Here Michelle reintroduces her orientation to the Garretts, as she understands that she, too, would be perceived as an encroachment on small-town life, but the clinic and its connection to the Garretts serve as more flagrant intrusions to Deerhorn. To a certain extent, the arrival of the Garretts overshadows Michelle's perceived racial abnormalities precisely because she is Charlie's biological kin, whereas the Garretts signify something unequivocally alien. As these passages show, the Garretts are read by many of the townsfolk as contaminants, corrupting the local land, its basic family structures, and its pastoral capital.[17]

Michelle's perspective helps clarify how race and sexuality both become markers of social difference that endanger one's livelihood. She and the Garretts signify as forms of contagion, pathogenic agents that bring to mind my reading of Chee's novel Edinburgh from Chapter 3. But recall that I show how, in *Edinburgh*, figurations of disease and monstrosity are reformulated as part of infectious genealogies that bind the queer Asian North American productively to a larger community that helps enable his long-term survival. In a similar manner, Michelle intervenes into discourses of race, place, and deviant sexuality by reorienting the lens of social difference. When Michelle first encounters Mr. Garrett at school, she describes him this way: "He was the brown of dark chocolate, a lush earth-brown, and the loose-shouldered way he carried himself suggested that he was friendly. What struck me most, besides the darkness, was that he was wearing a jacket and tie, which was more formal than what the rest of the teachers wore" (56–57). Certainly Mr. Garrett does not conform to the image expected by Michelle's adult counterparts, who might see him as a predatory figure, "lazy and ignorant" (38). Defying the whiteness undergirding the midwestern pastoral trope, Michelle resolutely claims Mr. Garrett as part of the land, through his "lush earth-brown" color, a hue that commands fecundity. Michelle moreover frames Mr. Garrett as someone fit to be a romantic lead: "And then I saw his face—the broad cheeks and strong jaw, the warm brown eyes, the hair cut almost military short. And I remember thinking, because I didn't understand white people yet, especially white men, that Mr. Garrett's good looks and physical impressiveness would make people like him better" (57). The point that Michelle "didn't understand white people yet" reminds us that this story is being actively revised in light of reflections she can give as an adult. Mr. Garrett is threatening not simply because he is a racial Other, but also because he is someone who is committed to his positions as role model and as teacher. Michelle's gaze can be described as non-normative—at least with respect to others in Deerhorn—insofar as it unmasks the ways that Mr. Garrett could be seen as both an attractive and a repulsive force for the community. Mr. Garrett dares to be just like what the white individuals in town value and emulate in their daily lives: friendly and well-mannered, a potential father, husband, or, if he were single, a suitor to women. Unfortunately, he just happens to be African American.

If Mr. Garrett is seen to be a suitable exemplar of the Deerhorn family man, despite his racial background, Michelle also offers us this progressive viewpoint of his marriage. At one point, Michelle comes upon the Garretts at the grocery store, where they look every bit the happy married couple: "I stood and watched them as he poked her like a teenage boy trying to get a girl's attention—and it was hard to believe that these two people, this playful man and his dignified wife, had thrown the town into such frenzy" (94–95). We must read this passage not only in relation to the Garretts' racial difference, but also their sexual significance. Here Michelle describes them as a couple very much in love, almost in a courtship phase. That they are showing such affection in a public space, of course, is potentially dangerous given how their fondness for each other might strike other locals as a transgressive act, as they place the weight of their romance on equal footing with any other townsfolk. Like Mr. Garrett, Mrs. Garrett is also depicted in terms that make her out to be charismatic: "She had strong, high cheekbones and slightly hollowed cheeks that were so polished and smooth they might have been carved of stone. There was something in her bearing and the set of her shoulders that made her look regal, even there in the freezer aisle. She was wearing a neat blue dress and carrying a handbag, as if they'd just come from church" (94). Words such as *regal* and *polished* designate Mrs. Garrett as an individual with a distinguished class bearing, someone that Michelle would admire. At the same time, the parenthetical thought process that follows this moment disrupts this fleeting and playful moment between the couple: "(And now I wonder—*had* they been at church? Did they drive up to Wausau or all the way to Steven's Point to find a community of other black congregants? Because they couldn't have worshipped in Deerhorn, of course. No local church would have had them.)" (94, emphasis original). The adult Michelle interrupts the narrative to reflect upon the fact that the Garretts, even on their idyllic Sunday grocery store trip, would have had to travel somewhere else simply to worship. Their love and their marriage are only minimally tolerated, but it is Michelle's gaze that astutely magnifies how alarming the model of their racialized romance might be.

The scene in the grocery store is especially pivotal to the construction of a tenuous inscrutable belonging precisely because the Garretts welcome Michelle by speaking with her in public, trying to coax her into conversation and, later still, helping her to find a grocery item she is looking for. But Michelle finds herself tongue-tied: "I couldn't get anything out of my mouth—it was like the muscles in my throat had cramped up—so I gestured toward the ice cream.

I took a few steps forward, opened the freezer door, and pulled out a frost-covered carton. It was strawberry, just like theirs" (95). Michelle later reflects on this moment: "I'd seen the Garretts, both of them. And they'd been nice to me. And they'd excused or overlooked my inability to speak, my awkwardness in their presence. I felt like I'd been in on a secret, and I knew instinctively that I couldn't tell my grandparents about it, or anyone at school. But something important had happened; I felt like part of something" (96). Her speculations over this chance meeting reframe her relationship to the Garretts as one of alliance. Given her classroom experiences and her sense of alien-ness from her peers, Michelle finds that the Garretts can be trusted, even liked. In this sense, her positive emotions toward them become something of a "secret," a moment of closeting precisely because she consciously goes against what she perceives as Deerhorn's social norms. In this process, she begins to imagine how she can be "part of something" other than her biological family unit, that the Garretts might factor in as part of what I earlier called interracial surrogacies.

Accordingly, the scene in the store is further notable for the way it registers these three characters as a collective. Given Michelle's age, they could be read as something akin to a nuclear family unit, with two parents and one child, perhaps going grocery shopping on any average Sunday. Naturally, the fact that Michelle's choice for ice cream perfectly mirrors the Garretts' creates the ideal familial fantasy: that they all might eventually enjoy the same flavor together during a dessert course, a form of gastronomic synchronicity that would have been a great comfort to this young child. Hence, we further see the importance of this couple to Michelle: the Garretts become momentary guardians. They serve, however ephemerally, as stand-ins for the parents who are not physically present with her, and they also model—as racial minorities—the possibility of romantic and professional futures she might herself attain. In this case, the fantasy of the nuclear family appears across racial lines and also violates the regime of blood relations, as Michelle obviously does not possess any common ancestry with the Garretts. It is the power and the potential of these interracial surrogate bonds that drives so much of Michelle's melancholy later as an adult.

In one of the most tender scenes of the novel, Mrs. Garrett attends to a minor surface wound Michelle has incurred while she bicycled out to the free clinic; she then carries Michelle inside to treat her: "Mrs. Garrett had one arm under my legs and the other beneath my back; my arms were around her neck for support. I remember being surprised that such a slight-looking woman could handle my weight so easily. And as I became aware of her thin shoulders, her strong hands, even the press of her breasts, I remember thinking that I couldn't recall the last time a woman had held me" (186). This memory reveals the ways in which Michelle's physical connection as a child to other women has been severely limited. Indeed, we recall that her mother by this time has abandoned her, and her grandmother shows a sense of reserve that stands in stark contrast to the way that Mrs. Garrett treats her here. This passage focuses on Mrs. Garrett's body, attending to the importance of the physical contact that implies a familial intimacy. We should pause on the use of the word *even* in relation to the "press of [Mrs. Garrett's] breasts." Though obviously not used with sexual connotations, Michelle remarks on Mrs. Garrett's breasts to frame the importance of her as a figure who could be looked upon as a surrogate mother. Not surprisingly, after a conversation discussing some of the tense issues boiling up in the community, the two embrace: "Then Mrs. Garrett stood up, crossed the room, and put her arms around me, holding me as she stood beside the table. My shoulder was against her stomach and I turned to her and cried, and it was Kevin, but it was Charlie too, and also my parents, because they had left me and I knew that they were never coming back" (190). In the space of Mrs. Garrett's physical body, Michelle articulates her many identifications that move beyond the heteronuclear family. First, she identifies with Kevin Watson, who like her, is a child who has been neglected by biological parents. Second, she understands how Charlie has come to function as her primary caregiver in the absence of her parents and that she cannot expect to have a normative family life.

With her physical embrace of Mrs. Garrett, Michelle releases some of the pent-up emotional turmoil regarding her feelings of familial disruption. The primary inscrutable belonging that the novel promotes here is one comprising a metaphorical genealogy of subjects labeled as deviant because of racial and sexual differences. The Garretts become the perfect surrogate parental figures precisely because their marriage and their blackness undermine the white heteronuclear family that is the Deerhorn norm. Michelle, as a biracial child, also stands as the physical embodiment of an unwelcome form of miscegenation. Crucially, their collective status as outsiders determines this elective social structure. But beyond this link, the Garretts do serve as powerful exemplars for Michelle in their occupational roles that stand to protect and to educate others. They are figures that command her respect. Further still, the Garretts, however brief their physical encounters with Michelle actually are, provide her with a moment of mutually constitutive recognition. In other words, Michelle is not seen as a contaminated entity in the eyes of the Garretts; they welcome the chance to engage in dialogue with her (57, 95) and comfort her when she is injured (190). The Garretts provide emotional and psychosocial support, however transitory, and thus enable the ephemeral emergence of this alternative kinship.

Though so much of the town frames the Garretts as a deviant couple, their marriage offers Michelle a site to reimagine the ways in which racial minorities might very well script reproductive, romantic, and professional futures. As a child, Michelle can believe that she lives in a town where her social difference will not entirely mark her as an outcast, but as an adult, she admits, "I *will never know who* they were beyond my limited perceptions, and in *not knowing*, I realize that my picture of them will always be incomplete. It's a picture I've burnished to an improbable sheen because I knew them when I was a child, because they were good to me, and because I see them through the lens of time and sadness" (185, emphasis mine). Looking back, Michelle fully realizes how important the Garretts were to an ideal she had concocted, but regardless of these "limited perceptions," she demonstrates exactly how indispensable they were to her. In this way, the Garretts shift out of the realm of being incidental figures and are recast as figures of great significance. Even as the Garretts are written out of their own survival plot, the dynamics that make their relationship untenable in Deerhorn are central to Michelle's later life, especially in her own faulty bid to engage in a same-sex romance. The Garretts model the possibility *and* the fragility of visibly pursuing romance and desire when one is considered a pariah.

Hunting Community

While Michelle is reevaluating her experience as a child, the readers also initiate this process. My critical practice operates to establish the bounds of other important social formations, showing how she, as well as the Garretts, complicate the conceptions of kinship, sexuality, and racial purity in one rural midwestern town. Michelle's recounting pinpoints how forms of difference brand certain individuals as aberrant. As she shows us how the Garretts threaten the racial harmony of Deerhorn, we see how their lives are very much intertwined with her own survival plot. Even as Michelle develops an inscrutable belonging through interracial surrogacies, she simultaneously narrates a form of communal integration involving another critical aspect of Deerhorn culture.

Thus I turn to another way in which the novel depicts how Michelle comes to formulate adjacent inscrutable belongings, ones involving a town invested in industry, farming, and hunting. Amid her occasional exchanges with the

Garretts, Michelle also interacts with a group of core characters, who find much meaning in the tracking and killing of game. As Michelle herself puts it, "By the age of eight, I knew how to shoot a gun. I could drive my grandparents' Pontiac, milk a cow, even operate a tractor if I had to, which I learned to do out on the old family farm still owned by my grandmother's brother" (103). Michelle's integration into the Deerhorn community requires her to master a set of tools—in this case, the gun, the car, and the tractor—that spotlight the largely rural, agrarian environment in which the novel is set. The centrality of the LeBeau lineage is made clear with respect to the property ownership of the "old family farm," and Michelle's fluency in the Deerhorn way of life signals her potential acceptance. Michelle further explains that the town's culture is one dominated by "blue collar sensibilities" (25), certainly embodied by her grandfather, who used to work in a shoe factory before he had retired. For Michelle, then, to be a part of Deerhorn means to take part in physical activity, in the form of manual labor on the farm or in the factory.

Essential to the novel's depiction of the town's values is the importance of hunting as a method by which communities come together. As Michelle recalls of her great-uncle, Pete Drexel: "Pete was my grandfather's usual hunting and fishing partner, a tall, easy-going man five years Charlie's junior who managed one of the cheese operations in town. Every weekend in the summer, we'd drive out to Pete and Bertha's place in the country, the men cooking ribs or venison over the large open grill while the women cut greens and made their mother's potato salad" (28). This depiction underscores how central the hunt is to the larger LeBeau clan, as the family breaks bread together and makes use of the game that is killed. This scene is also striking for the gender division, with the men being connected with the meat and the women taking on tasks passed down matrilineal lines. Beyond Charlie's blood relations, he comes to hunt with many other local men, including Earl Watson, Ray Davis, and Jim Riesling, who form the strong bonds of a sporting collective. In relation to such activities, Michelle's enthusiasm for hunting is conflicted: she describes being occasionally "taken hunting" with her grandfather and great-uncle "over the strenuous objection of [her] grandmother" (103). Her anomalous racial presence is mirrored by her unique status as a young female accomplice to the hunt. Her recounting in addition allows us to see how the novel redraws boundaries with respect to the killing of game.[18]

Michelle bonds with animals in ways that Charlie and his brethren might have found overly sentimental, but in doing so, she evolves the inscrutable belonging she creates through this hunting culture. Michelle's relationship to Charlie's dog, Brett, offers one explicit alteration to this collective, especially when they were once involved in the pursuit of prey: "When I arrived, Brett took to me right away—not because I had any special manner with dogs, but because I gave him attention. My grandfather was an old-fashioned owner of hunting dogs who believed that they were useful tools to flush and retrieve game, but otherwise belonged in the yard. I needed a companion, though, and couldn't have asked for a better one than Brett" (26). Michelle, in effect, repurposes Brett beyond his functional use as a hunting dog and institutes him as part of a human-animal family, thereby constructing a form of interspecies kinship.[19] The link between these two figures is clearly mapped in the novel; anytime Michelle is outdoors and in nature, it is in conjunction with Brett. At one point, Michelle reflects that she "belonged out here, where there were no other people, only the trees and lakes and rivers, and grazing animals" (61) and later adds, "Brett belonged here too, and out in the country in the fading light, I loved to watch him run" (61). For Michelle, hunting is just one aspect of the larger communion she imagines with the land, associated animals, and topographical features central to the area.

As a young girl involved with and knowledgeable about the local hunting culture, Michelle defies particular expectations of a more typical Deerhorn girl. It is perhaps not entirely surprising that she also sees the group of men engrossed in sport hunting through an idiosyncratic lens. About their love of hunting, Michelle recalls, "It was a heightened sense of excitement, the promise of possession and dominance, that I would have linked, had I been older, with the sexual. These men were never more alive than when they were just about to kill" (105). Certainly this moment reveals the homosocial bonding that occurs in the process of hunting, as it solidifies communal formations and reinforces their mutual goals.[20] This passage is the only time in the entire novel when the word *sexual* is used. For Michelle, this reflection is all the more singular because hunting is retrospectively defined in queer terms. That is, her older "self" ties sexuality to a non-normative desire, and by extension, she looks back on this moment as one defined by its queerness. Of course, this observation also associates queerness with a form of violent death, a voyeuristic gaze in which these Deerhorn men would watch something they had shot "struggle and die" (105), something that Michelle describes as "men at their purest, most primal state, the state of their highest fulfillment" (105). According to the philosopher Brian Luke, hunting can be described as sexualized ritual: "The pattern is that of a buildup and release of tension organized around the pursuit, phallic penetration, and erotic touching of a creature whom the hunter finds seductively appealing" (635). Luke clarifies this statement by asserting that hunting involves "a phallocentric sexuality. The weapon becomes an extension of the hunter's body and thereby the means by which he penetrates animal bodies . . ." (636). Luke's points provide a way to reconsider the white men of Deerhorn as a group who occasionally promote a metaphorical form of queer sexuality, though the tendency here is toward a destructive power that, without checks and balances, could become threatening.

As if bothered by the relationship between hunting and a predatory sexuality, Michelle retreats to reframe these men as individuals who offered her a different sense of family. She divulges, "there was more to those men than violence. They also had a warmth and openness that I never felt from women. In my family, it was the men who were the nurturers. They were the ones— my father included—who grinned widely when I did something funny, who bounced me on their knees, who ruffled my hair in affection" (105–106). This description of the Deerhorn men frames them through traits associated with maternity. Not only does this observation strike as a reversal in terms of gender norms, it also destabilizes the presumed heterosexuality undergirding motherhood. As fathers take the place of mothers, conceptions of reproduction become queer. For these Deerhorn men, hunting is a tradition that can be passed down from generation to generation; Michelle's inclusion in this community strikes as exceptional because it breaks the gendered restrictions that seemed to have been operating prior to that point. In this respect, Michelle not only reads this hunting collective as an alliance that fosters an alternative kinship, but also institutes another inscrutable belonging. For Michelle, whose own mother is absent (as is her father, largely), and who is raised by her grandparents, men like Charlie and Jim Riesling act in multiple roles that destabilize the heterosexuality assumed to form the core of the white American nuclear family that is the norm of 1970s Deerhorn culture. In addition, Michelle's rendering of this fellowship is based on situating the hunters through their maternal instincts and provides them with an unexpected connection to Mrs. Garrett, who as we have previously seen functions as a surrogate mother figure for Michelle. Her retrospective storytelling operates to bridge these seemingly unique, yet nevertheless adjacent inscrutable belongings.

Though hunting is so often associated with predation and killing, Michelle's perspective further clarifies the ethics that guide what is legitimate game.

While observing a flock of Canada geese, Michelle notes that her grandfather does not believe those birds fit for hunting: "'There's something about the idea of breaking up those families.' He smiled. 'Plus, they'll fight you, boy. They're not helpless little birdies'" (84). For Charlie and his collective, hunting follows a set of unspoken rules that in some ways preserve the possible futures of even those animals deemed as game. With respect to the most prized game—the buck—Charlie and his fellow sport hunters attempt to avoid killing does in the process: "I remember then one of my grandfather's steadfast rules: never hurt anything female" (147).[21] From a functional perspective, the special status of the does can be traced in part to the desire to keep game numbers up, as one male buck can impregnate multiple does (Marks 136; Willging 93). At the same time, the novel traces how this group is aware of the significance of animals within comparatively configured expressions of family and kinship. In other words, animals, both perceived as game or not, become refractive devices, as they allow Michelle and the hunters to meditate on the nature of social relations across species boundaries. The novel's representations of such unofficial regulations do follow in line with established ethnographic studies of hunters. Jan E. Dizard, for instance, explains that "hunting was a conscious choice borne, not of necessity, but of a desire for the experience of being an active and engaged participant in nature. The fact that this is a choice makes it necessary for hunters to do more than don the identity of predator. Killing may be normal, but *how one kills* is also crucial" (*Mortal Stakes* 129, emphasis original).[22] In the context of *Wingshooters*, the manner by which the hunter kills is understood as a pivotal part of this aggregation's codes of conduct. For Michelle, this respect for hunting allows her to understand the "somber" countenances of her grandfather and fellow hunters when they arrive back from one expedition having accidentally killed a doe in the process.

That Charlie and his fellow hunters do not intend to kill this doe also signals the obvious danger in their activities: unintended deaths can and will happen. Michelle herself is not given free rein to join the men; as she explains, "For deer, we would make our way deep into the woods, although not to the makeshift deer stand that Charlie and his friends had built; he would never take me to a place where we might run into other, less careful hunters" (104). In this respect, Michelle calls attention to the fact that—even in this alternative community in which she can defy gender and age expectations—the hunters must employ lethal force and, by virtue of this fact, possess the power to kill other human beings. Certainly Charlie's safety measures limiting Michelle's inclusion remind us that she herself can transform into game, and this passage in fact foreshadows the novel's later events. Thus to participate in the hunt is not only to operate by certain rules but also to understand the shared responsibility to keep group members safe. Following such rules, as Michelle notes, is a matter of life and death. Though it would seem that Michelle's own survival is not at stake when she is welcomed as part of this cadre, these policies indicate exactly how critical it is to operate by a set of baseline standards: they uphold ethical practices for killing nonhuman animals and ensure that humans do not become collateral damage. Despite the fact that this inscrutable belonging is in part conditioned upon the death of animals, their comradeship is dedicated to the propagation of vigorous cultural practices that extend intergenerationally and beyond family genealogies. Deerhorn's way of life is not only preserved but reproduced, a mode of parthenogenesis primarily involving men.

For Michelle, Deerhorn's sport hunting community offers her an inscrutable belonging that enables her to sidestep normative gender roles when she goes on these tracking expeditions. Further still, she reorients the stereotypical representations of hunters as inherently masculine figures, solely intent upon shoring up their power through the indiscriminate killing of animals. For these hunters, the companionship offered by their pursuit of game also extends to animals marked as prey. It is also in the rural spaces associated with the hunt that Michelle feels most at home: Deerhorn's landscape and its coterie of hunters afford Michelle the chance to believe, however briefly, that her social difference might still be accepted.

Not All in the Deerhorn Family

Though the novel imagines two alternative structures of social relations not solely based on biological bonds, those constructs become mutually exclusive. That these inscrutable belongings cannot find footing as a harmonious whole is attributable to the fact that blood relations that undergird the racially homogenous Deerhorn heteronuclear family exert the most powerful force within the novel. It is here that the novel's sequencing, that is, its plotting, takes on another level of significance. Michelle's observations reveal how the Garretts, who constitute one side of an inscrutable belonging, never appear in a sustained narrative frame alongside the community of hunters, individuals like Charlie and his compatriots who track and kill game. The plot takes on a zigzagging quality precisely because Michelle will make contact with the Garretts in one scene, but will find herself interacting with the hunters in another. In this sense, Michelle's survival plot illustrates how her two inscrutable belongings are unable to be narratively and thematically unified.

This inability to bring these alternative social formations together arises most conspicuously in the climax of Michelle's protoqueer childhood survival plot, as her life is put into mortal danger. As noted earlier, Earl Watson's custody of his son, Kevin, comes under question following claims of physical abuse; he blames the Garretts, even though they are not the ones to report the abuse that leads to his imprisonment. In one of the most violent scenes of the novel, Michelle comes upon Earl, who has just killed Mrs. Garrett (Mr. Garrett likely having been spared only because he was out of town visiting family). Michelle's life is obviously at stake, showing us the most tenuous moment in her ability to endure in the narrative. Charlie arrives soon after, hoping to diffuse the situation. Insidiously, Earl conveys a key piece of information regarding Mrs. Garrett: "Earl brought his arms together and covered the barrel of his gun with his hand, as if he was caressing it. 'It's only half done,' he answered. 'Only the female half.' And then the awful laugh again. 'She had one cooking, though, Charlie. She had one in the oven. She begged me not to kill her for the sake of the baby'" (225). This instance reminds us of Michelle's earlier description of hunting as a sexual activity, with Earl seemingly "caressing" his barrel here, as if in postcoital release. During this standoff, Earl also divulges that his custody of Kevin is in question and that his wife is leaving him. The Garretts thus come to be factored as the cause for the destruction of Earl's white heteronuclear family. If Earl cannot be with his wife and child, then—at least from Earl's perspective—the Garretts cannot be together, nor can they be allowed to procreate. The deaths of Mrs. Garrett and her unborn child signify the African American family as an aberrant kinship, one whose reproductive future must be terminated. By eliminating the Garretts, Earl serves simultaneously to shore up and to preserve the established Deerhorn familial order. Earl's crime also flagrantly upends the logics of the hunting rituals privileging particular lives over others. We recall that the preservation and safety of does is paramount, yet Mrs. Garrett, figured symbolically here as a kind of doe, is intentionally killed.[23] Earl's actions categorically abolish the potential intersection of two inscrutable belongings, one based on the integration of multiracial Others and the other founded upon the ethics of a local hunting community. When one of the Garretts and a hunter are brought into direct contact with each other a murder occurs, further signaling the perilous place of racial minorities in this fictional world.

If Earl seems intent on substituting the loss of his wife and child with the murder of the pregnant Mrs. Garrett, his mission remains undone. Indeed, as Michelle notes, "We all stood there in silence, taking in the horror of what [Earl had] just told us. 'I still have to find the buck, though,' he continued. 'You fellows want to help me?'" (225). The use of the term *buck* recalls the longer racial history in which African American men have been likened to male deer. As Lawrence M. Jackson notes, "Black men, in particular, approaching the concert stage had to cope with public perceptions of the 'Black Buck' or 'Coon' formed by the minstrel stereotypes of the 1800s. 'The Black Buck' was a racial slur used to describe a certain type of African American man. In particular, the caricature was used to describe black men who absolutely refused to bend to the law of white authority and were irredeemably violent" (76).[24] In *Wingshooters*, Earl's reference to Mr. Garrett as a "buck" can be read doubly. On the one hand, Earl draws upon the buck as a racial epithet, and on the other, Mr. Garrett is metaphorically related to the most prized game. In this process, Earl implies the subhuman status of Mr. Garrett's marriage and transforms Mr. Garrett into an animal that needs to be hunted. In an ethnographic study of deer hunting in central Pennsylvania, Simon J. Bronner explains the importance of hunting the buck: "In the drama of the hunt, configured as a male combat ritual between two physically imposing, and therefore sexually potent forces, the man needs to muster his phallic gun as the sign of prowess against the horned buck" ("Why We Hunt" 23–24).[25] Bronner's point applies as easily to the fictional town of Deerhorn as to Pennsylvania. After he loses his wife and son, Earl attempts to reclaim the potency of his white male heterosexuality by extending the hunt to Mr. Garrett.[26] Earl's willingness to kill the Garretts and his coded use of language demonstrate how hunting becomes a sexualized ritual in which racial hierarchies and sexual norms are reaffirmed. Scholars such as Tina Loo, Daniel Justin Herman, and others frame hunting as an activity used by white Americans to spotlight their mastery of the land and of nature.[27] In the context of the American South, Nicolas W. Proctor asserts that "the peculiarities of southern hunting owed a great deal to the existence of slavery. Part of its popularity arose from the fact that hunting was a particularly effective venue for the demonstration of white supremacy" (3). These scholars' perspectives extend to the novel's midwestern geographies, as the Garretts are framed through their threatening racialized sexuality, which must be vanquished to reinstitute the security of Earl's white heterosexual manhood and his claim to his nuclear family.

Earl's attempts to reassert his gendered, sexual, and racial power over the Garretts is, of course, also an extension of another preservation instinct related to the Deerhorn land. Indeed, if American sport hunting has part of its roots in plantation slave-owning, as scholars such as Scott E. Giltner and Proctor note, then the land becomes configured through a historical trajectory in which any African American presence must be maintained, regulated, and potentially expunged. Thus the queer racialized sexuality that enfolds the Garretts and stamps them as a baleful force polluting the local Deerhorn community is further compounded by their class status and the ways in which they bring with them the unwelcome prospect of social change. Earl's violation of the principles of hunting recasts the fluidity of human and animal relations that Michelle herself welcomes in her time as a young child, especially as he enforces a new regime in which the Garretts are prey. The pastoral impulse that largely grounds the early sections of this novel are catastrophically upended in this moment, as Earl's homicidal act destroys the proliferation of new social structures and reinforces long-existing social hierarchies and restrictive family formations.

Though Earl seems to desire recruiting both Michelle and Charlie into his fantasy of revenge, Michelle functions in a way similar to the Garretts: she is a mixed-race child, evidence of a sinister hybridity that is also fit to be exterminated. Michelle's beloved dog, Brett, is also killed in this scene, as he attempts to protect her from Earl's menacing posture. Brett's exit from the plotting is no less significant in this moment because he had offered Michelle another sense of family. Here Earl again violates the unspoken, assumed rules of his hunting community by killing an animal typically reserved to track and retrieve game. Later, Charlie, coming upon the clearing to find Brett dead, Earl's gun pointed at Michelle, and the body of Mrs. Garrett on the ground, fails to convince Earl to surrender his gun: "Now [Earl] turned in my direction. What I remember from his expression was that he didn't seem to see me. I was not a person to him, not a living thing, and I knew that he would kill me with as little concern as he'd shown for Brett and Mrs. Garrett. None of us were real to him" (228). Charlie must shoot and kill Earl to protect Michelle, but this passage continually emphasizes the equation that puts racial minorities and animals on a different plane of existence, not even "living things," as Mrs. Garrett, Brett, and Michelle are rendered as expendable and rearticulated as various forms of prey.

As Michelle pauses to reflect upon her experiences, she understands that her grandfather had cared for her, which he proved when he killed Earl in the clearing. Her survival plot is contingent here upon a biological family relation.

At the same time, her grandfather's regard for the Garretts is absent, even despite the fact of Mrs. Garrett's murder. Upon cradling Earl's dead body, Charlie states, "It wasn't worth it. Why'd you even have to let it get this far? Why'd you give everything up, for *this*?" (229, emphasis original). It is only later that Michelle is able to analyze what Charlie actually means in that moment: "But by what [Charlie] said to Earl's body in his moment of despair, it was clear that the Garretts weren't a part of it. He was not avenging them or defending them or punishing Earl; he didn't think about the Garretts at all" (240). Michelle adds that "for Charlie, the equation had been simple—his grandchild or his friend. That the Garretts were involved was incidental" (241). The problem with this logic, as Michelle points out, is that racial difference—and later, as an adult, we might add, sexual difference—links her and her mother with the Garretts. The moment in the clearing reveals the tenuousness of familial inclusion for Michelle, that her livelihood is dependent upon a blood connection made palatable only because she is partially white and therefore partially a LeBeau.

For Michelle, this event reorients her entire understanding of her childhood experiences. Most radically, the incident in the clearing encourages her to reconsider her own survival plot. If Mrs. Garrett was killed not only for her racial difference but also for how her blackness threatened the purity of white reproductive futures, so, too, is Michelle's life implicated. In other words, the Garretts were not "incidental" at all for Michelle; they are front and center precisely because she could have been in the same position. She could have been another murder victim, for the simple fact of a perceived racial perversity. In this way, she is a survivor, but one aware of the fragility of her survival. Consequently, we are not surprised when she admits, "And the child who lived in Deerhorn and was once a version of me is dead, or must be dead, in order for the grown-up to survive. In order for the grown-up to tolerate the life that her decisions have forever confined her to" (248). This perspective reveals how she believes that she had an indirect part in the murder of Mrs. Garrett and the death of her grandfather, while at the same time, part of her is "dead," the part that can be equated with someone like Mrs. Garrett. Her adulthood is predicated upon her knowledge of an asymmetrical yet collective form of both social and physiological death, as articulated in the ways that race, queer sexuality, and kinship can intertwine to produce such violence and brutality. Certainly Mrs. Garrett's physical death constitutes a fair share of Michelle's grief, but the novel simultaneously traces how Mrs. Garrett's marriage and her apparently aberrant kinship to Mr. Garrett are also socially unwelcome and therefore subject to termination. Michelle, too, by virtue of her mixed-race background, cannot escape the large shadow of social death, one that follows her into adulthood and is further compounded by her status as a queer woman.

The novel dispels Michelle's myth attached to her grandfather as her unadulterated hero and her protector. She reflects, "And [Charlie] left me with the harder knowledge that love is not enough; that it's those who love you the most who are most likely to hurt you, and whom you are most likely to betray" (249). Charlie never fully understands how traumatic the moment in the clearing was for his granddaughter, not simply because Michelle could have been shot by Earl and because her beloved dog was killed, but because love was contingent upon the coincidence of traditional familial kinship—that no love might have existed beyond those blood bonds once racial difference was factored in. The conclusion leaves Michelle wondering about whether or not Charlie could have ever cared for someone like her, if they had not been biologically related. Had she simply been a mixed-race child in danger from Earl's gun rather than Charlie's grandchild, Michelle leaves us to surmise, she would not necessarily have survived.

Given the horrendous circumstances surrounding Mrs. Garrett's murder, we are not surprised that Michelle holds such tortured feelings even decades after it has occurred (244–245). But the logic of blame that Michelle casts upon herself as a kind of peripheral perpetrator (in Mrs. Garrett's death and the eventual health decline of her grandfather) is deconstructed by her own attentiveness to the social contexts of 1974, a lens produced only by her reflections as an adult. In some ways, then, a critically engaged reading challenges Michelle's sense of culpability and brings us back to the centrality of the retrospective narration as presented to us by the queer Asian North American female storyteller. As Michelle recounts her experiences as a child, she helps revise how we understand the racial tensions that embroiled the Deerhorn community. We must look beyond Michelle's survivor's guilt precisely because the events of Deerhorn cannot be seen as exceptional or anomalous; instead, they reflect a larger national concern over racial purity and concomitant fears over expanding the definitions of the heteronuclear family.

Retrospection and the North American Family

In the fictions analyzed in this study, our queer Asian North American storytellers often turn to events and issues that may seem tangential to the plotting, but expand how the survival plot can be understood through external referents involving actual historical contexts. In the previous three chapters, for instance, I show that all these fictions include key instances that bind the storyteller to someone who has died of AIDS complications. In the second chapter, Bernard goes to the AIDS clinic and participates in a memorial for Li-Li, a graphic designer who had recently passed away from conditions arising out of his infection. In the third, Fee narrates how his fellow choirmate Freddy Moran eventually disintegrates as the infection progresses, while in the fourth, Bong Bong in one of his missives to Montgomery Clift implores him to save Rock Hudson, who at that point had announced in 1985 that he had contracted the HIV/AIDS virus. In all instances, Bernard, Fee, and Bong Bong deviate from their personal survival plots to recount the ways in which their social marginality reverberates alongside larger collectives and other individuals who face forms of material and structural violence.

In a similar fashion, Michelle uses her adult perspective to reframe and expand her childhood understanding of Deerhorn's racial tensions; her lens moves from local and regional perspectives to the implications of her personal experiences in national and transnational affairs. Her survival plot, then, which seems so centrally focused on Deerhorn, is actually interspersed with a multi-tiered narrative concerning collective dangers faced by racial Others. Her own mixed-race background is situated by way of the many wars fought in Asia, including World War II, the Korean War, and, most important in this novel, the Vietnam War: "And when the occasional child did venture to talk to me—out of sympathy or boredom or just plain curiosity—his parents would soon put a stop to it. Because of the war [in Vietnam], I'd hear them say, and I wouldn't understand until much later what they meant. Many of the older men in town had fought in World War II, and to them I wasn't just a foreigner; I was the Enemy" (22). Michelle's racial difference is articulated through her relationship to other children, who do not yet understand why she must be avoided. Her deviance originates not only because of the way she looks, but also in how she signifies as the culmination of a transgressive sexuality—the sexual union between a white man and an Asian woman. Her sequestration from the other children continues to cement her status as a protoqueer minority child. But the greater importance of this paragraph appears in its reference to the reification and racial formation of the white American family as it emerges in the shadow of the wars in Asia. In this case, what cannot be tolerated is the possibility of a white-Asian North American multiracial family. To embrace Michelle as a member of the American family would mean the symbolic welcoming of an individual whose very bloodlines trace back to an Asian enemy. Of course, these racist moments also bring into relief how often Michelle's own Japanese ethnic ancestry is obscured in light of anti-Asian prejudice. In this case, Michelle's indeterminate Asian-ness allows her to stand in for the enemy Japanese, North Korean, or Vietnamese child.

Michelle's retrospective viewpoint also enables her to correspond her personal experiences as a child with those of other American youths. For instance, Michelle refers to the racial tensions occurring in Boston: "Maybe if I'd been older, I might have had a better sense of how unsettled people were by all the changes going on in the country. Maybe I might have understood how what was happening in Boston was having effects that rippled all the way to Deerhorn" (93). She notes her "confused" observations of the "sight of buses full of black children being pelted with rocks, of white children walking nervously through hallways full of black faces, of police in riot gear being taunted by white youths with baseball bats and hockey sticks, of the Irish city councilwoman speaking about the coming race war, felt as far away to me as the images of the disgraced president stepping off his plane, of the bombings in Cambodia" (93). Here Michelle refers to an event that actually occurred, reaching a climax point during 1974 when Boston school systems were forced to desegregate (Delmont and Theoharis).[28] From her adult perspective, such scenes of unrest serve now as a way to situate the level of peril that forms of social difference can generate: "What I might have had with age was a healthier sense of fear regarding what was possible" (93). Indeed, the sight of "black children being pelted with rocks" is not unlike the treatment she received from many of her classmates. Thus her individual experience as an unwelcome biracial, protoqueer child in the Deerhorn community is largely emblematic of the unwelcome biracial, protoqueer child for America at large. These moments enable us to reconsider the novel through Michelle's retrospective narration and encourage a reading practice that explicitly aligns her personal adversities with national and transnational concerns over racial integration and the evolving American family.

One of the most curious passages of the entire novel involves Michelle's critique of her social consciousness. Reflecting upon Charlie's inability to understand the importance of the Garretts, Michelle explains that "he couldn't recognize that the kind of difference he'd rejected in the Garretts was also what he looked past in me. And in his failure to see, he showed me something that I should have known already—that in America, in 1974 and even today, blood does not run thicker than color" (241). Michelle is vague in her phrasing, "the kind of difference," but her wording opens up the space to continually link race, queer sexuality, and kinship. The Garretts are referred to again, reminding us that it is not only the fact of their racial background but also their marriage that present as objectionable to so many in Deerhorn. They are a minority, married couple who may reproduce, implicitly calling attention to a heterosexual pairing devastatingly unwelcomed by the community. Again, though, the Garretts' disruptive presence in Deerhorn indicates the larger tensions undergirding conceptions of the American family in this period. Indeed, only seven years prior to the fictionalized events depicted in the novel, the U.S. Supreme Court would legally recognize interracial marriage (*Loving v. Virginia* 1967).

This passage also brings up a question in relation to the phrase "something that I should have known already." Michelle's expectation for her eight-year-old self—that she should have understood the systemic nature of American social inequalities and the continuing unease over expanding kinship relations—is rather lofty, especially since she could not control the actions of the many others who participated and were privy to the events that led up to the shooting. Further still, recall that Michelle uses "what was happening in Boston" (93) as a way to frame her own myopia concerning national unrest over racial differences and its connection to her childhood troubles in Deerhorn. Of this historical period, Delmont and Theoharis have noted, newspapers and associated publications chose to obscure the Boston desegregation issue by using coded language, preferring instead to situate the conflict as one connected to busing students from one area of the city to another (192–194). In this sense, Michelle's ability to engage racial crises during that time period would have been frustrated by media rhetoric that cloaked the rising animosities at hand. In these multiple senses, we must push past her individual accountability and place these local events in relation to a sociohistorical milieu that establishes exactly why unorthodox hunting communities and interracial surrogacies cannot coexist.

Michelle's reframing of the idiom "blood is thicker than water" returns us to the frame of kinship. In reinventing the phrase as "blood does not run thicker than color," she charges her grandfather with an inability to embrace all of her social differences. Michelle realizes, then, that the primary obligations described in the original aphorism—to one's biological family—do not hold in her case. Her familial inclusion is a selective one in which the fact of her mixed-race heritage is ultimately unacknowledged. Michelle's "color" is precisely the fact of a racial hybridity that is always already queered, a deviant sexuality that takes embodied form. Since Michelle's familial love is conditionally rendered, the

Garretts present the potential of interracial surrogate bonds that are abruptly and violently terminated. The scene in which Michelle stands weeping but embraced by Mrs. Garrett (analyzed earlier in this chapter) is rivaled perhaps by only one other physical act: Charlie's willingness to shoot Earl to protect his granddaughter. But key to this act is her racial and biological connection to him, which he employs to obliterate the fact of her Japanese ethnic ancestry. For Michelle, only white American heteronuclear kinships can be allowed to endure, at least provisionally. Left unspoken is the issue of Michelle's queer sexuality. If Charlie cannot embrace Michelle for her biracial background, then could he have dealt with her queerness had he survived to the point when she pursues romances with women? This looming conundrum is one that casts a large pall over the novel, which in part serves to explain why this racially charged past is just one point along a longer trajectory of social issues—especially in relation to the queer sexuality she explores later as an adult—that haunts Michelle.

Only After: The Logics of Asian North American Queer Female Visibility

The revelation of Michelle's queer sexuality requires now a little more unpacking. Indeed, the logic of the novel's sequencing suggests that her queerness can be made apparent only in light of and in tandem with this narrative concerning racism and the impossibility of sustaining her competing inscrutable belongings. In this way, the novel parallels both *The Necessary Hunger* and *Southland*, precisely because the instability of a heterosexual relationship between two racial Others in an earlier generation serves as a harbinger of the difficult challenges faced by the queer Asian North American storyteller who is part of a later generation and who seeks to establish a same-sex romance. In this case, the catastrophic way in which the Garretts' marriage is terminated presages the many obstructions that Michelle must confront, as she more fully delves into her queer desires as an adult. Thus we can return to the pivotal paragraph in which Michelle finally divulges her sexuality to the readers, which occurs during a field trial competition. Michelle details how the woman she is dating expresses "dismay" at her interest: "She sat seething in the passenger seat of my Pontiac Grand Am—I'd refused to make the trip in her BMW—and rolled her window up to shut out the sound of gunfire. 'I always forget,' she said, arms crossed and cheeks flushed with anger, 'that you're half-Japanese and half-redneck'" (246). While this woman embraces Michelle's queer sexuality, she cannot fully accept

Michelle as a biracial individual with a midwestern, rural upbringing, one that was intimately connected with hunting, animals, and the landscape.[29] The term *redneck* also exposes a use of overt prejudice that denigrates Michelle's racial and class backgrounds. Her blue-collar upbringing is made to seem backward and barbaric, serving to obscure the fact that the culture of hunting did provide her with one instantiation of an inscrutable belonging. In the space of the private interaction between two individuals, this paragraph exposes the challenges that the mixed-race, queer Asian North American woman faces with respect to a partner who cannot fully recognize her.

Despite Michelle's feelings of failure, we read against the grain of this resignation because she has survived to tell the tale. Certainly we understand that the regime of social death casts a larger shadow over her life as an adult, but by looking back to her past, we can reread the narrative through the lens of her adult self. Her racial and sexual differences have influenced a grown-up Michelle in subtle and productive ways. It is perhaps not a surprise, then, that she finds the most promising social bonds in ones inspired by her childhood in Deerhorn. For instance, she reminisces about spending time hiking with her dog, Netty, but also admits, "The high, pine-scented mountains of California aren't the lush countryside of Wisconsin; Netty's not Brett, and fishing trout by myself is not the same as fishing bluegill with my grandfather. But it's the closest I can get with the way my life is now. It's enough; I have to make it be enough" (248). Michelle's sense of ambivalence, of course, relates to the impossibility of fully replicating what she once had in Wisconsin, the vital collectives that provided the sense of what could be achievable. Yet Michelle obviously does retain attachments to the inscrutable belongings she first created alongside the Garretts and the hunting cultures. First, she continues to find solace with her furry companion, Netty, while she traipses on long hikes through the Sierra Nevada mountain range. Second, despite Michelle's belief that her job working at an "alternative high school for troubled kids" (245) is only based on her desire to "try and shove down [her] anger and bitterness" (245), she channels her negative feelings into an occupation that still advocates for youth, many of whom no doubt come from backgrounds not unlike her own. In this sense, the interracial surrogacies that Michelle tentatively developed with the Garretts might be said to extend to her new career, as she takes a position as a sort of elder to these teenagers in high school. And even her attachment to Netty reveals Michelle's persistence in retaining a deep respect for the practice of hunting as well as her desire to keep closely affiliated to the land. Even with such a pessimistic viewpoint, then, the novel's conclusion must be reframed from Michelle's desire to reconstitute her inscrutable belongings, however unwilling she may be to admit to such motives.

The philosopher Sara Ahmed opens up important questions concerning social recognition as it relates to queer sexuality. She asks, "What kinds of alternative kinship stories are possible, which are not organized by the desire for reproduction, or the desire to be like other families, or by the promise of happiness as 'being like'?" (114). *Wingshooters* provides some answers in a fictional form, as Michelle's retrospective narration affords us multiple instantiations of "alternative kinship stories" through the construct of inscrutable belongings. The problem emerges insofar as they cannot be fostered at that time, an effect, as the narrative makes clear, of larger forces generating tensions and power struggles over how to define the American family. In *Antigone's Claim*, Judith Butler employs the titular tragedy and its central heroine to pose specific questions related to mourning and kinship: "[W]hich social arrangements can be recognized as legitimate love, and which human losses can be explicitly grieved as real and consequential loss? Antigone refuses to obey any law that refused public recognitions of her loss, and in this way prefigures the situation that those with publicly ungrievable losses—from AIDS, for instance—know too well. To what sort of living death have they been condemned?" (24). For Michelle, the only "public" space that allows her to grieve her grandfather, her beloved pet dog, and the Garretts—and her own social death—is that of literary communication. Only in her telling can her losses be recognized and mourned collectively.

Michelle's recounting is also a way to bridge her own status as a queer Asian North American woman and mixed-race subject to others who may suffer under the regimes of social and literal death—those like the Garretts, who cannot be embraced and are violently expelled from the local community. The reader is invited into this fictional world only insofar as he or she confronts Michelle's desire to unite the families that cannot yet be. It can only be in this space and time of acknowledging the tenuousness of these family structures that the queer Asian North American woman can surface. The narrative cannot resurrect these kinships, but for now, she has to "make it be enough."

In this chapter, I have focused on *Wingshooters* because of Revoyr's choice to use a first-person retrospective narrative voice: the queer Asian North American woman reflects upon her traumatic childhood and revises her understanding of the past. As with the other primary texts I have analyzed, this storytelling approach stymies a progressive logic that moves fictional narratives so often toward resolution. Most important, the novel resists the disarticulation of racial difference from queer sexuality, showing us how these intersectional, but often asymmetrically represented social rubrics enable the queer Asian North American woman to journey tentatively through the fictional world. Even without romance or courtship, the protagonist lasts to the final page, implying what the cultural critic Annamarie Jagose calls the "condition of its possibility" (7), that her same-sex desires may still proliferate in some unscripted tomorrow. Her queerness can only be provisional, as we see by the novel's conclusion, precisely because of the unfinished project of civil rights, the pervasiveness of social death, and the ever-present threat of physical harm to those who dare to embrace their otherness. Despite Michelle's sense that she has failed, the fact that she still exists to recount her story and still cherishes her affinity for the Garretts dramatically demonstrates the revolutionary nature of the survival plot. Though the Garretts may remain without larger social recognition in Deerhorn, Michelle enables representational resurrections to occur, revealing a mode of defiance that undercuts her pessimism. She engenders interracial surrogacies that gesture to the promise of what dynamic family formations can be, and at the same time, registers her crucial presence in the narrative space. The novel categorically encourages us to see how queerness, racialization, and modes of social difference are comparatively configured, and to ask ourselves how much the sustainability of the queer Asian North American woman in the fictional world depends on the conditions of collective survivals that involve an unexpected group of outcasts and pariahs, eccentrics and failures, and sexual and racial deviants, all in ephemeral, yet necessary inscrutable belongings.

CHAPTER 6

INSCRUTABLE BELONGINGS IN BONDAGE

DEGENERATE DESCENDANTS IN LYDIA KWA'S *PULSE*

THIS CHAPTER EXTENDS the bounds of the book by moving northward, across the border into Canada, a journey that progresses my argument to a new national dimension. Here the consideration of Canada emphasizes the binational framework of the book, linking queer Asian American and queer Asian Canadian texts under a larger grouping. As made evident already in the Introduction, although these two bodies of literature are far from interchangeable, their alignment is necessary given that queer Asian North Americans in both nation-states face common issues.[1] The connection holds especially true with respect to North American idealizations of traditional familial formations, which influence how writers construct their fictional worlds. But Canada is not the only national setting portrayed in Lydia Kwa's novel *Pulse*. Singapore provides a second backdrop for the action and firmly establishes the necessity of a queer diasporic critique alongside a queer of color critique. The two settings force us to attend to racial and ethnic registers that surface in multiple national contexts and in relation to our queer Asian North American storyteller.

The discussion begins with elucidation of the inscrutable belonging that the female narrator in *Pulse* must develop as a child. As posited in earlier chapters, inscrutable belongings offer dynamic social formations that help the queer Asian North American narrator to make sense of past traumas and to navigate the survival plot. The four fictional publications I have covered in the previous chapters depict a wide variation of inscrutable belongings: bathhouse patrons, hunters and the lands on which they track game, AIDS clinic volunteers and patients, individuals afflicted with infectious diseases, child sexual abuse survivors, racial minorities, even dead Hollywood film stars. What unites these seemingly disparate aggregations are the ways in which such collectives are consistently marked by their deviancy. These novels therefore remind us that the queer Asian North American subject cannot renounce his or her productive connection to the many communities that suffer from social misrecognition and outright prejudice.

But *Pulse* differs in some important ways from the other fictions discussed. First, the network of inscrutable belongings generated by Natalie, the protagonist-storyteller, is initially rooted in spiritual and mystical realms related to occult and divination practices. Second, the novel sets a major portion of the story in Natalie's country of ethnic origin. And third, most of the story occurs during the period in which she is already well into adulthood. The narrator's return to Singapore serves in several capacities: it requires Natalie to delve further into what occurred to her as a child and pushes her to reexamine the nature of family ties (both biological and elective), social formations, race, and religion. It also forms part of an extended survival plot in which she accounts for her own development alongside the lives (and deaths) of others, all amid violent historical contexts. Through this process, Natalie constructs a variety of dynamic social formations based on her identity as a degenerate descendant of the Singaporean nation-state: she aligns herself with other marginalized subjects facing erasure under official governance policies and restrictive cultural norms. Despite our storyteller's ability to withstand so many antagonistic forces, a similarly aligned character cannot: Selim, who also identifies as queer and happens to be the son of Natalie's closest childhood friend, commits suicide. In this sense, the novel reminds us that survival plots remain precarious.

In the first sections of the chapter I focus on the storyteller's personal traumas, which include loss, violence, and incest. The details concerning Natalie's life in Canada reveal that her survival plot remains unresolved, even though the novel opens with her having established a seemingly successful career and even a promising same-sex relationship. Natalie's endurance remains questionable precisely because she has not fully dealt with the nature of her childhood traumas, especially as they relate to the lives of those closest to her, many of whom remain in Singapore. In this sense, the survival plot widens and requires Natalie to reorient her understanding of inscrutable belongings, as they begin to enfold a wider group of people, forces, and entities that move her beyond her North American life.

The rest of the chapter engages the novel as a reflection of the queer Asian North American's unstable place in the postcolonial nation-state. As the setting primarily shifts to Singapore, Natalie returns to the land of her birth, which allows her to ponder over her past, present, and potential future through fresh perspectives. The novel critiques state-sanctioned policies engendered to maintain certain ethnoracial lineages, while simultaneously promoting a future-oriented ethos of modernization. In this sense, we can read Natalie's extended survival plot as an allegory for her position as the disobedient national daughter, who looks backward as a mode by which to temper and to balance narratives of progress. This part of the chapter is inspired, then, by the work of Geraldine Heng and Janadas Devan, who persuasively argue that political rhetoric (as espoused by Lee Kuan Yew, Singapore's first prime minister) founds a figurative "state" father who commands and expects undivided loyalty from an idealized citizenry (350). The novel institutes the queer Asian North American and Singaporean diasporic subject as a key figure in the reconfiguration of family, history, and national citizenship. Our storyteller commands her place as a degenerate descendant of the nation-state and, in the process, elaborates on an inscrutable belonging that comprises queers, BDSM practitioners, spiritualists, and mixed ethnoracial subjects.

Incest and Spiritual Inheritances

Pulse's survival plot originates with the issue of incestuous assault, and Natalie must find a way to recover from this brutal experience.[2] Of interest to me is the nature of incest-induced trauma, which strikes at the very heart of this study given that it is a form of sexual violence rooted in the family. Extending Judith Lewis Herman's perspectives on trauma and drawing from theories of power derived from Judith Butler, Jane Kilby argues that in this kind of intergenerational abuse "the adult is given the child's loving presence, and the child is given the adult's violence which means that neither the child nor the adult and his or her violence precede or follow the other" (262).[3] Kilby clarifies the problem related to kinship that arises in incest. The adult exploits a given power dynamic, bestowing violence on his or her own child, even as that same child provides love in return. This exchange system is further complicated because incest muddies the line between parent and child, as the two figures become bonded through sexual contact. This act catastrophically destroys the traditional familial roles of child and his or her adult parent.

Pulse depicts the traumatic ramifications of incest through an elliptical narrative in which Natalie delays revealing what had occurred to her as a young girl until late in the novel. Although she lives to tell her tale, she struggles to divulge this secret. In this sense, this novel generates its plot through a form of narrative sequencing necessitated by the protagonist's tortured psychic state. This anachronism brings to mind Susan Clancy's thesis in *The Trauma Myth*, in which she argues that child sexual abuse is most damaging when the adult fully understands the brutalities experienced in her youth. But even at that point, another issue manifests in the recounting of that trauma. As Butler notes of incest and its aftermath, "One will have to become a reader of the ellipsis, the gap, the absence, and this means that psychoanalysis will have to relearn the skill of reading broken narratives" (*Undoing Gender* 155).[4] *Pulse* does not so much depict the impossibility of representation in relation to trauma as it illuminates how the narrative of childhood sexual assault surfaces in inconspicuous ways. Butler would caution us to read *Pulse* through its "broken narratives," as they derive from Natalie's incestuous relationship with her father. As with the previous four chapters of *Inscrutable Belongings*, then, this one also reveals how a major trauma endured by the protagonist as a child haunts her well into adulthood.

When the novel opens, Natalie's parents are living with her in Toronto. For readers, nothing at first seems out of the ordinary. The first description of Natalie's father is one in which he rests in a chair. This rather innocuous description is then deconstructed by the information that he has experienced a stroke, which changes the way Natalie and her mother understand him. The only time that her father shows evidence of a dynamic personality appears when music plays: "Twice a week, during rehab at St. Michael's, he waltzes gracefully across the floor with his occupational therapist. Debonair. That's when I believe my mother's stories of the charming man who romanced her. Funny yet touching to watch the old man doing the cha-cha with young Miss Turner to the tune of 'Tea for Two'" (13). Natalie gestures to the abrupt shift that has occurred due to the stroke, a sense that her father is not the man he once was. But this change in him is recast by the late-stage revelation that her father had regularly sexually assaulted her when she was just a young girl.

To critique *Pulse* is to read and reread in order to situate how trauma for the queer Asian North American subject comes to be told, or, in these cases, how it comes to be narrated so often through a veiled subtext. Hence, a song like "Tea for Two," which revels in the future romance of lovers, takes on another insidious layer of meaning given Natalie's childhood experiences. The chorus of "Tea for Two" contains the following lyrics: "Just me for you / And you for me alone / Nobody near us to see us or hear us, / No friends or relations / On weekend vacations, / We won't have it known, dear, / That we own a telephone, dear" (Youmans and Caesar). In light of Natalie's traumas, these lyrics strike in a different way and remind us of the isolation and fear that she experiences even after the sexual assaults are over. Indeed, Natalie does not disclose her traumas to anyone and thus struggles in the shadow of what happened to her. The challenge in communicating—that is, there is a telephone, but it cannot be used—generates a narrative filled with absences and gaps that remain to be confronted. What can the family structure offer her when this social formation is the site of sexual violence? To answer this question, *Pulse* posits the necessity of elective social formations to counteract the duress produced by the home space. The novel continues a trend seen in every chapter of this book from the second onward: a protoqueer child's life is placed in danger, so he or she must look beside the bounds of more traditional social supports and guardians, such as parents or biological relatives, in order to endure.

Natalie's first inscrutable belonging emerges out of her connection to alternative therapies and spiritual philosophies, elements she is exposed to as a child living in Singapore. At that time, Natalie's grandparents—Mah-Mah and Kong-Kong—own an herbal shop called Cosmic Pulse, and her grandmother also uses the shop for divination consultations. During Mah-Mah's sessions, Natalie often watches and learns about her grandmother's spiritual views: "It was so unlike my father's Christianity. Instead of the Holy Trinity of Father, Son and Holy Spirit, her language consisted of Heaven, Man and earth, with each force influencing the others" (72). Natalie's grandparents believe that "there exist[s] a cosmic pulse throughout the universe, and that it behoove[s] . . . lowly humans to seek advice and direction from the myriad forces" that surround them. Her grandparents' non-Christian perspectives offer Natalie a foundation for relating to—indeed, surviving—the world around her. Natalie understands that Mah-Mah's divinations function as a form of inheritance: "[Mah-Mah] needed to pass on a legacy, wanted me not to forget why trigraph 52 was particularly significant in my life. But, being a Taoist, she also wanted to talk about change. That's why she referred to trigraph 53, where the presence of two figures in the middle row made all the difference, compared to the previous trigraph" (138). The trigraphs here refer to the various combinations of twelve tokens or chess pieces that provide 125 outcomes related to possible futures.[5] Mah-Mah attempts to bestow crucial information that will help Natalie withstand oncoming challenges. Indeed, trigraph 52 suggests that Natalie will face a dark threat, but that by remaining honest there was "hope of rescue following the prior surge of wickedness" (138). Of course, Mah-Mah's divination prefigures Natalie's experiences of childhood sexual abuse at the hands of her father. The possibility of "rescue" would certainly provide Natalie with a measure of solace in a threatening domestic space. Thus the use of the word *legacy* centrally locates Mah-Mah's divination as a tool that can be used for Natalie's benefit in the future, establishing how these spiritual and occult practices coalesce as the grounds of a nascent inscrutable belonging.

Mah-Mah and Kong-Kong's Taoist beliefs open up a world beyond the claustrophobic interiors of the home space. Interestingly, as a six-year-old, Natalie has her "first experience of the invisible realms" (76–77). Looking into a well, Natalie notices in the water's reflection, "Shapes began to form inside that light, shapes that did not reflect the landscape of the sky overhead. I could make out tall beings standing among white horses. The beings resembled humans, except they had slender, muscular wings along the length of their torsos. The vibrations from their wings reached me, penetrating me like pulses of light" (77). This event shifts the narrative into a super-realist register: Natalie realizes that another dimension may exist, the very one that her grandparents espouse as part of their professional work as diviners and herbalists.

In an episode recalled later by Natalie during the most climactic moment in the novel, these same beings seem to help save her life. Her father is about to strangle her, an act of violence arising out of jealousy: he realizes that Natalie is more than friends with her schoolmate Faridah. Natalie feels his hands around her throat and is about to lose consciousness, when he suddenly stops: "What had happened? He seemed to have seen something that alarmed him. He was staring into the water past my head. Something in the well? Or overhead, reflected in the water below?" (227). Though Natalie never directly states it, the suggestion is that her father sees the very same angel figures she saw as a child, here appearing at the precise moment that Natalie is in mortal danger. For Natalie, the "invisible realms" offer a set of otherworldly creatures who protect her, no doubt revealing the urgency of the mysticism and alternative therapies championed by her grandparents. These beings form the basis of Natalie's inscrutable belonging and enable her to survive, at least momentarily, the traumas sustained from incest.

By the time Natalie immigrates to Canada as a young teenager, the days of Cosmic Pulse are all but forgotten. As a University of Toronto student, she turns instead to the science of heredity as the foundation for a future career. But this biological discipline does not provide Natalie with the proper methodology to contextualize what has been passed down to her through the sexual violence she has experienced. Soon after this point, Natalie visits an acupuncturist for help with sleep disturbances. This visit transforms her life: "I decided not to pursue graduate studies in biology and instead switched to acupuncture, following in my grandfather's footsteps" (21). Natalie's decision places her firmly within a lineage of healers and focuses her to work in a way that reconstitutes the body's health. Through this process, Natalie reconstructs the meaning of a biological inheritance, moving away from genetic predispositions and toward a more mystical formulation of what can be extended intergenerationally.

Natalie's understanding of arts that others might consider occult or pseudoscientific represents a legacy and base of knowledge that also allow her to create a social formation outside of the traditional bounds of the family. For instance, she develops one of her most important extrafamilial bonds through her work as an acupuncturist. She meets her long-term same-sex partner, Michelle, through Michelle's father, Mr. Woo, a patient of Natalie's "for about seven years." Natalie "met Michelle when she came by the clinic to pick up her father one evening" (129). Natalie also acknowledges how "accepting" Mr. Woo is about their relationship and that she was "only open to Michelle because [Natalie] already had such a strong connection with her father and had heard lovely things about [Michelle]" (129). For Natalie, Mr. Woo and Michelle offer an example of a father-daughter dynamic far "different" from hers (129). Mr. Woo's acceptance validates Natalie's queer sexuality and provides an alternative kinship, one that emerges only after her embrace of the mystical arts first introduced to her by her maternal-side grandparents. In this sense, the novel's initial chapters set up the first act of Natalie's survival plot, as she makes a new life in Canada as an acupuncturist and as someone involved in a fulfilling same-sex relationship.

Bondage as Therapy, Bondage as Kinship

Though Natalie's adult life seems promising, her childhood experiences continue to plague her. As she survives to adulthood, she begins to explore her sexuality, one defined by same-sex desires. But this form of queerness becomes problematic because of its association with other non-normative sexual relationships such as incest. Concerning these kinds of overlaps, Butler asserts that "[w]hat counters the incest taboo offends not only because it often involves the exploitation of those whose capacity for consent is questionable, but because it exposes the aberration in normative kinship, an aberration that might also, importantly, be worked against the strictures of kinship to force a revision and expansion of those very terms" (*Undoing Gender* 160). Here the violation of the incest taboo moves beyond its exploitation of the child precisely because it also inherently renders any form of desire outside normative heterosexual relationships—between two consenting adults—as unintelligible. Incest, however destructive, is in some sense a mode of altering heteronormative and intergenerational kinship formation, though done in a traumatic way. If incest is outlawed, so then might be any other queer kind of desire, regardless of its construct, in order to eliminate any aberrant relationships: "In other words, there is no way that gay parenting or bisexuality might be acknowledged as a perfectly intelligible cultural formation and, thus, to escape its place as deviance. Similarly, there is no way to distinguish, as there must be, between deviations from the norm such as lesbian sexuality and incestuous practice" (*Undoing Gender* 159). Within the context of legal discourse, Courtney Megan Cahill makes a similar claim: "The degree to which the incest taboo has been used to inspire disgust against a range of consensual relationships—its sheer overinclusiveness—is perhaps the best reason why we should not dismiss the incest/same-sex marriage comparison so lightly" (1545). In light of Butler's and Cahill's perspectives, *Pulse*'s challenge is to actualize a definitive space between incestuous relationships and same-sex social formations.

Natalie's interest in *Kinbaku*, otherwise known as Japanese erotic bondage, represents one significant response to this challenge, as it allows her to contour the boundaries of her inscrutable belongings. Embracing such activities enables Natalie to revise the nature of power as it relates to her body, to her queerness, and to another individual, distinctly someone who is not biologically related.[6] Kinbaku possesses a nationally rooted history but, more recently, has been adopted by individuals outside of Japan. According to Nawashi Murakawa, "The contemporary Japanese terminology for Kinbaku is the simple term SM, and it has been accepted as the sex industry term for rope bondage. However, this must not be confused with the use of the very same definition in the West where SM (sado masochism) is more likely to be defined as something done between consenting partners, involved in what is described as submissive/masochist or dominant/sadist [roles]" (iv). Kinbaku does not always imply "physical gratification" (Murakawa viii), meaning it is not so easily defined as a sexual act. The critical and scholarly information on Kinbaku is quite limited, and my reading relies on an archive that largely engages BDSM (bondage and discipline, dominance and submission, sadism and masochism), which I employ throughout this chapter as "an umbrella term meant to be inclusive of all types of play involving the conscious, safe, sane, and consensual use of power dynamics" (Kolmes et al. 304).[7] Whether there are sexual exchanges at play in Kinbaku, most practitioners agree that Kinbaku falls within BDSM conventions.

It is very appropriate that Natalie comes to Kinbaku through her work as an acupuncturist. One of her patients actively pursues an interest in Kinbaku and is "convinced there [is] a way to do Japanese bondage to maximize the healing potential of the rope patterns, working the points of intersection as ways to tonify and regulate the blood or to disperse energy blockages" (95). In this sense, Natalie's interest in Kinbaku stems from her desire to heal. Though Kinbaku enthusiasts, especially in the West, do not link rope patterns and bondage with therapeutic methods, Mark Yu notes that Kinbaku can be reframed within the discourses of "healing, personal and spiritual development" (88). Taking Yu's point into account, I argue that *Pulse* depicts how Natalie links her queerness with erotic bondage and retools associated identities and (sexual) conventions to address past injuries in a healthful way.

Kinbaku functions to create new "bonds" for Natalie, as she makes productive contacts with other individuals though her BDSM interests. At one point, Natalie enters an Internet chat room to find a community among other practitioners.[8] That chat room is alive with debates about the philosophical ideals behind rope bondage. As Natalie believes, "binding the body with rope allowed us to transform our fears and develop trust; in addition, it was an erotic practice that not only gave pleasure in the moment, but also allowed further satisfaction after the fact, with the experience of touching or viewing the temporary markings left by the rope on the body" (40). For Natalie, then, Kinbaku does not so much emphasize strict power dynamics as it offers her a method to extract pleasure through rope bondage. Kinbaku allows her to delve further into her committed same-sex relationship with Michelle and hence provides her an avenue to pursue her queer desires.

But in relation to Natalie's childhood sexual traumas, her interest in Kinbaku and other forms of BDSM can take on another meaning. To be sure, Natalie's interest in Kinbaku cannot be understood as solely deriving from her sexual traumas. Yet in Natalie's case, I do gesture to a potential correlation, though not to a strict causality, between sexual trauma and the attraction to BDSM techniques. Indeed, scholars have shown that BDSM practitioners are far from pathological in the way they express their desires. Roy F. Baumeister, for instance, argues that "[m]any people apparently engage in sexual masochism without exhibiting any other unusual or deviant behavior patterns and without showing any signs of psychopathology" (134).[9] Rather than cast Natalie's affinity for Kinbaku as a psychopathological response to childhood traumas, I read this undertaking as another form of therapy that branches off from her original inscrutable belonging inspired by healing and psychic reconstitution. As Natalie notes, part of what attracts her to Kinbaku is its lasting impression. That is, evidence of the erotic bondage activity marks the body long after a session has completed. Kinbaku appears as a metaphorical and temporal reordering of sexual desire for Natalie, in which the restrictions placed on a partner are not from a force such as an abusive father. Instead, Kinbaku opens up the terrain of the body as a site for sexual pleasure while "transforming" fears of intimacy produced by past sexual trauma involving physical restraints and corporeal immobility.

My argument follows contentions introduced by Corie Hammers and by Danielle Lindemann, who show how BDSM functions as a therapeutic act that revises earlier experiences.[10] In a study focusing on survivors of rape traumas, Hammers notes that BDSM functions as a "*somatic intervention*" ("Corporeality" 2) that metamorphoses the ways in which sex acts are understood. For the participants in Hammers's study, "*consensual* rape play dislodged the 'bad pain' associated with the trauma such that a (re)connection to the body ensued" ("Corporeality" 20). BDSM alters the "rape script" ("Corporeality" 20) by coupling sexual acts with desire and play, rather than with brutal coercion. For Lindemann, a study of professional dominatrices yields the conclusion that these sex workers find their labor a form of therapy in which "clients are able to express these desires that have historically been conceptualized as problematic and pathological, in a context that is free from social judgment or reverberations" (168).[11] In aligning these studies with *Pulse*, I assert that Kinbaku enables Natalie to amend the incest "script" associated with her sexualized body by allowing her to regain control through the use of ropes and knots used to bind someone else. When her father almost strangles her when she is just a child, she is knocked unconscious, only to awaken in a state of confusion: "I was on the floor, tied up. The ropes ate into my skin. I winced from the pain" (225). By restraining another body but this time through Kinbaku, Natalie performs as an agent of pleasurable power rather than as a destructive force. She resists the narrative in which rope bondage is associated only with incest and childhood sexual traumas.

This experience psychologically liberates Natalie, even as it literally constrains her partner. In Sarah Sloane's understanding of Kinbaku, "[c]athartic play, at least in my ideal, is not a single scene, but an ongoing way to use BDSM as a touchstone for personal growth. Cathartic play, especially with someone that we have a deep level of trust in, can give us a chance to walk farther down a path of self-knowledge and self-awareness than we could easily walk by ourselves" (131). For Natalie, Kinbaku is precisely a form of "cathartic play," which licenses her to work through events in the past with the benefit of a willing participant. The sexual and nonsexual dynamics of both incest and BDSM might be regarded as non-normative, but for Natalie, Kinbaku refigures corporeal intimacy and rope bondage as a positive, pleasurable experience that allows her to explore both queer and non-sexual proclivities.

Queer, Intergenerational, Diasporic Kinships in Bondage

The first sections of the novel seem to suggest that Natalie has successfully negotiated her survival plot. She has moved to Canada and generated an inscrutable belonging based on spiritualism and folk-based religious customs to formulate a career in alternative healing therapies. Further still, her preoccupation with Kinbaku offers her a realm in which she can revise the traumatic narrative associated with her body.

But the novel begins to reveal fissures in Natalie's survival plot precisely because some of her past traumas continue to surface, often in inconspicuous ways. For instance, with Kinbaku, she acts only as the *nawashi*, or the individual who completes the binding of the partner. Her desire to remain the *nawashi* in all encounters suggests a block in remaining open and vulnerable to others. As Natalie admits after one session with Michelle, "How could I let Michelle bind me? I'm worried that I might feel something ugly when I'm bound. What if I snap? I don't want that to happen. And maybe I'm also scared that Michelle won't like what gets revealed if I let her bind me" (128). That this troubling realization occurs in the context of Kinbaku is apt because it is Selim, the other major character who engages in Kinbaku, who clarifies how Natalie's survival plot is hardly resolved. Selim is Faridah's adult son who, we learn late in the book, was sexually assaulted until he was sixteen by his father, Adam. Again, the revelation of Selim's sexual abuse mirrors Natalie's own in the sense that it is revealed out of sequence. This narrative anachrony helps model the traumas sustained by these characters, but also generates signifying forces behind the plotting itself: we must make meaning out of these belated divulgences. When Natalie first discovers from a letter penned by Faridah that Selim has committed suicide, she realizes that her own endurance is tied to the lives of others. At this point, her survival plot requires her to go back to Singapore and to reconsider her place within the nation-state as a diasporic subject. I accordingly move to probe how Natalie's survival plot intertwines with Selim's suicide and how her inscrutable belongings expand alongside her associations with Singaporean individuals, histories, and social forces.

Selim is central to Natalie's extended survival plot precisely because his life so closely parallels hers. He is queer, hails from Singapore, and cultivates a fervor for Kinbaku. If Selim cannot endure, then Natalie's own seemingly successful life in Canada becomes more tenuous. Natalie first meets Selim in February 2005, many years prior to his suicide. While visiting Singapore to see relatives, Natalie drops in on Faridah and attends a beach picnic hosted by Faridah's family. Natalie immediately witnesses a squabble, which makes her "an outsider, awkwardly witnessing a family drama that [she] had only the most superficial knowledge of" (32). Her alienation is amplified by the fact that no one in Faridah's family knows that she and Faridah "were lovers" (32) as young women. Her queer sexuality and former love affair have to be closeted in Singapore, circumstances that are made more palpable by Selim's close resemblance to his mother: "I was thinking how much Selim looked like Faridah: lean build, large black eyes, strongly sensuous mouth. It pleased yet pained me to watch him" (34). Natalie focuses on Selim as a physical embodiment of what became impossible: a lasting romantic partnership with Faridah. Selim, too, exhibits a significant affinity for Natalie. Some time after the beach scene, Selim confesses that he had already met Natalie, unbeknownst to her, through her online persona, Cosmic Pulse, the handle she had used in Kinbaku chat rooms. Because Selim knows that Natalie's grandparents once owned a shop by this name, he deduces that Cosmic Pulse is actually Natalie. These connections lay the foundation for each character's embrace of the other as a possible alternative social formation—that is, a branch of an inscrutable belonging.

Despite the fact that Selim is the product of a heteronormative kinship lineage, he is also firmly linked to Natalie through their collective interest in Kinbaku. Why does this association become so important? To answer this question, the novel provides two discursive strains concerning Kinbaku, one espoused by Natalie and the other by Selim. As previously mentioned, Natalie prefers not to emphasize strict power dynamics that position one practitioner as a "bottom" or "slave" and the other a "top" or "master" (41). Selim, through his online moniker as Benkulen Bound, believes otherwise; he "insisted that we must not get 'too soft' in our approach. It was clear that he was a gay man who used Kinbaku rope techniques within a Western BDSM practice" (40). In a conversation with Natalie, Selim further explains that Kinbaku allows him to "[r]elinquish control" and that "being a submissive doesn't mean not having power" (44). Selim believes ultimately that his approach to Kinbaku is also about "overcoming fears and developing trust" (44).[12] When Natalie discovers that Benkulen Bound is Selim, she also realizes that his queer sexuality and his interest in Kinbaku must remain closeted. Thus their parallels multiply: by their close proximity to Faridah, their shared queer sexuality, their interest in Japanese erotic bondage, and their tactical closeting while in Singapore.

The function of the chat room takes on greater meaning in transnational arenas, especially given Singapore's drive to support technological innovation (A. Lim) and its choice to render homosexuality illegal.[13] Only in cyberspace can Selim express directly his desire for men as well as pursue his interest in Kinbaku.[14] Natalie, too, finds a forum that allows her to explore her own philosophies among other enthusiasts and to initiate same-sex relationships.[15] Both characters are able to resist the nation-state's restrictive policies via technological innovations. In a study on political agitation and gay rights in Singapore, Lynette Chua argues that gay activists must adopt a strategy of "pragmatic resistance" (714), which involves aiming for "legal reform" while circumventing "tactics that directly confront the state, such as street protests, and avoid[ing] being seen as a threat to existing formal arrangements of power" (714). Though "pragmatic resistance" operates within the law, it does inspire the ways that queer characters in *Pulse* negotiate their outlawed sexualities. Selim's and Natalie's queerness remains illegible in public events such as family gatherings in parks. Because cyberspace provides them invisibility and anonymity, both characters can pursue their desires and erotic bondage relationships without explicitly endangering any legal policies. Certainly Natalie's and Selim's interest in Kinbaku offers them a way to work out their own positions as individuals *bound*—if I can pun briefly here—by the dictates of the nation-state as a figurative father.

But if Natalie establishes an inscrutable belonging with Selim, the son of a former lover and a fellow queer subject and Kinbaku practitioner, why does

Selim reciprocate by seeking out Natalie and subsequently confronting her about her Internet identity as Cosmic Pulse? The novel's sequencing suggests at first that Selim's connection to Natalie relates primarily to Kinbaku and to their queer sexuality, but they share another vital overlap—as incest survivors. As I mentioned earlier, this link is not made clear until well into the novel. Philip, Selim's lover, requests to meet with Natalie and gives her a letter written by Selim, explaining his suicide.[16] At the conclusion of the letter, he directs Philip to "*make sure you share this with [Faridah's] friend, Natalie*" (244) and adds that Natalie knows "*what it's like, to love someone who won't—can't—love you back. That father from whom we can never receive unconditional love*" (245). In this letter, Selim declares, "*You know he stopped bothering me a decade ago. Ever since I turned sixteen. So, from age nine to sixteen. A hell of a long time. Yeah, it sure helped that I got a whole lot stronger than him. He became afraid I would harm him. So what? The shadow of his crime darkens our household. His violence, the perverted desire he won't name*" (243–244). This moment reframes many prior conversations and requires a reading that moves back over the narrative to flesh out what had been ellipses or absences in speech or interactions between characters, the process that Butler so aptly describes in relation to individuals who attempt to tell their stories of traumatic survivals (*Undoing Gender* 155).

The parallels between Natalie and Selim as a result of their childhood sexual traumas thus become increasingly crucial to consider. When Faridah is first raising Selim, she tells him many stories about Natalie. One, in particular, is very important to Selim. One day, after suffering a beating from his father, Selim hides in a storage room. The only way that Faridah can coax Selim out is to tell the story about witnessing Natalie's father beating her so severely that he leaves marks on her body; realizing in a frenzy that his daughter's affection for Faridah is more than a friendship, he almost kills Natalie. The story somehow comforts Selim, as Natalie suspects that Selim saw the two of them as "joined together because [they] had both been marked by" their fathers' "rage" (55). This story takes on greater meaning when, prior to Selim's suicide, he mentions to Faridah that she must ask Natalie for forgiveness and then references both Cosmic Pulse and Godzilla, a monster figure that had been important to Natalie as a young girl. Why would Selim push his mother to ask Natalie for forgiveness? From Selim's perspective, Faridah must seek absolution from Natalie because Faridah could not be a proper witness to Natalie's trauma—or to his, for that matter—a fact that Selim seems to have accepted prior to his suicide. Selim's letter makes clear why Natalie's brutal beating fascinates him so much: because they share experiences of physical abuse, and because he realizes through that story that Natalie is an incest survivor. As Natalie herself reports,

> I see why Selim was drawn to the story of my life. He was such a good listener. Quite exceptional, because he must have heard not only what his mother was telling him, but also the implications between the lines. He heard what she could not. I never told her about being sexually abused by my father. But her son heard it, because of his own experiences. His psyche resonated with the implications of my father's rage at discovering that Faridah and I were lovers. (252–253)

Selim is a proxy for the reader, who must also reevaluate the novel to discover what direct speech or interior monologues have left out. He inspires the reader to be a better interpreter.

For instance, when Natalie arrives in Singapore, she and Faridah have another conversation about Selim's preoccupation with Natalie's childhood beating. Natalie figures out that Faridah's motivation for telling Selim that story was that the experience had "left a mark" on her and that she "carried that guilt with [her]. A terrible burden. Felt [she] had to say something to [her] son, who was also experiencing being hurt by his father. Like I had been" (185). After this direct speech act, the passage moves into interior monologue and Natalie reveals, "A long, chilling tremor grips my body. I feel a little crazy, unable to stop my body from shaking. No, it's the opposite of crazy. It's a kind of knowing, that reaches further. Closer to the core of truth" (185). At this point in the novel, Natalie has not admitted what that truth actually is: that Natalie's beating is very much implicated in incest. Here Natalie suggests that Faridah subconsciously understood the extent of Natalie's (and Selim's) traumas but could not face them. As Selim states in his letter, incest was "*[a] shadow my mother has not dared to name. She would rather think that her husband simply needed to be close to the son who survived. I know she's quite terrified of the truth*" (244). Natalie—not Faridah—becomes Selim's best witness, as she can testify to the violence he has experienced.

Selim thus employs Natalie's abuse as a tool for surviving his many years of incestuous trauma. Selim inherits Natalie's story and relates it to his own, further solidifying the inscrutable belonging between them. Natalie's survival plot inextricably intertwines with Selim's. Though Selim eventually commits suicide, his death still functions to enact a sort of rapprochement between Natalie and Faridah, as both characters must face the fact that they were hardly responsible for the horrific events that occurred in their youth. Selim's death also enables each woman to find a metaphorical rebirth. While Faridah never directly states that she knows "the truth," Selim's suicide does motivate her to end her marriage and perhaps script a new life beyond the "shadow" of incest that has destroyed her heteronuclear family. And Natalie returns to Singapore, which pushes her to confront directly her experiences of childhood sexual abuse.

Postcoloniality and Inscrutable Belongings

So far, I have limited my examination to a contained group of characters focusing on Natalie's inscrutable belongings that are constituted by her investments in alternative healing arts, erotic bondage, and individuals she meets while developing these passions. As argued throughout this book, the queer Asian North American's survival often hinges on a vital relationship with a character who dies (or has died), and the storyteller pushes us to ask why these two figures are so enmeshed in each other's lives. Natalie and Selim, I have shown, share multiple commonalities: both are incest survivors, both reorient their childhood traumas through erotic bondage methods, and both are queer Singaporean subjects who choose to remain closeted under certain conditions. Natalie's inscrutable belongings continue to transform, especially as she must resituate Selim's centrality to her survival plot and as she is pulled back to Singapore in the wake of his suicide. The novel further functions on a metadiscursive level, as Natalie uses first-person narration to reveal the complex nature of her trauma. This narrative choice allows Natalie to unveil her trauma to her reading audience without disclosing such information to other characters who directly interact with her in the fictional world.[17] Pressingly, readers are directed to return to the novel to see the ways that incest produces other representational fissures, linking the personal and the political, the individual and the transnational, the present and the past.

Pulse accordingly resonates with the preceding chapter, which focused on Revoyr's *Wingshooters*, precisely because the queer Asian North American female storyteller's inscrutable belongings are influenced by social contexts that embroil the nation-state. In this chapter's case, recall that I earlier stressed the importance of understanding the novel through the lens of a figurative father: the modernizing nation-state and all of the authoritarian policies enforced as Singapore emerges as an economic power and global leader. Hence, the novel must be reread in light of metaphorical disloyalties, as figures such as Natalie and Selim appear as disobedient national children, ones who engage in queer sexualities, who find power in Kinbaku, and who look deeply at history to undercut any simplistic narratives of progress. I have gestured to this line of inquiry in my comparative analysis of Natalie and Selim, who find ways to explore their sexual desires and BDSM penchants beyond the reach of Singaporean state policies through their use of chat room interfaces. But the novel requires a more comprehensive consideration of their collective recalcitrance and its relation to national paradigms. In this sense, we can say the novel interrupts nation-state modernization narratives, often too reliant upon chronological plottings, through Natalie's retrospective storytelling.

Pulse depicts a narrator attuned to the historical circumstances that propelled Singapore to independence. As Natalie tells it, "I turned forty-eight recently. June 6, to be exact. That makes me as old as modern Singapore. After all, I was born that momentous day in 1959 when the People's Action Party government, under Lee Kuan Yew, began to run the country, independent of British rule" (15). Here Natalie compares her birth to that of Singapore, a connection that invites another analysis. Technically, Natalie's understanding of history is flawed: Singapore did not achieve official independence until 1965, but her conception in this transitional moment is crucial, as she embodies the merging between past and future versions of the nation-state. If Natalie's "fate" is contingent upon having to confront the traumas related to incest, then how does such a challenge relate to a nation-state's origination?

To answer this question, we can return to the theorists and critics who have related incest to larger forces of social upheaval, such as racial difference and nation making. Discussing racial tensions in contemporary France, Judith Butler couples the incest taboo to miscegenation "insofar as the defense of culture that takes place through mandating the family as heterosexual is at once an extension of new forms of European racism" ("Is Kinship" 33). Butler goes on to note that "the incest taboo mandates exogamy, but the taboo against miscegenation limits the exogamy that the incest taboo mandates. Cornered, then, between a compulsory heterosexuality and a prohibited miscegenation, something called culture, saturated with the anxiety and identity of dominant European whiteness, reproduces itself in and as universality itself" (33). For Butler, the incest taboo and the miscegenation taboo require a lacuna in which racial purity could still be constructed. In other words, there must be a limit to exogamy, so it does not fall into the realm of deleterious inbreeding. U.S.

cultural critics and scholars make similar conclusions. Gillian Harkins argues that "[i]ncest and its twin figure, 'miscegenation,' marked the two symbolic limits of the familial nation: the dangers of endogamy posed by the demand for racial purity, and the dangers of racial impurity posed by the demand for exogamy" (20). Jolie A. Sheffer in addition remarks that representations of family in popular romances at the turn of the twentieth century generated a critical tension between incest and hybridity: "To underscore the familiality of racial difference, in these works, miscegenation is repeatedly linked to incest (that has already occurred or that threatens to occur) or incestuous eroticism (such as between non–blood relatives who treat each other like siblings)" (3). Whether in French or American contexts, Butler, Harkins, and Sheffer are united by their understanding of incest and miscegenation as taboos that function in tandem with idealized constructs of the nation-state.[18]

By exploring contemporary politics of ethnic, racial, and religious tensions in Singapore, *Pulse* presents a specific nation-state paradigm for thinking about social difference, kinship, and aberrations in familial formations. To further address these issues, I note Singapore's approach to addressing its diverse citizenry: "The official state policy towards managing the multi-cultural composition of Singapore is that it will never be a melting pot, as the different ethnic groups want to preserve their distinct traits in terms of customs, culture, language and in some cases where ethnicity and religion are closely correlated, faith" (Thio 198).[19] This view of "multi-cultural composition" is influenced by Singapore's path to nationhood.

Under British rule for more than a century, Singapore achieved independence in 1963 as part of the Federation of Malaya. Differences in governance approaches and continuing religious and racial tensions among the eleven different states constituting the Federation pushed Singapore to declare itself as an independent country in 1965.

While Singapore's official state policy suggests an egalitarian recognition of racial and religious identifications, the residues of colonialism and its policies toward social differences remain embedded in national governance (Goh, "From Colonial" 235). In this postcolonial milieu, three main ethnoracial categories achieve the most prominent legibility: "Under the CMIO (Chinese, Malay, Indian, Others) scheme, every Singaporean is officially racially typed at birth" (Huat, "Multiculturalism" 60).[20] The boundaries of ethnicity and race are further complicated by the conflation between ethnicity and religion.[21] In Singapore, the "stereotypical image" is that "Malays are Muslim," while the "Chinese practise Buddhism and Taoism and . . . Indians are Hindu, unless otherwise stated" (Thio 202).[22] The Singaporean citizen materializes most prominently through a combination of race, ethnicity, and religion, endangering or erasing those who fall outside those frameworks. Of course, compounding these issues are class designations, with Chinese descendants posted at the top and Malay descendants often denoted as a problem minority.[23] Even as Singapore attempts to bridge an ethos of diversity with a state policy of multiculturalism, divisions between groups result in power dynamics that ultimately fracture this idealized, unified national identity.

Such concerns obviously influence *Pulse*'s depictions, revealing a nation-state embroiled in factionalisms. In one conversation, Natalie and Selim weigh in on continuing social tensions in Singapore, a conversation I recount to address the embedded discourses of genealogy and kinship that surface repeatedly throughout the narrative. Selim first admits that he does not know much about his Malay heritage because his mother "hardly talks about" (38) this ancestry. Natalie responds with references to the 1964 race riots. The narrative breaks for analepsis here, as Natalie recalls a pivotal moment in which her and her father's lives were endangered during those riots: "I thought of the time Papa and I narrowly escaped being harmed in July 1964. We were in Geylang Serai when his scooter stalled on a dirt road next to a field of lalang grass. We spotted a gang of Malay men with parangs approaching us from the far side of the field. We were saved when a lorry drove by and blocked the path between the men and us, allowing Papa to finally start up his Vespa and drive away" (37). The conversation goes on, as Selim quotes from the National Pledge—"One united people regardless of race, language or religion"—in an ironic tone, precisely because fissures within the community continue to erupt, especially in light of 9/11 (37).[24] For Selim, the issue of religion becomes important in the post–9/11 moment: "Unlike [Natalie's] generation, it's not simply a question of race anymore. Especially when there's more and more of us in Singapore who are racially mixed. It's all about religion. Christianity against Islam" (39).[25] Though Selim suggests that the contemporary nation-state embraces racial differences, the strong tether between social categories reflects how Singaporean Muslims, most of whom are Malay, might be targeted through multiple identity markers in the post–9/11 era. As Rahil Ismail and Brian Shaw denote, in the period following 9/11 and the emergence of terrorist groups linked to Al-Qaeda, there was "the sense of pressure on Singapore Malay-Muslims to prove their loyalty and trustworthiness with a heightened sense of suspicion emanating from other Singapore communities" (41). In a novel concerned so much with personal traumas, incest, and childhood sexual abuse, how do we link Natalie's experiences with larger social contexts?

Looking back to Butler, Harkins, and Sheffer, I argue that the novel critically aligns personal traumas with larger postcolonial tensions involving the specter of miscegenation. If incest becomes a metaphor for an uncritical romance with a mode of endogamy that upholds ethnoracial purity in the ideal Singaporean citizen, then the nation-state itself—the figurative father—is implicated in an incestuous social construction. This deleterious inheritance is evident within the novel in elliptical ways. Indeed, Natalie's memory of her experience with her father in Geylang Serai, a precinct in Singapore known for its majority Muslim population, takes on greater meaning.[26] Natalie and her father, who primarily consider themselves Chinese and whose extended family practices a form of Taoism, would potentially be seen as deviant to the Malay men and targets for brutality during the riots. Natalie's memory never directly reveals why those Malay men would have been so intent on harming her and her father, so we must read beyond what is narrated to make sense of this frightening experience.

A broader example of this incestuous social construction transpires in the novel's staging of Singaporean historical tensions. On Chinese New Year's eve in 1965, Natalie's father comes home with his face bloodied. It is not entirely clear what has happened and why he is home late, but this temporal period falls in line with the civil unrest occurring as Singapore moved toward independence.[27] Natalie overhears a conversation in which her father explains, "I was trying to help. Otherwise, who knows what that man would have done to her?" (83). Because we hear this conversation from Natalie's distant perspective, we are uncertain of the context of her father's rhetorical question, but a plausible reading is that Natalie's father intervened to save a woman from sexual violence, perhaps related to animosities arising out of racial, ethnic, and religious identifications.

In the climactic sequence in which Natalie's father punishes her after discovering her same-sex relationship with Faridah, the novel again subtly relates incest to larger issues of racial and religious identity. In his tirade prior to the moment he begins to strangle her, Natalie's father states, "God saved your life in 1964, and what for? What kind of daughter? You are garbage!" (226). In this instance, Natalie's father is clearly jealous of her romance with Faridah, as he states that Natalie has "betrayed" him (226). Natalie functions as a lover rather than a daughter, punctuating her father's continued incestuous demands. At the same time, the reference to 1964 recalls the pair's dangerous experience in Geylang Serai. His father's evocation of this memory represents another attempt to reassert control over the daughter's body: that only he can establish Natalie's proper worth. Faridah, too, is indirectly referenced in this moment, precisely because of her part-Malay background and because she becomes a sexual and racial competitor. The queer, interethnic romance between Natalie and Faridah is a sign of a deleterious hybridity that Natalie's father desperately tries to delegitimize. The father's explosive reaction might be said to stem from his insecure racialized heterosexual masculinity, a vulnerability that is mirrored by the tumultuous evolution of Singapore's national history.

In this way, the novel highlights how incestuous personal relationships relate to Singapore's uneasy road to independence. If Natalie signifies as a body that will not be constrained by ideals of sexual and racial purity, especially as evidenced by her fledgling desires for Faridah, then she further exemplifies a defiant figure who must be controlled. Incest not only functions to destroy familial social relations but also symbolically acts as a mode by which to counter, however traumatically, forms of unwelcome exogamy.

Peranakan Kinships

The novel obsessively returns to questions concerning race, ethnicity, religion, and sexuality, notably when Natalie invokes her ancestral lineages. Here Natalie's recounting undercuts how the nation-state's narrative of unified progression operates to expunge the presence of ethnoracial hybridity. Concerning her maternal side, Natalie explains, "My family never talked about our Malay lineage. On Mum's side, Mah-Mah was Nonya, the female offspring of a Chinese father and a Malay mother. But Kong-Kong never commented on it, as if this uncomfortable reality didn't exist" (64). Kong-Kong "came to discover truths about Malays and could proclaim them with such certainty. Laced with vehemence" (64). The erasure of Natalie's Malay background follows within the identity paradigms set forth and supported by state policy. Natalie's acknowledgment of her maternal-side grandmother as a Nonya is important insofar as she readily understands the possibility of mixture and hybridity in Singaporean society.

"The Peranakans, otherwise known as Babas and Nonyas, or Straits Chinese," were an "an ethnic group which traced its descent to seventeenth century

Chinese migrants who married local women in Southeast Asia" (Rocha 100). The Peranakans historically were elevated to an elite status in Singapore because of their cultural familiarity with British customs and their long-term settlement in the area,[28] but their social position eroded during the postcolonial period (Joan Henderson, "Ethnic" 35).[29]

The official movement toward the CMIO classification system further has contributed to the decline of Peranakan cultures and communities: "All racial identities are determined within the CMIO framework . . . and the Peranakans are classed as Chinese for the purposes of identity cards, official forms and the census" (Joan Henderson, "Ethnic" 36). Rocha further notes that those of mixed descent are "often unable to identify with their allocated label, or being arbitrarily defined by phenotype" (116). Henderson's and Rocha's points reveal the illegibility of certain mixed groups within Singapore, explicitly those who do not hail from a genealogy that can be strictly traced to Chinese, Malay, or Indian backgrounds.[30] Given these contexts, *Pulse*'s inclusion of major Peranakan characters serves to undercut the bounded formations of race and ethnicity functioning in Singapore.[31]

Natalie's family attempts to resolve the issue of miscegenation through Kong-Kong's aggressive promotion of their diasporic Chinese heritage. The obsession with ethnoracial preservation, of course, is reinvoked through incest as a form of endogamy in which the daughter's body becomes the site of regulation. Natalie is the appropriate bearer of inscrutable belongings because she refuses to conform to these regimes of purity, a disobedience that connects her more intimately with Faridah, Faridah's husband, Adam, and their son, Selim, because these four characters all hail from mixed backgrounds. Whereas Natalie's family obscures their Peranakan ancestry, Faridah's family more willingly acknowledges their hybrid genealogies, despite the nation-state's rather rigid perspective on ethnoracial mixing. At the same time, Selim, in particular, pushes back against the ways his father attempts to police how their hybridity should be maintained. I accordingly move to an exploration of Faridah's family and the ways in which multiple ancestries function as the site of familial containment.

As Natalie notes, Faridah eventually marries Adam, who is also of Peranakan background. But this genealogy is partially shrouded, patently in relation to Faridah and Adam's son, Selim: "On his identity card, Selim was listed as Chinese, in accordance with Adam's ethnicity. But that's part of the inconsistency. Adam is really a Baba, a male of mixed Malay and Chinese heritage.

But neither Babas nor Nonyas would be acknowledged on their identity cards. I knew from Faridah that Adam was infuriated by his son's decision to privilege his Malay name over his Christian one" (30). The National Registry Identification Card that Natalie references allows a citizen to mark a racial background but not to account for mixed backgrounds. Enforcing only one racial identification at the expense of more complicated lineages again figures into the state's implicit co-optation of its citizens' personal lives. As Angelia Poon notes, "The patrilineal inheritance of race foregrounds the extent to which claiming a racial identity in official terms is not largely a matter of personal choice in Singapore, a point seen most clearly in the case of children from mixed-race marriages who cannot automatically, for example, use a hyphenated or hybrid racial category to describe themselves within the bureaucratic machinery of the state" (72). When *Pulse* was published in 2010, the one-race rule was still enforced, but the Identification Card form now allows more than one option. But the order of the races chosen still makes a difference. For instance, if Selim had been listed as Chinese and then Malay, he would have been slotted into governmental services and programs on the basis of the first racial identification. Of course, Selim introduces another wrinkle into this equation by choosing his Malay name over "Gabriel," the Christian one given to him by his father. Selim follows the path of his maternal-side grandfather Osman, who "picked the name [Selim] and that particular spelling to reflect the connection to their Arabic lineage—albeit distant—tracing their history back to the Ottoman Empire" (30).[32] A Peranakan like Selim can obscure his many possible identifications just as thoroughly as state policy can. But Selim's decision to honor an ethnic lineage outside of his Chinese ancestry reveals his push to expand the boundaries of kinship models implicitly enforced by state regulations and directly expected by immediate family members.

For Selim, heritage is more than a matter of blood; it is also a political orientation. As Natalie explains, Selim's father, Adam, was distantly related to "Munshi Abdullah, the famous tutor and interpreter for Sir Stamford Raffles" (41). This mention of Sir Stamford Raffles, founder of Singapore, firmly places nation, race, ethnicity, and religion back within the colonial framework. Raffles was more infamously known for "developing the myth of Malay backwardness, so much so that for most of the nineteenth century, his arguments about the so-called decay of Malay society were implicitly accepted by Europeans" (41–42). This viewpoint follows the work of Syed Muhd Khairudin Aljunied, who argues that Raffles promoted Hinduism and Buddhism ("Sir Thomas") while denigrating Malays for their Islamic faith ("From Noble"). Natalie calls Selim's grandfather a "proud descendant" (42) of Abdullah, and Selim sees this distant ancestry as a way to resist how Singaporean citizens should identify themselves through racialized regimes based in part on outdated colonial paradigms that generated rigid hierarchies. Like his grandfather, Selim "was obviously very proud of being related to Munshi Abdullah, the learned tutor to Raffles who, unlike popularly disseminated views, did not unequivocally support the views of his British master" (59).[33] Selim's decision to honor his Malay-Arabic heritage serves both to sidestep postcolonial classification rubrics and to escape his father's religious impositions.

As noted earlier, unlike Natalie's progenitors, Selim's family embraces their Peranakan heritage. The family retains its hybrid consciousness, despite the force of a national milieu so intent on maintaining a fantasy of the ideal, pure citizen. At the same time, Selim's choice to push back against Adam's Christian faith signals a way in which the Peranakan future is still endangered. In this sense, even within the framework of mixed ethnicity and mixed race, the novel posits the problematic function of the state father's rule of law as a mode by which children's bodies become mastered. That is, the child must act as the vessel for the ethnoracially insulated and ensured future, one instituted on the domestic scale by the (sexual) mastery of the father over the child's body. In Selim's case, his father's ability to preserve ethnoracial and religious purities of their Peranakan heritage through his child is threatened, and thus this child must be dominated and reclaimed.

Both Natalie's and Selim's approaches to their ethnoracial backgrounds underlie their alignment with ancestries in danger of erasure. For Natalie, the avowal of her Peranakan background despite her father's best efforts signals the importance of a rebellious hybridity that is itself a useful metaphor for all the ways that she is already a disobedient national daughter: as a queer, as a practitioner of Kinbaku, as a believer in alternative therapies and spiritual beings, as one who constructs inscrutable belongings. For Selim, choosing to identify through a Malay-Arab ancestor undermines how hybridity can still be controlled in the context of biological family relations and more largely reveals how his choice to promote one lineage functions to critique neocolonial discourses that still shroud Singaporean policies. Like Natalie, Selim can be understood as a disobedient national child through his queerness, his interest in Kinbaku, and his incisive favoring of his Malay-Arab background. The inscrutable belonging between Natalie and Selim also flourishes in their collective resistance of their biological fathers and the nation-state's dictates that govern how an individual must identify and how families come to be socially constructed through regimes of purity and endogamy. But this oppositional approach is precisely why these two characters become targets for regulation, control, and domination at both familial and national levels.

Godzilla and Other Historical Monstrosities

Natalie's trip back to Singapore forces her to confront her buried traumas. By placing her past into conversation with Selim's death, she begins to navigate the unresolved psychic issues that stem from her father's abuse and the nation-state's limited social recognition of those marked as somehow different. The extended national discourse around racial hybridity and the nation-state's reconfiguration of colonial apparatuses reproduce regimes of oppression on its own citizens: as Selim and Natalie resist being regulated on both individual and social levels, they are branded by their status as disobedient national children. At the same time, Natalie's survival plot requires her to reconsider how violence is wielded at both personal and national scales. If both her biological father and figurative state father are intimately associated with the production of trauma, then Natalie must evaluate such brutalities through their sociocultural dimensions. In doing so, she models a form of historical consciousness, one that is essential to maintaining and evolving her inscrutable belongings. I accordingly turn to an exploration of ways in which Natalie refigures monstrosity, especially with respect to the novel's depiction of Godzilla.

As a child, Natalie does not explicitly link Godzilla with her father, but her recollections already begin to gesture to this pairing. Her obsession with Godzilla appears rooted in how to understand the creature's psyche: was he inherently evil, or did his environment shape his destructive actions? Determined to discuss the issue further, she goes to her schoolteacher, Miss Rajah, and theorizes that "the monster was full of atomic radiation. So I think Godzilla must have something to do with the A-bomb" (116). This conversation turns in another direction as Natalie asks Miss Rajah why there isn't "anything in our history syllabus about the atomic bombings of Hiroshima and Nagasaki?" (116). Miss Rajah explains that "Singaporeans of our parents' generations are still bitter about the Japanese occupation of the island. Some Chinese lost relatives during the Nanking Massacre in China. So it was a double blow for those people" (117). Miss Rajah's point, of course, forms part of a larger national conversation concerning this occupation, one that emphasizes the period's brutality, massacres, and cultural denigration and economic instability.³⁴ At the same time, Miss Rajah reminds us that Singapore itself comprises many citizens who have had diasporic trajectories. In this sense, the novel continually subverts any essentialist characterization of the ideal citizen-subject, thus interlacing Natalie's own flagrantly queer, hybrid identity to the discourses of diaspora that show how Singaporeans cannot be tethered to a pure origin point or an indigenous ancestral community. Natalie's migration to Canada extends and enriches the diasporic nature of Singaporean citizenry.

The conversation later returns to the question of Godzilla. Natalie muses, "Maybe Godzilla would have been fine if it weren't for the nuclear accident. People did that to him. I mean, the atomic bomb" (118). This conversation clearly operates on two levels. On the personal level, it reveals Natalie's desire to rationalize her father's sexual abuse, that his monstrosity can be explained by some motivation. As I have earlier argued, Natalie's father is consumed by the desire to retain power over defining his ethnic heritage and his reproductive future, which are both endangered by the chaotic forces of nation-state construction. Unfortunately, he attempts to maintain stability in these tempestuous circumstances by abusing his own child.

On another level, we must recall the fact of Natalie's use of Kinbaku, a Japanese erotic bondage practice. Kinbaku always returns us to the issues of domination and submission, and further positions us to account for any reference to the Japanese imperial enterprise. The novel's allusion to the Japanese occupation adds another wrinkle to Singapore's elaborate history. Scholars such as Kevin Blackburn ("Reminiscence" 95) and Ernest Koh (77) reveal that this period directly influenced the move toward Malayan and later Singaporean independence. Japanese colonialism is rendered as the oppositional force spurring nation-state development. Certainly the period following the occupation becomes the defining point for Singapore's arrival onto the stage of a global capitalism, but this economic advancement cannot be seen as entirely beneficial, given the emphasis on futurity and neoliberalism that promotes an amnesiac nation-state.³⁵

If Singaporean curricula pose the Japanese as monsters without cause, then Natalie's response evades such a reading, showing us how power is situational and villainy a matter of perspective. Natalie shows her astute critical thinking here, following what Susan J. Napier argues is the crucial reversal of the film: "[I]t demonizes American nuclear science in an obvious reference to the atomic tragedies of Hiroshima and Nagasaki. Second, it allows for the traditional happy ending (another important convention in the traditional science fiction movie genre), by allowing 'good' Japanese science to triumph against the evil monster" (331–332).[36] As Napier points out, the film introduces a critique of American nuclear science, complicating the terrain of blame that surfaced in the period following World War II. Natalie undermines any simplistic categorization of the Japanese as the primary antagonist of the Singaporean nation-state. For Natalie, the sites of war and conquest as well as war's aftermath generate numerous caustic forces and transnational currents that reverberate into the present day.

But *Pulse*'s invocation of the film introduces another perspective through Natalie's retrospective storytelling. If Natalie is bound—at least metaphorically speaking—by Japanese culture and associated contexts, then she is bound in a way that reconstitutes the imperial enterprise and nation-state modernization. As an adult, Natalie watches the film on her return to Singapore, and her experience is slightly changed. She "notic[es] aspects of the movie [she doesn't] remember from the first time [she] watched it. [She doesn't] think the American version went into such detail about the presence of strontium-90. It was so much clearer in the original film, the link between the destructiveness of the monster and the atomic bomb, a creation of humanity" (233). This moment solidifies her belief that monstrosity is self-perpetuating: violent acts such as dropping an atomic bomb generate more such acts. As already noted, neoliberal and neocolonial policies, which the novel suggests are partially derived out of Singapore's traumatic historical emergence, can also engender other iniquities: they shape a modern nation-state in which a model citizen is valued at the destructive cost of others who are deemed as too deviant. For Natalie, then, to look back at this film is to bring to light a larger historical tapestry involving this unending cycle of retribution and widespread regulation of social differences.

At the same time, this perspective does not absolve the savagery wrought by colonialism and its aftermath. Natalie makes mention of two important visits that she makes while in Singapore, one to the Raffles Hotel and another to the Changi Prison. Of the Raffles Hotel, Natalie muses about the fact that the past is "sanitized—suffering and carnage concealed under the mantle of creeping ivy" (236). She goes on to note the exclusion of Asians on the property "until 1930" (236), clarifying the British policies that created damaging racial divisions; her observations further thwart the "sanitized" depiction of the past. Natalie's narration hence provides a window into the problematic display of what has already occurred: touristic venues suggest that the visitor can consume colonial encounters in a hedonistic way. Walking through the Raffles Hotel, Natalie can appreciate aspects of the location, calling it "restful" to sit on a "wrought-iron bench and look up to the rooms on the second storey. Rooms once occupied by Joseph Conrad, Somerset Maugham, Ava Gardner and Charlie Chaplin" (236).[37] Certainly legions of visitors still seek out the hotel's picturesque vistas, a place generating an important source of income for a country intent on displaying its textured heritage. The site also beckons to visitors as a harmonious melding of Eastern (its geographical location, for instance) and Western (the writers who stayed here) elements.

While this space is conditioned for the amusement of the tourists, the presentation of the Raffles Hotel produces a mode of historical amnesia concerning the detrimental effects of colonialism. Daniel P. S. Goh argues that venues like the Raffles Hotel, which have been renovated and restored to pre-independence facades—the most sustained alterations occurring in 1989—function as "monument[s] to the neoliberal globalization of Singapore" ("Capital" 177) in which "the cosmopolitan-vernacular hybridities of globalization are celebrated" ("Capital" 189).[38] According to Joan C. Henderson, "Raffles Hotel is presented in the context of colonial society and its values, and nostalgia for this era is constantly evoked, especially the 1920s and 1930s which are generally accepted as its heyday. Connections with literary figures like Somerset Maugham are emphasised, such personalities clearly belonging to a Western and not an Asian culture. A very partial view of history is thus communicated" ("Conserving" 22–23).[39] In this vein, Natalie intervenes in the ways that "hybridities of globalization," in the form of tourist sites and revitalized areas, are selectively chosen and redesigned to highlight specific narratives of the nation-state, offering only a "partial view of history."[40]

For Natalie, the Raffles Hotel is a site of contested meanings. She accordingly wonders, "[h]ow many people of this current generation of youths know that when the Japanese occupied Singapore from 1942 to 1945, they named Raffles Hotel *Syonan Ryokan*? *Syonan* meaning 'Light of the South,' their name for Singapore, and *Ryokan* meaning a Japanese inn. Such euphemistic detail that the hotel had served as a transit camp for British prisoners of war" (236). Here Natalie looks past the Raffles Hotel as the popular tourist site it has become, tracing more colonial violence that occurred there. In this instance, Natalie's perspective shows us how the once-powerful British colonial subjects can transform into the vanquished and be subjected to domination. Even in such an idyllic space, one that Natalie describes as "restful" (236), she understands not only how much time and labor it takes to redevelop any location but also the ways that such sanitization covers over a lineage of traumas derived out of conquest.

Natalie accordingly functions as a diasporic nonconformist and disobedient national daughter, refusing to identify wholeheartedly with a nationalist project that recasts only certain portrayals of historical contact as pleasurable and culturally enriching. As Natalie points out, "When Lord Mountbatten and his naval fleet entered Singapore on September 4, 1945, and demanded surrender from the Japanese troops on the island, three hundred Japanese soldiers refused to surrender and killed themselves with grenades at *Syonan Ryokan*. Perhaps even on this very spot where I am now resting. How things have changed: many of the guests at Raffles these days are tourists from Japan" (236). Natalie emphasizes the incongruity between tourist sites and their historical pasts, illuminating which significations can be embraced and which cannot.[41]

Of the Changi Prison site, Natalie ponders the mind-set of the Japanese invading forces. She muses: "I wonder how it was then, to be a member of the conquering army. Did the Japanese soldiers allow themselves to feel the horrors of war? Some of them must have" (264).[42] Here Natalie again acts to avoid any simple categorization of the Japanese as evil. For Natalie, history can be unsanitized only by complicating the line separating heroes and villains, while still acknowledging past brutalities. This message is strikingly salient for Natalie, as she comes to promote a life philosophy and occupational trajectory so focused on healing and alternative therapies. Indeed, Natalie offers a corrective to the way that Singapore's national consciousness erases—or at least rhetorically simplifies—the country's history and produces an idealized, but circumscribed citizen-subject who functions as the metaphorical, docile state child.

Natalie comes to see the ambivalences that shape Singapore's violent colonial history. This process of working through national traumas helps to inform her understanding of her father, which undergoes a kind of metamorphosis. Though Natalie does not absolve her father of past actions, she attempts to rationalize his past actions; in this sense, she reformulates the nature of psychic wounds as they modify the creation of families, both traditionally conceived and alternatively constructed. Natalie elucidates how her tortured life is one informed by the riotous structural forces that have generated the postcolonial nation-state. Indeed, a national genealogy of trauma is handed to her, one that simultaneously haunts the intergenerational brutalities apparent in the incestuous relationship she is forced to endure. Natalie's awareness of and engagement with these cycles of past violence (on both personal and national levels) continues to spur her down dynamic paths, solidifying her inscrutable belongings comprising figures such as otherworldly spiritual beings, film monsters, Kinbaku practitioners, acupuncturists, and queer Singaporeans.

Beyond Cosmopolitan Hybridities of the Future: Embracing the Degenerate Descendant

With elegant nuance, Natalie reframes how we can understand Singapore through its legacies of colonial trauma. At the same time, I must further address how Natalie becomes enmeshed in discourses related to the nation-state's futurity, which primarily involve an idealized tomorrow in which economic supremacy and urban revitalization projects loom large. Scholars certainly have noted Singapore's relentless drive toward innovation with the intent of becoming an "important global player" (Baum 1098) as well as a "global city with total business capacities" (Yeung 143).[43] C. J. W.-L. Wee argues that the central governing entity, the People's Action Party (PAP), "remains faithful to its core mission since 1965 of matching up to the modern West, using all the relevant sociocultural engineering tools to bring that goal about" ("End" 989).[44]

Stephan Ortmann argues that Singapore's modernization has occurred in two phases, the first between independence and 1980, and then from 1980 onward. In the first phase, Singaporean leaders emphasized economic strength and looked to the future to shape a new narrative of nation-state progression. Of the lasting ramifications of this first phase, "Old buildings, which were in the way of development, were torn down. There are not many remnants of Singapore's colonial past that still survive today, and those that do stand in the shadow of Singapore's gigantic skyline" (Ortmann 29). In the second phase, Singaporean leaders sought to unify the citizenry through an authoritarian political system, a strategy that ultimately has backfired because it simultaneously led to increased social, cultural, and legislative restrictions. The justification for this strict and pragmatic mode of governance was that a tenuous economy makes the nation-state fragile.[45]

Given the turbulent postcolonial history that shrouds Singapore, the desire to stabilize the nation-state is understandable. But this approach fails to find value in anything deemed unproductive or aberrant in construct. The queer Asian North American and diasporic Singaporean comes to be instituted as a figure who intervenes in this ethos by embracing a retrogressive consciousness, recognizing the importance of obsolescence and deterioration. Natalie's narrative endurance requires her to continue to generate alternative perspectives of the past, bringing to light communities and spaces deemed unfit to be welcome into the modernized, future-oriented economy productive and its associated, heterosexually fecund national family. Because she is only visiting Singapore, Natalie's inscrutable belongings are finally inspired by her fully assuming her place as a degenerate descendant; she is a figure who flourishes outside the traditional construct of the physical home and the domestic space idealized by the figurative state father.

This spatial exile explains Natalie's itinerancy in the novel's last fifty pages, and I turn to investigate Natalie as a kind of postcolonial *flaneuse*: she claims an ambulatory mobility that emphasizes her tactical place within the final arc of the survival plot.[46] At one point, after finishing a meal, Natalie goes to "walk along New Bridge Road, heading north, passing shopping complexes interspersed with office buildings. Turning right at Upper Hokkien Street, "[she spies] a few older HDB [Housing and Development Board] government flats in an area where, one hundred years ago, brothels would have lined the side streets. Instead of its former seediness, the street has been tidied up, with the old facades carefully restored to attract tourists" (235). Here urban renewal functions selectively on the basis of how a given space signifies to the nation-state and its policymakers, and its potential impact on the global consumer. That is, the old facades can be restored because they offer a cultural heritage auguring a normative reproductive future that can advance nation building, while the legacy of sex work must be expunged because of its association with deviant sexuality (even as prostitution in Singapore remains legal).[47] As Nicole Tarulevicz puts it in her study of Singaporean discourses of history, "Buildings may serve as the embodiment of national identity, but only certain buildings" (424). The brothels, though sites of hedonistic pleasure connected to neoliberal economic consumption, do not signify properly in relation to sexual practices—namely, those leading to increased numbers of Singaporean heteronuclear families and obedient national children. Therefore, brothels cannot be recognized as part of an official discourse of state-sanctioned locations, so Natalie must function to undermine this effacement.

The reference to the "older HDB government flats" is important in the rather inconspicuous way that Natalie calls attention to processes of gentrification and social control. The HDB flats ensure structural integration of different ethnic groups, making them a central signifier of Singapore's modernization.[48]

These HDB flats have become what Sishir Chang calls a Singaporean architectural "vernacular" (102). As Robbie B. H. Goh further notes, "The first decade of the HDB's activities was marked most significantly by the relocation of residents out of pre-modern housing, which was usually organised along the racial lines of immigrant communities, into radically different housing environments designed to create multiracial, integrated communities" (1590).[49] The dream of such "multiracial, integrated communities" would seem to be a great success given the ubiquity of HDB flats,[50] but the discourse of hybridity is advanced only insofar as these residences enable the government to favor a spatial ideology that lends itself to nation building.

The HDB flats, while arguably decreasing ethnic and racial divisions, simultaneously engendered other changes in social formations. For instance, Sishir Chang explains that "the large extended families that existed previously in Singaporean society have been broken apart and now the focus of family life is in the nuclear family" (104–105). Chang argues that this alteration in family form was spurred in part by "limited space in HDB housing and the emphasis on total community planning in HDB new towns which have greatly reduced the need for the support of an extended family" (105). The propagation of the HDB flats and the concomitant reconstruction of Singaporean social relations around the nuclear family contextualize how Natalie's reference to these buildings appears in diametric opposition to the brothels. Indeed, the HDB flats materialize the heart of the modernized Singaporean nation-state replete with the fertile promise of the reproductive future, while the brothels represent retrogression that must be wiped out.[51] Natalie, our queer Asia North American storyteller, must look back in order to remind us of the vestiges of locations that generated alternative social formations and sexual cultures.

This focus on capital, spatial innovation, and neoliberal economic policies does bring us back to the question of the individual subject and her participation in nation making. Because Natalie's inclusion in the national citizenry is always jeopardized by her status as a mixed ethnicity diasporic subject and as a queer woman who also engages in BDSM activities, she fails to uphold the futurity that the nation-state, as symbolic father, would affirm. On her way to the Raffles Hotel, Natalie observes, "The merlion sculpture on Marina Bay comes into view, endlessly spewing water out its mouth back into the ocean. Whoever thought up this hybrid symbol—combining the story of Sanga Nila Utama spotting lions on the island in the eleventh century with the Western myth of the mermaid—was a marketing genius" (229). Natalie again points out the importance of hybridity to the nationalist ethos, which attempts to bring together Eastern and Western cultural elements to endorse intercultural harmony and the nation-state's cosmopolitan virtues. The "marketing genius" of that symbol is evident in the way that the sculpture, as part of public works and state-sanctioned beautification efforts, helps to advocate for a robust tourism sector. The Marina Bay, of course, is one of the most prominent sites that spotlight Singapore's modernization, brimming with sweeping nighttime vistas of illuminated skyscrapers and hotels. But Natalie notices too that "[i]n contrast, past the end of the new highway stand the remnants of Clifford Pier: all boarded up and no longer the busy international passenger terminal it used to be. Degeneration *is* the way of Tao" (229–230). Natalie's turn to the word *degeneration* reveals the ways the nation-state views certain objects, places, and even people as excessive and requiring some sort of reharnessing.

In this specific case, the Clifford Pier, though a prominent site of colonial-era transit, might seem to be the appropriate location to abandon given its history with British rule, but the site would eventually be "gazetted" and refurbished so it could "house an international restaurant with alfresco dining" (Hao 17). In this sense, the pier only becomes properly productive once it can be updated and then enfolded into the project of international tourism. Thus Natalie's focus on a period in which the pier is defunct is fitting, as it fails to uphold a state-sanctioned postcolonial productivity. She relates to this place as metaphorical haven for those that may not always offer the nation-state the innovation and transformation it demands.

Natalie reconfigures degeneration with respect to Taoism—alternatively denoted as Daoism—to bring into focus the ways that nation-state policies artificially create distinctions between the useful and the outdated, the loyal and the treasonous. According to Hans-Georg Moeller, "By introducing the distinction between good and bad, the Confucians, from a Daoist point of view, not only create goodness but also badness. Without the Confucian attempt to make the world a better place, the world would be 'beyond good and evil.' To prevent badness means, from a Daoist point of view, also to prevent goodness. You cannot have one without the other" (118). The Daoist sees the world as one in flux; she "accepts the fact of being born into a civilizational order but does not accept the possibility that civilizational values define what it means to be fully alive and human. The acceptance of phenomenal existence requires a more profound recognition of the fact that the fulfillment and renewal of human life depends on a periodic return to a chaotic or primitive condition"

(Girardot 75). These viewpoints on Daoism help articulate what is at stake for Natalie when she describes the Clifford Pier as in "degeneration," repurposing this word as part of a process as crucial to human life as progression or what Girardot calls "civilizational order." Indeed, implicit in Natalie's perspective is the fact that degeneration is immediately dismissed as a pejorative directed at a location that has outlasted its use value.[52] Natalie helps us to see that such sites and associated individuals (like herself) can help to create balance and actually restore a sense of order.

If degeneration is the way of Tao, Natalie's embrace of it is significant because she herself constantly looks back to temper the desire to move forward. As a queer diasporic Asian North American who returns to the homeland, she bears no children in service of nation-state initiatives or policies, continues her interest in the mystical arts, and avows her mixed ancestry.[53] Natalie endorses her status as the insubordinate figurative child who unveils buried narratives of Singapore's past in ways that seem chaotic and uncontrollable, especially from a governing regime so intent on harnessing the country's biopower and corralling its complicated and diverse citizenry into a unified plot of progress.[54] I follow Maurizio Peleggi's point that "[i]t is not surprising that cities and particular sites therein should be imagined, experienced and remembered in substantially different terms according to whether one is a native of the place, a long-term resident or a temporary visitor" (264). As a figure who cannot and does not claim Singapore as a national homeland, but nevertheless has strong ties to the country based on her childhood experiences, Natalie's liminality continually colors her observations. Her relationship to home and family, already being so parlous and inflected by rupture, influences how she interfaces with local places. Sites of unproductivity (such as the pier) and sexual deviance (such as the brothel) function as metaphorical spaces in which the storyteller finds a sense of comfort and refuge, however fleeting. By instituting such sites in order to generate alternative value systems for the nation-state, Natalie also reminds us that the development of inscrutable belongings engenders another form of harmony by placing heteronuclear families in a dynamic equilibrium with non-normative kinships.

Queer Asian North American Diasporic Survivals

Natalie's approach to history reverberates alongside her personal traumas. She reconfigures the past postcolonial atrocities to avoid vilifying her father as an inherently monstrous figure. She begins to see that his actions could have derived from the chaotic period of national independence. In this sense, Natalie's inscrutable belongings ultimately involve the critical intertwinement of her personal life with larger structural, spatial, and historical forces that have shaped Singapore as a nation. Given all of the ways that Selim and Natalie are juxtaposed, it is not surprising that the novel poses the strength of their inscrutable belonging. As I have shown, though these two characters are biologically unrelated, they initially make contact by virtue of their association with Faridah. But they share another commonality through the pleasure they find in Kinbaku. Another parallel emerges late in the novel as Natalie realizes that they are both incest survivors. A final overlap arises in their mixed-race backgrounds. But what tragically separates these characters and destroys their inscrutable belonging is Selim's suicide. The novel poses Selim as a melancholic subject who cannot work through the problematic nature of attachment. As Selim acknowledges in his note to Philip, "*Impossible to ask for something that won't be given freely. So there you have it. I've had enough*" (245). That "something" is an unconditional love from his father not based within or sullied by incestuous abuse. Though Selim is undone by Godzilla's touch, Natalie is able to repurpose what that death means, giving his suicide a sense of sacrifice. If he cannot live, then he must be able to help those who still remain.

But we cannot be too surprised that a queer Asian character might "choose" death over life. In a country in which male homosexual acts are still illegal (as of 2018) and the cultural milieu still actively denigrates queerness, most patently in the media (Detenber et al.), Natalie, Faridah, Selim, and others who affirm their same-sex desires flounder under the regime of social death: their romances must remain closeted for fear of potential sociocultural and, in Selim's case, legal reprisals.[55] If the novel posits that characters can be a product of their circumstances, then Selim's choice makes more sense; he exits a milieu in which he is constantly buffeted by antagonistic forces. The problem that the novel sets up is the hypocrisy of both individual and national viewpoints on kinship, family, sexuality, and a narrative of progressive, linear nation-state advancement.

In the wake of Selim's death, Natalie gets to sit down with Faridah, Adam, and their daughter over dinner. It is one of the few moments in which the novel takes place in a localized domestic space, but the scene is far from peaceful. Indeed, Adam immediately brings up the question of homosexuality in Canada, suggesting that he already understands the undercurrent of erotic attachments going on at the dinner table. As Adam divulges, "We read that the country now allows for marriage for homosexuals" (202), something that he attributes to the West's degradation of morality. Natalie responds in kind: "I beg to differ. Loving someone of the same sex isn't merely a Western phenomenon. And it's not a problem" (203). This scene is notable for a number of reasons, largely because Adam's discourse reminds us that queers do not have a spot at the Singaporean family's proverbial dinner table. His argument parallels what party leaders have at times echoed. For instance, Diane K. Mauzy and R. S. Milne detail how "[f]rom the 1970s the PAP government had been concerned that Asian values were being eroded or superceded by Western values" (62). Mauzy and Milne note that these decadent "Western values" prioritize individual thinking and desire at the expense of community building and an interdependent ethos (62).[56] Thus the novel continually links the biological father—in this case, Adam—to the figurative state father through the discourse of sexual normativity and the exaltation of the heteronuclear family. With the nation-state's viewpoint in mind, Natalie's sexual desire is seen as too individualistic and unpatriotic because of its correspondence with the West. At the same time, the dinner table includes at least three characters who are queer or have engaged in non-normative sex acts: Adam, in his incestuous relationship with his son, and Faridah and Natalie, who were once lovers. The novel continually confronts the multifaceted nature of the closet as it extends to the domestic space and casts a pall over the relationships that characters forge with each other.

The tenuousness of *Pulse*'s representation of one inscrutable belonging (comprising queer individuals such as Natalie and Selim) is made apparent by state policies concerning the illegality of homosexuality and the larger implications of these sexual restrictions. As Simon Obendorf explains, "Queer identities—due to their largely non-procreative and non-normative nature—have come to be understood by post-colonial state managers as threatening national survival and viability. The existence of such fears can be detected in the Singapore government's response to the issue of population growth—specifically the decline in the numbers of babies born to Singaporean families" (236).[57] This issue of population growth has long been central to state policy precisely because fertility decline started in the 1970s and clearly threatens any stable notion of Singaporean national identity, as indigeneity cannot be maintained.[58] Women are specifically targeted for national duty with respect to bearing children (Williams 147); this policy emphasizes not only a heterosexual reproductive future but the primacy of the biological family, which is itself oriented around marriage.[59] The state as a figurative father fosters the construct of an ideal Singaporean heteronuclear family by providing certain incentives for its citizens, such as baby bonuses and prioritized housing options in government flats.[60]

Of course, the social recognition of only certain kinds of family formations leads us to wonder about queer Singaporeans (or queer diasporic Singaporeans, in Natalie's case). What place is there for those marked by nonprocreative potential and non-normative desires? Kinbaku, in particular, appears as an unpatriotic, hedonistic, and disobedient activity that does little to advance national initiatives centered on biological, heterosexual procreation and the stability of the future population. Natalie is implicated in a form of gendered and sexualized dereliction: she is a Singaporean woman of a marriageable age, with the appropriate class bearing and, to a certain extent, the proper ethnoracial background—though we recall that her legibility here is directly as a result of her family's decision to obscure their ancestral hybridities—who should be using her body/vessel to produce more heterosexual Singaporeans. At the same time, we must read beyond the state as this figurative father who determines the right kind of children: Natalie and Selim procreate in the sense that they construct their inscrutable belonging, one that functions across generations and links past, present, and future. Kinbaku is further contextualized from the frame of Natalie's understanding of this bondage activity as therapeutic and healing rather than as solipsistic and self-serving. For Natalie, Kinbaku is not only a literalized form of connection to others but also a metaphorical conceit, binding her to a postcolonial history that makes apparent the insecurity of the nation-state in its continual attempt to define the ideal citizen subject through pragmatic policies involving the inextricable knots of reproductive futurism, modernization imperatives, and economic progress. Inscrutable belongings are central to the novel, as I argue, because they articulate why Natalie and Selim need each other to attempt to navigate the thorny terrains of nation-state modernization, postcolonial history, sexual abuse, incest, BDSM behaviors, and queer sexualities.

As degenerate descendants, they function to undermine the restrictive bonds of normative social formations. Singaporean policy constructs only one nationally sanctioned postcolonial family: "The married, monogamous, heterosexual, procreative couple is thus firmly located at the centre of the public housing landscape. This was a central contribution to the narrowing of intimate possibilities in the postcolonial period in order to achieve what the colonial administration never could—a nation of subjects" (Oswin 263). But, as Lindy Williams et al. reveal, "the increasing participation of women in the labor force, attitudinal changes among the younger generation, and adoption of values compatible with modern life styles, such as increasing emphasis on career and material success" (297) have changed the structures of Singaporean families, which is not necessarily viewed as a positive.

If the heteronormative family continues to exist at the center of the Singaporean conception of home and nation, then characters like Natalie and Selim can never find a stable place within these social constructs. Outlawed and rendered as excess, these two characters find a crucial bridge to each other that affords but does not guarantee survival.[61] On the one hand, Selim's suicide reveals the fragility of these alternative social formations. On the other, Natalie's return to Canada at the novel's conclusion signals a return to her life as a healer, to her romance with Michelle, and to a national space that perhaps offers more fecund grounds for inscrutable belongings.[62] But the novel's final scene occurs in the space of the airplane, with Natalie shuttling between Singapore and Canada. This state of suspension is, of course, apt because it reminds us that the storyteller's survival plot retains its disquiet, with no guarantee of a better tomorrow.

CODA

IN 2014, the Asian Pride Project (APP) and the National Queer Asian and Pacific Islander Alliance (NQAPIA) teamed up to create the Visibility Project, a set of public service announcements in which Asian North American immigrant parents express their support for their queer progeny. In one video, a mother addresses the audience in Mandarin and then again in English, in both cases proclaiming her love for her queer son. The camera at first focuses on the mother's speech, but later it cuts to an image of the mother and her son together. Other videos are structured similarly: the immigrant parent or parents speak to an audience in one of six Asian languages—Mandarin, Hindi, Laotian, Korean, Japanese, and Tagalog—with the intent of showing their love for their queer children. These videos are monumental in that they shift the weight of coming out onto parents and biological families, suggesting that the problem of queer visibility is not solved simply by the act of the child speaking about his experiences as a desiring subject. The conundrums facing queer Asian North Americans are often rooted in social formations in which an open declaration of sexuality can result in disavowal, disapproval, open rejection, physical abuse, and generally negative feelings, perpetrated by close biological family members. By making these parents visible and audible, the APP and the NQAPIA rescript how Asian North Americans as a group confront issues of queerness in their familial and kinship formations. It becomes a collective rather than an individual process.

In addition to examining these public service announcements, I want to acknowledge briefly the larger terrain of visual culture, especially with respect to fictional films. Indeed, beyond the Visibility Project, cinematic depictions draw upon many of the same issues and themes concerning the intricacies and complications of coming out and finding acceptance from the family. For instance, Andrew Ahn's *Spa Night* (2016) is a nuanced and arresting depiction of an eighteen-year-old Korean American named David Cho (played by Joe Seo), who must negotiate the expectations of his parents concurrently with the development of same-sex yearnings. The film's title is a nod to the fact that David eventually gains employment at a Korean spa (to circumvent his family's dire financial situation), a location that allows him transitory, queer encounters with some of the patrons. David functions in many parallel ways to Bernard, our narrator from "Camouflage" (analyzed in Chapter 2), as both find a sense of refuge in the torrid space of spas and bathhouses. The similarities in these characters' lives make a film still from *Spa Night*—with a pensive David looking into a fogged up mirror—the appropriate cover image for this book. In this moment, David not only looks at himself but uses the mirror's reflective surfaces as a vantage point to cruise other men at the spa. In this space of visual yearnings, David achieves an ephemeral sense of queer recognition. As the film moves toward its conclusion, David begins to act out on his desires, even as he has yet to come out to his parents. Though out of the formal bounds of this study, this film is undoubtedly revolutionary and reminds us that there are other modes by which endurance and survival might be depicted and critically analyzed.

The darker underbelly of the public service announcements, gestured to by the ambivalent conclusion of *Spa Night*, of course, is the alternative narrative: the one in which parents do not support their children, or children cannot find the guidance they require to explore safely their emergent queer desires. This alternative narrative is the focus of this book: that is, how fiction writers imagine the survival plots of queer Asian North Americans who may not find support from blood relations or who cannot expect a romantic partner to serve as part of a viable kinship as a result of the continuing struggles for same-sex and queer couples to achieve fully integrated social, cultural, and legislative recognitions.

Many of the fictions I analyze in this book present substantial obstacles to the queer Asian North American storyteller's embrace not only by immediate family members but also by adults who are expected to function in caretaking capacities. I began my sustained readings by exploring Leong's short story "Camouflage," in which the narrator is subjected to incestuous violence by his uncle. I followed this examination with a consideration of Chee's *Edinburgh*; this novel unfolds as a protagonist works through the traumas that linger long after he is the target of sexual abuse from his choir director. In the subsequent chapter, I analyzed Alumit's *Letters to Montgomery Clift*, in which a storyteller moves to the United States as a young child and is raised by an extended family member, who is abusive. In the next, I critiqued Revoyr's *Wingshooters*. In this fictional narrative, the protagonist's parents leave her with extended family members when she is just a young child. Her relationship with her paternal-side grandfather is negatively affected when a murder occurs in their small town, and the conclusion reveals a grown-up narrator defined by an almost crippling sense of resignation. And in the final chapter, which reads Kwa's *Pulse*, the storyteller's father sexually abuses her and creates an incredible rift in the heart of the family.

Fortunately, in one novel the relationship between the storyteller and his biological family does remain primarily salubrious rather than harmful. In Alexander Chee's *Edinburgh*, the narrator's parents seem to accept and support his queer sexuality. At the same time, his father pushes him to learn English at the expense of his Korean heritage, encouraging him to follow a path of deracination in the pursuit of a normative Americanization. Familial ties, at least in their more traditional sense, exist as a site of conflict in all four novels in some form or another. These concerns explain the dire necessity of inscrutable belongings, however ephemeral or even self-destructive in their manifestations.

The conclusion of *Letters to Montgomery Clift* is perhaps most radical in how it unifies inscrutable belongings and more normative kinships. Indeed, as Bong comes to embrace his place with the Arangans, his relationship to Logan, and his complex connection to Clift, he also brings his mother into this fold, which suggests a larger social formation that reconstructs the boundaries of the queer Asian North American's family. This blueprint thus encourages multiple filiations, and in ending here, the novel provides the most optimistic, though nonformulaic, resolution to the survival plot.

At this point, I would like to return to the APP and NQAPIA videos to establish what is *not* being represented in them. Certainly their reconfiguration of how sexual and racial identities might find fruitful harmony within traditional homes is a welcome engagement with the actual social contexts affecting queer Asian North Americans today. But the videos must be seen beyond the content directly depicted. To better understand this dynamic, I look first at the organizations themselves because they are vital parts of the apparatus that will be foundational for reconstructing kinships. The APP states its mission to be "an online space for family and friends of lesbian, gay, bisexual and transgender (LGBT) Asian & Pacific Islander (API) people. It is a place to share our stories and experiences with each other, in the languages of our communities, in video, sound, pictures, and words." Allowing individuals who identify as queer and API to volunteer their own stories, the Asian Pride Project employs the virtual space to rescript conceptions of community and social formation.[1] The NQAPIA is a federation that comprises local organizations, with the aim of providing these smaller communal entities with general support. An annual conference allows members to "network, organize, agitate, educate, and build capacity" and functions with a goal similar to the APP's.[2]

The Visibility Project and its public service announcements can be cast in light of the production process itself, which extends beyond the traditional family constructs represented in the videos. In this sense, I am also foregrounding the importance of authorship and its relationship to activist representation. The videos cannot be divorced from activist communities that helped conceive of and produce them. These activist communities might be seen as variations of the dynamic social formations that I have been exploring in the fictions at the heart of this study. Without the communities and social formations that exist beyond the bounds of the heteronuclear family, the queer Asian North American's narrative of survival remains ever tenuous.

The question of authorship is where I would like to leave this book. The cultural productions at the center of this study, although fictionalizing queer Asian North Americans' lives, serve as activist documents. These writers, avowing their own status as queer Asian North Americans, are "volunteering" stories not necessarily about themselves, but about individuals who could be like themselves. In this process, they contribute to the possibilities of queer Asian North American lives without foregrounding an uplift narrative. In this sense, their emphasis on sequencing—that is, their desire to plot out survival from a retrospective positionality and to make explicit the link between endurance and the need for inscrutable belongings—reveals why these fictions are so singular and are able to accomplish a feat that the Visibility Project cannot.

Drawing on the social death miring the queer Asian North American, these works compel in their imaginative attempts to reconstruct the bonds of sociality and, in so doing, remind us of the perils and promises of inscrutable belongings. In this process, they script fruitful variations on the storyteller's ability to survive a hostile fictional world, and they gesture to the ways that such life trajectories must extend from these imagined landscapes to prescribe the demand to recognize and support the material endurance of all those—queer Asian North Americans and others—still subjected to the violent forces of social death and physical violence.

These fictions charge readers of all backgrounds to expand their understanding of social formations and, at the same time, to develop spaces and places and to devote time, energy, and resources to cultivate and to expand these inscrutable belongings.

NOTES

Introduction

1. As of 2017, some policies concerning the LGBTQI community are finding some obvious resistance from the new presidential administration. Trump recently ordered a ban on transgender individuals serving in the U.S. military.

2. For legal consideration of marriage equality and race, see Khuu.

3. See Barnard; Somerville; Ordover; and Canaday.

4. By using the term *postracial*, I mean a period in which a discourse emerges that suggests that racism is an artifact of the past. For considerations of postracial discourse, see Squires; Carbado and Gulati; D. T. Goldberg; and Tesler.

5. For consideration of the drop in marriage rates and changes in long-term social relationships in the American context, see Cherlin; and Heuveline and Timberlake; for an exploration of the decline in Canadian marriage rates as a result of social relationships such as cohabitation, see Kerr, Moyser, and Beaujot; and Beaujot and Ravanera.

6. In the context of a study involving interracial dating, Rocío García introduces her topic in this way: "Despite the increase in U.S. 'alternative' families from divorce, cohabitation, interracial relationships, and adoption, the nuclear family remains the form of family institution that accrues various economic, legal, and emotional benefits" (807). Canadian scholars have made similar findings from the perspective of a study involving couples and their ideals about monogamy and marriage. Green, Valleriani, and Adam note that, despite harboring liberal views concerning various sexual arrangements within a marriage, most heterosexual couples interviewed nevertheless retained a private ideal that marriage was a monogamous arrangement and expected as such in their own relationship (427). These studies help elucidate the cultural ideals concerning marriage and family that are still being retained on both sides of the U.S.-Canadian border.

7. LGBTQI stands for lesbian, gay, bisexual, transgender, queer, and intersex. I often

use the term *queer* as a shorthand for that acronym. Additional letters are sometimes added, including a Q to mean "questioning," a T to mean "two-spirited" in the context of Indigenous individuals, an A to mean "ally" and/or "asexual/aromantic." In addition, this manuscript chooses to employ gender-based terminology that may seem to reinscribe a binaristic formulation between male and female, but I have chosen to use this approach as a measure of grammatical standardization rather than of a political orientation concerning this issue. Indeed, I am well aware of the construct of gender. My use of gender-based pronouns must be conditioned with the understanding that my use of terms such as *him* and *her* necessarily implicates the complicated discourses that help us engage these terms as occasionally limiting (and reductive) and, in some cases, in need of radical transformation.

8. The motif of camouflage dovetails with Kenji Yoshino's consideration of "covering," a tactic employed by minorities involving assimilation into mainstream cultures. In the case of Leong's short story, Bernard seeks to express his sexuality in such a way that he cannot be deemed a public target.

9. For reconsiderations of Patterson's social death in a U.S. context, see Holland; Castronovo; JanMohamed; Peterson; and Cacho.

10. See also Backus for an exploration of social death in a lesbian context.

11. In the specific context of Canada, various scholars have shown some of the continued challenges facing queers and those identifying as LGBTQI, despite the fact that same-sex marriage has now been legal for over a decade. Margaret F. Gibson explains that gay adoption continues to be mired in complicated paperwork and politicized rhetoric (417). Giwa and Greensmith further explain that ethnic minorities who identify as queer and who experience racial prejudices experience multiple modes of exclusion (179). Finally, Wendy Pearson details the issues that may arise as Canadian same-sex marriages potentially define a new neoconservative norm for queer couples (160). Gibson (419) and Heather Macintosh, Elke D. Reissing, and Heather Andruff (88) make similar remarks about the dangers of normalizing a specific kind of queer relationship and the impact it might have on the larger community.

12. Judith Butler cautions against the promotion of marriage rights over a larger reconception of sexuality in relation to the nation-state, especially as it extends to kinship relationships ("Is Kinship" 16).

13. Connie M. Kane adds that "the family's honor and reputation are highly valued, so that individual wishes and needs may be suppressed for the sake of family loyalty" (96).

14. Not surprisingly, given the importance of family to queer Asian North Americans, "the most important personal issue surrounding Asian North American gays and lesbians seems to be coming out to parents" (Ishii-Kuntz 378). At the same time, given the fact that discussions or expressions of sexuality are often absent from the family dynamics of queer Asian North Americans, "Asian North American gays and lesbians may be more likely to come out to people from other ethnic groups rather than their own families or ethnic communities" (R. Green 172).

15. Citing an earlier study, Okazaki also reveals that only approximately one-quarter of respondents had come out to their parents "because of fear of rejection" (39).

16. I refer specifically to cultural productions such as big-budget Hollywood films and television shows.

17. By using the phrase *traditional kinship system*, I refer to the foundational conceptions offered by the anthropologist David Schneider, who defined American kinship through genealogy (blood) or the *order of nature* and marriage or the *order of law* (*American Kinship* 27). The American family system by contrast is a specific unit of kinship, which is based on the nuclear model (Sarkisian and Gerstel 1).

18. For more on the "rice queen" dynamic, which involves a same-sex relationship between a Caucasian man and an Asian man, see Metzger; and E. Lim. For more on queer Asian North American sexual and racial formation, see Fung; Chong-suk Han "Geisha of a Different Kind"; Eguchi; and Han, Proctor, and Choi.

19. See Eng's *Racial Castration* on representations of masculinity and Asian North American men. R. Lee's *Orientals* also offers a useful chapter on the "third sex" phenomenon used to describe Chinese immigrants during the late nineteenth and early twentieth centuries. Though the term *bottom* has often been used in a pejorative sense when connected to queer Asian North American men, Nguyen Tan Hoang reminds us that we must also consider the possible pleasures in positions of racialized and sexual subjection.

20. For more on queer Asian North American women and the problem of social recognition, see JeeYeun Lee; and Gopinath.

21. See Lenon; and R. K. Robinson. Other studies consider the problematic connections between movements for racial and queer equality in the United States context; please consult Franke; Bassichis and Spade; West; Stone and Ward; and Reddy. For more general considerations of same-sex marriage, see Trott. For issues related to same-sex marriage equality in Canada, see Cotler; P. W. Hogg; Mulé; and Pettinicchio.

22. For more on U.S. homonormativity, in relation to same-sex marriage, see Carter; Hopkins, Sorensen, and Taylor; and M. Bernstein. For general critical considerations of U.S. homonormativity, see Tilsen and Nylund; and E. Ng.

23. In the latter case, the census encouraged a roots-based classification system over monoracial backgrounds, allowing mixed ancestry identities to predominate and for Indigenous populations to gain more social recognition.

24. Along these lines, Marie Lo, in a reading of Joy Kogawa's *Obasan*, argues that the novel in some ways shows a stronger national connection through the interlocking histories of Indigenous populations and Japanese Canadians than any binational alignments between Japanese Canadians and Japanese Americans.

25. See Goellnicht ("A Long Labour"); and L. Cho.

26. Canadian multiculturalism policies have been critiqued, so I do not mean to suggest that this approach has been unequivocally successful. For more on the problems and debates concerning Canadian multiculturalism, see Banting and Kymlicka; and Wong and Guo.

27. While federal recognition arguably occurred in 2013 with *U.S. v. Windsor*, *Obergefell v. Hodges* forced all states to recognize gay marriage.

28. While the United States favored policies that restricted immigration from a

larger group of countries located in Asia, as demonstrated by the sweeping Immigration Act of 1924, Canadian policy more specifically targeted Chinese ethnic migrants, reaching an apotheosis with the Chinese Immigration Act of 1923. Both countries also targeted Asian North Americans from the framework of national security. Following the attacks on Pearl Harbor, both nations passed laws that granted their governments the power to intern Japanese ethnic populations located on the west coast of North America.

29. Brotman, Ryan, and Cormier further note, "Discrimination in health care is particularly salient for today's gay and lesbian elders" (192) and add, "Many of these people lived their youth and young adult lives in very hostile environments, prior to the development of the modern day gay liberation movement that began in the late 1960s in Canada and the United States" (192).

30. As Miriam Smith specifically notes, the Canadian gay liberation movement modeled itself on the earlier emergence of the gay liberation and civil rights discourses in the United States ("Social Movements and Equality Seeking"). The binational developments in LGBTQI contexts, for instance, have led scholars Jason Pierceson, Miriam Smith (*Political Institutions*), and David Rayside to produce book-length studies on the interconnected legal histories related to same-sex-identifying individuals in Canada and the United States.

31. For more on this coalitional connection, see http://www.aidsactionnow.org/?page_id=38.

32. For other approaches to literary studies that consider Asian American and Asian Canadian as an interconnected textual genealogy, see Ty (*Politics of the Visible*); Ty and Goellnicht; Davis (*Begin Here*); and Chiu.

33. The novel has already been the subject of considerable academic criticism, particularly from Canadian scholars. Please see Chao; Calder; Martin; and N. Gordon.

34. He comes to the United States just before the Tydings-McDuffie Act (1934), which enabled the Philippines to become an independent nation, but at the cost of ending any widespread migration from that country until 1965. The Luce-Cellar Act in 1946 did allot for one hundred migrants from the Philippines.

35. In this sense, I follow the logic offered by Sau-ling C. Wong, who considers Asian American literature as "an emergent and evolving textual coalition, . . ." (9).

36. The documentation concerning queer Asian North American writers prior to the 1970s is scant. One exception is Yone Noguchi, a queer Asian North American writer who engaged in affairs with both women and men around the turn of the century. For more on Noguchi, see Sueyoshi. Another is Mai-Mai Sze, who is the author of one novel, *Silent Children* (1948). Though she was engaged in a same-sex relationship with another woman, references to that relationship in print apparently did not appear (Bendix).

37. Eng and Fujikane's critical bibliographic work on queer Asian North American cultural productions begins with a consideration of a small number of texts published in the 1970s, including selections penned by Russell Leong (under the pseudonym of Wallace Lin) and Lonny Kaneko's "Shoyu Kid" in *Aiiieeeee! An Anthology of Asian American Writers* (Chan et al.). In this earlier period, a number of poetry collections were also produced; see Noda; and Woo.

38. To draw upon the wide range of queer Asian North American fiction writers who published within the past two decades, I occasionally avoided listing works published by the same author. Suri is also author of *The Age of Shiva* and *The Death of Vishnu*. K. Ali is also author of *The Disappearance of Seth*. R. Mehta is also author of *No Other World*. Revoyr is also author of *Lost Canyon*. Working with J. Tamaki, M. Tamaki is also co-author of the graphic novel *This One Summer*. Tamaki has also published other single-authored novels, including *(you) Set Me on Fire* and *Cover Me*. Han Ong is also author of *The Disinherited*. Dawesar is also author of *Miniplanner* and *That Summer in Paris*. Selvadurai is also author of *Funny Boy*, *Cinnamon Gardens*, and *Swimming in the Monsoon Sea*. Mootoo is also author of *Cereus Blooms at Night*, *He Drowns She in the Sea*, *Out on Main Street*, and *Valmiki's Daughter*. Goto is also author of *Hopeful Monsters*, *Darkest Light*, and *The Water of Possibility*. Choy is also author of *All That Matters*. I have not been comprehensive here, but I highlight the sheer volume of fictions being produced by queer Asian North Americans in the past decades.

39. In the context of Canada, legislative aims such as the multiculturalism act (1988) certainly signaled a strong shift in a direction that would support a heterogeneous creative arts community.

40. In an interview, Rahul Mehta also notes that Rakesh Satyal was the acquisitions editor at HarperCollins for his first manuscript, which became *Quarantine* (Centrone). One of the most robust networks emerged in the Queer Asian Canadian context, as Larissa Lai's acknowledgments to *Salt Fish Girl* cite the support of Hiromi Goto, Tamai Kobayashi, and Shani Mootoo. These writers have also listed each other in various iterations in their publications (Mootoo praises Lai in *Out on Main Street*; Kobayashi and Goto note the other respectively in their novels *Prairie Ostrich* and *The Kappa Child*).

41. David Eng specifically focuses his readings on family and kinship, but not necessarily on their relationship to queer Asians or queer Asian North Americans, as they are imagined in fictional worlds. Nevertheless, my book is very much influenced by his call to reassociate sexuality and race (2010). Thus this study finds its strongest analytical "switchpoints" (Stockton, *Beautiful Bottom* 21) constituted by Asian North American racial formation and queer sexuality.

42. Refreshing about Hom's study is its emphasis on more positive coming out experiences. Other studies have shown a far more pessimistic viewpoint concerning the disclosure of sexuality for queer Asian North Americans. For instance, Chung and Szymanski note, "Further, the participants felt that it was particularly difficult to come out to their parents because of their Asian background. Most of them chose not to come out to their parents or to avoid the topic" (88).

43. The damage produced out of a bad coming out experience is perhaps dramatically evident in the revenge fantasy film *Ethan Mao* (Bui 137).

44. Eric Wat notes, "Many of the narrators—people whom I have interviewed for their life histories—agree that there was not a sense of community before the formation of Asian/Pacific Lesbians and Gays (A/PLG) in late 1980, although there had been venues, especially gay bars, where gay Asian men could congregate in large numbers

in Los Angeles in the 1970s. A/PLG was the first formal organization representing the interests of gay and lesbian Asians in Los Angeles" (2). What is important to note about Wat's study is that the community's development is reliant upon a large urban center in which queer Asian North Americans aggregate.

45. For some of these studies, see Li and Orleans; Kimmel and Yi; Ohnishi, Ibrahim, and Grzegorek; Singh, Chung, and Dean; Hahm and Adkins; Szymanski and Gupta; Narui; Szymanski and Sung; and Sung, Szymanski, and Henrichs-Beck.

46. There have been some tentative considerations of queer Asian North American lives within the context of poststructural kinship studies. Eng's work intriguingly offers very few examples of poststructural kinships involving individuals who actually identify as queer and as Asian North American. Other studies such as by Arora and by Badruddoja focus on filmic and sociological methodologies respectively and cannot be fully applied to the archive at this book's center.

47. This critical oversight reflects a problematic related to Asian North American and queer communities at large. As Dana Takagi contends, "If anything, I expect many of us [queer Asian North Americans] view ourselves as on the margins of both communities [queer and Asian North American]" (21).

48. For other useful studies that employ a queer of color critique, see Barnard; Alexander; Esquibel; Dunning; D. Scott; Gerstner; and Martinez.

49. Here I refer to the work of early scholars and writers such as Audre Lorde, Cherríe Moraga and Barbara Smith, whose publications and considerations of race and sexuality preceded the birth of queer theory as its own viable discipline. The pioneering *This Bridge Called My Back* (Moraga and Anzaldúa), would, for instance, showcase the work of many writers who would go on to be formative in the field of women of color feminisms, such as the aforementioned Lorde, Moraga, Smith, as well as Gloria Anzaldúa, Nellie Wong, Merle Woo, and Barbara Noda.

50. The motif of disease nevertheless relates to the novel's brief invocation of Rock Hudson, who, though appearing in Golden Age film productions, was also known for the fact that he was the first major celebrity to die of the AIDS virus in the 1980s.

Chapter 1

1. For academic studies on the subject, see Ninh; and Song. Memoirs such as Evelyn Lau's *Runaway: Diary of a Street Kid* and Val Wang's *Beijing Bastard* reveal the challenges of growing up under the shadow of model minority expectations. Akhil Sharma's novel *Family Life* dramatically reveals the burdens of the model minority plot on a child who must achieve not only for himself but also for his brother, whose life is irreparably altered in a tragic accident.

2. My typology of queer Asian North American fictions is not exhaustive, and there is certainly murkiness among these three categories. For instance, Tamai Kobayashi's *Prairie Ostrich* involves a main narrative perspective granted to a child, nicknamed Egg, who is not necessarily marked by protoqueerness. At the same time, Egg's older teenage sister is certainly suggested to be a queer character. This novel fits best within the protoqueer category, even as its main character does not exhibit any same-sex yearnings.

3. Leung's novel is based on actual historical events. For more on the riots that occurred in Wyoming in 1885, see Laurie.

4. For more on Hayakawa, see Miyao.

5. *Huntress*, however, serves as a historical precursor to another of Lo's novels, *Ash*; thus the novel is critically invested in an expansive temporality in the construction of the story world.

6. This first mode of tactical diversion is probably the most prevalent in the fictions penned by queer Asian North American writers.

7. My work is inspired by Kathryn Bond Stockton, whom I cited previously in relation to her work on queerness and child figures (*The Queer Child*).

8. For some key pieces on *Rolling the R's*, see Nubla; and E. E. Reyes.

9. See T. Lawrence; and Hilderbrand.

10. Krishna's connection to queer sexuality is not without precedent. As Rohit K. Dasgupta notes, Krishna's friendship with Arjuna has been read through its homoerotic potentialities (652–653).

11. For more on sexual and gender politics in contemporary pagan cultures and communities, see Kraemer. Of the gothic subculture, Amy C. Wilkins explains that "the scene prides itself on its inclusivity" (334), while acknowledging that "it is demographically homogeneous" (334) given certain racial and class significations. This context does have an impact on how to consider the graphic novel, especially with respect to the fact that Skim might stand out due to her status as a mixed-race individual.

12. For instance, Norman Wong's linked-story collection *Cultural Revolution* follows the trajectory of a Chinese immigrant family across several generations.

13. While the structure of the South Asian Indian family is undergoing change, especially in light of modernization imperatives, the "majority of family forms continue to be nuclear" (Dommaraju 1240), with an emphasis on parents and their children.

14. The climax of this flashback occurs in the period of unrest after a coup attempt in 1982 in which South Asian Indians were targeted.

Chapter 2

1. In the context of incest and women's literature, Rosaria Champagne argues that "'fictions' are not lies. Rather, they are narrative recastings of events unrecognized by history" (3). My study is influenced by her understanding of the murky boundaries between fiction and history.

2. I work off the definition of the "love-plot" as articulated by Joseph Boone, in which two characters of the opposite sex court each other, finally ending with an "everlasting union . . . sexual love transcends all material concerns; emotions are more valuable than reason in matters of the heart" (6–7). Of the courtship and marriage plot, William H. Magee provides the most traditional understandings of these narrative constructs (198). Many scholars, of course, have come to redefine the marriage plot in its myriad variations; see, for example, Marcus; and Hager.

3. For more studies on Asian North American literature and the form of the bildungsroman, see Ho; and Otano.

4. For other studies involving Asian North American cultural production and racial formalisms, see Davis's *Transcultural Reinventions*, Ling's *Narrating Nationalisms*, Jeon's *Racial Things, Racial Forms*, and Otano's *Speaking the Past*.

5. For more considerations of queer sexuality as it exerts pressure on form and aesthetics within literary narratives, see Warhol; Matz; Miller; and Ohi.

6. See Tsou; Christopher Lee (*Semblance*); and Tang.

7. Edith Hall's definition of the "survivor" reminds us that "virtually everyone" (145) has a story of trauma. In this way, comparative relationality suggests that the queer Asian North American subject must place certain claims of loss in conversations with others.

8. The trauma theorist Cathy Caruth marks the importance of trauma through the impact of survival and its relation to temporality ("Violence and Time" 25). Caruth's point applies as well to these fictions, as the queer Asian North American storyteller attempts to make a "claim" on his or her survival by looking backward. The construction of the storytelling perspective is an attempt by the queer Asian North American protagonist to make more comprehensible the fact of his or her survival. Both Greenberg and Vickroy make similar points concerning the nature of time and the survivor of a trauma. Greenberg argues, "A survivor of trauma has withstood a threat to the body. However, while the body recovers (or if it doesn't fully recover, continues to live), the impact upon the mind lingers" (324–325), while Vickroy asserts, "Survivors' experience resists normal chronological narration or normal modes of artistic representation" (5). A critical difference in my book is that the distinction between past and present is more differentiated in the narratives I study, in part because one of the linking elements is that "social death," in both fact and spirit, appears as a "structural trauma" (LaCapra, "Trauma," 722) that is not necessarily associated with a specific event or injury but remains far more abstracted in the way that it can cause damage.

9. Within race and ethnic studies, the concept of survivorship finds an associated genealogy within the work of Gerald Vizenor. Vizenor focuses on "survivance" as "creat[ing] an active presence, more than the instincts of survival, function, or subsistence." (*Native Liberty* 88). In disarticulating survivance from survival, Vizenor suggests that survival cannot be the basis of a collective cultural struggle. In using the term *survivorship*, I mean to push how queer Asian North American writers always place the individual in relation to the larger field of social relations. For more on Vizenor and survivance, see *Manifest Manners* (5, 11).

10. Peter Brooks defines plot as "an embracing concept for the design and intention of narrative, a structure for those meanings that are developed through temporal succession, or perhaps better: a structuring operation elicited by, and made necessary by, those meanings that develop through succession and time" (12). For other definitions of plot, see Prince (71–72). For useful cultural studies concerning plots, see Heller; Hirsch; and Tate. For a clinical and therapeutic approach to plots, see Mattingly.

11. Some, such as Tilley's *Plot Snakes*, focus on a classical theorization of narrative sequence, while others such as Booker's *The Seven Basic Plots* focus more on different kinds of narrative sequences based on content.

12. Though kinship and family studies stagnated in light of David M. Schneider's trenchant critique of the field (*Critique*), it has of late experienced an incredible resurgence due to the evolving nature of social relations. For some useful theoretical approaches of these changes, see Carsten; Godelier; and Sahlins.

13. From a geographical and comparative (post)colonial perspective, Richard Phillips notes, "The nuclear family has been accorded a privileged place in histories and historical geographies of colonialism in Canada and other resettlement societies"(240).

14. One primary example would be the use of concubines in China.

15. For more on Asian North Americans in relation to issues of betrayal and cultural representation, see Bow; and Parikh.

16. For instance, Jan Dizard and Howard Gadlin argue that "the fact still remains that it is the husband-wife-children-unit that is the family in our culture: its needs predominate, or are supposed to, and its *raison d'être* is autonomy, emotional and financial" (23). While agreeing that the definition of the American family is evolving, the authors of *Counted Out* (Powell et al.) make similar claims concerning the traditional structure of this social unit (20). For more working definitions of the American family in this vein, see Hansen (1); and Sarkisian and Gerstel (1).

17. See Nancy E. Levine for an excellent overview of alternative kinship studies. For some alternative kinship studies regarding queer families, see Weston; and Mallon. For some alternative kinship studies regarding adoption, see Brian; and Briggs. For some alternative kinship studies regarding reproductive technologies and associated issues, see Strathern; Mamo; and Cahn (*The New Kinship*). For variations on queer motherhoods, see S. Park.

18. For Freeman, alternative kinship for queers is defined by practices that function through revitalization and retrospection ("Queer Belongings" 309–311).

19. For an excellent overall historical consideration of Asian Americans, see Sucheng Chan.

20. For a book-length study related to the construction of paper families in the United States, see Estelle T. Lau. For more on the historical trajectory of Chinese Canadians, see Arlene Chan.

21. For instance, see Xiaojian Zhao's *Remaking Chinese America* for the historical emergence of families as legislation changed and offered the opportunities for more women to migrate.

22. For more book-length studies regarding Korean American adoptees and issues of kinship, see E. Kim (*Adopted Territory*); Palmer; Tuan and Shiao; Brian; C. C. Choy; and Prébin.

23. Xiaobei Chen explores a different issue within the Asian Canadian context involving the desire by white adoptive parents to push their adoptive children to form strong ethnic and cultural ties, a problem insofar as it "misses and masks the contradictions engendered by the racialised structuring of adoptions, a characteristic of international and interracial adoption that has been the focus of analysis for an increasing number of scholars" (1).

24. Sociological and anthropological studies of queer Asian North Americans are

not entirely absent. See Manalansan for a work that does some engagement with queer Asian North Americans and associated social formations.

25. Here I am referencing the work of Wendy Brown from "Wounded Attachments," the third chapter from *States of Injury*, in which she explores the limits of protest politics and the inability to move past an uncritical embrace of a traumatic past.

26. For studies concerning the emergence of queer political conservatism, see Goldstein; and P. Robinson.

27. My viewpoint here follows Alan Bérubé, who argues that "for the gay community, gay bathhouses represent a major success in a century-long political struggle to overcome isolation and develop a sense of community and pride in their sexuality. . . ." (34). Richard Tewksbury makes a similar remark at the end of his anthropological study of bathhouses (109). Corie J. Hammers articulates a parallel argument with respect to lesbian bathhouses ("Making Space"). In contrast to these positive viewpoints, Leo Bersani famously excoriated the bathhouse: "Anyone who has ever spent one night in a gay bathhouse knows that it is (or was) one of the most ruthlessly ranked, hierarchized, and competitive environments imaginable" (206). For more academic considerations of the bathhouse, see Chapter 1 from Chisholm's *Queer Constellations*.

28. For studies on the correlations between bathhouse sex and HIV transmission rates, see Rabin; Haubrich et al.; Faissol et al.; and Binson et al.

Chapter 3

1. Kathryn Bond Stockton describes another version of such a "Child" in *The Queer Child* (2009), a youthful figure who apparently exhibits "normative strangeness," which "may explain why children, as an idea, are likely to be both white and middle-class. It is a privilege to need to be protected—and to be sheltered—and thus to have a childhood" (31).

2. By the term *proto-LGBTQI* child, I refer to the identities that typically fall under queer groups: lesbian, gay, bisexual, transgender, queer, and intersex.

3. Edelman's argument rarely touches on race as a direct subject, but at the end of his second chapter he does gesture to the fact that the Child cannot be a racialized figure.

4. According to Henry A. Giroux, "Historically poor kids and children of color have been considered to be beyond the boundaries of both childhood and innocence, they have been associated with the cultures of crime, rampant sexuality, and drug use" (9). Robin Bernstein further notes the importance of childhood innocence in relation to racial discourses emerging in the nineteenth and early twentieth centuries.

5. As Ninh shows, the Asian North American nuclear family is wrapped up in the mythos of the model minority paradigm, leaving daughters vulnerable to the expectation that they deliver on a seemingly never-ending promise: they will forward the family economically, socially, and culturally, all the while remaining ever filial. As Song argues in his monograph, Asian North American children can never live up to the fantasy that has been constructed pertaining to their own existence, one related to their trajectories as model minorities.

6. Virginia L. Blum explores the ways in which children can be written out of fic-

tional plots, especially as they struggle under the power dynamics of an adult world, in her work *Hide and Seek*.

7. Two integral Asian North American literary texts that explore the topic of comfort women are Nora Okja Keller, *Comfort Woman*, and Chang-rae Lee, *A Gesture Life*. For some scholarly studies on the topic of comfort women, see Kang; Hicks; Tanaka; Yoshimi; and Soh.

8. In *Breaking the Magic Spell*, the cultural critic Jack Zipes provides one of the foundational differences between the forms: folktales are generally understood to be orally transmitted, while fairy tales tend to be literary adaptations found in written form.

9. I follow the classic viewpoints advanced by both William Bascom and Bruno Bettelheim that the folktale and fairy tale genres function through their didactic capacities. For other useful considerations of genre and form in relation to the fairy tale, folktale, myth, or legend, see C. Goldberg; Bottigheimer; and Somoff. Bettelheim focuses on the amalgamation of these forms, calling it the "folk fairy tale." For others on fairy tales, see von Franz (*Interpretation*); and Tatar (*Hard Facts*). For the classic study on the folktale, see Propp, which is a structuralist account of the form and attempts to break down the component parts of the "folk" narrative.

10. From this point forward, I shorten the full name of this figure for Lady Tamamo when referring to the established figure.

11. In T. W. Johnson's study of fox imagery in Far Eastern culture, he notes that "the Japanese tale looks as if it is a native grafting onto an earlier Chinese legend which, in turn, may have been built on an even earlier Indian legend" (36). Asian studies scholar U. A. Casal elaborates that the fox was considered to be "one of the most cunning, cautious, and skeptical animals all over the world. It also possesses lecherous and covetous propensities . . . the worst kind of mercenary and shameless women are termed *kitsune*, foxes, vixen" (29). Given the complicated background of this tale, Chee inscribes a pan-Asian myth about female seduction and sexuality into the novel by pushing its boundaries onto Korean culture and identity.

12. There are various significations of the fox in Far Eastern folklore. For instance, see Blust (490); and Heine (*Shifting Shape*). For more studies of the goddess Inari and fox imagery, see Opler and Hashima; Smyers ("'My Own Inari'"; *Fox*).

13. As Jennifer Freyd notes, "Childhood sexual abuse, whether molestation or even penetration, usually leaves no lasting physical evidence. It is neither explained nor understandable to the child" (3).

14. Judith Levine also corroborates this point, explaining that "research confirms what is intuitively clear: that the worst devastation is wrought not by sex per se but by betrayal of the child's fundamental trust" (28).

15. According to Jo Woodiwiss, the context of the child sexual abuse is extremely important in order to uncover the impact of the trauma from that experience over time. Susan A. Clancy argues that it is often the aftermath of the sexual abuse that is the most problematic because the victim comes to reconsider the nature of childhood sexual experiences in the light of the exploitative power dynamics, thus leading to a delayed reaction.

16. Caruth defines trauma as the "wound of the mind . . . [which] is not, like the wound of the body, a simple and healable event, but rather an event that . . . is experienced too soon, too unexpectedly" (*Unclaimed Experience* 3). Ruth Leys provides an excellent example of psychic injury in practice through an investigation of soldiers who fought in World War I (623). Dominick LaCapra's exploration of trauma stresses the importance of temporality ("Trauma" 699).

17. Abraham and Torok distinguish the transgenerational phantom from the experience of the melancholic because the child deals with the psychic effects from someone older, particularly of a different age group. As a result, the child must contend with the "tombs of others" that return in the form of an unconsciously excavated secret (172). For Warden, the "tomb" is the secret of his father's status as a pedophile, something that plays out unconsciously: he not only has a sexual relationship with a man who had been molested by Big Eric, but also discovers the secret in such a way that it encourages him to kill his father.

18. For explorations of the plague in the context of Edinburgh, see Seafield; and J.-A. Henderson. For some general academic studies of the bubonic plague, see Horrox; and Herlihy.

19. See Crimp (33); and Denneny (46).

20. I am attuned to the ways in which the queer racialized subject, especially one associated with AIDS or HIV, can be situated as the diametric opposite to family values. As Simon Watney notes, "the Spectacle of AIDS thus promises a stainless world in which we will only be recalled, in textbooks and carefully edited documentary 'evidence,' as signs of plagues and contagions averted—intolerable interruptions of the familial" (86).

21. Thomas Piontek takes up the ethical and moral imperative of AIDS representations, arguing that such topical analyses should contain both political and literary components (148).

22. For other useful sources on AIDS narratives and related discourses of representation, see Chandler; Piontek; Clum; S. Warner; Román; Piggford; Castiglia and Reed; and Pearl.

23. AIDS narratives have been read in relation to discourses of witnessing and testimonials. For some other sources, see Brophy; De Moor; Diedrich; and Hallas.

24. James W. Jones cautions against the use of a plague discourse in relation to AIDS and HIV, precisely because it connotatively communicates the fact that queers, in particular, are somehow deserving of these diseases due to the religious signification of the term (76).

25. As C. J. Duncan and S. Scott note, "Once a plague case had been identified, the family was locked up in the house, the well known cross was daubed on the door, and a watchman was appointed to stand guard" (315). Barbara Tuchman adds that the plague's "loathsomeness and deadliness did not herd people together in mutual distress, but only prompted their desire to escape each other" (96). Following the work of John Hatch, Robert A. Scott notes the social crises that arose during the plague (17).

26. The importance of knowing or not knowing the donor's identity is the subject of much study. Naomi Cahn explores a new legal paradigm that encourages even anony-

mous sperm donors to allow donor-conceived children access to their identities at some point ("The New Kinship"). For studies on the issue of donor insemination and kinship, see Strathern (Chapter 1); Hargreaves; Freeman et al.; Hertz and Mattes; and Franklin.

27. According to Charis Thompson, "The widespread availability of ART procedures for reproduction without heterosexual intercourse has also helped normalize single and homosexual parenting and kinship" (13).

28. Issues related to kinship and assisted reproductive technologies are often mediated through state law. As of 2011, for instance, Maine does not have any statutes related to surrogacy laws (Dana 390).

29. For more on queer men as fathers, see Bergman et al.; Patterson and Tornello; Dana; and Greenfield and Seli.

30. For an in-depth critical discussion of Chua's work, see Koshy.

Chapter 4

1. Alumit is also author of *Talking to the Moon* (2007). Other important queer Filipino American fiction works include Linmark's *Rolling the R's* (1995) and its semi-sequel *Leche* (2011), and Realuyo's *The Umbrella Country* (1999).

2. Though I am reliant here on Western conceptions of folk and fairy tales, the didactic and moral elements of such forms would have potentially been available to Bong. In the context of a Filipino appropriation of Western fairy tales in relation to *Mga Kuwento ni Lola Basyang* (The Stories of Grandmother Basyang), Rhoda Myra Garces-Bacsal, Ruanni Tupas, and Jesus Federico Hernandez argue, "While the moralistic and didactic tone in children's literature has been decried as infantilizing and old-fashioned, librarians and children's literature experts acknowledge that there are stories that can be both subversive and moralistic at the same time . . ." (22). This perspective is useful for considering how Bong would have been exposed to multiple traditions of the make-believe.

3. Leonardo N. Mercado notes, "That Filipinos associate food with health is seen in rituals which always have food offerings" (292).

4. The syncretism of religion and animism is also seen in the Filipino Muslim context. As Paul A. Rodell notes, "Like the Christian, the Muslim Filipino pays attention to the local spirit world even while praying in the great tradition of his adopted religion. So, for example, he will make an offering to his pre-Islamic rice spirits before planting a crop, but later give a portion of the profit to the mosque to support the zakat (religious tithe)" (44).

5. Of this pre-Hispanic and precolonial spirit world, Herminia Q. Meñez explains, "The Spanish chroniclers during the period of colonization referred to these spirits as nono, diwata, anito, or tumao. All these terms are still used today, including those that designate specific types, such as duwende (Tagalog: dwarf), matanda sa punso (Tagalog: old man of the mound), lamang-lupa (Tagalog: underground spirit), mae-am (Aklan: old woman), and sapat sa taeon (Aklan: spirits of the forest)" ("Encounters" 252). For explorations of Filipino animistic beliefs in various cultural, tribal, and ethnic contexts, see Krieger (101); Dichoso (62); Vanoverbergh (79); and Gaioni (391).

6. Virgil Mayor Apostol also notes that "[m]odern-day offerings can be found disguised in Christian observances, such as those dedicated to ancestral spirits. For example, it is still a practice among people, especially in rural areas, to present a food offering to ancestral spirits during wakes and death anniversaries" (89). Mellie Leandicho Lopez makes a similar point: "Food is used in religious rituals. Both Christian and non-Christian make food offerings to appease angry spirits of the environment. Despite their Christian religion, many lowland Filipinos practice animism with their Christian faith..." (379).

7. One of the best-known examples of the ritual in which food is offered to the gods occurs in the Cebuano cultural context, an event known as the Halad Festival. While there's never any direct reference to this kind of festival in the novel (indeed, Bong speaks Ilocano and Tagalog, so the association here seems distant), we can see that Bong is certainly influenced by ritualistic activities, as they are connected to food offerings. For more on the Cebuano halad festival, see Mojares; Seki (120); Sabanpan-Yu; and Sala-Boza. For considerations of Halad in other Filipino cultural contexts, see Olofson (192); and Aparece (141).

8. For an exploration of the Cinderella story in the Filipino context, see, for example, Hart and Hart; and Gil.

9. According to Maximo Ramos, "The aswang concept in the Philippines is most usefully understood as a congeries of beliefs about five types of mythical beings identifiable with certain creatures of the European tradition: (1) the blood-sucking vampire, (2) the self-segmenting viscera sucker, (3) the man-eating weredog, (4) the vindictive witch, and (5) the carrion-eating ghoul" (238). For other considerations of the aswang, see De Jesus (7); Demetrio (97); Cannell (144–145); McAndrew (94–96); Woods and Ellington (28); and B. C. Lim (179–225). For more on sorcery and witchcraft in various Filipino cultural contexts, see Meñez ("Performance" 67); and Baes (265).

10. For those who experience torture, as the philosopher Elaine Scarry reminds us, the world and the body are remade in violent ways (40–41). The reconstruction of the world into objects through torture shatters the individual's comprehension of the world. For Bong, his childhood experiences resemble a form of pedestrian torture, as Auntie Yuna is able to transform the meaning of common objects such as brooms.

11. For scholarship on Medusa and Greek myth, see Silverman. For a consideration of Haitian voodoo practices, see McGee.

12. According to Jack Zipes, "The fairy tale celebrates the marks as magical: marks as letters, words, sentences, signs. More than any other literary genre, the fairy tale has persisted in emphasizing transformation of the marks with spells, enchantments, disenchantments, resurrections, recreations" ("Changing Function," 7). In relation to Alumit's novel, we can see how language and the world are transformed for Bong in these darkly magical ways.

13. Though Clift seems to be the perfect overseer, the film's ending suggests that his protection and his offering of kinship are no longer even needed.

14. The nature of Clift's sexuality has been the subject of some debate. For references to Clift's gay sexuality, Patricia Bosworth employs quotations directly from people Clift had known (74, 113, 195). Amy Lawrence is more adamant that Clift can only be

read as a gay actor through a revisionist labeling, since the "conviction only became widespread a decade after Clift's death" (142). For another useful biography on Clift, see LaGuardia.

15. In the Visayan cultural context, William Henry Scott explains, "Sorcerers were believed to derive their secret knowledge of black magic—spells and charms—from unnatural forces. Habit was a spell and ginhabit, the one bewitched by it: bakwit was a spell by which women detained their lovers; lumay, a love potion; and buringot, the opposite" (83). For more on the lumay, see Lieban (154) and Cannell (40). Madale further defines the love spell in terms of the Maranaws: "Another Maranaw magical practice consists of the use of love-charms or kakasi or kata-o sa kabakagowi a tao (charm or art of love)" (63).

16. According to Michael McGhee, the most important way to define whether the psychotic break has become pathological is to examine how the affected individual relates to the world (345). In McGhee's estimation, the importance is the level of disassociation that the individual experiences, so much so that "the psychotic person falls into a state of delusion" while "the spiritual practitioner falls out of delusion" (345).

17. Rather than pathologizing Bong's visions as nonsensical, I argue that they help explain his psychic state. In this sense, I follow the Mohammed Abouelleil Rashed patient-centered approach to diagnosis, which involves being attentive to "the patient's own language" and to "frame the problem in terms that would meet [his] approval" (200). In Bong's case, the hallucinatory visions serve a great purpose for reconstructing the order to his childhood world. Matthew R. Broome reminds us that "there are degrees of psychosis and rationality" (39). I take into account the rather murky line between the spiritual aspect of Bong's experience and the ways in which it can be read as a psychotic break from reality.

18. In the context of the Subic Bay area, Kathleen Barry notes, "In 1989 there were 11,600 women in prostitution who were registered as entertainers, with an estimated 6,000 bar girls, 14,000 unlicensed streetwalkers, and 500 go-go bars, massage parlors and brothels (10% of which are owned by retired U.S. military)" (146). For more on this social context, see also Enloe (149); Kuo (72); Niu (97–98); Ringdal (366); and V. Gonzalez (36).

19. For other studies that explore conceptions of evil and morality in fairy tales, see Tatar (*Off with Their Heads*); and von Franz (*Shadow and Evil*).

20. See A. Cheng; and Eng and Han.

21. The short list includes Anna May Wong, Sessue Hayakawa, and Philip Ahn. For book-length studies on Anna May Wong, see Anthony Chan; Hodges; Leibfried and Lane; and K. Leong; on Sessue Hayakawa, see Miyao; on Philip Ahn, see Chung.

22. Chapter 2 of Brian Eugenio Herrera's *Latin Numbers* explores the ways in which Latinx actors often are forced to portray other ethnic and racial groups.

23. For more on the controversies related to cross-ethnic and cross-racial casting, please see W. H. Sun; and Davé ("Racial Accents").

24. In this sense, Bong might be said to have more in common with early Asian American actors such as Anna May Wong and Philip Ahn. Wong, who was of Chinese descent, famously played the part of a Mongolian slave in *The Thief of Baghdad*. Ahn,

who was of Korean descent, often was cast in roles for characters of Chinese ancestry. For more on Ahn's cross-ethnic roles, see Chung.

25. See the "Apocalypse Now" section from *Simulacra and Simulation*.

26. For more on the biases of (racialized) representation in relation to the Vietnam War, see Kinney; Nguyen; and Chong.

27. For studies of Asian North Americans in the cinema and film industry and associated contexts, see Marchetti; Xing; Feng (*Identities*); C. P. Shimizu (*Hypersexuality*; *Straitjacket*); Locke; Park; and Davé ("Racial Accents"). For studies of Asian North Americans in relation to television representation, see Hamamoto; and Davé (*Indian Accents*).

28. Joann Lee makes a similar observation: "Asians are often cast as adjuncts to main characters to fulfill various functions—often ethnic parts—as dictated by particular genres" (177). For a book-length study on these concerns, see Yuen.

29. For some studies on yellowface and Orientalist performance, see the introduction to R. Lee's *Orientals*; Moon; Josephine Lee (*Pure Invention*), and Fuller's *Hollywood Goes Oriental*.

30. Lee infamously was overlooked for the part of a Eurasian character in *Kung Fu*, the role later given to David Carradine, who was Caucasian. As Crystal S. Anderson notes, "Hollywood designated Lee as too 'Oriental,' which had implications for ethnic and national identities" (14).

31. Films such as Wayne Wang's *The Joy Luck Club* (1993) and Justin Lin's *Better Luck Tomorrow* (2002) demonstrate the inroads made in shooting films that deal with Asian North American issues. Asian North Americans have also been involved in independent and experimental cinema for many decades, providing venues for minority actors to showcase their talents. On these issues, see Mimura; and Okada.

32. For an excellent general study of the history of extras in Hollywood, see Slide. For studies of extras in earlier periods, see Regester; and Holmes (99).

33. I use the word *queer-ish* here because Amada, though not identifying as queer, nevertheless finds herself cast in roles in which her sexuality is deemed as deviant or subversive.

34. Karen D. Pyke and Denise L. Johnson describe the lotus blossom stereotype as a figuration in which the Asian North American woman is "hyperfeminine: passive, weak, excessively submissive, slavishly dutiful, sexually exotic, and available for white men" (36).

35. Amada's experiences in Hollywood mirror those of many Asian North American actresses, who continue to contend with the circumscription of their racial, gendered, and sexual differences in stereotypical roles, most famously Anna May Wong. Hanying Wang also provides a short reading of *The World of Suzie Wong*, the movie that starred Nancy Kwan and helped perpetuate the stereotype of the hypersexual and subservient Oriental woman (84). For more critical explorations of Asian North American actresses, stereotypes, and the racial politics of performance, see Tajima; C. Liu; Feng ("Suzie Wong"); C. F. Sun; C. P. Shimizu (*Hypersexuality*); and L. K. Lopez.

36. Hemant Shah notes that Hollywood representations of Asian North Americans serve to shore up white supremacy (8).

37. In a study concerning viewers of the film *Rush Hour 2* and the perception of stereotypes, Ji Hoon Park, Nadine G. Gabbadon, and Ariel R. Chernin discovered that "[d]espite participants' emphasis on the fictional nature of *Rush Hour 2*, they perceived a sense of realism in its racial representations; few participants stated that racial stereotypes in the film were unreal or incorrect. . . ." (172). The important element here is to note that Gorham's central thesis is supported: individuals, though aware of the inaccuracy of stereotype, may nevertheless react in such a way as to cement the authenticity of a given representation.

38. For a study of Asian North American men and how they perceive stereotypes about themselves, see Y. J. Wong et al.

39. For critical considerations of Asian North Americans specifically in theater and performance contexts, see Moy; Josephine Lee (*Performing*); Kurahashi; Shimakawa; and Esther Kim Lee.

40. This list of major actors and performers who died of AIDS includes Anthony Perkins, Robert Reed, Liberace, and Freddie Mercury.

Chapter 5

1. I provide epidemiological data from two recent studies concerning U.S. and Canadian populations, respectively. As Jennifer Pellowski et al note, since 1990, men who have sex with men have the highest HIV infection rates. In data obtained for the period "1995 to 2001," R. S. Hogg et al. reveal that "[i]n Canada, there are an estimated 71 300 (range 58 600–84 000) individuals infected with HIV, of whom 54 700 (44 400–65 000) are men. The majority reside in Ontario, Quebec and British Columbia and their routes of infection are men who have sex with men (MSM) (46.7%), heterosexual contact (34.5%) or injecting drug use (16.9%)" (581, lack of commas in original).

2. I use the terms *lesbian desire*, *queer female desire*, and *same-sex female desire* for similar things. While understanding connotative discursive differences among these terms, I find the need to separate them distracting to my overall argument. For early critical studies on lesbian culture, see Douglas's *Love and Politics* and Zimmerman's *The Safe Sea of Women*. The philosopher Judith Roof defines lesbian sexuality as "women's real or imagined sexual desire for or sexual activity with a woman" (*Lure* 6). Lesbianism is further characterized as a "collective, multiple position" (Case 1). For other useful considerations of lesbianism, see Engelbrecht; Martindale; Villarejo; Rohy; Garber; and Guess. For more on psychoanalytic approaches to lesbian desire, see Hamer; de Lauretis (*Practice*); Traub; and Adams. For considerations of lesbian communities through cultural geographies, see Valentine ("Negotiating"; "Desperately"); and Inness (Chapter 6). For a philosophical approach to lesbian identity, see Card (*Lesbian Choices*); Roof (*Lure*); and Emery. I further follow Cheshire Calhoun's point that "[f]eminist theory must treat lesbian oppression as a special case of patriarchal oppression and remain blind to the irreducibly lesbian nature of lesbian lives" ("Separating" 559). Calhoun also approaches this topic in the article "The Gender Closet: Lesbian Disappearance Under the Sign 'Women.'" Finally, the term *lesbian* has also been critiqued by queer theorists in general for its reliance on binaristic gender-sex categories. I follow Suzanna Danuta Walters's point that it is occasionally important to separate lesbian sexuality as a distinct social identity category ("From Here" 843).

3. For a consideration of same-sex female desire in early American literature, see K. R. Kent.

4. Hoogland makes a similar point: "The myth of the devouring lesbian is still going strong. . . ." (*Lesbian*, 119). If and when women do engage in queer sexual practices or acts do emerge, such moments can often be followed by what Patricia Juliana Smith calls "lesbian panic" (2), which results in such figures committing harm to herself and/or to someone else, as a way to sublimate her anxieties and fear.

5. Ann M. Ciasullo makes a similar point about how queer women in general have been mainstreamed in the American culture in the 1990s, as the more feminine-looking queer woman becomes acceptable to audiences.

6. The problem of invisibility as a trope in the writings of queer American women is not solely confined to the archive that constitutes this chapter. Teresa de Lauretis makes note of this fact ("Sexual Indifference" 159).

7. Though I focus on Nina Revoyr in this chapter, I note that queer Asian North American female writers have published in a variety of genres and forums. For examples of poetry collections by queer Asian North American women, see W. Kim (*Curtains*; *Artichokes*; *Rolling Sky*); Noda; Woo; C. Cheng; Minahal; Naca; and Beyer. For examples of performance work by queer Asian North American women, see Sam; and Uyehara. For some fictions penned by openly queer Asian North American women, see W. Kim (*Dancer Dawkins* and *Dead Heat*); and Lo (*Ash*). Kim's novels derive inspiration from the dime novel western and the lesbian pulp fiction. For articles on the lesbian pulp, see Walters ("As Her Hand"); Hermes; Elliott; Nealon; Foote; Y. Keller; and Meeker. In the Canadian contexts, queer Asian North American writers Lydia Kwa, Shani Mootoo, and Larissa Lai explore same-sex female relationships in fictions that do involve a prominent character who is of Asian descent; see *This Place Called Absence*, *Valmiki's Daughter*, and *Salt Fish Girl*, respectively. The relative death of such fictional publications is made apparent in Karin Aguilar-San Juan's 1993 review article on the field ("Landmarks," 940). As of 2018, the list still remains fairly short.

8. For more considerations of lesbianism in relation to narrative theory, see Stimpson; Kennard; Juhasz; and J. Abraham.

9. For the purposes of standardization, I refer specifically to the narrator of *Wingshooters* as Michelle, rather than Mike, her childhood nickname.

10. My reading is influenced by Judith Halberstam's point that "[u]nder certain circumstances failing, losing, forgetting, unmaking, undoing, unbecoming, not knowing may in fact offer more creative, more cooperative, more surprising ways of being in the world" (*Queer Art* 2–3).

11. For more on alternative kinships related to queer and same-sex communities, see Lewin (*Gay Fatherhood, Lesbian Mothers*); Carrington; M. Sullivan; Mallon; Mezey; Dean (6); Moore; and A. Goldberg. For studies on single motherhood and alternative kinship, see Hertz.

12. For more on transracial adoptions in the American context and associated kinship issues, see Callahan; Briggs; and Prébin.

13. For an excellent overview of alternative kinship structures in both American and transnational contexts, see N. E. Levine.

14. In this sense, the novel gestures to the import of understanding racial difference through its sexual valences, ones that render such bodies as queer. The link between racial difference and queer sexuality has been made by a number of scholars, such as Somerville (*Queering*) and Stockton (*Beautiful*) in black and white contexts.

15. For other considerations of the Midwest in the representational imagination, see Shortridge; Watts; Pichaske; Balken; and Ryden.

16. For some studies on the Midwest in relation to industry and economic change, see Teaford; Fink; and W. J. Warren.

17. The social contexts for a couple like the Garretts moving to a small town in the Midwest might be challenging to conceive of on national terms, but the movement of African Americans more generally into the urban Midwest has been detailed by a number of academics. For specific studies involving African American presence in Wisconsin, see Dougherty; Trotter; Schwalm; and P. D. Jones.

18. With respect to the presence of women in hunting, Mary Zeiss Stange contends that "women's identity with nature . . . and nonviolence" (2) somehow eliminates them from the possibility that they could track and kill game. In relation to the shifting gender boundaries of hunting, Jon Littlefield explains that "hunting is no longer a strictly male pursuit—approximately 9% of hunters are female" (114).

19. For more studies on interspecies kinships, see Kuzniar; Haraway; and Steiner.

20. As Lisa M. Fine notes in her ethnographic study, "The activity of hunting, as it came to be understood in the twentieth century, tapped into a number of enduring sources of masculine identity which changed slowly over time" (810). For more on the gender dynamics of hunting, see Wonders (270). Though hunting is clearly most associated with men, Daniel Justin Herman reminds us that gender norms have been upturned over time, enabling women a space in the wild (229).

21. In general, deer are considered to be one of the most difficult species to sport hunt (Dizard, *Going Wild* 116).

22. For a book-length study on the ethical issues related to hunting, see Wood.

23. We can read this moment as one in which Mrs. Garrett is "ungendered" (Spillers 69), especially as Earl's actions reinforce the social order in which the African American female subject only registers under the regime of violence and brutality, as it is visited upon the physical body.

24. Ronald L. Jackson II describes the buck in similar racialized terms (41). For a foundational source concerning the stereotype of the "buck" in reference to African Americans, see Bogle. In separate studies, Lendrum (366) and McIlwain (178) show how African Americans attempted to revise the "buck" stereotype in their own terms during the era of blaxploitation films.

25. For other ethnographic studies of hunting, see Boglioli for this activity in Vermont and Willging for this activity in Wisconsin. Bronner has also published a book-length study on hunting (*Killing*) and an article on pigeon shooting ("Contesting").

26. According to Matt Cartmill, "Some hunters think that their sport affirms their virility as well as their masculine identity" (233).

27. See Loo (299–301); and D. J. Herman (88). In considerations of transnationalism and American hunting, cultural critics have focused on the work of Ernest Hemingway; for instance, see Hediger; and Armengol-Carrera. For some other critical studies of American literature and hunting, see Coupe; Rivers; Altherr (on Henry David Thoreau); Walsh (on Harriette Arnow); Parker (on D'Arcy McNickle); and Cook (on James Welch). Scholars have noted the connection between hunting and colonialism more broadly; see McKenzie; McNairn; and Mukherjee. See Sramek for considerations and readings of hunting in relation to the United Kingdom, and see Wonders for a study of hunting in connection with Canada.

28. For another useful source on this event, see Formisano.

29. Though Michelle is not necessarily embraced for her "rural" roots as elucidated here, a number of scholars have explored the vitality of queer communities and cultures outside of cities and metropolitan areas. See Howard; Gray; and Herring.

Chapter 6

1. See Goellnicht ("A Long Labour") for one of the foundational pieces on this issue.

2. For a useful review of major studies and considerations of incest and the incest taboo, see Seery, who interestingly reconsiders this topic in light of political theory. For psychotherapeutic and psychoanalytic approaches, see Agentieri; J. L. Herman (*Father-Daughter*); Dinsmore; Freud; and Ambrosio. For socioanthropological approaches, see Lévi-Strauss; Cohen; Arens; Leavitt; and Evans and Maines. For evolutionary and biological approaches to incest, see Bischof; Erickson; and Wolf. For literary critical approaches and cultural studies approaches, see Doane; Harkins; Sacco; Sheffer; and Connolly.

3. As Kilby points out, J. L. Herman's refutation of psychoanalytic approaches to incest too heavily draws on the psyche of the father figure. For Herman's study, see *Father-Daughter Incest*. For a useful genealogy of Judith Butler's critical considerations of incest, the incest taboo, and kinship more broadly, see Strong.

4. In the context of general subject formation, Butler also explores the challenges of narrating identity in *Giving an Account of Oneself*.

5. For a useful source on Chinese divination and trigraphs, see Sawyer and Sawyer.

6. Given the relative paucity of established studies on Kinbaku (also called Shibari), the practices are indeed difficult to mark down in one way or another. As Douglas Kent points out, "Shibari evolved through countless experts developing their individual style. Subsequent generations built on the developments of their predecessors. However, at no point was shibari *defined*" (vol. 1: 7). For more sources on Shibari, see Harrington; Master "K"; and D. Kent (vol. 2).

7. Kolmes et al. further explain the variations on BDSM (304).

8. For more on the ways that BDSM communities develop, see R. D. K. Herman and Margot Weiss.

9. Numerous studies are devoted to the issue of bias in therapeutic treatment, especially calling for increased training by therapists who encounter patients who

engage in BDSM. For these studies, see Barker et al.; Lawrence and Love-Crowell; Easton; and Kelsey et al. Other studies reveal that the psychological profiles of the vast majority of BDSM practitioners do not evidence "a pathological symptom of past abuse" (Richters et al. 1667). Andreas A. J. Wismeijer and Marcel A. L. M. van Assen conclude that "[w]e showed that the psychological profile of BDSM participants is characterized by a set of balanced, autonomous, and beneficial personality characteristics and a higher level of subjective well-being compared with non-BDSM participants" (9).

10. In an ethnographic study, Robin Bauer makes a similar claim that BDSM enables "personal growth and healing" and possesses "political potential in that it enabled them to question cultural assumptions about power in general and sex and gender specifically" (235–236).

11. For other ethnographic accounts of BDSM communities that move beyond a pathological recounting of such groups, see Newmahr.

12. Selim's viewpoint dovetails with that of Madison Young, a Kinbaku practitioner who argues, "Submissives are often strong and powerful wo/men who wish to set aside or give their 'power' to another person. Submissives are willing to make themselves vulnerable, open to experiences" (56).

13. For considerations of homosexuality in relation to Singaporean law, see Stewart Chang ("Postcolonial" and "Gay Liberation").

14. Gary L. Atkins (185–219) and Robert Phillips (191–192) have separately noted the instrumentality of the Internet in providing Singaporean queers with an avenue to explore their sexualities without fear of nation-state reprisal and oppressive regulation.

15. These fictional portrayals mirror real life in that the Internet has contributed to a new wave of interest in Kinbaku (Midori 3).

16. All of the contents from this letter are formatted in italics in the novel.

17. For other considerations of trauma in relation to narrative and recovery, see Caruth (*Unclaimed Experience*); J. L. Herman (*Trauma*); Horvitz; LaCapra (*Writing History*); and Vickroy.

18. For more sources on the connections between incest and miscegenation, see Fenton; and Lahr-Vivaz.

19. For more on the context of state-sponsored multiculturalism and the problems associated with this policy, see Liu et al.; Law; and D. Goh ("State Carnivals").

20. On the issue of multiracialism as an underpinning of the nation-state, Michael Hill and Kwen F. Lian argue that "[a]s one of the founding myths of Singapore it is a 'charter' for social action" (93–94).

21. "Given that the identity of certain groups is shaped by a conflation of religious and ethnic identity, inter-group conflict can be precipitated by both religions and racial factors" (Thio 202).

22. For more on Hinduism in Singapore, see Sebastian and Parameswaran; and Sinha ("'Hinduism'" and "Unraveling"), and for more on Taoism in Singapore, see Sinha ("'Hinduism'"). As Thio further notes, "Christianity alone transcends the ethnic boundary" (202). For more on Christianity in Singapore, see D. Goh ("State and Social").

23. For more on the issue of Malay and Muslim minority problems, see Roach; Rahman (112–114); and Mutalib.

24. Selim refers to the terrorist group called Jemaah Islamiah, which was targeted by the Singaporean government in 2001 and 2002. For an article exploring these contexts and implementing an effective counterterrorism strategy, see Hassan and Pereire.

25. In the context of issues raised in dining practices and ethnic Malays, Gabriele Marranci would corroborate Selim's viewpoint: "While in the past the loyalty question had focused on the ethnic identity of the Singaporean Malays and their links with Malaysia, today it focuses more on their identity as Muslims" (87).

26. Alhabshi notes that Geylang Serai is a heavily populated Malay settlement that had once suffered from blight and impoverishment but was targeted for urban renewal.

27. Though the race riots were far more prominent in 1964, Kin Wah Chin notes that "[s]ignificantly, the height of Confrontation (from September 1964 to February 1965) overlapped with the communal riots and also with the vituperative exchanges between the Alliance Party and the PAP between January and April 1965" (103). As Lily Zubaidah Rahim further notes, "Indeed, by mid-1965, racial tensions were so explosive that foreign observers in Malaysia believed that any prolongation of the friction between KL and Singapore would have resulted in bloodshed" (34).

28. Nirmala Srirekam Purushotam explains that a number of factors including "anglicisation" enabled the Straits Chinese "a disproportionate influence . . . in Singapore British society" (41).

29. As Lee Su Kim notes, "With modernization and the introduction of Western ideas, the clannishness of the Babas gradually eroded, and family ties became weak. . . ." (166).

30. In this sense, I follow Philip Holden's claim regarding English-language Singaporean literature: "Careful attention to such literary texts complicates a historical account that legitimizes state multiracialism as simply managing primordial communities, insisting rather on state multiracialism's own implication in recreating and redeploying racialization" (34).

31. Peranakan communities contain more subgroups. See Kershaw (esp. 75); and Moorthy.

32. Historically, Singapore has sustained a small and distinct Arab population known as the Hadramis (Talib).

33. For more on Munshi Abdullah, see Alatas (138–140).

34. For a study on the economic changes that occurred in Singapore during its occupation, see H. Shimizu (115–122); for cultural and educational control, see Kwang (31–32).

35. Because the occupation period most directly affected those of Chinese descent, trauma can be seen as asymmetrically felt by those of Singaporean backgrounds (Blackburn, "Recalling" 244). Miss Rajah's comments concerning Japanese colonialism might be seen as nationally situated.

36. For some useful critical considerations of Godzilla and associated representations of monsters, see Ryfle; Szasz and Issei; and Stymeist.

37. Using examples of Singaporean revitalization projects, T. C. Chang argues that tourism paradigms should be rethought as ones that benefit both transnational and visiting consumers as well as locals (47). In relation to *Pulse*, Chang's argument resonates insofar as sites marked for tourism can be a draw for a diverse set of visitors. Natalie complicates the nature of tourist-driven sites, as she is a diasporic subject yet could still claim status as a local.

38. For more on Singapore and neoliberal economic models, see A. Ong; and Liow.

39. Maurizio Peleggi takes a balanced look at the Raffles Hotel, arguing that "[t]he monumentalisation of colonial hotels, on the contrary, transforms—or more precisely redoubles—economic value into use value at the same time that it increases marketability by 'restoration'" (264). His point is to move beyond the paradigm that links historical restorations to an apolitical amnesia.

40. Roy Jones and Brian J. Shaw note that "selection and approval of suitable sites is not quite as straightforward as it may seem owing to the high degree of subjectivity involved between the unquantifiable elements of historic, aesthetic or cultural value, the competing claims of various ethnic groups and the need to support national development priorities" (126). Their point reveals a more balanced view of the nation-state's role in the process of sites reserved for restoration and conservation. On the other hand, *Pulse* functions with a more critical viewpoint of the nation-state's role in the process of constructing a collective memory.

41. For more on the culture of consumption on Singapore, see Huat ("Multiculturalism").

42. For a study of the politics around collective memory, Singapore, and World War II sites, see Muzaini and Yeoh.

43. Singapore has been conceptualized as a form of the global city called the global city-state (Olds and Yeung 507).

44. Wee ("Suppressed") explores similar issues in a critique of filmic representations.

45. Ortmann (37) and Leow (119) explore the importance of cultural production in the process of intervening in discourses of national identity and development. Influenced by Ortmann's and Leow's points, I argue that *Pulse* participates in a reconsideration of national identity.

46. I riff off the term employed by Elizabeth Wilson in *The Sphinx in the City*. The modernist *flaneuse*, who is female, is a variation on the male urban wanderer, who moves about the city with a detached but observant gaze.

47. For a history of Singaporean prostitution from the late nineteenth to the mid-twentieth centuries, see J. F. Warren.

48. For more studies of HDB flats and public housing in Singapore, see V. Lee; Tu and Wong; and Phang.

49. Chua Beng Huat explains the housing policy in relation to ethnicity and race through the government's focus on the regulation of social difference (see "Singapore" 46).

50. I use the conditional phrase *would* because scholars take diverging viewpoints on the success of social integration through public housing in Singapore. For instance, Sim et al. contend that the HDB flats have functioned to reduce ethnic differences while

enhancing social integration. In contrast, Sin ("Politics" and "Quest") questions the success of HDB's policies to reduce ethnic and racial residential segregation.

51. According to Chris Hudson, "Ethnic and cultural differences that might engender different family forms" in Singapore "are subsumed, and the nuclear family is given primacy as the core unit of the nation" (22).

52. We can see how appropriate it is that she turns to alternative therapies, Kinbaku and acupuncture, forms of healing sometimes considered by the policymakers to be pre-modern and even uncivilized (D. Goh, "Chinese" 118).

53. Catherine Gomes notes how important it is for the nation-state to create a transnational citizenry with loyalty to the Singaporean homeland (39). For more on the issue of brain drain in Singaporean context and its connection to a transnational citizenship, see A. Koh.

54. For a study of demolition and urban renewal in the context of Singaporean *kampungs*, connoting a village-type settlement often inhabited by those of Malay background, see Seng.

55. Though the law (designated section 377 in the Penal Code) targeting homosexual acts between men was upheld, Singapore has not levied the legal control over lesbian sexualities. Despite the perception, then, that lesbianism might be more accepted, the work of Detenber et al. reveals that "this study found that most Singaporeans hold negative attitudes toward lesbians and gay men, and are rather intolerant toward media portrayals of homosexuality" (373). For more on the issue of this law, see Stewart Chang "Legacies"; J. T. Lee; Shing; Sanders; and J. Chen.

56. For more on the discourse of Western decadence and immorality in relation to Singaporean social policies, see Wilkinson (165).

57. As Youyenn Teo explains, the ideal Singaporean family is a "heterosexual, married couple. Both man and woman are educated and formally employed. The couple should have children—three, or more, if they can afford it" (338). Wong Kai Wen notes in addition, "Current policies that promote childbearing continue to be framed within the dominant ideology of the heterosexual nuclear family" (96).

58. For more on the issue of fertility decline in Singapore, see Swee-Hock; Fawcett and Khoo; Palen; Lee, Alvarez, and Palen; G. Jones ("Late Marriage"); and S. Sun.

59. Gavin W. Jones notes that "[i]n Singapore, marriage is the gatekeeper to fertility. As in other East Asian countries, fewer than 2 percent of birth[s] occur out of wedlock" ("Population" 317). For more on the place of women in relation to reproduction and Singapore policy, see Pyle.

60. See G. Jones ("Population" 323) and Williams (147–148) for more on housing policies favoring married couples. See Yap (655–656) and G. Jones ("Late Marriage" 95) for more on the baby bonus.

61. Thus I mentioned earlier the tactic of pragmatic resistance taken up by recent queer activists in Singapore, which involves mediating their goals through less subversive means (Tan and Jin 198). Kwa's *Pulse* resists this mode of mainstreaming by articulating its radical inscrutable belongings.

62. Canada is not depicted as a panacea for queer same-sex relationships. Though

Natalie returns to Canada less haunted by her past, it is too reductive to state that she somehow concludes the novel completing a successful courtship plot.

Coda

1. Asian Pride Project, "Share Your Story," http://asianprideproject.org/share-your-story/ (accessed on October 25, 2016).

2. National Queer Asian and Pacific Islander Alliance, http://www.nqapia.org/wpp/about-the-conference/ (accessed on October 25, 2016).

REFERENCES

Abboud, Soo Kim, and Jane Kim. *Top of the Class: How Asian Parents Raise High Achievers—and How You Can Too*. New York: Berkley, 2006.
Abraham, Julie. *Are Girls Necessary? Lesbian Writing and Modern Histories*. Minneapolis: U of Minnesota P, 1996.
Abraham, Nicolas, and Maria Torok. *The Shell and the Kernel: Renewals of Psychoanalysis*. Vol. 1. Chicago: U of Chicago P, 1994.
Adams, Alice E. "Making Theoretical Space: Psychoanalysis and Lesbian Sexual Difference." *Signs* 27.2 (2002): 473–499.
Agentieri, Simona. "Incest Yesterday and Today: From Conflict to Ambiguity." *On Incest: Psychoanalytic Perspectives*. Ed. Giovanna Ambrosio. London: Karnac, 2005. 17–50.
Aguilar, Filomeno V., Jr. *Clash of Spirits: The History of Power and Sugar Planter Hegemony on a Visayan Island*. Honolulu: U of Hawai'i P, 1998.
Aguilar-San Juan, Karin. "Going Home: Enacting Justice in Queer Asian America." *Q&A: Queer in Asian America*. Ed. David L. Eng and Alice Y. Hom. Philadelphia: Temple UP, 1998. 25–40.
———. "Landmarks in Literature by Asian American Lesbians." *Signs* 18.4 (1993): 936–943.
Ahmed, Sara. *The Promise of Happiness*. Durham: Duke UP, 2010.
Alatas, Syed Hussein. *The Myth of the Lazy Native: A Study of the Image of the Malays, Filipinos and Javanese from the 16th to the 20th Century and Its Function in the Ideology of Colonial Capitalism*. New York: Routledge, 2010.
Alexander, Bryant Keith. *Performing Black Masculinity: Race, Culture, and Queer Identity*. Walnut Creek: AltaMira, 2006.
Alhabshi, Sharifah Mariam. "Urban Renewal of Traditional Settlements in Singapore

and Malaysia: The Cases of Geylang Serai and Kampung Bharu." *Asian Survey* 50.6 (2010): 1135–1161.

Ali, Kazim. *The Disappearance of Seth*. Wilkes-Barre: Etruscan Press, 2009.

———. *Quinn's Passage*. Kenmore: BlazeVox, 2005.

———. *The Secret Room*. Los Angeles: Kaya, 2017.

Aljunied, Syed Muhd Khairudin. "From Noble Muslims to Saracen Enemies: Thomas Stamford Raffles' Discourse on Islam in the Malay World." *Sari* 21 (2003): 13–29.

———. "Sir Thomas Stamford Raffles' Discourse on the Malay World: A Revisionist Perspective." *Sojourn: Journal of Social Issues in Southeast Asia*, 20.1 (2005): 1–22.

Altherr, Thomas L. "'Chaplain to the Hunters': Henry David Thoreau's Ambivalence Toward Hunting." *American Literature* 56.3 (1984): 345–361.

Alumit, Noël. *Talking to the Moon*. New York: Carroll & Graf, 2007.

———. *Letters to Montgomery Clift*. San Francisco: MacAdam/Cage, 2002.

Ambrosio, Giovanna, ed. *On Incest: Psychoanalytic Perspectives*. London: Karnac, 2005.

Anderson, Crystal S. *Beyond the Chinese Connection: Contemporary Afro-Asian Cultural Production*. Jackson: UP of Mississippi, 2013.

Anzaldúa, Gloria E. *Borderlands/La Frontera: The New Mestiza*. San Francisco: Aunt Lute, 1987.

Aparece, Ulysses B. "Lunas: The 'Mother' of All Sukdan Shamans' Curing Rituals." *Philippine Quarterly of Culture and Society* 34.2 (2006): 135–187.

Apostol, Virgil Mayor. *Way of the Ancient Healer: Sacred Teachings from the Philippine Ancestral Traditions*. Berkeley: North Atlantic, 2010.

Arens, William. *The Original Sin: Incest and Its Meaning*. Oxford. Oxford UP, 1986.

Armengol-Carrera, Josep M. "Race-ing Hemingway: Revisions of Masculinity and/as Whiteness in Ernest Hemingway's *Green Hills of Africa* and *Under Kilimanjaro*." *Hemingway Review* 31.1 (2011): 43–61.

Arora, Anupama. "Rituals of Queer Diaspora in Nisha Ganatra's *Chutney Popcorn*." *South Asian Popular Culture* 5.1 (April 2007): 31–43.

Atkins, Gary L. *Imagining Gay Paradise: Bali, Bangkok, and Cyber-Singapore*. Hong Kong: Hong Kong UP, 2012.

Backus, Margot Gayle. "Judy Grahn and the Lesbian Invocational Elegy: Testimonial and Prophetic Responses to Social Death in *A Woman Is Talking to Death*." *Signs* 18.4 (1993): 815–837.

Badruddoja, Roksana. "Queer Spaces, Places, and Gender: The Tropologies of Rupa and Ronica." *NWSA Journal* 20.2 (Summer 2008): 156–188.

Baes, Jonas. "*Marayaw* and the Changing Context of Power Among the Iraya of Mindoro, Philippines." *International Review of the Aesthetics and Sociology of Music* 19.2 (1988): 259–267.

Balken, Debra Bricker. *After Many Springs: Regionalism, Modernism, and the Midwest*. Des Moines: Des Moines Art Center, 2009.

Bankoff, Greg. "Devils, Familiars and Spaniards: Spheres of Power and the Supernatural in the World of Seberina Candelaria and Her Village in Early 19th Century Philippines." *Journal of Social History* 33.1 (1999): 37–55.

Banting, Keith, and Will Kymlicka. "Canadian Multiculturalism: Global Anxieties and Local Debates." *British Journal of Canadian Studies* 23.1 (2010): 43–72.

Barillas, William. *Midwestern Pastoral: Place and Landscape in Literature of the American Heartland*. Athens: Ohio UP, 2006.

Barker, Meg, et al. "Kinky Clients, Kinky Counselling? The Challenges and Potentials of BDSM." *Feeling Queer or Queer Feelings: Radical Approaches to Counselling Sex, Sexualities and Genders*. Ed. Lyndsey Moon. New York: Routledge, 2007. 106–124.

Barnard, Ian. *Queer Race: Cultural Interventions in the Racial Politics of Queer Theory*. New York: Peter Lang, 2004.

Barry, Kathleen. *The Prostitution of Sexuality*. New York: New York UP, 1995.

Bascom, William. "The Forms of Folklore: Prose Narratives." *Journal of American Folklore* 78.307 (1965): 3–20.

Bassichis, Morgan, and Dean Spade. "Queer Politics and Anti-Blackness." *Queer Necropolitics*. Ed. Jin Haritaworn, Adi Kuntsman, and Silvia Posocco. New York: Routledge, 2014.

Bathgate, Michael. *The Fox's Craft in Japanese Religion and Culture: Shapeshifters, Transformations, and Duplicities*. New York: Routledge, 2004.

Baudrillard, Jean. *Simulacra and Simulation*. Ann Arbor: U of Michigan P, 1995.

Bauer, Robin. "Transgressive and Transformative Gendered Sexual Practices and White Privileges: The Case of the Dyke/Trans BDSM Communities." *WSQ: Women's Studies Quarterly* 36.3 and 4 (2008): 233–253.

Baum, Scott. "Social Transformations in the Global City: Singapore." *Urban Studies* 36.7 (1999): 1095–1117.

Baumeister, Roy F. "The Enigmatic Appeal of Sexual Masochism: Why People Desire Pain, Bondage, and Humiliation in Sex." *Journal of Social and Clinical Psychology* 16 (1997): 133–150.

Beaujot, Roderic, and Zenaida Ravanera. "Family Change and Implications for Family Solidarity and Social Cohesion." *Canadian Studies in Population* 35.1 (2008): 73–101.

Bendix, Trish. "Queer History Women Forgot: Mai-Mai Sze." *GOMAG: The Cultural Road Map for City Girls Everywhere*. March 7, 2017, gomag.com/article/queer-women-history-forgot-mai-mai-sze. Accessed August 2, 2017.

Bergman, Kim, et al. "Gay Men Who Become Fathers via Surrogacy: The Transition to Parenthood." *Journal of GLBT Family Studies* 6 (2010): 111–141.

Bernstein, Mary. "Same-Sex Marriage and the Future of the LGBT Movement: SWS Presidential Address." *Gender & Society* 29.3 (June 2015): 321–337.

Bernstein, Robin. *Racial Innocence: Performing American Childhood from Slavery to Civil Rights*. New York: New York UP, 2011.

Bersani, Leo. "Is the Rectum a Grave?" *October* 43 (Winter 1987): 197–222.

Bérubé, Alan. "The History of Gay Bathhouses." *Journal of Homosexuality* 44.3 (2003): 33–53.

Bettelheim, Bruno. *The Uses of Enchantment: The Meaning and Importance of Fairy Tales*. New York: Vintage, 2010.

Beyer, Tamiko. *We Come Elemental*. Farmington: Alice James, 2013.

Binson, Diane, et al. "HIV Transmission Risk at a Gay Bathhouse." *Journal of Sex Research* 47.6 (2010): 580–588.
Bischof, Norbert. "The Biological Foundations of the Incest Taboo." *Social Science Information* 11.6 (1972): 7–36.
Blackburn, Kevin. "Recalling War Trauma of the Pacific War and the Japanese Occupation in the Oral History of Malaysia and Singapore." *Oral History Review* 36.2 (2009): 231–252.
———. "Reminiscence and War Trauma: Recalling the Japanese Occupation of Singapore, 1942–1945." *Oral History* 33.2 (2005): 91–98.
Blum, Virginia L. *Hide and Seek: The Child Between Psychoanalysis and Fiction.* Urbana: U of Illinois P, 1995.
Blust, Robert. "The Fox's Wedding." *Anthropos* 94.4/6 (1999): 487–499.
Bogle, Donald. *Toms, Coons, Mulattoes, Mammies, and Bucks: An Interpretive History of Blacks in American Films.* New York: Viking, 1973.
Boglioli, Marc. *A Matter of Life and Death: Hunting in Contemporary Vermont.* Amherst: U of Massachusetts P, 2009.
Booker, Christopher. *The Seven Basic Plots: Why We Tell Stories.* New York: Continuum, 2004.
Boone, Joseph Allen. *Tradition Counter Tradition: Love and the Form of Fiction.* Chicago: U of Chicago P, 1987.
Bosworth, Patricia. *Montgomery Clift: A Biography.* Milwaukee: Limelight, 2004.
Bottigheimer, Ruth B. "Fairy Tales, Folk Narrative Research and History." *Social History* 14.3 (1989): 343–357.
Bourque, Dawn M. "'Reconstructing' the Patriarchal Nuclear Family: Recent Developments in Child Custody and Access in Canada." *Canadian Journal of Law and Society* 10.1 (1995): 1–24.
Bow, Leslie. *Betrayal and Other Acts of Subversion: Feminism, Sexual Politics, Asian American Women's Literature.* Princeton: Princeton UP, 2001.
Brett, Caroline. "Psychotic and Mystical States of Being: Connections and Distinctions." *Philosophy, Psychiatry, & Psychology* 9.4 (2002): 321–341.
Brian, Kristi. *Reframing Transracial Adoption: Adopted Koreans, and the Politics of Kinship.* Philadelphia: Temple UP, 2012.
Briggs, Laura. *Somebody's Children: The Politics of Transracial and Transnational Adoption.* Durham: Duke UP, 2012.
Bronner, Simon J. "Contesting Tradition: The Deep Play and Protest of Pigeon Shoots." *Journal of American Folklore* 118.470 (Fall 2005): 409–452.
———. *Killing Tradition: Inside Hunting and Animal Rights Controversies.* Lexington: UP of Kentucky, 2008.
———. "'This Is Why We Hunt': Social-Psychological Meanings of the Traditions and Rituals of Deer Camp." *Western Folklore* 63.1–2 (2004): 11–50.
Brooks, Peter. *Reading for the Plot: Design and Intention in Narrative.* Reprint ed. Cambridge: Harvard UP, 1992.

Broome, Matthew R. "The Rationality of Psychosis and Understanding the Deluded." *Philosophy, Psychiatry, & Psychology* 11.1 (2004): 35–41.
Brophy, Sarah. *Witnessing AIDS: Writing, Testimony, and the Work of Mourning.* Toronto: U of Toronto P, 2004.
Brotman, Shari, Bill Ryan, and Robert Cormier. "The Health and Social Service Needs of Gay and Lesbian Elders and Their Families in Canada." *The Gerontologist* 43.2 (2003): 192–202.
Brown, Wendy. *States of Injury: Power and Freedom in Late Modernity.* Princeton: Princeton UP, 1995.
Browne, Nick. "The Spectator-in-the-Text: The Rhetoric of *Stagecoach*." *Film Quarterly* 29.2 (Winter 1975–1976).
Bui, Long. "Breaking into the Closet: Negotiating the Queer Boundaries of Asian American Masculinity and Domesticity." *Culture, Society & Masculinities* 6.2 (Fall 2014): 129–149.
Butler, Judith. *Antigone's Claim: Kinship Between Life and Death.* Ithaca: Columbia UP, 2002.
———. *Giving an Account of Oneself.* New York: Fordham UP, 2005.
———. "Is Kinship Always Already Heterosexual?" *differences: A Journal of Feminist Cultural Studies* 13.1 (2002): 14–44.
———. *The Psychic Life of Power: Theories in Subjection.* Stanford: Stanford UP, 1997.
———. *Undoing Gender.* New York: Routledge, 2004.
Cacho, Lisa Marie. *Social Death: Racialized Rightlessness and the Criminalization of the Unprotected.* New York: New York UP, 2012.
Cahill, Courtney Megan. "Same-Sex Marriage, Slippery Slope Rhetoric, and the Politics of Disgust: A Critical Perspective on Contemporary Family Discourse and the Incest Taboo." *Northwestern University Law Review* 99.4 (2005): 1543–1612.
Cahn, Naomi. "The New Kinship." *Georgetown Law Journal* 100 (2012): 367–429.
———. *The New Kinship: Constructing Donor-Conceived Families.* New York: New York UP, 2013.
Cain, Roy. "Disclosure and Secrecy Among Gay Men in the United States and Canada: Shift in Views." *Journal of the History of Sexuality* 2.1 (July 1991): 25–45.
Calder, Alison. "Paper Families and Blonde Demonesses: The Haunting of History in SKY Lee's *Disappearing Moon Cafe*." *ARIEL* 31.4 (October 2000): 7–21.
Calhoun, Cheshire. "The Gender Closet: Lesbian Disappearance Under the Sign 'Women.'" *Feminist Studies* 21.1 (1995): 7–34.
———. "Separating Lesbian Theory from Feminist Theory." *Ethics* 104.3 (1994): 558–581.
Callahan, Cynthia. *Kin of Another Kind: Transracial Adoption in American Literature.* Ann Arbor: U of Michigan P, 2010.
Canaday, Margot. *The Straight State: Sexuality and Citizenship in Twentieth-Century America.* Princeton: Princeton UP, 2009.
Cannell, Fenella. *Power and Intimacy in the Christian Philippines.* New York: Cambridge UP, 1999.

Carbado, Devin W., and Mitu Gulati. *Acting White?: Rethinking Race in "Post-Racial" America*. New York: Oxford UP, 2015.
Card, Claudia. "Genocide and Social Death." *Hypatia* 18.1 (2003): 63–79.
———. *Lesbian Choices*. New York: Columbia UP, 1995.
Carrington, Christopher. *No Place Like Home: Relationships and Family Life Among Lesbians and Gay Men*. Chicago: U of Chicago P, 2002.
Carsten, Janet. *After Kinship*. West Nyack: Cambridge UP, 2003.
Carter, Julian. "Gay Marriage and Pulp Fiction: Homonormativity, Disidentification, and Affect in Ann Bannon's Lesbian Novels." *GLQ* 15.4 (2009): 583–609.
Cartmill, Matt. *A View to a Death in the Morning: Hunting and Nature Through History*. Cambridge: Harvard UP, 1993.
Caruth, Cathy. "Unclaimed Experience, Trauma and the Possibility of History." *Yale French Studies* 79 (1991): 181–192.
———. *Unclaimed Experience: Trauma, Narrative, and History*. Baltimore: Johns Hopkins UP, 1996.
———. "Violence and Time: Traumatic Survivals." *Assemblage* 20 (April 1993): 24–25.
Casal, U. A. "The Goblin Fox and Badger and Other Witch Animals of Japan." *Folklore Studies* 18 (1959): 1–93.
Case, Sue-Ellen. *The Domain-Matrix: Performing Lesbian at the End of Print Culture*. Bloomington: U of Indiana P, 1996.
Cashdan, Sheldon. *The Witch Must Die: The Hidden Meaning of Fairy Tales*. New York: Basic, 1999.
Castiglia, Christopher, and Christopher Reed. *If Memory Serves: Gay Men, AIDS, and the Promise of the Queer Past*. Minneapolis: U of Minnesota P, 2012.
Castle, Terry. *The Apparitional Lesbian: Female Homosexuality and Modern Culture*. New York: Columbia UP, 1993.
Castronovo, Russ. *Necro Citizenship: Death, Eroticism, and the Public Sphere in the Nineteenth-Century United States*. Durham: Duke UP, 2001.
Cayton, Andrew R. L., and Peter S. Onuf. *The Midwest and the Nation: Rethinking the History of an American Region*. Bloomington: Indiana UP, 1990.
Centrone, Brian. "Rahul Mehta on Pushing Through Writer's Block and Exploring Pain Through Fiction." *Lambda Literary*. April 16, 2017, https://www.lambdaliterary.org/interviews/04/16/rahul-mehta-on-pushing-through-writers-block-memory-and-exploring-pain-through-fiction. Accessed September 1, 2017.
Chadda, Rakesh K., and Koushik Sinha Deb. "Indian Family Systems, Collectivistic Society and Psychotherapy." *Indian Journal of Psychiatry* 55.6 (2013): 299–309.
Chambers, Ross. *Untimely Interventions: AIDS Writing, Testimonial & the Rhetoric of Haunting*. Ann Arbor: U of Michigan P, 2004.
Champagne, Rosaria. *The Politics of Survivorship: Incest, Women's Literature, and Feminist Theory*. New York: New York UP, 1996.
Chan, Anthony. *Perpetually Cool: The Many Lives of Anna May Wong, 1905–1961*. Lanham: Scarecrow, 2003.
Chan, Arlene. *The Chinese Community in Toronto: Then and Now*. Toronto: Dundurn, 2013.

Chan, Jeffrey Paul, et al., eds. *Aiiieeeee! An Anthology of Asian American Writers*. New York: New American Library, 1974.

Chan, Kenneth. "Rice Sticking Together: Cultural Nationalist Logic and the Cinematic Representations of Gay Asian-Caucasian Relationships and Desire." *Discourse* 28.2/3 (2006): 178–196.

Chan, Sucheng. *Asian Americans: An Interpretive History*. New York: Twayne, 1991.

Chandler, Marilyn. "No Immunity: AIDS in Recent Fiction." *Northwest Review* 27.3 (1989): 144–151.

Chang, Robert S. "The Invention of Asian Americans." *UC Irvine Law Review* 3.4 (2013): 947–964.

Chang, Sishir. "A High-Rise Vernacular in Singapore's Housing Development Board Housing." *Berkeley Planning Journal* 14 (2000): 97–116.

Chang, Stewart. "Gay Liberation in the Illiberal State." *Washington International Law Journal* 24.1 (2015): 1–46.

———. "Legacies of Exceptionalism and the Future of Gay Rights in Singapore." *Hong Kong Law Journal* 46.1 (2016): 71–88.

———. "The Postcolonial Problem for Global Gay Rights." *Boston University International Law Journal* 32.2 (2014): 309–354.

Chang, T. C. "Heritage as a Tourism Commodity: Traversing the Tourist-Local Divide." *Singapore Journal of Tropical Geography* 18.1 (1997): 46–68.

Chao, Lien. "The Collective Self: A Narrative Paradigm in SKY Lee's *Disappearing Moon Cafe*." *Cross-Addressing: Resistance Literature and Cultural Borders*. Ed. John C. Hawley. Albany: State U of New York P, 1996. 237–255.

Chee, Alexander. *Edinburgh*. Reprint. New York: Picador, 2002.

Chen, Jianlin. "Singapore's Culture War Over Section 377A: Through the Lens of Public Choice and Multilingual Research." *Law & Social Inquiry* 38.1 (2013): 106–137.

Chen, Xiaobei. "Not Ethnic Enough: The Cultural Identity Imperative in International Adoptions from China to Canada." *Children & Society* 29.6 (2014): 1–11.

Cheng, Anne Anlin. *The Melancholy of Race: Psychoanalysis, Assimilation, and Hidden Grief*. London: Oxford UP, 2001.

Cheng, Ching-In. *The Heart's Traffic*. Los Angeles: Arktoi, 2009.

Cherlin, Andrew J. "The Deinstitutionalization of American Marriage." *Journal of Marriage and Family* 66 (November 2004): 848–861.

Chin, Justin. *98 Wounds*. San Francisco: Manic D, 2011.

Chin, Kin Wah. *The Defence of Malaysia and Singapore: The Transformation of a Security System, 1957–1971*. Cambridge: Cambridge UP, 2009.

Chisholm, Diane. *Queer Constellations: Subcultural Space in the Wake of the City*. Minneapolis: U of Minneapolis P, 2005.

Chiu, Monica. *Scrutinized! Surveillance in Asian North American Literature*. Honolulu: U of Hawai'i P, 2014.

Cho, Grace. *Haunting the Korean Diaspora: Shame, Secrecy, and the Forgotten War*. Minneapolis: U of Minneapolis P, 2008.

Cho, Lily. "Asian Canadian Futures: Diasporic Passages and the Routes of Indenture." *Canadian Literature* 199 (Winter 2008): 181–201.
Chong, Sylvia Shin Huey. *The Oriental Obscene: Violence and Racial Fantasies in the Vietnam Era*. Durham: Duke UP, 2012.
Chou, Rosalind S., and Joe R. Feagin. *Myth of the Model Minority: Asian Americans Facing Racism*. Boulder: Paradigm, 2008.
Choy, Catherine Ceniza. *Global Families: A History of Asian International Adoption in America*. New York: New York UP, 2013.
Choy, Wayson. *All That Matters*. Toronto: Doubleday Canada, 2004.
———. *The Jade Peony*. Vancouver: Douglas & McIntyre, 1995.
Chu, Patricia P. *Assimilating Asians: Gendered Strategies of Authorship in Asian America*. Durham: Duke UP, 2000.
Chua, Amy. *Battle Hymn of the Tiger Mother*. New York: Penguin, 2011.
Chua, Lawrence. *Gold by the Inch*. New York: Grove, 1998.
Chua, Lynette J. "Pragmatic Resistance, Law, and Social Movements in Authoritarian States: The Case of Gay Collective Action in Singapore." *Law & Society Review* 46.4 (2012): 713–747.
Chuh, Kandice. "Discomforting Knowledge: Or, Korean 'Comfort Women' and Asian Americanist Critical Practice." *Journal of Asian American Studies* 6.1 (2003): 5–23.
Chung, Hye Seung. *Hollywood Asian: Philip Ahn and the Politics of Cross-Ethnic Performance*. Philadelphia: Temple UP, 2006.
Chung, Y. Barry, and Dawn M. Szymanski. "Racial and Sexual Identities of Asian American Gay Men." *Journal of LGBT Issues in Counseling* 1.2 (2006): 67–93.
Ciasullo, Ann M. "Making Her (In)Visible: Cultural Representations of Lesbianism and the Lesbian Body in the 1990s." *Feminist Studies* 27.3 (2001): 577–608.
Clancy, Susan A. *The Trauma Myth: The Truth About the Sexual Abuse of Children and Its Aftermath*. New York: Basic, 2009.
Clum, John M. "'And Once I Had It All': AIDS Narratives and Memories of an American Dream." *Writing AIDS: Gay Literature, Language, and Analysis*. Ed. Timothy Murphy and Suzanne Poirier. New York: Columbia UP, 1993. 200–224.
Coale, Sam. "*Red Noses*, the Black Death, and AIDS: Cycles of Despair and Disease." *Confronting AIDS Through Literature: The Responsibilities of Representation*. Ed. Judith Laurence Pastore. Urbana: U of Illinois P, 1993. 95–102.
Cohen, Yéhudi. "The Disappearance of the Incest Taboo." *Human Nature* 1 (1978): 72–78.
Connolly, Brian. *Domestic Intimacies: Incest and the Liberal Subject in Nineteenth-Century America*. Philadelphia: U of Pennsylvania P, 2014.
Cook, Barbara. "A Tapestry of History and Reimagination: Women's Place in James Welch's *Fools Crow*." *The American Indian Quarterly* 24.3 (Summer 2000): 441–453.
Cotler, Irwin. "Marriage in Canada—Evolution or Revolution." *Family Court Review* (January 2006): 60–73.
Coupe, Lynda Wolfe. *Images of the Hunter in American Life and Literature*. New York: Peter Lang, 2000.

Crimp, Douglas. *Melancholia and Moralism: Essays on AIDS and Queer Politics*. Boston: MIT Press, 2004.
Cvetkovich, Ann. *An Archive of Feelings: Trauma, Sexuality, and Lesbian Public Cultures*. Durham: Duke UP, 2003.
Dana, Anne R. "The State of Surrogacy Laws: Determining Legal Parentage for Gay Fathers." *Duke Journal of Gender Law & Policy* 18 (2011): 353–390.
Dasgupta, Rohit K. "Queer Sexuality: A Cultural Narrative of India's Historical Archive." *Rupkatha Journal on Interdisciplinary Studies in Humanities* 3.4 (2011): 651–670.
Davé, Shilpa S. *Indian Accents: Brown Voice and Racial Performance in American Television and Film*. Urbana: U of Illinois P, 2013.
———. "Racial Accents, Hollywood Casting, and Asian American Studies." *Cinema Journal* 56.3 (Spring 2017): 142–147.
Davidson, Arnold E. *Coyote Country: Fictions of the Canadian West*. Durham: Duke UP, 1994.
Davis, Rocío G. *Begin Here: Reading Asian North American Autobiographies of Childhood*. Honolulu: U of Hawai'i P, 2007.
———. *Transcultural Reinventions: Asian American and Asian Canadian Short Story Cycles*. Toronto: TSAR, 2001.
Dawes, James. "Narrating Disease: AIDS, Consent, and the Ethics of Representation." *Social Text* 43 (Fall 1995): 27–44.
Dawesar, Abha. *Babyji*. New York: Random House, 2007.
———. *Miniplanner*. Berkeley: Cleis, 2000.
———. *That Summer in Paris*. New York: Nan A. Talese, 2006.
Day, Iyko. "Must All Asianness Be American? The Census, Racial Classification, and Asian Canadian Emergence." *Canadian Literature* 199 (Winter 2008): 45–70.
de Certeau, Michel. *The Practice of Everyday Life*. Berkeley: U of California P, 1984.
De Jesus, Melinda L. "Of Monsters and Mothers: Filipina American Identity and Maternal Legacies in Lynda J. Barry's *One Hundred Demons*." *Meridians: Feminism, Race, Transnationalism* 5.1 (2004): 1–26.
de Lauretis, Teresa. *The Practice of Love: Lesbian Sexuality and Perverse Desire*. Bloomington: Indiana UP, 1994.
———. "Sexual Indifference and Lesbian Representation." *Theatre Journal* 40.2 (1988): 155–177.
De Moor, Katrien. "The Doctor's Role of Witness and Companion: Medical and Literary Ethics of Care in AIDS Physicians' Memoirs." *Literature and Medicine* 22.2 (2003): 208–229.
Dean, Tim. *Unlimited Intimacy: Reflections on the Subculture of Barebacking*. Chicago: U of Chicago P, 2009.
Delmont, Matthew, and Jeanne Theoharis. "Introduction: Rethinking the Boston 'Busing Crisis.'" *Journal of Urban History* 43.2 (2017): 191–203.
Demetrio, Francisco. "Towards a Classification of Bisayan Folk Beliefs and Customs." *Asian Folklore Studies* 28.2 (1969): 95–132.
Denneny, Michael. "AIDS Writing and the Creation of Gay Culture." *Confronting AIDS*

Through Literature: The Responsibilities of Representation. Ed. Judith Laurence Pastore. Urbana: U of Illinois P, 1993. 36–54.

Detenber, Benjamin H., et al. "Singaporeans' Attitudes Toward Lesbians and Gay Men and Their Tolerance of Media Portrayals of Homosexuality." *International Journal of Public Opinion Research* 19.3 (2007): 367–379.

Dhalla, Ghalib Shiraz. *Ode to Lata.* Los Angeles: Really Great, 2002.

———. *The Two Krishnas.* New York: Magnus, 2011.

Dichoso, Fermin. "Some Superstitious Beliefs and Practices in Laguna, Philippines." *Anthropos* 62.1/2 (1967): 61–67.

Diedrich, Lisa. "'Without Us All Told': Paul Monette's Vigilant Witnessing to the AIDS Crisis." *Literature and Medicine* 23.1 (2004): 112–127.

Dinh, Viet. *After Disasters.* Seattle: Little A, 2016.

Dinsmore, Christine. *From Surviving to Thriving: Incest, Feminism, and Recovery.* State U of New York P, 1991.

Dizard, Jan E. *Going Wild: Hunting, Animal Rights, and the Contested Meaning of Nature.* Rev. ed. Amherst: U of Massachusetts P, 1999.

———. *Mortal Stakes: Hunters and Hunting in Contemporary America.* Amherst: U of Massachusetts P, 2003.

Dizard, Jan E., and Howard Gadlin. *The Minimal Family.* Amherst: U of Massachusetts P, 1990.

Doane, Janice L. *Telling Incest: Narratives of Dangerous Remembering from Stein to Sapphire.* Ann Arbor: U of Michigan P, 2001.

Dommaraju, Premchand. "One-Person Households in India." *Demographic Research* 32.45 (June 2015): 1239–1266.

Dougherty, Jack. *More Than One Struggle: The Evolution of Black School Reform in Milwaukee.* Chapel Hill: U of North Carolina P, 2003.

Douglas, Carol Anne. *Love and Politics: Radical Feminist and Lesbian Theories.* San Francisco: Ism Press, 1990.

Du, Nang, Hendry Ton, and Elizabeth J. Kramer. "New Immigrants." *Praeger Handbook of Asian American Health.* Vol 1. Ed. William Baragar Bateman, Noilyn Abesamis-Mendoza, and Henrietta Ho-Asjoe. Santa Barbara: Praeger, 2009. 329–342.

Duncan, C. J., and S. Scott. "What Caused the Black Death?" *Postgraduate Medical Journal* 81 (2005): 315–320.

Dunning, Stefanie K. *Queer in Black and White: Interraciality, Same Sex Desire, and Contemporary African American Culture.* Bloomington: Indiana UP, 2009.

Easton, Dossie. "Cultural Competence with BDSM Lifestyles." *Counselling Ideologies: Queer Challenges to Heteronormativity.* Ed. Lyndsey Moon. Farnham: Ashgate, 2010. 219–232.

Edelman, Lee. *No Future: Queer Theory and the Death Drive.* Durham: Duke UP, 2004.

Eguchi, Shinsuke. "Cross-National Identity Transformation: Becoming a Gay 'Asian-American' Man." *Sexuality & Culture* 15:1 (2011): 19–40.

Elliott, Mary. "When Girls Will Be Boys: 'Bad' Endings and Subversive Middles in Nineteenth-Century Tomboy Narratives and Twentieth-Century Lesbian Pulp Novels." *Legacy* 15.1 (1998): 92–97.

Emery, Kim. *The Lesbian Index: Pragmatism and Lesbian Subjectivity in the Twentieth-Century United States*. Albany: State U of New York P, 2002.

Eng, David L. *The Feeling of Kinship: Queer Liberalism and the Racialization of Intimacy*. Durham: Duke UP, 2010.

———. *Racial Castration: Managing Masculinity in Asian America*. Durham: Duke UP, 2001.

Eng, David L., and Alice Y. Hom, eds. *Q&A: Queer in Asian America*. Philadelphia: Temple UP, 1998.

Eng, David L., and Candace Fujikane. "Asian American Literature." *glbtq: An Encyclopedia of Gay, Lesbian, Bisexual, Transgender, and Queer Culture*. 2002, http://www.glbtq.com/literature/asian_am_lit,3.html. Accessed January 10, 2011.

Eng, David L., and Shinhee Han. "A Dialogue on Racial Melancholia." *Loss: The Politics of Mourning*. Ed. David L. Eng and David Kazanjian. Berkeley: U of California P, 2003. 343–371.

Engelbrecht, Penelope J. "'Lifting Belly Is a Language': The Postmodern Lesbian Subject." *Feminist Studies* 16.1 (1990): 85–114.

Enloe, Cynthia H. *The Morning After: Sexual Politics at the End of the Cold War*. Berkeley: U of California P, 1993.

Erickson, Mark. "Nature Disrupted: Evolution, Kinship and Child Sexual Abuse." *Clinical Neuropsychiatry* 3.2 (2006): 110–120.

Eschholz, Sarah. "Symbolic Reality Bites: Women and Racial/Ethnic Minorities in Modern Film." *Sociological Spectrum* 22 (2002): 299–334.

Esquibel, Catrióna Rueda. *With Her Machete in Her Hand: Reading Chicana Lesbians*. Austin: U of Texas P, 2006.

Evans, Wendy T., and David R. Maines. "Narrative Structures and the Analysis of Incest." *Symbolic Interaction* 18.3 (1995): 303–322.

Faissol, Daniel M., et al. "The Role of Bathhouses and Sex Clubs in HIV Transmission: Findings from a Mathematic Model." *Journal of Acquired Immune Deficiency Syndromes* 44.4 (2007): 386–394.

Farwell, Marilyn R. *Heterosexual Plots & Lesbian Narratives*. New York: New York UP, 1996.

Fawcett, James T., and Siew-Ean Khoo. "Singapore: Rapid Fertility Transition in a Compact Society." *Population and Development Review* 6.4 (1980): 549–579.

Feng, Peter X. *Identities in Motion: Asian American Film and Video*. Durham: Duke UP, 2002.

———. "Recuperating Suzie Wong: A Fan's Nancy Kwan-dary." *Countervisions*. Ed. Darrell Hamamoto and Sandra Liu. Philadelphia: Temple UP, 2000. 40–56.

Fenton, Zanita. "An Essay on Slavery's Hidden Legacy: Social Hysteria and Structural Condonation of Incest." *Howard Law Journal* 55.2 (2012): 319–338.

Ferguson, Roderick. *Aberrations in Black: Toward a Queer of Color Critique*. Minneapolis: U of Minneapolis P, 2003.

Fine, Lisa M. "Rights of Men, Rites of Passage: Hunting and Masculinity at Reo Motors of Lansing, Michigan, 1945–1975." *Journal of Social History* 33.4 (2000): 805–823.
Fink, Deborah. *Cutting into the Meatpacking Line: Workers and Change in the Rural Midwest*. Chapel Hill: U of North Carolina P, 1998.
Fludernik, Monica. *An Introduction to Narratology*. New York: Routledge, 2006.
Foote, Stephanie. "Deviant Classics: Pulps and the Making of Lesbian Print Culture." *Signs* 31.1 (2005): 169–190.
Formisano, Ronald P. *Boston Against Busing: Race, Class, and Ethnicity in the 1960s and 1970s*. 2nd rev. ed. Chapel Hill: U of North Carolina P, 2004.
Franke, Katherine. *Wedlocked: The Perils of Marriage Equality*. New York: New York UP, 2017.
Franklin, Sarah. *Biological Relatives: IVF, Stem Cells, and the Future of Kinship*. Durham: Duke UP, 2013.
Freeman, Elizabeth. "Queer Belongings: Kinship Theory and Queer Theory." *A Companion to Lesbian, Gay, Bisexual, Transgender, and Queer Studies*. Ed. George E. Haggerty and Molly McGarry. Hoboken: Blackwell, 2007. 295–314.
———. *Time Binds: Queer Temporalities, Queer Histories*. Durham: Duke UP, 2010.
Freeman, T., et al. "Gamete Donation: Parents' Experiences of Searching for Their Child's Donor Siblings and Donor." *Human Reproduction* 24.3 (2009): 505–516.
Freud, Sigmund. *Totem and Taboo*. Trans. James Strachey. New York: Routledge, 2001.
Freyd, Jennifer J. *Betrayal Trauma: The Logic of Forgetting Childhood Abuse*. Cambridge: Harvard UP, 1996.
Fulford, K. W. M., and Mike Jackson. "Spiritual Experience and Psychopathology." *Philosophy, Psychiatry, & Psychology* 4.1 (1997): 41–65.
Fuller, Karla Rae. *Hollywood Goes Oriental—CaucAsian Performance in American Film*. Detroit: Wayne State U Press, 2010.
Fung, Richard. "Looking for My Penis: The Eroticized Asian in Gay Video Porn." *A Companion to Asian American Studies*. Ed. Kent A. Ono. Hoboken: Blackwell, 2004. 236–253.
Gaioni, Dominic T. "The Tingyans of Northern Philippines and Their Spirit World." *Anthropos* 80.4/6 (1985): 381–401.
Garber, Linda. *Identity Poetics: Race, Class, and the Lesbian-Feminist Roots of Queer Theory*. New York: Columbia UP, 2001.
Garces-Bacsal, Rhoda Myra, Ruanni Tupas, and Jesus Federico Hernandez. "A Filipino Grandmother Grimm: Subversion of Foreign Fairy Tales Through Indigenization and Cultural Appropriation in *Mga Kuwento ni Lola Basyang* (The Stories of Grandmother Basyang)." *Bookbird: A Journal of International Children's Literature* 54.1 (2016): 19–30.
García, Rocío. "Normative Ideals, 'Alternative' Realities: Perceptions of Interracial Dating Among Professional Latinas and Black Women." *Societies* 5 (2015): 807–830.
Gerstner, David A. *Queer Pollen: White Seduction, Black Male Homosexuality, and the Cinematic*. Champaign: U of Illinois P, 2011.
Gibson, Margaret F. "Adopting Difference: Thinking Through Adoption by Gay Men in Ontario, Canada." *Signs* 39.2 (2014): 407–432.

Gil, Avelina. "Mayyang and the Crab: A Cinderella Variant." *Philippine Quarterly of Culture and Society* 1.1 (1973): 26–32.

Giltner, Scott E. *Hunting and Fishing in the New South: Black Labor and White Leisure After the Civil War*. Baltimore: Johns Hopkins UP, 2008.

Girardot, N. J. *Myth and Meaning in Early Daoism: The Theme of Chaos (Hundun)*. St. Petersburg: Three Pines, 2009.

Giroux, Henry A. *Stealing Innocence: Corporate Culture's War on Children*. New York: St. Martin's, 2000.

Giwa, Sulaimon, and Cameron Greensmith. "Community of Toronto: Perceptions of Gay and Queer Social Service Providers of Color." *Journal of Homosexuality* 59 (2012): 149–185.

Go, Fe Susan. "Mothers, Maids and the Creatures of the Night: The Persistence of Philippine Folk Religion." *Philippine Quarterly of Culture and Society* 7.3 (1979): 186–203.

Godelier, Maurice. *The Metamorphoses of Kinship*. Trans. Nora Scott. New York: Verso, 2011.

Goellnicht, Donald. "A Long Labour: The Protracted Birth of Asian Canadian Literature." *Essays on Canadian Writing* 72 (Winter 2000): 209–247.

———. "Of Bones and Suicide: SKY Lee's *Disappearing Moon Cafe* and Fae Myenne Ng's *Bone*." *MFS Modern Fiction Studies* 46.2 (Summer 2000): 300–330.

Goh, Daniel P. S. "Capital and the Transfiguring Monumentality of Raffles Hotel." *Mobilities* 5.2 (2010): 177–195.

———. "Chinese Religion and the Challenge of Modernity in Malaysia and Singapore: Syncretism, Hybridisation and Transfiguration." *Asian Journal of Social Science* 37 (2009): 107–137.

———. "From Colonial Pluralism to Postcolonial Multiculturalism: Race, State Formation and the Question of Cultural Diversity in Malaysia and Singapore." *Sociology Compass* 2.1 (2008): 232–252.

———. "State and Social Christianity in Post-Colonial Singapore." *Sojourn: Journal of Social Issues in Southeast Asia* 25.1 (2010): 54–89.

———. "State Carnivals and the Subvention of Multiculturalism in Singapore." *British Journal of Sociology* 62.1 (2011): 111–133.

Goh, Robbie B. H. "Ideologies of 'Upgrading' in Singapore Public Housing: Post-Modern Style, Globalisation and Class Construction in the Built Environment." *Urban Studies* 38.9 (2001): 1589–1604.

Goldberg, Abbie E. *Gay Dads: Transitions to Adoptive Fatherhood*. New York: New York UP, 2012.

Goldberg, Christine. "The Construction of Folktales." *Journal of Folklore Research* 23.2/3 (1986): 163–176.

Goldberg, David Theo. *Are We All Postracial Yet?* Boston: Polity Press, 2015.

Goldstein, Richard. *The Attack Queers: Liberal Society and the Gay Right*. New York: Verso, 2002.

Gomes, Catherine. "Keeping Memories Alive: Maintaining Singaporean Nationalism Abroad." *Asia Journal of Global Studies* 3.1 (2009): 37–50.

Gomez, Jewelle. "A Cultural Legacy Denied and Discovered: Black Lesbians in Fiction by Women." *Home Girls: A Black Feminist Anthology.* Ed. Barbara Smith. New Brunswick: Rutgers UP, 2000. 110–123.
Gonzalez, Vernadette Vicuña. "Military Bases, 'Royalty Trips,' and Imperial Modernities: Gendered and Racialized Labor in the Postcolonial Philippines." *Frontiers: A Journal of Women Studies* 28.3 (2007): 28–59.
Gopinath, Gayatri. *Impossible Desires: Queer Diasporas and South Asian Public Cultures.* Durham: Duke UP, 2005.
Gordon, Avery F. *Ghostly Matters: Haunting and the Sociological Imagination.* Minneapolis: U of Minnesota P, 1997.
Gordon, Neta. "Charted Territory: Canadian Literature by Women, the Genealogical Plot, and SKY Lee's *Disappearing Moon Cafe*." *Narrative* 14.2 (May 2006) 163–179.
Gorham, Bradley W. "Considerations of Media Effects: The Social Psychology of Stereotypes: Implications for Media Audiences." *Beyond Blackface: Africana Images in US Media.* Ed. A. Houston. Dubuque: Kendall Hunt, 2010. 93–101.
Goto, Hiromi. *Chorus of Mushrooms.* Edmonton: NeWest Press, 1993.
———. *Darkest Light.* Toronto: Razorbill Canada, 2012.
———. *Half World.* New York: Viking Books for Young Readers, 2010.
———. *Hopeful Monsters: Stories.* Vancouver: Arsenal Pulp Press, 2004.
———. *The Kappa Child.* Markham: Red Deer Press, 2002.
———. *The Water of Possibility.* Regina: Coteau Books, 2001.
Gray, Mary L. *Out in the Country: Youth, Media, and Queer Visibility in Rural America.* New York: New York UP, 2009.
Green, Adam Isaiah, Jenna Valleriani, and Barry Adam. "Marital Monogamy as Ideal and Practice: The Detraditionalization Thesis in Contemporary Marriages." *Journal of Marriage and Family* 78 (April 2016): 416–430.
Green, Robert-Jay. "Gay and Lesbian Family Life: Risk, Resilience, and Rising Expectations." *The Psychology of Ethnic Groups in the United States.* Ed. Pamela Balls Organista, Gerardo Marin, and Kevin M. Chun. Thousand Oaks: Sage, 2009. 172–195.
Greenberg, Judith. "The Echo of Trauma and the Trauma of Echo." *American Imago* 55.3 (1998): 319–347.
Greenfield, Dorothy A., and Emre Seli. "Gay Men Choosing Parenthood Through Assisted Reproduction: Medical and Psychosocial Considerations." *Fertility and Sterility* 95.1 (2011): 225–229.
Guess, Carol. "Que(e)rying Lesbian Identity." *Journal of the Midwest Modern Language Association* 28.1 (1995): 19–37.
Haase, Donald. "Children, War, and the Imaginative Space of Fairy Tales." *Lion and the Unicorn* 24.3 (2000): 360–377.
Hagedorn, Jessica. "Asian Women in Film: No Joy, No Luck." *Ms.* (January/February 1994): 74–79.
Hager, Kelly. *Dickens and the Rise of Divorce: The Failed-Marriage Plot and the Novel Tradition.* Farnham: Ashgate, 2010.

Hahm, Hyeouk Chris, and Chris Adkins. "A Model of Asian and Pacific Islander Sexual Minority Acculturation." *Journal of LGBT Youth* 6.2–3 (2009): 155–173.

Halberstam, Judith. *In a Queer Time and Place*. New York: New York UP, 2005.

———. *The Queer Art of Failure*. Durham: Duke UP, 2011.

Hall, Edith. "Subjects, Selves, and Survivors." *Helios* 34.2 (2007): 125–159.

Hallas, Roger. *Reframing Bodies: AIDS, Bearing Witness, and the Queer Moving Image*. Durham: Duke UP, 2009.

Hamamoto, Darrell Y. *Monitored Peril: Asian Americans and the Politics of TV Representation*. Minneapolis: U of Minnesota P, 1994.

Hamer, Diane. "Significant Others: Lesbianism and Psychoanalytic Theory." *Feminist Review* 34 (Spring 1990): 134–151.

Hammers, Corie J. "Corporeality, Sadomasochism and Sexual Trauma." *Body & Society* (March 2013): 1–23.

———. "Making Space for an Agentic Sexuality? The Examination of a Lesbian/Queer Bathhouse." *Sexualities* 11.5 (2008): 547–572.

Han, C. Winter. *Geisha of a Different Kind: Race and Sexuality in Gaysian America*. New York: New York UP, 2015.

Han, Chong-suk. "Geisha of a Different Kind: Gay Asian Men and the Gendering of Sexual Identity." *Sexuality & Culture* 10.3 (2006): 3–28.

Han, Chong-suk, Kristopher Proctor, and Kyung-Hee Choi. "I Know a Lot of Gay Asian Men Who Are Actually Tops: Managing and Negotiating Gay Racial Stigma." *Sexuality & Culture* 18.2 (2014): 219–234.

Hansen, Karen V. *Not-So-Nuclear Families: Class, Gender, and Networks of Care*. New Brunswick: Rutgers UP, 2005.

Hao, Wan Meng. *Heritage Places of Singapore*. Singapore: Marshall Cavendish, 2011.

Haraway, Donna. *When Species Meet*. Minneapolis: U of Minnesota P, 2007.

Harder, Lois, and Michelle Thomarat. "Parentage Law in Canada: The Numbers Game of Standing and Status." *International Journal of Law, Policy and the Family* 26.1 (2012): 62–87.

Hargreaves, Katrina. "Constructing Families and Kinship Through Donor Insemination." *Sociology of Health & Illness* 28.3 (2006): 261–283.

Harkins, Gillian. *Everybody's Family Romance: Reading Incest in Neoliberal America*. Minneapolis: U of Minnesota P, 2009.

Harrington, Lee "Bridgett." *Shibari You Can Use: Japanese Rope Bondage and Erotic Macramé*. Anchorage: Mystic Productions Press, 2006–2007.

Hart, Donn V., and Harriett C. Hart. "Cinderella in the Eastern Bisayas: With a Summary of the Philippine Folktale." *Journal of American Folklore* 79.312 (1966): 307–337.

Hart, Lynda. *Fatal Women: Lesbian Sexuality and the Mark of Regression*. Princeton: Princeton UP, 1994.

Hassan, Muhammad Haniff Bin, and Kenneth George Pereire. "An Ideological Response to Combating Terrorism—The Singapore Perspective." *Small Wars and Insurgencies* 17.4 (2006): 458–477.

Haubrich, Dennis J., et al. "Gay and Bisexual Men's Experiences of Bathhouse Culture and Sex: Looking for Love in All the Wrong Places.'" *Culture, Health & Sexuality* 6.1 (2004): 19–29.

Heath, Stephen. "Notes on Suture." *Screen* 18.4 (Winter 1977): 48–76.

Hediger, Ryan. "Hunting, Fishing, and the Cramp of Ethics in Ernest Hemingway's *The Old Man and the Sea*, *Green Hills of Africa*, and *Under Kilimanjaro*." *Hemingway Review* 27.2 (2008): 35–59.

Heine, Steven. *Shifting Shape, Shaping Text: Philosophy and Folklore in the Fox Koan.* Honolulu: U of Hawai'i P, 1999.

Heller, Dana. *Family Plot: The De-Oedipalization of Popular Culture.* Philadelphia: U of Pennsylvania P, 1995.

Henderson, Jan-Andrew. *Edinburgh: City of the Dead.* Edinburgh: B&W, 2010.

Henderson, Joan C. "Conserving Colonial Heritage: Raffles Hotel in Singapore." *International Journal of Heritage Studies* 7.1 (2001): 7–24.

———. "Ethnic Heritage as a Tourist Attraction: The Peranakans of Singapore." *International Journal of Heritage Studies* 9.1 (2003): 27–44.

Heng, Geraldine, and Janadas Devan. "State Fatherhood: The Politics of Nationalism, Sexuality, and Race in Singapore." *Nationalisms and Sexualities.* Ed. Andrew Parker, Mary Russo, Doris Sommer, and Patricia Yaeger. New York: Routledge, 1992. 343–364.

Herlihy, David. *The Black Death and the Transformation of the West.* Cambridge: Harvard UP, 1997.

Herman, Daniel Justin. *Hunting and the American Imagination.* Washington: Smithsonian Institution Press, 2001.

Herman, Judith Lewis. *Father-Daughter Incest.* Cambridge: Harvard UP, 1981.

———. *Trauma and Recovery.* New York: Basic, 1997.

Herman, R. D. K. "Playing with Restraints: Space, Citizenship and BDSM." *Geographies of Sexualities: Theory Practices and Politics.* Ed. Kath Browne et al. Farnham: Ashgate, 2007. 89–100.

Hermes, Joke. "Sexuality in Lesbian Romance Fiction." *Feminist Review* 42 (Autumn 1992): 49–66.

Herrera, Brian Eugenio. *Latin Numbers: Playing Latino in Twentieth-Century U.S. Popular Performance.* Ann Arbor: U of Michigan P, 2015.

Herring, Scott. *Another Country: Queer Anti-Urbanism.* New York: New York UP, 2010.

Hertz, Rosanna. *Single by Chance, Mothers by Choice: How Women Are Choosing Parenthood Without Marriage and Creating the New American Family.* New York: Oxford UP, 2008.

Hertz, Rosanna, and Jane Mattes. "Donor-Shared Siblings or Genetic Strangers: New Families, Clans, and the Internet." *Journal of Family Issues* 32.9 (2011): 1129–1155.

Heuveline, Patrick, and Jeffrey M. Timberlake. "The Role of Cohabitation in Family Formation: The United States in Comparative Perspective." *Journal of Family and Marriage* 66.5 (December 2004): 1214–1230.

Hicks, George. *The Comfort Women: Japan's Brutal Regime of Enforced Prostitution in the Second World War.* New York: Norton, 1997.

Hilderbrand, Lucas. "'Luring Disco Dollies to a Life of Vice': Queer Pop Music's Moment." *Journal of Popular Music Studies* 25.4 (2013): 415–438.

Hill, Michael, and Kwen F. Lian. *The Politics of Nation Building and Politics in Singapore*. New York: Routledge, 1995.

Hirsch, Marianne. *The Mother/Daughter Plot: Narrative, Psychoanalysis, Feminism*. Bloomington: Indiana U Press, 1989.

Ho, Jennifer Ann. *Consumption and Identity in Asian American Coming-of-Age Novels*. New York: Routledge, 1995.

Hoang, Nguyen Tan. *A View from the Bottom: Asian American Masculinity and Sexual Representation*. Durham: Duke UP, 2014.

Hodges, Graham Russell Gao. *Anna May Wong: From Laundryman's Daughter to Hollywood Legend*. New York: Palgrave Macmillan, 2004.

Hogg, Peter W. "Canada: The Constitution and Same-Sex Marriage." *International Journal of Constitutional Law* 4.3 (2006): 712–721.

Hogg, R. S., et al. "Rates of New Infections in British Columbia Continue to Decline at a Faster Rate Than in Other Canadian Regions." *HIV Medicine* 14 (2013): 581–582.

Holden, Philip. "Reading Singapore Literature in English in an Historical Frame." *Race and Multiculturualism in Malaysia and Singapore*. Ed. Daniel P. S. Goh et al. New York: Routledge, 2009. 19–35.

Holland, Sharon Patricia. *Raising the Dead: Readings of Death and (Black) Subjectivity*. Durham: Duke UP, 2000.

Holmes, Sean P. "The Hollywood Star System and the Regulation of Actors' Labour, 1916–1934." *Film History* 12 (2000): 97–114.

Hom, Alice Y. "Stories from the Homefront: Perspectives of Asian American Parents with Lesbian Daughters and Gay Sons." *Asian American Sexualities: Dimensions of the Gay & Lesbian Experience*. Ed. Russell Leong. New York: Routledge, 1996. 37–50.

Hong, Grace Kyungwon, and Roderick A. Ferguson. "Introduction." *Strange Affinities: The Gender and Sexual Politics of Comparative Racialization*. Ed. Grace Kyungwon Hong and Roderick A. Ferguson. Durham: Duke UP, 2011. 1–22.

Hoogland, Renée C. "Hard to Swallow: Indigestible Narratives of Lesbian Sexuality." *Modern Fiction Studies* 41.3–4 (1995): 467–481.

———. *Lesbian Configurations*. New York: Columbia UP, 1997.

Hopkins, Jason J., Anna Sorensen, and Verta Taylor. "Same-Sex Couples, Families, and Marriage: Embracing and Resisting Heteronormativity." *Sociology Compass* 7.2 (2013): 97–110.

Hornsey, Richard. "After the Bathhouse; Or, In Praise of Awkwardness." *English Language Notes* 5.2 (Fall/Winter 2007): 49–62.

Horrox, Rosemary. *The Black Death*. Manchester: Manchester UP, 1994.

Horvitz, Deborah M. *Literary Trauma: Sadism, Memory, and Sexual Violence in American Women's Fiction*. Albany: State U of New York P, 2000.

Howard, John. *Men Like That: A Southern Queer History*. Chicago: U of Chicago P, 2001.

Hsu, Madeline. *The Good Immigrants: How the Yellow Peril Became the Model Minority*. Princeton: Princeton UP, 2015.

Huang, Philip. *A Pornography of Grief*. Hong Kong: Signal 8 Press, 2011.

Huang, Quanyu. *The Hybrid Tiger: Secrets of the Extraordinary Success of Asian-American Kids*. Amherst: Prometheus, 2014.

Huat, Chua Beng. "Multiculturalism in Singapore: An Instrument of Social Control." *Race & Class* 44.3 (2003): 58–77.

———. "Singapore as Model: Planning Innovations, Knowledge Experts." *Worlding Cities: Asian Experiments and the Art of Being Global*. Ed. Ananya Roy and Aihwa Ong. Malden: Blackwell, 2011. 29–54.

Hudson, Chris. "We Need 50,000 Babies a Year: Marriage and the Family in Singapore." *Education About Asia* 13.1 (2008): 21–24.

Inness, Sherrie A. *The Lesbian Menace: Ideology, Identity, and the Representation of Lesbian Life*. Amherst: U of Massachusetts P, 1997.

Ishii-Kuntz, Masako. "Asian North American Families: Diverse History, Contemporary Trends and the Future." *Handbook of Contemporary Families: Considering the Past, Contemplating the Future*. Ed. Marilyn Coleman and Lawrence H. Ganong. Thousand Oaks: Sage, 2004. 369–384.

Ismail, Rahil, and Brian J. Shaw. "Singapore's Malay-Muslim Minority: Social Identification in a Post-'9/11' World." *Asian Ethnicity* 7.1 (2006): 37–51.

Jackson, Lawrence M. "The Black Male Dancer Physique: An Object of White Desirability." *Journal of Pan African Studies* 4.6 (2011): 75–81.

Jackson, Ronald L., II. *Scripting the Black Masculine Body: Identity, Discourse, and Racial Politics in Popular Media*. Albany: State U of New York P, 2006.

Jagose, Annamarie. *Inconsequence: Lesbian Representation and the Logic of Sexual Sequence*. Ithaca: Cornell UP, 2002.

JanMohamed, Abdul. *The Death-Bound-Subject: Richard Wright's Archaeology of Death*. Durham: Duke UP, 2005.

Jeon, Joseph Jonghyun. *Racial Things, Racial Forms: Objecthood in Avant-Garde Asian North American Poetry*. Iowa City: U of Iowa P, 2012.

Johnson, T. W. "Far Eastern Fox Lore." *Asian Folklore Studies* 33.1 (1974): 35–68.

Jones, Gavin. "Late Marriage and Low Fertility in Singapore: The Limits of Policy." *The Japanese Journal of Population* 10.1 (2012): 89–101.

———. "Population Policy in a Prosperous City-State: Dilemmas for Singapore." *Population and Development Review* 38.2 (2012): 311–336.

Jones, James W. "The Plague and Its Texts: AIDS and Recent American Fiction." *Journal of American Culture* 16.1 (1993): 73–80.

Jones, Patrick D. *The Selma of the North: Civil Rights Insurgency in Milwaukee*. Reprint. Cambridge: Harvard UP, 2010.

Jones, Roy, and Brian J. Shaw. "Palimpsests of Progress: Erasing the Past and Rewriting the Future in Developing Societies—Case Studies of Singapore and Jakarta." *International Journal of Heritage Studies* 12.2 (2006): 122–138.

Joshi, Paramjit T., and Kenneth E. Towbin. "Psychosis in Childhood and Its Management." *Neuropsychopharmacology: The Fifth Generation of Progress*. Ed. Kenneth L. Davis et al. Philadelphia: Lippincott Williams & Wilkins, 2002. 613–624.

Juhasz, Suzanne. "Lesbian Romance Fiction and the Plotting of Desire: Narrative Theory, Lesbian Identity, and Reading Practice." *Tulsa Studies in Women's Literature* 17.1 (1998): 65–82.

Kane, Connie M. "Differences in Family of Origin Perceptions Among African American, Asian North American, and Hispanic American College Students." *Journal of Black Studies* 29.1 (1998): 93–105.

Kang, Laura Hyun Yi. "Conjuring 'Comfort Women': Mediated Affiliations and Disciplined Subjects in Korean/American Transnationality." *Journal of Asian American Studies* 6.1 (2003): 25–55.

Keeling, Kara. "'Ghetto Heaven': *Set It Off* and the Valorization of Black Lesbian Butch-Femme Sociality." *Black Scholar* 33.1 (2003): 33–46.

Keller, Nora Okja. *Comfort Woman*. New York: Penguin, 1998.

Keller, Yvonne. "'Was It Right to Love Her Brother's Wife So Passionately?' Lesbian Pulp Novels and U.S. Lesbian Identity, 1950–1965." *American Quarterly* 57.2 (2005): 385–410.

Kelly, Fiona. "Producing Paternity: The Role of Legal Fatherhood in Maintaining the Traditional Family." *Canadian Journal of Women and the Law* 21.2 (2009): 315–351.

Kelsey, Katherine, et al. "Assessment of Therapists' Attitudes Towards BDSM." *Psychology & Sexuality* 4.3 (2013): 255–267.

Kennard, Jean E. "Ourself Behind Ourself: A Theory for Lesbian Readers." *Signs* 9.4 (1984): 647–662.

Kent, Douglas. *Douglas Kent's Complete Shibari*. Vol. 1. *Land*, Ottawa: Mental Gears, 2010.

———. *Douglas Kent's Complete Shibari*. Vol. 2. *Sky*, Ottawa: Mental Gears, 2010.

Kent, Kathryn R. *Making Girls into Women: American Women's Writing and the Rise of Lesbian Identity*. Durham: Duke UP, 2003.

Kerr, Don, Melissa Moyser, and Roderic Beaujot. "Marriage and Cohabitation: Demographic and Socioeconomic Differences in Quebec and Canada." *Canadian Studies in Population* 33.1 (2006): 83–117.

Kershaw, Roger. "Toward a Theory of Peranakan Chinese Identity in an Outpost of Thai Buddhism." *Journal of the Siam Society* 69 (1981): 74–106.

Khayatt, Didi. "Toward a Queer Identity." *Sexualities* 5.4 (2002): 487–501.

Khuu, Neo. "*Obergefell v. Hodges*: Kinship Formation, Interest Convergence, and the Future of LGBTQ Rights." *UCLA Law Review* 64 (2017): 184–229.

Kilby, Jane. "Judith Butler, Incest, and the Question of the Child's Love." *Feminist Theory* 11.3 (2010): 255–265.

Kim, Eleana. *Adopted Territory: Transnational Korean Adoptees and the Politics of Belonging*. Durham: Duke UP, 2010.

———. "Our Adoptee, Our Alien: Transnational Adoptees as Specters of Foreignness and Family in South Korea." *Anthropological Quarterly* 80.2 (2007): 497–531.

Kim, Lee Su. "The Peranakan Baba Nyonya Culture: Resurgence or Disappearance?" *Sari* 26 (2008): 161–170.

Kim, Willyce. *Curtains of Light*. Self-published, 1971.
———. *Dancer Dawkins and the California Kid*. Boston: Alyson, 1985.
———. *Dead Heat*. New York: Alyson, 1988.
———. *Eating Artichokes*. Oakland: Women's Press Collective, 1972.
———. *Under the Rolling Sky*. N.P.: Maud Gonne Press, 1976.
Kim, Younghan. "Representation of People of Asian Descent in Mainstream Mass Media Within the United States." *Multicultural Education Review* 5.2 (2013): 20–48.
Kimmel, Douglas C., and Huso Yi. "Characteristics of Gay, Lesbian, and Bisexual Asians, Asian Americans, and Immigrants from Asia to the USA." *Journal of Homosexuality* 47.2 (2004): 143–172.
Kinney, Katherine. *Friendly Fire: American Images of the Vietnam War*. Oxford: Oxford UP, 2000.
Kobayashi, Tamai. *Prairie Ostrich*. New Brunswick: Goose Lane, 2013.
Koh, Aaron. "Global Flows of Foreign Talent: Identity Anxieties in Singapore's Ethnoscape." *Sojourn: Journal of Social Issues in Southeast Asia* 18.2 (2003): 230–256.
Koh, Ernest. "The Chinese of Singapore and Their Imperial Second World War 1939–1945." *Chinese Southern Diaspora Studies* 5 (2012): 57–78.
Kolmes, Keely, et al. "Investigating Bias in Psychotherapy with BDSM Clients." *Journal of Homosexuality* 50.2/3 (2006): 301–324.
Koshy, Susan. "Neoliberal Family Matters." *American Literary History* 25.2 (2013): 344–380.
Kraemer, Christine Hoff. "Gender and Sexuality in Contemporary Paganism." *Religion Compass* 6/8 (2012): 390–401.
Krieger, Herbert W. "Races and Peoples in the Philippines." *Far Eastern Quarterly* 4.2 (1945): 94–101.
Kumar, Mala. *The Paths of Marriage*. Fairfield: Bedazzled Ink, 2014.
Kumashiro, Kevin. "Supplementing Normalcy and Otherness: Queer Asian American Men Reflect on Stereotypes, Identity, and Oppression." *Qualitative Studies in Education* 12.5 (1999): 491–508.
Kuo, Lenore. *Prostitution Policy: Revolutionizing Practice Through a Gendered Perspective*. New York: New York UP, 2002.
Kurahashi, Yuko. *Asian American Culture on Stage: The History of the East West Players*. New York: Garland, 1999.
Kuzniar, Alice A. *Melancholia's Dog: Reflections on Our Animal Kinship*. Chicago: U of Chicago P, 2006.
Kwa, Lydia. *Pulse*. Key Porter, 2010.
———. *This Place Called Absence*. New York: Kensington, 2002.
Kwang, Tan Yap. *Examinations in Singapore: Change and Continuity (1891–2007)*. Singapore: World Scientific, 2008.
LaCapra, Dominick. "Trauma, Absence, Loss." *Critical Inquiry* 25.4 (1999): 696–727.
———. *Writing History, Writing Trauma*. Baltimore: Johns Hopkins UP, 2001.
LaGuardia, Robert. *Monty: A Biography of Montgomery Clift*. New York: D.I. Fine, 1988.

Lahr-Vivaz, Elena. "Passing for Solitude: Incest and Ideology in the *Lone Star* State." *Journal of American Studies* 46.1 (2012): 203–217.
Lai, Larissa. *Salt Fish Girl*. 2nd ed. Toronto: Thomas Allen, 2012.
Lau, Estelle T. *Paper Families: Identity, Immigration Administration, and Chinese Exclusion*. Durham: Duke UP, 2006.
Lau, Evelyn. *Runaway: Diary of a Street Kid*. Toronto: Coach House, 1995.
Laurie, Clayton D. "Civil Disorder and the Military in Rock Springs, Wyoming: The Army's Role in the 1885 Chinese Massacre." *Montana: The Magazine of Western History* 40.3 (1990): 44–59.
Law, Kam-Yee. "The Myth of Multiracialism in Post-9/11 Singapore: The *Tudung* Incident." *New Zealand Journal of Asian Studies* 5.1 (2003): 51–71.
Lawrence, Amy. *The Passion of Montgomery Clift*. Berkeley: U of California P, 2010.
Lawrence, Anne E., and Jennifer Love-Crowell. "Psychotherapists' Experience with Clients Who Engage in Consensual Sadomasochism: A Qualitative Study." *Journal of Sex & Marital Therapy* 34 (2008): 67–85.
Lawrence, Tim. "Disco and the Queering of the Dance Floor." *Cultural Studies* 25.2 (2011): 230–243.
Leavitt, Gregory C. "Disappearance of the Incest Taboo: A Cross-Cultural Test of General Evolutionary Hypotheses." *American Anthropologist* 91.1 (1989): 116–131.
Lee, Chang-rae. *A Gesture Life*. New York: Riverhead, 2000.
Lee, Christopher. "The Lateness of Asian Canadian Studies." *Amerasia Journal* 33.2 (2007): 1–17.
———. *The Semblance of Identity: Aesthetic Mediation in Asian American Literature*. Stanford: Stanford UP, 2012.
Lee, Esther Kim. *A History of Asian American Theatre*. New York: Cambridge UP, 2006.
Lee, Jack Tsen-Ta. "The Limits of Liberty: The Crime of Male Same-Sex Conduct and the Rights to Life and Personal Liberty in Singapore." *Hong Kong Law Journal* 46.1 (2016): 49–70.
Lee, JeeYeun. "Why Suzie Wong Is Not a Lesbian." *A Lesbian, Gay, Bisexual & Transgender Anthology*. Ed. Brett Beemyn and Mickey Eliason. New York: New York UP, 1996. 115–132.
Lee, Joann. "Asian American Actors in Film, Television and Theater: An Ethnographic Case Study." *Race, Gender & Class* 8.4 (2001): 176–184.
Lee, Josephine. *The Japan of Pure Invention: Gilbert and Sullivan's The Mikado*. Minneapolis: U of Minnesota P, 2010.
———. *Performing Asian America: Race and Ethnicity on the Contemporary Stage*. Philadelphia: Temple UP, 1997.
Lee, Robert G. *Orientals: Asian Americans in Popular Culture*. Philadelphia: Temple UP, 1999.
Lee, Sharon M., Gabriel Alvarez, and J. John Palen. "Fertility Decline and Pronatalist Policy in Singapore." *International Family Planning Perspectives* 17.2 (1991): 65–73.
Lee, SKY. *Disappearing Moon Cafe*. Vancouver: Douglas & McIntyre, 1990.

Lee, Vasoo J. "Singapore: Social Development, Housing and the Central Provident Fund." *International Journal of Social Welfare* 10 (2001): 276–283.
Leibfried, Philip, and Chei Mi Lane. *Anna May Wong: A Complete Guide to Her Film, Stage, Radio, and Television Work.* Jefferson: McFarland, 2004.
Lendrum, Rob. "The Super Black Macho, One Baaad Mutha: Black Superhero Masculinity in 1970s Mainstream Comic Books." *Extrapolation* 46.3 (2005): 360–372.
Lenon, Suzanne. "What's So Civil About Marriage? The Racial Pedagogy of Same-Sex Marriage in Canada." *darkmatter* 3 (2008): 26–36.
Leong, Karen J. *The China Mystique: Pearl S. Buck, Anna May Wong, Mayling Soong, and the Transformation of American Orientalism.* Berkeley: U of California P, 2005.
Leong, Russell. *Asian American Sexualities: Dimensions of the Gay and Lesbian Experience.* New York: Routledge, 1995.
———. *Phoenix Eyes & Other Stories.* Seattle: U of Washington P, 2000.
Leow, Joanne. "The Future of Nostalgia: Reclaiming Memory in Tan Pin Pin's *Invisible City* and Alfian Sa'at's *A History of Amnesia*." *Journal of Commonwealth Literature* 45 (2010): 115–130.
Leung, Brian. *Take Me Home.* New York: Harper, 2010.
———. *World Famous Love Acts.* Louisville: Sarabande, 2004.
Lévi-Strauss, Claude. *The Elementary Structures of Kinship.* Boston: Beacon, 1971.
Levine, Judith. *Harmful to Minors: The Perils of Protecting Children from Sex.* Minneapolis: U of Minneapolis P, 2002.
Levine, Nancy E. "Alternative Kinship, Marriage, and Reproduction." *Annual Review of Anthropology* 37 (2008): 375–389.
Lewin, Ellen. *Gay Fatherhood: Narratives of Family and Citizenship in America.* Chicago: U of Chicago P, 2009.
———. *Lesbian Mothers: Accounts of Gender in American Culture.* Ithaca: Cornell UP, 1993.
Leys, Ruth. "Traumatic Cures: Shell Shock, Janet, and the Question of Memory." *Critical Inquiry* 20.4 (1994): 623–662.
Li, Lusha, and Myron Orleans. "Coming Out Discourses of Asian American Lesbians." *Sexuality and Culture* 5.2 (2001): 57–79.
Lieban, Richard Warren. *Cebuano Sorcery: A Study of Malign Magic in the Philippines.* Berkeley: U of California P, 1967.
Lim, Alywn. "The Culture of Technology of Singapore." *Asian Journal of Social Science* 30.2 (2002): 271–286.
Lim, Bliss Cua. "Queer Aswang Transmedia: Folklore as Camp." *Kritika Kultura* 24 (2015): 178–225.
Lim, Eng-Beng. *Brown Boys and Rice Queens: Spellbinding Performance in the Asias.* New York: New York UP, 2013.
Lim, Imogene L. "Pacific Entry, Pacific Century: Chinatowns and Chinese Canadian History." *Re/collecting Early Asian America: Essays in Cultural History.* Ed. Josephine Lee, Imogene L. Lim, and Yuko Matsukawa. Philadelphia: Temple UP, 2002. 15–30.

Lindemann, Danielle. "BDSM as Therapy." *Sexualities* 14.2 (2011): 151–172.
Ling, Jinqi. *Narrating Nationalisms: Ideology and Form in Asian American Literature.* Oxford: Oxford UP, 1998.
Linmark, R. Zamora. *Leche.* Minneapolis: Coffee House Press, 2011.
———. *Rolling the R's.* Los Angeles: Kaya, 1995.
Liow, Eugene Dili. "The Neoliberal-Developmental State: Singapore as Case Study." *Critical Sociology* 38.2 (2011): 241–264.
Littlefield, Jon. "Men on the Hunt: Ecofeminist Insights into Masculinity." *Marketing Theory* 10.1 (2010): 97–117.
Liu, Cynthia W. "When Dragon Ladies Die, Do They Come Back as Butterflies? Re-Imagining Anna May Wong." *Countervisions.* Ed. Darrell Hamamoto and Sandra Liu. Philadelphia: Temple UP, 2000. 23–39.
Liu, James H., et al. "Social Representations of History in Malaysia and Singapore: On the Relationships Between National and Ethnic Identity." *Asian Journal of Social Psychology* 5 (2002): 3–20.
Lo, Malinda. *Ash.* New York: Little, Brown, 2009.
———. *Huntress.* New York: Little, Brown, 2011.
Lo, Marie. "Passing Recognition: *Obasan* and the Borders of Asian American and Canadian Literary Criticism." *Comparative American Studies: An International Journal* 5.3 (2007): 307–332.
Locke, Brian. *Racial Stigma on the Hollywood Screen from World War II to the Present: The Orientalist Buddy Film.* New York: Palgrave Macmillan, 2009.
Loo, Tina. "Of Moose and Men: Hunting for Masculinities in British Columbia, 1880–1939." *The Western Historical Quarterly* 32.3 (Autumn 2001): 296–319.
Lopez, Lori Kido. "Fan Activists and the Politics of Race in *The Last Airbender*." *International Journal of Cultural Studies* 15.5 (2012): 431–445.
Lopez, Mellie Leandicho. *A Handbook of Philippine Folklore.* Quezon City: U of the Philippines P, 2006.
Lorde, Audre. *Sister Outsider: Essays and Speeches.* Berkeley: Crossing, 1984.
Love, Heather. *Feeling Backward: Loss and the Politics of Queer History.* Cambridge: Harvard UP, 2007.
Lowe, Lisa. *Immigrant Acts: On Asian American Cultural Politics.* Durham: Duke UP, 1996.
Lu, Lynn. "Critical Visions: The Representation and Resistance of Asian Women." *Dragon Ladies: Asian American Feminists Breathe Fire.* Ed. Sonia Shah. Brooklyn: South End, 1999. 17–28.
Luke, Brian. "Violent Love: Hunting, Heterosexuality, and the Erotics of Men's Predation." *Feminist Studies* 24.3 (Autumn 1998): 627–655.
Macintosh, Heather, Elke D. Reissing, and Heather Andruff. "Same-Sex Marriage in Canada: The Impact of Legal Marriage on the First Cohort of Gay and Lesbian Canadians to Wed." *Canadian Journal of Human Sexuality* 19.3 (2010): 79–90.
Madale, Abdullah T. *The Maranaws, Dwellers of the Lake.* Manila: Rex Book Store, 1997.
Magee, William H. "Instrument of Growth: The Courtship and Marriage Plot in Jane Austen's Novels." *Journal of Narrative Technique* 17.2 (1987): 198–208.

Mallon, Gerald P. *Gay Men Choosing Parenthood*. New York: Columbia UP, 2004.
Mamo, Laura. *Queering Reproduction: Achieving Pregnancy in the Age of Technoscience*. Durham: Duke UP, 2007.
Manalansan, Martin. *Global Divas: Filipino Gay Men in the Diaspora*. Durham: Duke UP, 2003.
Marchetti, Gina. *Romance and the "Yellow Peril": Race, Sex, and Discursive Strategies in Hollywood Fiction*. Berkeley: U of California P, 1994.
Marcus, Sharon. *Between Women: Friendship, Desire, and Marriage in Victorian England*. Princeton: Princeton UP, 2007.
Markens, Susan. *Surrogate Motherhood and the Politics of Representation*. Berkeley: U of California P, 2007.
Marks, Stuart A. *Southern Hunting in Black and White: Nature, History, and Ritual in a Carolina Community*. Princeton: Princeton UP, 1991.
Marranci, Gabriele. "Defensive or Offensive Dining? Halal Dining Practices Among Malay Muslim Singaporeans and Their Effects on Integration." *Australian Journal of Anthropology* 23 (2012): 84–100.
Martin, Daniel. "Ghostly Foundations: Multicultural Space and Vancouver's Chinatown in SKY Lee's *Disappearing Moon Cafe*." *Studies in Canadian Literature/Etudes en Littérature Canadienne* 29.1 (2004): 85–105.
Martindale, Kathleen. *Un/Popular Culture: Lesbian Writing After the Sex Wars*. Albany: State U of New York P, 1997.
Martinez, Ernesto Javier. *On Making Sense: Queer Race Narratives of Intelligibility*. Stanford: Stanford UP, 2013.
Marzanski, Marek, and Mark Bratton. "Psychopathological Symptoms and Religious Experience: A Critique of Jackson and Fulford." *Philosophy, Psychiatry, & Psychology* 9.4 (2002): 359–371.
Master "K." *The Beauty of Kinbaku: Or Everything You Ever Wanted to Know About Japanese Erotic Bondage When You Suddenly Realized You Didn't Speak Japanese*. New York: King Cat Ink, 2008.
Mattingly, Cheryl. *Healing Dramas and Clinical Plots: The Narrative Structure of Experience*. New York: Cambridge UP, 1998.
Matz, Jessie. "*Maurice* in Time." *Style* 34.2 (2000): 188–211.
Mauzy, Diane K., and R. S. Milne. *Singapore Politics Under the People's Action Party*. New York: Routledge 2002.
McAndrew, John P. *People of Power: A Philippine Worldview of Spirit Encounters*. Quezon City: Ateneo de Manila UP, 2001.
McGee, Adam M. "Haitian Vodou and Voodoo: Imagined Religion and Popular Culture." *Studies in Religion* 41.2 (2012): 231–256.
McGhee, Michael. "Mysticism and Psychosis: Descriptions and Distinctions." *Philosophy, Psychiatry, & Psychology* 9.4 (2002): 343–347.
McIlwain, Charlton D. "Race, Pigskin, and Politics: A Semiotic Analysis of Racial Images in Political Advertising." *Semiotica* 167 (2007): 169–191.
McKenzie, Callum. "The British Big-Game Hunting Tradition, Masculinity and Frater-

nalism with Particular Reference to 'The Shikar Club.'" *The Sports Historian* 20.1 (May 2000): 70–96.

McNairn, Jeffrey L. "Meaning and Markets: Hunting, Economic Development and British Imperialism in Maritime Travel Narratives to 1870." *Acadiensis* 34.2 (Spring 2005): 3–25.

Meeker, Martin. "A Queer and Contested Medium: The Emergence of Representational Politics in the 'Golden Age' of Lesbian Paperbacks, 1955–1963." *Journal of Women's History* 17.1 (Spring 2005): 165–188.

Mehta, Rahul. *No Other World*. New York: Harper, 2017.

———. *Quarantine*. New York: Harper Perennial, 2011.

Meñez, Herminia Q. "Encounters with Spirits: Mythology and the *Ingkanto* Syndrome in the Philippines." *Western Folklore* 37.4 (October 1978): 249–265.

———. "The Performance of Folk Narrative in Filipino Communities in California." *Western Folklore* 36.1 (1977): 57–69.

Mercado, Leonardo N. "Soul and Spirit in Filipino Thought." *Philippine Studies* 39 (1991): 287–302.

Metzger, Sean. "Ice Queens, Rice Queens, and Intercultural Investments in Zhang Yimou's *Turandot*." *Asian Theatre Journal* 20.2 (2003): 209–217.

Mezey, Nancy J. *New Choices, New Families: How Lesbians Decide About Motherhood*. Baltimore: Johns Hopkins UP, 2008.

Midori. *The Seductive Art of Japanese Bondage*. Emeryville: Greenery Press, 2001.

Miller, D. A. *Jane Austen, or The Secret of Style*. Princeton: Princeton UP, 2003.

Mimura, Glen M. *The Ghostlife of Third Cinema: Asian American Film and Video*. Minneapolis: U of Minnesota P, 2009.

Minahal, Maiana. *Legend Sondayo*. Berkeley: Civil Defense Poetry, 2009.

Miyao, Daisuke. *Sessue Hayakawa: Silent Cinema and Transnational Stardom*. Durham: Duke UP, 2007.

Moeller, Hans-Georg. *Daoism Explained: From the Dream of the Butterfly to the Fishnet Allegory*. Chicago: Open Court, 2004.

Mojares, Resil B. "Where Is the Center? Ideology Formation and the Constitution of a Rural Cebuano Community: 1582–1988." *Philippine Quarterly of Culture and Society* 28.1 (2000): 1–78.

Mok, Teresa. "Getting the Message: Media Images and Stereotypes and Their Effect on Asian Americans." *Cultural Diversity and Mental Health* 4.3 (1998): 185–202.

Moon, Krystyn R. *Yellowface: Creating the Chinese in American Popular Music and Performance, 1850s–1920s*. New Brunswick: Rutgers UP, 2004.

Moore, Mignon. *Invisible Families: Gay Identities, Relationships, and Motherhood Among Black Women*. Berkeley: U of California P, 2011.

Moorthy, Ravichandran. "The Evolution of the *Chitty* Community of Melaka." *Jebat* 36 (2009): 1–15.

Mootoo, Shani. *Cereus Blooms at Night*. New York: Grove, 1998.

———. *He Drowns She in the Sea*. New York: Grove, 2005.

———. *Moving Forward Sideways Like A Crab*. Toronto: Doubleday Canada, 2014.

———. *Out on Main Street: & Other Stories*. Vancouver: Raincoast, 2002.

———. *Valmiki's Daughter*. Toronto: House of Anansi, 2008.
Moraga, Cherríe, and Gloria Anzaldúa, eds. *This Bridge Called My Back: Writings by Radical Women of Color*. 2nd ed. New York: Kitchen Table: Women of Color P, 1983.
Moy, James S. *Marginal Sights: Staging the Chinese in America*. Iowa City: U of Iowa, 1993.
Mukherjee, Pablo. "Nimrods: Hunting, Authority, Identity." *Modern Language Review* 100.4 (2005): 923–939.
Mulé, Nick J. (2010) "Same-Sex Marriage and Canadian Relationship Recognition—One Step Forward, Two Steps Back: A Critical Liberationist Perspective." *Journal of Gay & Lesbian Social Services* 22.1–2 (2010): 74–90.
Muñoz, José Esteban. *Cruising Utopia: The Then and There of Queer Futurity*. New York: New York UP, 2009.
Murakawa, Nawashi. Foreword. *Kinbaku: The Art of Rope Bondage*. Ed. Philip Blakely. Cambridge: Kahboom Media, 2013. iii–viii.
Murphy, Timothy F. *Ethics in an Epidemic: AIDS, Morality, and Culture*. Berkeley: U of California P, 1994.
Mutalib, Hussin. "The Singapore Minority Dilemma." *Asian Survey*, 51.6 (2011): 1156–1171.
Muzaini, Hamzah, and Brenda S. A. Yeoh. "War Landscapes as 'Battlefields' of Collective Memories: Reading the *Reflections at Bukit Chandu*, Singapore." *Cultural Geographies* 12 (2005): 345–365.
Naca, Kristin. *Bird Eating Bird*. New York: Harper Perennial, 2009.
Nadal, Kevin L. "Sexual Orientation Identity Development and Mental Health Experiences of Gay and Bisexual Asian American Men: Implications for Culturally Competent Counseling." *Culturally Responsive Counseling with Asian American Men*. Ed. William Ming Liu, Derek Kenji Iwamoto, and Mark H. Chae. New York: Routledge, 2010. 213–234.
Napier, Susan J. "Panic Sites: The Japanese Imagination of Disaster from Godzilla to Akira." *Journal of Japanese Studies* 19.2 (1993) 327–351.
Narui, Mitsu. "Understanding Asian/American Gay, Lesbian, and Bisexual Experiences from a Poststructural Perspective." *Journal of Homosexuality* 58.9 (2011): 1211–1234.
Nealon, Christopher S. "Invert-History: The Ambivalence of Lesbian Pulp Fiction." *New Literary History* 31.4 (2000): 745–764.
Nelson, Emmanuel S. "AIDS and the American Novel." *Journal of American Culture* 13.1 (Spring 1990): 47–53.
Newmahr, Staci. *Playing on the Edge: Sadomasochism, Risk, and Intimacy*. Bloomington: Indiana UP, 2011.
Ng, Eve. "A 'Post-Gay' Era? Media Gaystreaming, Homonormativity, and the Politics of LGBT Integration." *Communication, Culture & Critique* 6 (2013): 258–283.
Ng, Mark Tristan. "Searching for Home: Voices of Gay Asian North American Youth in West Hollywood." *Asian American Youth: Culture, Identity, Citizenship*. Ed. Jennifer Lee and Min Zhou. New York: Routledge, 2004. 269–284.
Nguyen, Viet Thanh. "Speak of the Dead: Speak of Viet Nam: The Ethics and Aesthetics of Minority Discourse." *CR: The New Centennial Review* 6.2 (2006): 7–37.

Ninh, erin Khuê. *Ingratitude: The Debt-Bound Daughter in Asian American Literature.* New York: New York UP, 2011.
Niu, Greta Ai-Yu. "Wives, Widows, and Workers: Corazon Aquino, Imelda Marcos, and the Filipina 'Other.'" *NWSA Journal* 11.2 (1999): 88–102.
Noda, Barbara. *Strawberries.* Berkeley: Shameless Hussy, 1979.
Nubla, Gladys. "The Politics of Relation: Creole Languages in *Dogeaters* and *Rolling the R's*." *MELUS: The Journal of the Society for the Study of the Multi-Ethnic Literature of the United States* 29.1 (2004): 199–218.
Obendorf, Simon. "A Few Respectable Steps Behind the World? Gay and Lesbian Rights in Contemporary Singapore." *Human Rights, Sexual Orientation and Gender Identity in the Commonwealth: Struggles for Decriminalisation and Change.* Ed. Corinne Lennox and Matthew Waites. London: Institute of Commonwealth Studies, 2013. 231–259.
Ohi, Kevin. *Henry James and the Queerness of Style.* Minneapolis: U of Minnesota P, 2011.
Ohnishi, Hifumi, Farah A. Ibrahim, and Jennifer L. Grzegorek. "Intersections of Identities." *Journal of LGBT Issues in Counseling* 1.3 (2006): 77–94.
Okada, Jun. "'Noble and Uplifting and Boring as Hell': Asian American Film and Video, 1971–1982." *Cinema Journal* 49.1 (2009): 20–40.
Okazaki, Sumie. "Influences of Culture on Asian Americans' Sexuality." *Journal of Sex Research* 39.1 (2002): 34–41.
Olds, Kris, and Henry Wai-Chung Yeung. "Pathways to Global City Formation: A View from the Developmental City-State of Singapore." *Review of International Political Economy* 11.3 (2004): 489–521.
Olofson, Harold. "St. Vincent and the Thunder-God: Narratives of Play and Apocalypse in Relation to a Central Visayan Island Fiesta." *Philippine Quarterly of Culture and Society* 30.1/2 (2002): 172–229.
Ong, Aihwa. "Boundary Crossings: Neoliberalism as a Mobile Technology." *Transactions of the Institute of British Geographers* 32 (2007): 3–8.
Ong, Han. *The Disinherited.* New York: Farrar, Straus and Giroux, 2004.
———. *Fixer Chao.* New York: Picador, 2002.
Opler, Morris E., and Robert Seido Hashima. "The Rice Goddess and the Fox in Japanese Religion and Folk Practice." *American Anthropologist* 48.1 (1946): 43–53.
Ordover, Nancy. *American Eugenics: Race, Queer Anatomy, and the Science of Nationalism.* Minneapolis: U of Minneapolis P, 2003.
Ortmann, Stephan. "Singapore: The Politics of Inventing National Identity." *Journal of Current Southeast Asian Affairs* 28.4 (2009): 23–46.
Oswin, Natalie. "The Modern Model Family at Home in Singapore: A Queer Geography." *Transactions of the Institute of British Geographers* 35 (2010): 256–268.
Otano, Alicia. *Speaking the Past: Child Perspective in the Asian North American Bildungsroman.* Hamburg: Lit Verlag, 2004.
Oudart, Jean-Pierre. "Cinema and Suture." *Screen* 18.4 (Winter 1977): 35–47.
Palen, J. John. "Fertility and Eugenics: Singapore's Population Policies." *Population Research and Policy Review* 5.1 (1986): 3–14.

Palmer, John D. *The Dance of Identities: Korean Adoptees and Their Journey Toward Empowerment*. Honolulu: U of Hawai'i P, 2010.

Pao, Angela C. *No Safe Spaces: Re-casting Race, Ethnicity, and Nationality in American Theater*. Ann Arbor: U of Michigan P, 2010.

Parikh, Crystal. *An Ethics of Betrayal: The Politics of Otherness in Emergent U.S. Literatures and Culture*. New York: Fordham UP, 2009.

Park, Jane Chi Hyun. *Yellow Future: Oriental Style in Hollywood Cinema*. Minneapolis: U of Minnesota P, 2010.

Park, Ji Hoon, Nadine G. Gabbadon, and Ariel R. Chernin. "Naturalizing Racial Differences Through Comedy: Asian, Black, and White Views on Racial Stereotypes in *Rush Hour 2*." *Journal of Communication* 56 (2006) 157–177.

Park, Shelley M. *Mothering Queerly, Queering Motherhood: Resisting Monomaternalism in Adoptive, Lesbian, Blended, and Polygamous Families*. Albany: State U of New York P, 2013.

Parker, Robert Dale. "Who Shot the Sheriff? Storytelling, Indian Identity, and the Marketplace of Masculinity in D'Arcy McNickle's *The Surrounded*." *Modern Fiction Studies* 43.4 (1997): 898–932.

Pate, SooJin. *From Orphan to Adoptee: U.S. Empire and Genealogies of Korean Adoption*. Minneapolis: U of Minnesota P, 2014.

Paterson, Rab. "The Fall of Fortress Singapore: Churchill's Role and the Conflicting Interpretations." *Sophia International Review* 30 (2008): 31–68.

Patterson, Charlotte J., and Samantha L. Tornello. "Gay Fathers' Pathways to Parenthood: International Perspectives." *Journal of Family Research* 22 (2010): 103–116.

Patterson, Orlando. *Slavery and Social Death: A Comparative Study*. Cambridge: Harvard UP, 1985.

Pearl, Monica B. *AIDS Literature and Gay Identity: The Literature of Loss*. New York: Routledge, 2013.

Pearson, Wendy. "Investigating the Epistemology of the Bedroom: Same-Sex Marriage and Sexual Citizenship in Canada." *Discourse* 26.3 (2004): 136–165.

Peleggi, Maurizio. "Consuming Colonial Nostalgia: The Monumentalisation of Historic Hotels in Urban South-East Asia." *Asia Pacific Viewpoint* 46.3 (2005): 255–265.

Pellowski, Jennifer, et al. "A Pandemic of the Poor: Social Disadvantage and the U.S. HIV Epidemic." *American Psychologist* 68.4 (May 2013): 197–209.

Peterson, Christopher. *Kindred Specters: Death, Mourning, and American Affinity*. Minneapolis: U of Minnesota P, 2007.

Pettinicchio, David. "Public and Elite Policy Preferences: Gay Marriage in Canada." *International Journal of Canadian Studies* 42 (2010): 125–153.

Pham, Minh-Ha T. "The Asian Invasion (of Multiculturalism) in Hollywood." *Journal of Popular Film & Television* 32.3 (2004): 121–131.

Phang, Sock-Yong. "The Singapore Model of Housing and the Welfare State." *Housing and the New Welfare State: Perspectives from East Asia and Europe*. Ed. R. Groves et al. Farnham: Ashgate, 2007. 15–44.

Phillips, Richard. "Settler Colonialism and the Nuclear Family." *The Canadian Geographer* 53.2 (2009): 239–253.
Phillips, Robert. "'Singaporean by Birth, Singaporean by Faith': Queer Indians, Internet Technology, and the Reconfiguration of Sexual and National Identity." *Queer Singapore: Illiberal Citizenship and Mediated Cultures*. Ed. Audrey Yue and Jun Zubillaga-Pow. Hong Kong: Hong Kong UP, 2012. 187–196.
Pichaske, David R. *Rooted: Seven Midwest Writers of Place*. Iowa City: U of Iowa P, 2006.
Pierceson, Jason. *Courts, Liberalism, and Rights: Gay Law and Politics in the United States and Canada*. Philadelphia: Temple UP, 2005.
Piggford, George. "'In Time of Plague': AIDS and Its Significations in Hervé Guibert, Tony Kushner, and Thom Gunn." *Cultural Critique* 44 (Winter 2000): 169–196.
Piontek, Thomas. "Unsafe Representations: Cultural Criticism in the Age of AIDS." *Discourse* 15.1 (1992): 128–153.
Ponce, Martin Joseph. *Beyond the Nation: Diasporic Filipino Literature and Queer Reading*. New York: New York UP, 2012.
Poon, Angelia. "Pick and Mix for a Global City: Race and Cosmopolitanism in Singapore." *Race and Multiculturalism in Malaysia and Singapore*. Ed. Daniel P. S. Goh et al. New York: Routledge, 2009. 71–85.
Powell, Brian, et al. *Counted Out: Same-Sex Relations and Americans' Definitions of Family*. New York: Russell Sage Foundation, 2010.
Prébin, Elise M. *Meeting Once More: The Korean Side of Transnational Adoption*. New York: New York UP, 2013.
Prince, Gerald. *Dictionary of Narratology*. Lincoln: U of Nebraska P, 1989.
Proctor, Nicolas W. *Bathed in Blood: Hunting and Mastery in the Old South*. Charlottesville: U of Virginia P, 2002.
Propp, Vladimir. *The Morphology of the Folktale*. 2nd ed. Austin: U of Texas P, 1968.
Puar, Jasbir K. "Mapping US Homonormativities." *Gender, Place & Culture* 13.1 (2006): 67–88.
———. *Terrorist Assemblages: Homonationalism in Queer Times*. Durham: Duke UP, 2007.
Purushotam, Nirmala Srirekam. *Negotiating Multiculturalism: Disciplining Difference in Singapore*. Berlin: Walter de Gruyter, 2000.
Pyke, Karen D., and Denise L. Johnson. "Asian American Women and Racialized Femininities: 'Doing' Gender Across Cultural Worlds." *Gender & Society* 17.1 (2003): 33–53.
Pyle, Jean L. "Women, the Family, and Economic Restructuring: The Singapore Model?" *Review of Social Economy* 55.2 (1997): 215–223.
Rabin, Judith A. "The AIDS Epidemic and Gay Bathhouses: A Constitutional Analysis." *Journal of Health Politics, Policy and Law* 10.4 (1986): 729–747.
Rahim, Lily Zubaidah. *Singapore in the Malay World: Building and Breaching Regional Bridges*. New York: Routledge, 2009.
Rahman, Noor Aisha Abdul. "The Dominant Perspective on Terrorism and Its Impli-

cation for Social Cohesion: The Case of Singapore." *Copenhagen Journal of Asian Studies* 27.2 (2009): 109–128.

Ramos, Maximo. "The *Aswang* Syncrasy in Philippine Folklore." *Western Folklore* 28.4 (1969): 238–248.

Rashed, Mohammed Abouelleil. "Religious Experience and Psychiatry: Analysis of the Conflict and Proposal for a Way Forward." *Philosophy, Psychiatry, & Psychology* 17.3 (2010): 185–204.

Rayside, David. *Queer Inclusions, Continental Divisions: Public Recognition of Sexual Diversity in Canada and the United States*. Toronto: U of Toronto P, 2008.

Realuyo, Bino. *The Umbrella Country*. New York: Ballantine, 1999.

Reddy, Chandan. "Time for Rights? *Loving*, Gay Marriage, and the Limits of Legal Justice." *Fordham Law Review* 76.6 (2008): 2849–2872.

Regester, Charlene. "African American Extras in Hollywood During the 1920s and 1930s." *Film History* 9 (1997): 95–115.

Revoyr, Nina. *The Age of Dreaming*. New York: Akashic, 2008.

———. *Lost Canyon*. New York: Akashic, 2015.

———. *The Necessary Hunger*. New York: St. Martin's, 1998.

———. *Southland*. New York: Akashic, 2008.

———. *Wingshooters*. New York: Akashic, 2011.

Reyes, Eric Estuar. "American Developmentalism and Hierarchies of Difference in R. Zamora Linmark's *Rolling the R's*." *Journal of Asian American Studies* 10.2 (2007): 117–140.

Reyes, Raquel A. G. *Love, Passion and Patriotism: Sexuality and the Philippine Propaganda Movement, 1882–1892*. Singapore: NUS Press; Seattle: In association with U of Washington P, 2008.

Richardson, Matt. "Our Stories Have Never Been Told: Preliminary Thoughts on Black Lesbian Cultural Production as Historiography in *The Watermelon Woman*." *Black Camera* 2.2 (Spring 2011): 100–113.

Richters, Juliet, et al. "Demographic and Psychosocial Features of Participants in Bondage and Discipline, Sadomasochism or Dominance and Submission (BDSM)." *Journal of Sexual Medicine* 5 (2008): 1660–1668.

Ringdal, Nils Johan. *Love for Sale: A World History of Prostitution*. New York: Grove, 2004.

Rivers, Jacob F., III. *Cultural Values in the Southern Sporting Narrative*. Columbia: U of South Carolina P, 2002.

Roach, Kent. "National Security, Multiculturalism and Muslim Minorities." *Singapore Journal of Legal Studies* (2006): 405–438.

Robinson, Paul. *Queer Wars: The New Gay Right and Its Critics*. Chicago: U of Chicago P, 2006.

Robinson, Russell K. "Marriage Equality and Postracialism." *UCLA Law Review* 61 (2014): 1010–1081.

Rocha, Zarine. "Multiplicity Within Singularity: Racial Categorization and Recognizing 'Mixed Race' in Singapore." *Journal of Current Southeast Asian Affairs* 30.3 (2011): 95–131.

Rodell, Paul A. *Culture and Customs of the Philippines*. Westport: Greenwood, 2002.
Rohy, Valerie. *Impossible Women: Lesbian Figures & American Literature*. New York: Cornell UP, 2000.
Román, David. *Acts of Intervention: Performance, Gay Culture, and AIDS*. Bloomington: Indiana UP, 1998.
Roof, Judith. *Come as You Are: Sexuality & Narrative*. New York: Columbia UP, 1996.
———. *A Lure of Knowledge: Lesbian Sexuality and Theory*. New York: Columbia UP, 1991.
Roy, Sandip. *Don't Let Him Know*. New York: Bloomsbury, 2015.
Ryden, Kent C. *Sum of the Parts: The Mathematics and Politics of Region, Place, and Writing*. Iowa City: U of Iowa P, 2011.
Ryfle, Steve. "Godzilla's Footprint." *VQR: Virginia Quarterly Review* (Winter 2005): 45–63.
Sabanpan-Yu, Hope. "Cebuano Food Festivals: A Matter of Taste." *Philippine Quarterly of Culture and Society* 35.4 (2007): 384–392.
Sacco, Lynn. *Unspeakable: Father-Daughter Incest in American History*. Baltimore: Johns Hopkins UP, 2009.
Sahlins, Marshall. *What Kinship Is—And Is Not*. Chicago: U of Chicago P, 2013.
Sala-Boza, Astrid. "Towards Filipino Christian Culture: Mysticism and Folk Catholicism in the Señor Sto. Niño de Cebu Devotion." *Philippine Quarterly of Culture and Society* 36.4 (2008): 281–308.
Salesses, Matthew. "Interview with Alexander Chee." *Redivider: A Journal of New Literature and Art*, December 2009, http://www.redividerjournal.org/interview-with-alexander-chee. Accessed October 30, 2017.
Sam, Canyon. "The Dissident." *Amazon All Stars: Thirteen Lesbian Plays*. Ed. Rosemary Keefe Curb. New York: Applause, 1996. 377–393.
Sanders, Douglas E. "377 and the Unnatural Afterlife of British Colonialism in Asia." *Asian Journal of Comparative Law* 4.1 (2009): 1–49.
Sarkisian, Natalia, and Naomi Gerstel. *Nuclear Family Values, Extended Family Values*. New York: Routledge, 2012.
Satyal, Rakesh. *Blue Boy*. New York: Kensington, 2009.
Sawyer, Ralph D., and Mei-chün Sawyer. *Ling Ch'i Ching: A Classic Chinese Oracle*. Boulder: Westview, 2004.
Scarry, Elaine. *The Body in Pain: The Making and Unmaking of the World*. New York: Oxford UP, 1985.
Schneider, David M. *American Kinship: A Cultural Account*. 2nd ed. Chicago: U of Chicago P, 1980.
———. *A Critique of the Study of Kinship*. Ann Arbor: U of Michigan P, 1984.
Schultz, Pamela. *Not Monsters*. Lanham: Rowman & Littlefield, 2005.
Schwalm, Leslie A. *Emancipation's Diaspora: Race and Reconstruction in the Upper Midwest*. Chapel Hill: U of North Carolina P, 2010.
Scott, Darieck. *Extravagant Abjection: Blackness, Power, and Sexuality in the African American Literary Imagination*. New York: New York UP, 2010.

Scott, Robert A. *Miracle Cures: Saints, Pilgrimage, and the Healing Powers of Belief.* Berkeley: U of California P, 2011.

Scott, William Henry. *Barangay: Sixteenth-Century Philippine Culture and Society.* Manila: Ateneo de Manila UP, 1994.

Seafield, Lily. *Scottish Ghosts.* Gretna: Pelican, 2001.

Sebastian, Rodney, and Ashvin Parameswaran. "Hare Krishnas in Singapore: Agency, State, and Hinduism." *Sojourn: Journal of Social Issues in Southeast Asia* 23.1 (2008): 63–85.

Sedgwick, Eve Kosofsky. *Touching Feeling: Affect, Pedagogy Performance.* Durham: Duke UP, 2003.

Seery, John. "Stumbling Toward a Democratic Theory of Incest." *Political Theory* 41.1 (2013): 5–32.

Seki, Koki. "The Folk Notion of Power Among Cebuano Migrant Fisher Folk." *Philippine Quarterly of Culture and Society* 30.1/2 (2002): 111–137.

Selvadurai, Shyam. *Cinnamon Gardens.* Toronto: McLelland and Stewart, 1998.

———. *Funny Boy.* Toronto: McLelland and Stewart, 1994.

———. *The Hungry Ghosts.* Toronto: Doubleday Canada, 2013.

———. *Swimming in the Monsoon Sea.* Toronto: Tundra, 2005.

Seng, Loh Kah. "History, Memory, and Identity in Modern Singapore: Testimonies from the Urban Margins." *Oral History Review* 36.1 (2009): 1–24.

Shah, Hemant. "'Asian Culture' and Asian American Identities in the Television and Film Industries of the United States." *Studies in Media & Information Literacy Education* 3.3 (2003): 1–10.

Shah, Nayan. *Stranger Intimacy: Contesting Race, Sexuality and the Law in the North American West.* Berkeley: U of California P, 2012.

Shahani, Nishant. *Queer Retrosexualities: The Politics of Reparative Return.* Bethleham: Lehigh UP, 2011.

Sharma, Akhil. *Family Life.* New York: Norton, 2014.

Sheffer, Jolie A. *Romance of Race: Incest, Miscegenation, and Multiculturalism in the United States, 1880–1930.* New Brunswick: Rutgers UP, 2012.

Shimakawa, Karen. *National Abjection: The Asian American Body on Stage.* Durham: Duke UP, 2002.

Shimizu, Celine Parreñas. *The Hypersexuality of Race: Performing Asian/American Women on Screen and Scene.* Durham: Duke UP, 2007.

———. *Straitjacket Sexualities: Unbinding Asian American Manhoods.* Stanford: Stanford UP, 2012.

Shimizu, Hiroshi. *Japan and Singapore in the World Economy: Japan's Economic Advance into Singapore.* New York: Routledge, 2002.

Shing, Lynette J. Chua Kher. "Saying No: Sections 377 and 377A of the Penal Code." *Singapore Journal of Legal Studies* (2003): 209–261.

Shohat, Ella, and Robert Stam. *Unthinking Eurocentrism: Multiculturalism and the Media.* New York: Routledge, 1994.

Shortridge, James R. *The Middle West: Its Meaning in American Culture*. Lawrence: UP of Kansas, 1989.

Sie, James. *Still Life Las Vegas*. New York: St. Martin's, 2015.

Silverman, Doris K. "Medusa: Sexuality, Power, Mastery, and Some Psychoanalytic Observations." *Studies in Gender and Sexuality* 17.2 (2016): 114–125.

Sim, Loo Lee, et al. "Public Housing and Ethnic Integration in Singapore." *Habitat International* 27 (2003): 293–307.

Simpson, Caroline Chung. "Asian American Literature." *Encyclopedia of Lesbian Histories and Cultures*. Ed. Bonnie Zimmerman. New York: Routledge, 2013. 71–72.

Sin, Chih Hoong. "The Politics of Ethnic Integration in Singapore: Malay 'Regrouping' as an Ideological Construct." *International Journal of Urban and Regional Research* 27.3 (2003): 527–544.

———. "The Quest for a Balanced Ethnic Mix: Singapore's Ethnic Quota Policy Examined." *Urban Studies* 39.8 (2002): 1347–1374.

Singh, Anneliese A., Y. Barry Chung, and Jennifer K. Dean. "Acculturation Level and Internalized Homophobia of Asian American Lesbian and Bisexual Women." *Journal of LGBT Issues in Counseling* 1.2 (2006): 3–19.

Sinha, Vineeta. "'Hinduism' and 'Taoism' in Singapore: Seeing Points of Convergence." *Journal of Southeast Asian Studies* 39.1 (2008): 123–147.

———. "Unraveling 'Singaporean Hinduism': Seeing the Pluralism." *International Journal of Hindu Studies* 14.2/3 (2010): 253–279.

Slide, Anthony. *Hollywood Unknowns: A History of Extras, Bit Players, and Stand-Ins*. Jackson: UP of Mississippi, 2012.

Sloane, Sarah. "Bondage and Vulnerability." *Ropes, Bondage, and Power: Power Exchange Books' Resource Series*. Ed. Lee "Bridgett" Harrington. Las Vegas: Nazca Plains, 2009. 129–134.

Smith, Barbara. *Home Girls: A Black Feminist Anthology*. New Brunswick: Rutgers UP, 2000.

Smith, Miriam. *Political Institutions and Lesbian and Gay Rights in the United States and Canada*. New York: Routledge, 2008.

———. "Social Movements and Equality Seeking: The Case of Gay Liberation in Canada." *Canadian Political Science Association* 31.2 (June 1998): 285–309.

Smith, Patricia Juliana. *Lesbian Panic: Homoeroticism in Modern British Women's Fiction*. New York: Columbia UP, 1997.

Smyers, Karen A. *The Fox and the Jewel: Shared and Private Meanings in Contemporary Japanese Inari Workship*. Honolulu: U of Hawai'i P, 1999.

———. "'My Own Inari': Personalization of the Deity in Inari Worship." *Japanese Journal of Religious Studies* 23.1/2 (1996): 85–116.

Soh, C. Sarah. *The Comfort Women: Sexual Violence and Postcolonial Memory in Korea and Japan*. Chicago: U of Chicago P, 2009.

Somerville, Siobhan. *Queering the Color Line: Race and the Invention of Homosexuality in American Culture*. Durham: Duke UP, 2000.

Somoff, Victoria. "On the Metahistorical Roots of the Fairytale." *Western Folklore* 61.3/4 (2002): 277–293.

Song, Min Hyoung. *The Children of 1965: On Writing, and Not Writing, as an Asian American*. Durham: Duke UP, 2013.

Soto, Sandra K. *Reading Chican@ Like a Queer: The De-Mastery of Desire*. Austin: U of Texas P, 2010.

Spillers, Hortense. "Mama's Baby, Papa's Maybe: An American Grammar Book." *Diacritics* 17.2 (1987): 65–81.

Spa Night. Directed by Andrew Ahn. Strand Releasing, 2016.

Spivey, Sue E., and Christine M. Robinson. "Genocidal Intentions: Social Death and the Ex-Gay Movement." *Genocide Studies and Prevention* 5.1 (2010): 68–88.

Squires, Catherine R. *The Post-Racial Mystique: Media and Race in the Twenty-First Century*. New York: New York UP, 2014.

Sramek, Joseph. "'Face Him Like a Briton': Tiger Hunting, Imperialism, and British Masculinity in Colonial India, 1800–1875." *Victorian Studies* 48.4 (2006): 659–680.

Stange, Mary Zeiss. *Woman the Hunter*. New York: Beacon, 1997.

Steiner, Gary. *Animals and the Moral Community: Mental Life, Moral Status and Kinship*. New York: Columbia UP, 2008.

Stewart, Jacqueline. *Migrating to the Movies: Cinema and Black Urban Modernity*. Berkeley: U of California Press, 2005.

Stimpson, Catharine R. "Zero Degree Deviancy: The Lesbian Novel in English." *Critical Inquiry* 8.2 (1981): 363–379.

Stockton, Kathryn. *Beautiful Bottom, Beautiful Shame: Where Black Meets Queer*. Durham: Duke UP, 2006.

———. *The Queer Child, or Growing Sideways in the Twentieth Century*. Durham: Duke UP, 2009.

Stone, Amy L., and Jane Ward. "From 'Black People Are Not a Homosexual Act' to 'Gay Is the New Black': Mapping White Uses of Blackness in Modern Gay Rights Campaigns in the United States." *Social Identities* 17.5 (2011): 605–624.

Strathern, Marilyn. *Kinship, Law and the Unexpected: Relatives Are Always a Surprise*. New York: Cambridge UP, 2005.

Straw, Will. "The Small Parts, Small Players." *Screen* 52.1 (2011): 78–81.

Strong, Thomas. "Kinship Between Judith Butler and Anthropology? A Review Essay." *Ethnos: Journal of Anthropology* 67.3 (2002): 401–418.

Stymeist, David H. "Myth and the Monster Cinema." *Anthropologica* 51.2 (2009): 395–406.

Sueyoshi, Amy. *Queer Compulsions: Race, Nation, and Sexuality in the Affairs of Yone Noguchi*. Honolulu: U of Hawai'i P, 2012.

Sullivan, Laura L. "Chasing Fae: *The Watermelon Woman* and Black Lesbian Possibility." *Callaloo* 23.1 (Winter 2000): 448–460.

Sullivan, Maureen. *The Family of Woman: Lesbian Mothers, Their Children, and the Undoing of Gender*. Berkeley: U of California P, 2004.

Sun, Chyng Feng. "Ling Woo in Historical Context: The New Face of Asian American Stereotypes on Television." *Gender, Race, and Class in Media*." Ed. Gail Dines and Jean M. Humez. Thousand Oaks: Sage, 2002. 656–664.

Sun, Shirley Hsiao-Li. *Population Policy and Reproduction in Singapore: Making Future Citizens.* New York: Routledge, 2012.
Sun, William Huizhu. "Power and Problems of Performance Across Ethnic Lines: An Alternative Approach to Nontraditional Casting." *TDR: The Drama Review* 44.4 (Winter 2000): 86–95.
Sung, Mi Ra, Dawn M. Szymanski, and Christy Henrichs-Beck. "Challenges, Coping, and Benefits of Being an Asian American Lesbian or Bisexual Woman." *Psychology of Sexual Orientation and Gender Diversity* 2.1 (2015): 52–64.
Suri, Manil. *The Age of Shiva.* New York: Norton, 2008.
———. *The City of Devi.* New York: Norton, 2013.
———. *The Death of Vishnu.* New York: Norton, 2001.
Swee-Hock, Saw. "Singapore: Resumption of Rapid Fertility Decline in 1973." *Studies in Family Planning* 6.6 (1975): 166–169.
Szasz, Ferenc M., and Takechi Issei. "Atomic Heroes and Atomic Monsters: American and Japanese Cartoonists Confront the Onset of the Nuclear Age, 1945–80." *Historian* 69.4 (2007): 728–752.
Sze, Mai-Mai. *Silent Children.* New York: Harcourt, Brace, 1948.
Szymanski, Dawn M., and Arpana Gupta. "Examining the Relationships Between Multiple Oppressions and Asian American Sexual Minority Persons." *Psychological Distress, Journal of Gay & Lesbian Social Services* 21.2–3 (2009): 267–281.
Szymanski, Dawn M., and Mi Ra Sung. "Asian Cultural Values, Internalized Heterosexism, and Sexual Orientation Disclosure Among Asian American Sexual Minority Persons." *Journal of LGBT Issues in Counseling* 7.3 (2013): 257–273.
Tajima, Renee E. "Lotus Blossoms Don't Bleed: Images of Asian Women." *Making Waves: An Anthology of Writings By and About Asian American Women*. Ed. Asian Women United of California. Boston: Beacon, 1989. 308–317.
Takagi, Dana. "Maiden Voyage: Excursion into Sexuality and Identity Politics in Asian America." *Asian American Sexualities: Dimensions of the Gay and Lesbian Experience.* Ed. Russell Leong. New York: Routledge, 1996. 21–35.
Talib, Ameen Ali. "Hadramis in Singapore." *Journal of Muslim Minority Affairs* 17.1 (1997): 89–96.
Tamaki, Mariko. *Cover Me.* Toronto: McGilligan, 2000.
———. *Saving Montgomery Sole.* New York: Roaring Brook, 2016.
———. *(you) Set me on Fire.* Toronto: Razorbill, 2014.
Tamaki, Mariko, and Jillian Tamaki. *Skim.* Toronto: Groundwood, 2010.
———. *This One Summer.* New York: First Second, 2014.
Tan, Kenneth Paul, and Gary Lee Jack Jin. "Imagining the Gay Community in Singapore." *Critical Asian Studies* 39.2 (2007): 179–204.
Tan, Michael T. *Revisiting Usog, Pasma, Kulam.* Diliman, Quezon City: U of the Philippines P, 2008.
Tanaka, Yuki. *Japan's Comfort Women.* New York: Routledge, 2002.
Tang, Amy C. *Repetition and Race: Asian American Literature After Multiculturalism.* New York: Oxford UP, 2016.

Tarulevicz, Nicole. "History Making in Singapore: Who Is Producing the Knowledge?" *New Zealand Journal of Asian Studies* 11.1 (2009): 402–425.

Tatar, Maria. *The Hard Facts of Grimms' Fairy Tales*. Boston: Shambhala, 2003.

———. *Off with Their Heads: Fairy Tales and the Culture of Childhood*. Princeton: Princeton UP, 1992.

Tate, Claudia. *Domestic Allegories of Political Desire: The Black Heroine's Text at the Turn of the Century*. New York: Oxford UP, 1992.

Teaford, Jon C. *Cities of the Heartland: The Rise and Fall of the Industrial Midwest*. Bloomington: Indiana UP, 1993.

Tenorio, Lysley. *Monstress*. New York: Ecco, 2012.

Teo, Youyenn. "Shaping the Singapore Family, Producing the State and Society." *Economy and Society* 39.3 (2010): 337–359.

Tesler, Michael. *Post-Racial or Most-Racial?: Race and Politics in the Obama Era*. Chicago: U of Chicago P, 2016.

Tewksbury, Richard. "Bathhouse Intercourse: Structural and Behavioral Aspects of an Erotic Oasis." *Deviant Behavior: An Interdisciplinary Journal* 23 (2002): 75–112.

Thio, Li-Ann. "Control, Co-Optation and Co-Operation: Managing Religious Harmony in Singapore's Multi-Ethnic, Quasi-Secular State." *Hastings Constitutional Law Quarterly* 33.2 and 3 (2006): 197–253.

Thompson, Charis. *Making Parents: The Ontological Choreography of Reproductive Technologies*. Cambridge: MIT P, 2005.

Tilsen, Julie, and Dave Nylund. "Resisting Normativity: Queer Musings on Politics, Identity, and the Performance of Therapy." *International Journal of Narrative Therapy and Community Work* 3 (2010): 66–72.

Tilley, Allen. *Plot Snakes and the Dynamics of Narrative Experience*. Gainesville: UP of Florida, 1992.

Traub, Valerie. "The Psychomorphology of the Clitoris." *GLQ: A Journal of Lesbian and Gay Studies* 2 (1995): 81–113.

Trott, Ben. "Same-Sex Marriage and the Queer Politics of Dissensus." *The South Atlantic Quarterly* 115.2 (2016): 411–423.

Trotter, Joe William, Jr. *Black Milwaukee: The Making of an Industrial Proletariat, 1915-45*. Champaign: U of Illinois P, 2006.

Tsou, Elda. *Unquiet Tropes: Form, Race, and Asian American Literature*. Philadelphia: Temple UP, 2015.

Tu, Yong, and Grace K. M. Wong. "Public Policies and Public Resale Housing Prices in Singapore." *International Real Estate Review* 5.1 (2002): 115–132.

Tuan, Mia, and Jiannbin Lee Shiao. *Choosing Ethnicity, Negotiating Race: Korean Adoptees in America*. New York: Russell Sage Foundation, 2011.

Tuchman, Barbara. *A Distant Mirror: The Calamitous 14th Century*. Reissue ed. New York: Random House Trade Paperbacks, 1987.

Ty, Eleanor. *Asianfail: Narratives of Disenchantment and the Model Minority*. Champaign: U of Illinois P, 2017.

———. *The Politics of the Visible in Asian North American Narratives*. Toronto: U of Toronto P, 2004.

———. *Unfastened: Globality and Asian North American Narratives*. Minneapolis: U of Minneapolis P, 2010.

Ty, Eleanor, and Donald C. Goellnicht, eds. *Asian North American Identities: Beyond the Hyphen*. Bloomington: Indiana UP, 2004.

Uyehara, Denise. *Maps of City and Body: Shedding Light on the Performances of Denise Uyehara*. Los Angeles: Kaya, 2004.

Valentine, Gill. "Desperately Seeking Susan: A Geography of Lesbian Friendships." *Area* 25.2 (1993): 109–116.

———. "Negotiating and Managing Multiple Sexual Identities: Lesbian Time-Space Strategies." *Transactions of the Institute of British Geographers* 18.2 (1993): 237–248.

Vanoverbergh, Morice. "Kankanay Religion (Northern Luzon, Philippines)." *Anthropos* 67.1/2 (1972): 72–128.

Vickroy, Laurie. *Trauma and Survival in Contemporary Fiction*. Charlottesville: U of Virginia P, 2002.

Villarejo, Amy. *Lesbian Rule: Cultural Criticism and the Value of Desire*. Durham: Duke UP, 2003.

Vizenor, Gerald. *Manifest Manners: Narratives of Postindian Survivance*. 2nd ed. Lincoln: U of Nebraska P, 1999.

———. *Native Liberty: Natural Reason and Cultural Survivance*. Lincoln: U of Nebraska P, 2009.

Von Franz, Marie-Louise. *The Interpretation of Fairy Tales*. Rev. ed. Boston: Shambhala, 1996.

———. *Shadow and Evil in Fairy Tales*. Rev. ed. Boston: Shambhala, 1995.

Walsh, Kathleen. "'Hunter's Horn': Harriette Arnow's Subversive Hunting Tale." *Southern Literary Journal* 17.1 (1984): 54–67.

Walters, Suzanna Danuta. "As Her Hand Crept Slowly Up Her Thigh: Ann Bannon and the Politics of Pulp." *Social Text* 23 (Autumn-Winter 1989): 83–101.

———. "From Here to Queer: Radical Feminism, Postmodernism, and the Lesbian Menace (Or, Why Can't a Woman Be More Like a Fag?)." *Signs* 21.4 (1996): 830–869.

Wang, Hanying. "Portrayals of Chinese Women's Images in Mainstream Films—An Analysis of Four Representative Films of Different Periods." *Intercultural Communication Studies* 21.3 (2012): 82–92.

Wang, Val. *Beijing Bastard: Into the Wilds of a Changing China*. New York: Gotham, 2014.

Warhol, Robyn R. "Making 'Gay' and 'Lesbian' into Household Words: How Serial Form Works in Armistead Maupin's *Tales of the City*." *Contemporary Literature* 40.3 (1999): 378–402.

Warner, Michael. *The Trouble with Normal: Sex, Politics, and the Ethics of Queer Life*. Cambridge: Harvard UP, 1999.

Warner, Sharon Oard. "The Way We Write Now: The Reality of AIDS in Contemporary Short Fiction." *Studies in Short Fiction* 30.4 (1993): 491–500.

Warren, James Francis. *Ah Ku and Karayuki-San: Prostitution in Singapore 1880–1940.* Singapore: National U of Singapore P, 2003.

Warren, Wilson J. *Tied to the Great Packing Machine: The Midwest and Meatpacking.* Iowa City: U of Iowa P, 2006.

Wat, Eric. *The Making of a Gay Asian Community: An Oral History of Pre-AIDS Los Angeles.* Lanham: Rowman & Littlefield, 2002.

Watney, Simon. "The Spectacle of AIDS." *AIDS: Cultural Analysis Cultural Activism.* Ed. Douglas Crimp. Cambridge: MIT P, 1996. 71–86.

Watts, Edward. *An American Colony: Regionalism and the Roots of Midwestern Culture.* Athens: Ohio UP, 2002.

Weber, Ronald. *The Midwestern Ascendancy in American Writing.* Bloomington: Indiana UP, 1992.

Wee, C. J. W.-L. "The End of Disciplinary Modernisation? The Asian Economic Crisis and the Ongoing Reinvention of Singapore." *Third World Quarterly* 22.4 (2001): 987–1002.

———. "The Suppressed in the Modern Urbanscape: Cultural Difference and Film in Singapore." *positions* 20.4 (2012): 983–1007.

Weiss, Margot D. "Working at Play: BDSM Sexuality in the San Francisco Bay." *Anthropologica* 48.2 (2006): 229–245.

Wen, Wong Kai. "Futures of Ageing in Singapore." *Journal of Futures Studies* 17.3 (2013): 81–102.

West, Isaac. "Analogizing Interracial and Same Sex Marriage." *Philosophy and Rhetoric* 48.4 (2015): 561–582.

Weston, Kath. *Families We Choose: Lesbians, Gays, Kinship.* New York: Columbia UP, 1991.

Wilkins, Amy C. "'So Full of Myself as a Chick': Goth Women, Sexual Independence, and Gender Egalitarianism." *Gender & Society* 18.3 (2004): 328–349.

Wilkinson, Barry. "Social Engineering in Singapore." *Journal of Contemporary Asia* 18.2 (1988): 165–188.

Willging, Robert C. *On the Hunt: The History of Deer Hunting in Wisconsin.* Madison: Wisconsin Historical Society Press, 2008.

Williams, Lindy. "W(h)ither State Interest in Intimacy? Singapore Through a Comparative Lens." *Sojourn: Journal of Social Issues in Southeast Asia* 29.1 (2014): 132–158.

Williams, Lindy, et al. "Intergenerational Influence in Singapore and Taiwan: The Role of the Elderly in Family Decisions." *Journal of Cross-Cultural Gerontology* 14 (1999): 291–322.

Wilson, Elizabeth. *The Sphinx in the City: Urban Life, the Control of Disorder, and Women.* Berkeley: U of California Press, 1992.

Wismeijer, Andreas A. J., and Marcel A. L. M. van Assen. "Psychological Characteristics of BDSM Practitioners." *Journal of Sexual Medicine* 10.8 (2013): 1943–1952.

Wolf, Arthur. *Incest Avoidance and the Incest Taboos: Two Aspects of Human Nature.* Stanford: Stanford Briefs, 2014.

Woloch, Alex. *The One vs. the Many: Minor Characters and the Space of the Protagonist in the Novel.* Princeton: Princeton UP, 2003.

Wonders, Karen. "Hunting Narratives of the Age of Empire: A Gender Reading of Their Iconography." *Environment and History* 11.3 (2005): 269–291.
Wong, Lloyd, and Shibao Guo. "Revisiting Multiculturalism in Canada: An Introduction." *Revisiting Multiculturalism in Canada: Theories, Policies, and Debates.* Ed. Shibao Guo and Lloyd Wong. Rotterdam: Sense Publishers, 2015. 1–14.
Wong, Nellie. *Dreams in Harrison Railroad Park.* Berkeley: Kelsey St. Press, 1977.
Wong, Norman. *Cultural Revolution.* New York: Ballantine, 1995.
Wong, Sau-ling Cynthia. *Reading Asian American Literature: From Necessity to Extravagance.* Princeton: Princeton UP, 1993.
Wong, Y. Joel, et al. "Asian American Male College Students' Perceptions of People's Stereotypes About Asian American Men." *Psychology of Men & Masculinity* 13.1 (2012): 75–88.
Woo, Merle. *Yellow Woman Speaks.* Expanded ed. Seattle: Red Letter, 2003.
Wood, Forrest, Jr. *The Delights and Dilemmas of Hunting.* Lanham: UP of America, 1997.
Woodiwiss, Jo. *Contesting Stories of Childhood Sexual Abuse.* New York: Palgrave MacMillan, 2009.
Woods, Damon L., and Lucien Ellington. *The Philippines: A Global Studies Handbook.* Santa Barbara: ABC-CLIO, 2005.
Wu, Ellen D. *The Color of Success: Asian Americans and the Origins of the Model Minority.* Princeton: Princeton UP, 2015.
Xia, Yan, Kieu Anh Do, and Xiaolin Xie. "The Adjustment of Asian American Families to the U.S. Context: The Ecology of Strengths and Stress." Ed. G. W. Peterson and K. R. Bush. *Handbook of Marriage and the Family.* New York: Springer, 2013. 705–722.
Xing, Jun. *Asian America Through the Lens: History, Representations, and Identity.* Walnut Creek: AltaMira, 1998.
Yanagisako, Sylvia Junko. *Transforming the Past: Tradition and Kinship Among Japanese Americans.* Stanford: Stanford UP, 1992.
Yap, Mui Teng. "Fertility and Population Policy: The Singapore Experience." *Journal of Population and Social Security (Population)*, supp. to vol. 1 (2003): 643–658.
Yeung, Henry Wai-chung. "State Intervention and Neoliberalism in the Globalizing World Economy: Lessons from Singapore's Regionalization Programme." *Pacific Review* 13.1 (2000): 133–162.
Yook, Eunkyong Lee. *Culture Shock for Asians in U.S. Academia: Breaking the Model Minority Myth.* Lanham: Lexington, 2013.
Yoshimi, Yoshiaki. *Comfort Women.* Trans. Suzanne O'Brien. New York: Columbia UP, 2002.
Yoshino, Kenji. *Covering: The Hidden Assault on Civil Rights.* New York: Random House, 2006.
Youmans, Vincent, and Irving Caesar. "Tea for Two." Song. 1925.
Young, Madison. "Thoughts on Rope, Submission and Feminism." *Ropes, Bondage, and Power.* Ed. Lee "Bridgett" Harrington. Las Vegas: Nazca Plains, 2009. 51–61. Power Exchange Books' Resource Series.
Yu, Mark. "Personal Rope, Universal Power." *Ropes, Bondage, and Power.* Ed. Lee "Bridgett"

Harrington. Las Vegas: Nazca Plains, 2009. 87–96. Power Exchange Books' Resource Series.

Yuen, Nancy Wang. *Reel Inequality: Hollywood Actors and Racism*. New Brunswick: Rutgers UP, 2016.

Zhao, Xiaojian. *Remaking Chinese America: Immigration, Family, and Community, 1940–1965*. New Brunswick: Rutgers UP, 2002.

Zia, Helen. *Asian American Dreams*. New York: Farrar, Straus & Giroux, 2001.

Zimmerman, Bonnie. *The Safe Sea of Women: Lesbian Fiction, 1969–1989*. Boston: Beacon, 1991.

Zipes, Jack. *Breaking the Magic Spell: Radical Theories of Folk and Fairy Tales*. Rev. ed. Lexington: UP of Kentucky, 2002.

———. "The Changing Function of the Fairy Tale." *The Lion and the Unicorn* 12.2 (December 1988): 7–31.

INDEX

AAN! (AIDS ACTION NOW!), 11
Abboud, Soo Kim, 29–30
Aberrations in Black (Ferguson), 20
Abraham, Nicolas, 92
abuse, 38, 54, 64–65, 77. *See also* molestation; physical abuse; sexual abuse; trauma
ACT UP (AIDS Coalition to Unleash Power), 11
adoption, 19, 69, 71, 131, 137, 148, 168, 249n23. *See also* families; guardian figures; racial identity
African American, 20, 25, 54, 60, 83, 164–66, 172, 174, 184–86, 259n17, 259n23, 259n24
After Disasters (Dinh), 16
Age of Dreaming (Revoyr), 33–35, 37
Aguilar, Filomeno V., 128
Aguilar-San Juan, Karin, 18
Ahmed, Sara, 194
Ahn, Andrew, 236
AIDS/HIV: activist groups, 11; epidemic of, 11, 16, 23–24, 69, 92, 111, 123, 160; inscrutable belonging and, 73–75, 80, 82–86, 112–15, 189; sex practices and, 73–75, 83–84. *See also* plague

Ali, Kazim, 16, 245n38
Allison, Dorothy, 77
alternative kinship: adult formations of, 68–71, 82, 112–13, 118–21, 154–57, 168–70, 203, 208; childhood formations of, 46–48, 128–30, 137, 142, 176–83, 194, 201. *See also* families; inscrutable belonging
Alumit, Noël, 4, 16, 24, 59, 123–57, 159–60, 189, 237
Alyson Books, 16
And the Band Played On (Shilts), 111
anonymity, 74–75, 78–79, 84, 209–10, 242n8
Antigone's Claim (Butler), 194
Anzaldúa, Gloria, 162
Apocalypse Now, 145
APP (Asian Pride Project), 235, 237–38
Apparitional Lesbian, The (Castle), 164
Arab, 219–220, 262n32
artistry, 29–30, 40, 70, 96, 110
Ash (Lo), 37
Asian American Sexualities (Leong), 18
Asian American studies, 10
Asian Canadian studies, 10
Asian North American: studies, 32, 70–72, 88; use of term, xv

308　INDEX

Austen, Jane, 2, 4, 64
authorial background, 59–60, 161, 163, 238

Babas. *See* Peranakan
Babyji (Dawesar), 16
Barillas, William, 173
Barnard, Ian, 2, 171
Bastard Out of Carolina (Allison), 77
Bathgate, Michael, 94
bathhouses, 81–85, 236, 250n27
Battle Hymn of the Tiger Mother (A. Chua), 29, 31, 89–91
Baudrillard, Jean, 145
Baumeister, Roy F., 206
BDSM, 204–7, 209, 213, 222, 228, 233, 260n9
belonging. *See* adoption; families; inscrutable belonging; national identity; racial identity; sexual identity
Bernard Amador Angelo Tan (character), 3–4, 72–88, 111, 124, 189, 236
Bettelheim, Bruno, 127
Beyond the Nation (Ponce), 18
Blackburn, Kevin, 222
Black Death. *See* plague
Blue Boy (Satyal), 16, 38, 40–44
Boccaccio, Giovanni, 109
bondage. *See* BDSM
Bong Bong Luwad (character), 124–57, 189, 237
Boston, 190–191
Bourque, Dawn, 67
Bow, Leslie, 50
Bratton, Mark, 135
Brett, Caroline, 135–36
Brian, Kristi, 168
Bronner, Simon J., 185
Brown Boys and Rice Queens (E. B. Lim), 18
Browne, Nick, 131
Buddhism (Buddhist), 215, 219. *See also* religion; mysticism; spirituality
Butler, Judith, 7, 76, 97, 170, 194, 199, 203–4, 210–16

Cahill, Courtney Megan, 204
California, 14–15, 33, 151, 166, 193
"Camouflage" (Leong), 3–4, 23–25, 59, 72–88, 111, 123–26, 159–60, 189, 236
Canaday, Margot, 2
Caruth, Cathy, 100, 248n8
Cashdan, Sheldon, 138–39
Castle, Terry, 164
Cayton, Andrew R. L., 173
Cereus Blooms at Night (Mootoo), 16
Chadda, Rakesh K., 50
Chambers, Ross, 112
Chang, Sishir, 228
Chee, Alexander, 4, 24, 59, 88–124, 159–60, 174, 189, 237
Cheng, Anne Anlin, 143
Children of 1965, The (Song), 89
Chin, Justin, 16
China, 72, 94, 221, 249n14, 251n11
Chinatown, 70
Chinese American, 33, 70, 243n19, 247n112, 249nn20,21, 255n24
Chinese Canadian, 12–13, 46, 49–50, 71, 161, 244n28, 249n20
Chinese Singaporean, 214–19, 262n35. *See also* Peranakan
Chiu, Monica, 11
Cho, Grace, 92–93
Chorus of Mushrooms (Goto), 15
Choy, Wayson, 15, 245n38
Christian (Christianity), 128, 201, 215, 219–20, 253n4, 254n6, 261n22. *See also* religion; mysticism; spirituality
chrononormativity, 63
Chu, Patricia P., 61–62
Chua, Amy, 29, 89–91, 120
Chua, Lawrence, 16
Chua, Lynette, 209
Chuh, Kandice, 92
Chung, Jamie, 146
cinema, 24, 34, 125–26, 132, 136, 141, 142–47, 149, 151–52, 155–57, 236, 256nn27,31. *See also* film; movie

City of Devi, The (Suri), 16
civil rights movement, 2, 5, 16, 86, 145
Clancy, Susan A., 99, 200, 251n15
class identity, 2, 9, 17, 20, 55, 64, 171–73, 175, 179, 186, 193, 218, 233, 247n11; middle class and, 60, 159, 250n1
Clift, Montgomery, 124–43, 147–48, 153–57, 189, 237
closet (closeting), 5, 15, 18, 35, 51, 54, 57, 93, 155–56, 176, 208–9, 212, 231–32. *See also* coming out
CMIO Classification system, 214, 218
Coale, Sam, 115
colonialism, 92–96, 105, 138–39, 212–21, 226, 229, 233
comfort women. *See* sex work
coming out, 56–57, 209, 212, 216, 231, 235–36, 245n42. *See also* closet
courtship plots, 2–3, 56, 60, 64, 165–66, 247n2, 265n62. *See also* marriage plots
Crimp, Douglas, 111
Crouching Tiger Hidden Dragon (film), 146
Cruising Utopia (Muñoz), 21
Cvetkovich, Ann, 77

Dancer Dawkins and the California Kid (W. Kim), 15
Davidson, Arnold E., 13
Davis, Rocío, 11
Dawes, James, 111–12
Dawesar, Abha, 16, 245n38
Day, Iyko, 10
Dead Heat (W. Kim), 15
death narratives, 64–65. *See also* social death
Deb, Koushik Sinha, 50
Decameron, The (Boccaccio), 109
Deerhorn (setting), 166–67, 169–81, 183–91, 193, 195
degenerate descendants, 25, 198–99, 226–27, 233. *See also* inscrutable belonging
Delmont, Matthew, 191

Denneny, Michael, 111, 115
Desperate Housewives (TV series), 147
Devan, Janadas, 199
Dhalla, Ghalib Shiraz, 16, 49
Dichoso, Fermin, 132
Dinh, Viet, 16
Disappearing Moon Cafe (SKY Lee), 12–15, 49–50, 160–61
Dizard, Jan E., 182
Don't Ask, Don't Tell, 1
Don't Let Him Know (Roy), 49, 52–54, 56
Du, Nang, 5

East West Players, 151
Edelman, Lee, 21, 24, 72, 88–90, 120
Edinburgh (Chee), 4, 24–25, 59, 88–124, 159–60, 174, 189, 237
Eng, David L., 2, 18–20, 32, 245n41
Entourage (TV series), 147
Eschholz, Sarah, 150
Esquibel, Catrióna Rueda, 162

families: dynamics of, 5–6, 179, 184–85, 225, 237; heteronormativity and, 38, 40–43, 49, 52–53, 63, 213, 233; homosexuality and, 18, 51, 54–57, 113, 119, 216, 232, 235, 238, 242n14; model minority stereotypes and, 27–31, 250n5; race and, 71, 89, 169, 171–72, 176, 187–92, 219–20; sexual abuse and, 199–204, 210, 217, 222; structure and, 50, 67, 82, 125–26, 186, 194, 197, 228. *See also* alternative kinship; guardian figures; inscrutable belonging
fantastical elements, 44–47, 93–94, 104, 107, 121, 127–29, 135–36. *See also* folk tradition; fox-demon mythology; Lady Tammamo myth
Farwell, Marilyn, 61–62
Fatal Women (Hart), 162
Fee (character), 89–121, 123–24, 189, 237
Feeling Backward (Love), 63
Feeling of Kinship, The (Eng), 2, 18, 20

Feng, Peter X., 152
Ferguson, Roderick, 20
Filipino American, 3, 13–14, 20, 70, 82, 125, 126, 128–29, 132, 137, 145, 253n1
film, 4, 6, 19, 20, 34–35, 80, 126, 128, 130–32, 136–37, 140–48, 150–57, 198, 222–23, 226, 236, 243n16, 245n43, 246nn46,50, 254n13, 256nn27,31, 257n37, 259n24, 263n44. *See also* cinema; movie
filmic lineages, 24, 137, 142–43, 147, 155. *See also* inscrutable belonging
Fixer Chao (Ong), 16
flashbacks. *See* retrospective storytelling
folk tradition, 129, 132, 136, 198, 201–3, 207, 229–30, 254n6. *See also* fantastical elements; fox-demon mythology; Lady Tammamo myth; religion
fox-demon mythology: generally, 91–97, 101, 104–5, 107, 117, 121, 251n11; *The Tempest* (Shakespeare) and, 96–97. *See also* fantastical elements; folk tradition; Lady Tammamo myth
Freeman, Elizabeth, 63, 69–70
Fulford, K. W. M., 135
Funny Boy (Selvadurai), 15

Garber, Linda, 163
Geisha of a Different Kind (C. W. Han), 18
Gerstel, Naomi, 67
Giltner, Scott E., 186
Global Divas (Manalansan), 18
Go, Fe Susan, 128
Godzilla, 221–23, 231
Goellnicht, Donald C., 11–12
Goh, Daniel P. S., 224
Goh, Robbie B. H., 228
Gold by the Inch (Lawrence Chua), 16
Gomez, Jewelle, 162
Gopinath, Gayatri, 18, 20, 163
Gordon, Avery, 7
Gorham, Bradley, 150
Goto, Hiromi, 15–16, 245n38

guardian figures: parental absence, 39, 43–48, 87, 124, 141, 152–53; parental substitutes, 125–32, 136–37, 139, 142–43, 155, 169, 175–77, 181, 237. *See also* adoption; alternative kinship; families

Haase, Donald, 136
Hagedorn, Jessica, 149
Halberstam, Judith, 63
Half World (Goto), 38, 45–48
Hammers, Corie, 206
Han, Chong-suk, 6
Han, C. Winter, 18
Harder, Lois, 67
Harkins, Gillian, 214, 216
Hart, Lynda, 65, 162
Hayakawa, Sessue, 146
Heath, Stephen, 132
Henderson, Joan, 218, 224
Heng, Geraldine, 199
Herman, Daniel Justin, 183
Herman, Judith Lewis, 199
heteronormativity, 18, 57, 81
heteronuclear. *See* family
Hindu (Hinduism), 40, 50, 55, 215, 219, 261n22. *See also* religion; mysticism; spirituality
Hoang, Nguyen Tan, 18
Hollywood, 24, 34, 125–26, 137, 143–44, 146–48, 150–51, 153–54, 156, 159, 198, 243n16, 256nn30,32,35,36. *See also* Los Angeles; film
Hollywood culture, 126, 143–52, 156, 256n35
Holst, Gustav, 98
Hom, Alice Y., 18
homicide, 33, 52, 64–65, 81, 102, 167, 184–88
homonormativity, 9, 69, 73, 243n22
homosexuality: families and, 18, 51–57, 113, 119, 216, 232–38, 242n14; interracial relationships and, 54–56, 217. *See also* protoqueer figures; sexual identity

INDEX 311

Hoogland, Renée C., 162
Hornsey, Richard, 83–84
Huang, Philip, 16
Huang, Quanyu, 29–30
Hudson, Rock, 156, 246n50
Hungry Ghosts, The (Selvadurai), 16
hunting, 94, 179–86, 191, 193; deer and, 172, 182, 185, 259n21, 259n24
Huntress (Lo), 16, 33, 35–36, 37, 38, 45
Hybrid Tiger (Q. Huang), 29–31
hybridity, 35–36, 52, 128, 130, 172, 186, 191, 214, 217–222, 224, 226, 228–229, 233. *See also* mixed race

identity. *See* class identity; national identity; racial identity; sexual identity
immigration, 70–71, 94, 124, 132, 139, 153, 202. *See also* families; racial identity
Impossible Desires (Gopinath), 18
In a Queer Time and Place (Halberstam), 63
incest, 12–13, 49, 76–79, 85, 88, 198–207, 210–17, 231, 237
India: 50, 52, 53, 55, 247n13; folklore and, 94, 251n11
Indian (South Asian) American, 40–41, 50, 51, 53–56, 70
Indian Kenyan 51, 247n14
Indian Singaporean, 214–15, 218
Indiscretion of an American Wife (film), 140–42, 154
infectious genealogies, 91, 116–17, 120, 174. *See also* inscrutable belonging
Ingratitude (Nihn), 89
Inness, Sherrie, 65, 162
inscrutable belonging: AIDS and, 73–75, 82–86, 112–13, 115; mystical traditions and, 198, 201, 203; race and, 169, 175–77, 187, 218, 228; sexual abuse and, 97, 101–2, 109, 114, 159, 210–11; shared interest-based, 180–83, 204–10; social death and, 8, 81–82, 155, 170, 187–88; survival plots and, 8, 22–27, 60–73, 82–86, 125–26, 143–44, 157, 193–97, 238. *See also* alternative kinship; degenerate descendants; families; filmic lineages; infectious genealogies; intergenerational transmission; interracial surrogacies
intergenerational transmission, 92–94, 110, 115, 121, 181, 201, 203. *See also* inscrutable belonging
interracial relationships: heterosexual, 71, 125, 164–65, 218; homosexual, 54–56, 217; tension from, 14, 32–37, 171–72, 177, 189, 213
interracial surrogacies, 25, 169, 176, 178, 191–93, 195. *See also* inscrutable belonging
invisibility, 162–63, 170
Ismail, Rahil, 215
It Gets Better Campaign, 1, 3

Jackson, Lawrence M., 185
Jackson, Mike, 135
Jade Peony, The (Choy), 15
Jagose, Annamarie, 195
Japan, 46, 93–94, 105, 171, 204, 221, 251n11, 262n35
Japanese American, 34, 70, 73, 82, 84, 164, 165, 166, 168, 171, 190, 192, 243n24, 244n28
Japanese Canadian, 46, 243n24, 244n28
Jewish, 130. *See also* religion; mysticism; spirituality
Joshi, Paramjit T., 135–36

Kappa Child, The (Goto), 16
Kaya, 16
Keeling, Kara, 162
Kelly, Fiona, 67
Khairudin Aljunied, Syed Muhd, 219
Khayatt, Didi, 17
Kilby, Jane, 199
Kim, Eleana, 168
Kim, Jane, 29–30

312 INDEX

Kim, Willyce, 15
Kim, Younghan, 150
Kinbaku, 204–10, 212–13, 220, 222, 231, 233
kinship. *See* alternative kinship; families; inscrutable belonging
Kobayashi, Tamai, 16
Koh, Ernest, 222
Korea 92, 94–96, 251n11; adoptee from, 19, 71
Korean American, 89, 236–37
Korean War, 189
Kramer, Elizabeth J., 5
Kumar, Mala, 49, 54–55
Kwa, Lydia, 4, 25, 59, 197–234, 237

Lady Tammamo myth, 93–96, 104–5, 117. *See also* fantastical elements; folk tradition; fox-demon mythology
Lai, Larissa, 16
Latinx (Latin@), 83, 255n22
Lee, Bruce, 146
Lee, Christopher, 62, 71
Lee, JeeYeun, 163
Lee, Josephine, 145
Lee, Rex, 147
Lee, SKY, 12–13, 49, 160
legislation: anti-miscegenation, 32, 35, 218–19; racial, 10–14, 50, 71, 160, 190–91, 244n28; sexual, 5, 56, 83, 155, 209, 227, 231–32, 264n55
Lenon, Suzanne, 8
Leong, Russell, 3, 23, 59, 72, 111, 123–24, 159–60, 189, 236
Lesbian Menace, The (Inness), 162
lesbian stereotypes, 162–63, 257n2
Letters to Montgomery Clift (Alumit), 4, 24–25, 59, 123–57, 159–60, 189, 237
Leung, Brian, 16, 33–34
Lim, Eng-Beng, 18
Lim, Imogene L., 70
Lindemann, Danielle, 206
Linmark, R. Zamora, 16
Little, Brown, 16

Liu, Lucy, 146
Lo, Malinda, 16, 33
Loo, Tina, 185
Lorde, Audre, 162
Los Angeles, 72, 79, 125, 138, 167, 246n44. *See also* Hollywood
Love, Heather, 63
Loving v. Virginia, 191
Lu, Lynn, 149
Luke, Brian, 180–81

Maine, 89, 102, 108, 112–13, 118–19, 253n28
Manalansan, Martin, 18, 20
Mapa, Alec, 147
marginality, 7, 37, 56, 62–63, 68, 116–17, 126, 144–46, 148–50, 152–53, 156, 189, 198
marriage, 171–72, 175. *See also* same-sex marriage
marriage plots, 2–3, 9, 60, 64, 85, 247n2. *See also* courtship plots
Marzanski, Marek, 135
Mauzy, Diane K., 232
McClelland & Stewart, 16
Mehta, Rahul, 16, 245n38
mental health, 125, 130, 133–35, 147, 255n16
Michelle LeBeau (character), 166–95, 237
Midwest, 25, 160, 162, 166, 173–74, 178, 185, 193, 259nn15–17
Miller, Terry, 1
Milne, R. S., 232
Miss Saigon, 80
model minority stereotypes, 28–32, 40, 89
Moeller, Hans-Georg, 229
Mok, Teresa, 145
molestation, 4, 24, 75–81, 106. *See also* pederastic relationships; protoqueer figures; sexual abuse; trauma
Monstress (Tenorio), 12
Mootoo, Shani, 16, 245n38
Moraga, Cherríe, 162
movie, 24, 34–35, 54, 124, 126, 130–31, 140, 143–45, 147–49, 151–54, 156–57, 223, 256n35. *See also* cinema; film

INDEX 313

Moving Forward Sideways Like a Crab (Mootoo), 16
Muñoz, José Esteban, 21–22
Murakawa, Nawashi, 204
Murphy, Timothy F., 112
Muslim (and Islam), 214–16, 253n4, 262n23, 262n25. *See also* religion; mysticism; spirituality
mysticism, 37, 44, 47, 94, 128–29, 132–33, 198, 202–3, 230. *See also* religion; spirituality

Napier, Susan J., 222–23
narrative: death, 64–65; ellipticts, 27, 31–37, 57, 62; ensemble, 27, 31, 48–58, 72, 164; intergenerational, 12–13, 49, 55, 104–5; protoqueer, 27, 31, 37–48, 57, 87, 164, structure, 60–62, 75–76, 124–27, 152, 154–56, 183, 192, 200. *See also* survival plots; tactical diversions
natal alienation, 63
Natalie (character), 198–235, 237
national identity, 199, 208, 212–16, 221–25, 230
Native American (indigenous), 242n7, 243n13
Native Canadian (First Nations, indigenous), 10
Necessary Hunger, The (Revoyr), 16, 161, 163–65, 167, 192
Nelson, Emmanuel S., 111
NeWest Press, 16
New York, 11, 102
New York City, 20
Ng, Mark Tristan, 5–6
98 Wounds (Chin), 16
Ninh, erin Khuê, 89
No Future (Edelman), 21, 72, 89–90
No Other World (Mehta), 16
Nonyas. *See* Peranakan
Northanger Abbey (Austen), 2
NQAPIA (National Queer Asian and Pacific Islander Alliance), 235, 237–38

Obendorf, Simon, 232
Ode to Lata (Dhalla), 16
One vs. the Many, The (Woloch), 64
Ong, Han, 16, 245n38
Onuf, Peter S., 173
Ordover, Nancy, 2
Ortmann, Stephan, 226
Oudart, Jean-Pierre, 131
Out on Main Street & Other Stories (Mootoo), 16

pastoral, 173–74, 186
Pate, SooJin, 71
Paths of Marriage, The (Kumar), 49, 54–56
Patterson, Orlando, 5, 63
pederastic relationships, 39, 97–104, 113. *See also* molestation; protoqueer figures; sexual abuse; trauma
Peleggi, Maurizio, 230
Peranakan, 217–20, 262n31; Babas, 217–19, 262n29; Nonyas, 217, 219; Straits Chinese, 217, 262n28
performance, 39–40, 70, 73–74, 79–80, 83–84, 143, 148, 151, 153, 156, 256nn29,35, 257n39, 258n7. *See also* film; theater
Peterson, Christopher, 69–70
Pham, Mihn-ha T., 146
Philippines: 75–76, 124–25, 128, 131, 134, 136–39, 145, 244n34, 254n9; folk beliefs, religious practices, and customs of, 253nn2–9. *See also* Filipino American
Phoenix Eyes & Other Stories (Leong), 72
photography, 99, 143
physical abuse, 127–29, 132–34, 137, 155, 167, 184, 210–11
Picador, 16
Place in the Sun, A (film), 147
plague, 109–11, 114–17, 252n25. *See also* AIDS/HIV
Ponce, Martin Joseph, 18, 130, 140, 147

Poon, Angelia, 219
pop culture, 38–39
Pornography of Grief, A (P. Huang), 16
power dynamics, 91, 97–101, 103, 185–86, 199–200, 204–6, 209–10, 222
Prairie Ostrich (Kobayashi), 16
Proctor, Nicolas W., 185–86
protoqueer figures: Asian North American children as, 87, 91–95, 101, 120, 128, 142, 160, 170, 190; development of, 21, 37–48, 53, 66; sexual abuse and, 24, 89, 92, 116, 199–202, 217, 225; suicide and, 42, 90, 102, 198; survival plots and, 77, 87, 123, 184; trauma and, 24–25, 38–39, 75, 99, 114, 131, 198
Psychic Life of Power, The (Butler), 77
Puar, Jasbir K., 9, 18
Pulse (Kwa), 4, 25, 59, 197–234, 237

Q&A (Eng & Hom), 18
Quarantine (Mehta), 16
queer Asian North American fictions, 15–17
Queer Compulsions (Sueyoshi), 18
queer critical genealogies, 17–22
queer diasporic critique, 20–21, 75, 118, 144, 172
queer of color critique, 20–21, 75, 118, 144, 167, 172
queer pessimism, 21, 88
queer racial formalisms, 28–30, 58, 60–63
Queer Retrosexualities (Shahani), 63
queer studies, 69–70, 72, 88
Quinn's Passage (Ali), 16

racial barriers, 144–51, 156, 175, 223
Racial Castration (Eng), 18, 20, 32
racial identity: isolation and, 41, 143, 145–46, 192–94; mixed-race and, 166, 170–72, 177, 186–90, 217–20, 228, 230–31; protoqueer figures and, 89–91, 94–95, 109, 131. *See also* interracial relationships

racial stereotypes, 6, 68, 80, 149–51, 171–74, 185, 190, 214–15
racism, 167–69, 171–75, 178, 185–92
Raffles, Sir Stamford, 219
Raintree Country (film), 147
realist novels, 64
Realuyo, Bino, 16
religion, 128, 135–37, 201–2, 214–15, 220, 229–30. *See also* mysticism; spirituality
reproductive future, 88–91, 119–20, 161–62, 169, 178, 184, 191, 222
reproductive past, 62, 91, 97, 121
retributive justice, 105, 108
retrospective storytelling: analepses and, 66, 73, 75–76; family dynamics and, 142, 181, 186, 188–92; survival plots and, 88–91, 107–10, 112–13, 124–27, 156, 163, 174, 238; trauma and, 62–63, 99–101, 116–20, 166–70, 178. *See also* tactical diversions
Revoyr, Nina, 4, 16, 25, 33, 59, 159–95, 237, 245n38
Richardson, Matt, 163
Robinson, Russell K., 8
Rocha, Zarine, 218
Rolling the R's (Linmark), 16, 38–40, 42–44
Roof, Judith, 61–62, 257n2
Roy, Sandip, 49
Rubens, Paul Peter, 98
Rush Hour (film), 146

Salesses, Matthew, 94
Salt Fish Girl (Lai), 16
same-sex marriage, 1, 8–10, 56, 155, 232
Sarkisian, Natalia, 67
Satyal, Rakesh, 16
Savage, Dan, 1
"Save the I-Hotel" (Tenorio), 12–13, 15
Saving Montgomery Sole (Tamaki), 16
Schneider, David, 67
Search, The (film), 130–32, 137, 140–42

Secret Room, The (Ali), 16
Selvadurai, Shyam, 15, 245n38
Seo, Joe, 236
sexual abuse: cycle of, 102–3, 105, 108; inscrutable belonging and, 97, 101–2, 109, 114, 159, 210–11; power dynamics and, 98–101, 103, 106, 199–200; protoqueer figures and, 24, 89, 92, 116, 199–202, 217, 225; survival plots and, 91, 98, 102, 107, 118, 200, 210. *See also* molestation; pederastic relationships; trauma
sexual consent, 89, 99–103, 205–7
sexual desire, 64, 74–81, 87, 101, 157, 164, 192, 205–6, 232, 236
sexual development, 73, 77–78, 81, 85, 103
sexual experiences, concealed, 51–54
sexual identity: adult figures and, 146, 155, 157, 192, 194, 203–10, 220, 228, 233; protoqueer figures and, 90, 133, 216
sex work, 39, 72–76, 79–80, 88, 92–93, 104, 138–39, 227
Shah, Nayan, 70–71
Shahani, Nishant, 63
shame, 40–41, 77–80, 101, 201
Shaw, Brian, 215
Sheffer, Jolie A., 214, 216
Shigeta, James, 146
Shilts, Randy, 111
Shimizu, Celine Parreñas, 80
Sie, James, 16
Simpson, Caroline Chung, 50
Singapore, 198–99, 208–34
Skim (Tamaki & Tamaki), 38, 42–44
Sloane, Sarah, 207
Smith, Barbara, 162
social death: inscrutable belonging and, 8, 81–82, 155, 170, 187–88; survival plots and, 5, 57, 60, 63, 65, 85, 118, 123, 193–95, 238
Somerville, Siobhan, 2
Song, Min Hyoung, 89
Soto, Sandra K., 162

Southland (Revoyr), 16, 161, 164–65, 167, 192
Spa Night (film), 236
speculative fiction, 93
spirituality, 41–42, 45, 47, 48, 78, 94, 96, 128, 131–32, 135–37, 198–99, 201–2, 205, 207, 220, 226, 242n7, 253nn4,5, 255nn16,17. *See also* mysticism; religion
Stewart, Jacqueline, 152
Still Life Las Vegas (Sie), 16
St. Martin's Press, 16
Straits Chinese. *See* Peranakan
Straw, Will, 144
Suddenly, Last Summer (film), 147
Sueyoshi, Amy, 18
suicide: protoqueer figures and, 42, 90, 94–95, 102, 198; race and, 148–50; survival plots and, 24–25, 52–53, 108, 116, 208–12, 231
Sullivan, Laura L., 163
supernatural: 45–47, 94, 121, 127; occult and, 44, 132–34, 138, 198, 202; divination and, 198, 201–2; 260n5
Suri, Manil, 16, 245n38
survival plots: evolution of, 144, 155–56, 171, 186–87, 207, 227, 233, 237; gender and, 160; incest and, 199; inscrutable belonging and, 8, 22–27, 60–73, 82–86, 125–26, 143–44, 157, 193–98, 238; molestation and, 78–79, 81; narrative structure and, 124, 133, 137, 163; protoqueer figures and, 77, 87, 123, 184; retrospective storytelling and, 90, 108–9, 112–13, 127; sexual abuse and, 91, 98, 102, 107, 118, 200, 210; social death and, 5, 57, 60, 63, 65, 85, 118, 123, 193–95; suicide and, 24–25, 52–53, 108, 116, 208–12, 231; trauma and, 63, 92, 133–34, 188, 237

Taoism (Daoism), 215–216, 229–230, 261n22. *See also* religion; mysticism; spirituality

316   INDEX

tactical diversions, 22, 27, 31–59, 72, 87, 163–64, 247n6. *See also* narrative, ensemble; narrative, elliptics; narrative, protoqueer
Takagi, Dana, 19
Take Me Home (Leung), 33, 35, 37
Talking to the Moon (Alumit), 16
Tamaki, Jillian, 38, 245n38
Tamaki, Mariko, 16, 38, 245n38
Tan, Michael T., 129
Tang, Amy C., 62
Tarulevicz, Nicole, 227
Tate, Claudia, 60
Taylor, Elizabeth, 147
television, 6, 39, 143–45, 148, 151–52, 156, 243n16, 256n27. *See also* film; performance
Tenorio, Lysley, 12
Terminal Station (film), 140
Terrorist Assemblages (Puar), 18
theater, 34, 145, 151, 257n39. *See also* film; performance
Theoharis, Jeanne, 191
Thomarat, Michelle, 67
Time Binds (Freeman), 63
Ton, Hendry, 5
Top of the Class (Abboud & J. Kim), 29–31
Torok, Maria, 92
Toronto, 11, 42, 45, 200, 202
Towbin, Kenneth E., 135–36
trauma: confrontation of, 159, 167, 170, 194, 203–13, 221–22; protoqueer figures and, 24–25, 38–39, 75, 77, 99, 114, 131, 198; survival plots and, 63, 92, 133–34, 188, 237. *See also* homicide; molestation; sexual abuse; suicide

Trauma Myth, The (Clancy), 200
Tsou, Elda, 62
Two Krishnas, The (Dhalla), 49, 51–52, 54, 56
Ty, Eleanor, 11

Umbrella Country, The (Realuyo), 16
Undoing Gender (Butler), 7

Vancouver, 71
Vietnam, 145, 189, 256n26
View from the Bottom, A (Hoang), 18
violence, 52, 57, 76–77, 81, 85, 133–34, 137, 186, 215–16. *See also* homicide; physical abuse; trauma
Visibility Project, 235–36, 238

Walters, Suzanna Danuta, 17
Warner, Michael, 84
Wee, C. J. W.-L., 226
Weston, Kath, 168
Williams, Lindy, 234
Wingshooters (Revoyr), 4, 25, 59, 159–95, 237
Wisconsin, 14, 166, 193, 259nn17,25
Woloch, Alex, 64
Wong, Anna May, 146
World Famous Love Acts (Leung), 16
World of Suzie Wong, The (film), 152
W. W. Norton, 16

Yanagisako, Sylvia Junko, 168
Yew, Lee Kuan, 199
Yu, Mark, 205

Zia, Helen, 146, 151
Zipes, Jack, 127